A
CLINICAL
HYPNOSIS
PRIMER

CONTRIBUTORS

Elgan L. Baker, PhD., director of psychology training and associate professor, Department of Psychiatry, Indiana University School of Medicine. Diplomate (clinical), ABPP, ABPH; fellow, SCEH; member, ASCH; member, Executive Committee, Division 30, American Psychological Association.

Errol R. Korn, MD, gastroenterologist in private practice, San Diego. Clinical faculty, University of California, San Diego, School of Medicine. Fellow, ASCH; past president, San Diego Society of Clinical Hypnosis; member, SCEH; member, American Pain Society.

Gerald L. McCracken, DDS, private practice in dentistry, San Diego. Member, ASCH, San Diego Society of Clinical Hypnosis, AGD, ADA, International Academy of Gnathology, Laguna Beach Gnathological Research and Study Group.

Robert L. Magnuson, MD, private practice, Scripps Memorial Hospitals, La Jolla. Former chief, Rehabilitative Medicine Service, Naval Regional Medical Center, San Diego. Past president, San Diego Society of Clinical Hypnosis; member, ASCH.

Jesse James Thomas, PhD, private practice in psychotherapy, La Jolla. Adjunct faculty, San Diego State University and the California School of Professional Psychology. Member ASCH and San Diego Society of Sex Therapists and Educators.

The authors would like to extend their thanks to the following people who contributed their thoughts on the future of hypnosis for Chapter 19, Other Voices: **Simon W. Chiasson, MD**, assistant professor, North Ohio University College of Medicine, and past president, ASCH; **Harold B. Crasilneck, PhD**, clinical professor of psychiatry and anesthesiology at the University of Texas Health Science Center, and past president, SCEH; **Ann Damsbo, PhD**, former chief, Pain Clinic, Naval Regional Medical Center, San Diego; **Michael J. Diamond, PhD**, associate clinical professor, Department of Psychiatry and Biobehavioral Sciences, UCLA, and past president, Division 30, APA; **A. David Feinstein, PhD**, private practice, San Diego; **Elliot V. Feldbau, DMD**, clinical instructor, Harvard School of Dental Medicine; **Lillian E. Fredericks, MD**, assistant professor of anesthesiology, Hospital of the University of Pennsylvania; **Clyde W. Jones, MD**, chief, Department of Anesthesiology, Kaiser Permanente Medical Center, San Diego; **Joan Murray-Jöbsis** (formerly **Scagnelli**), **PhD**, clinical professor, Chapel Hill, North Carolina, and past president ASCH; **Karen Olness, MD**, director of research in behavioral pediatrics at the Minnesota Children's Medical Center and president elect, ASCH; **David Spiegel, MD**, director of the Adult Psychiatric Outpatient Clinic, Stanford University School of Medicine; **Herbert Spiegel, MD**, faculty of psychiatry at the College of Physicians and Surgeons at Columbia University; **Eric C. Steese, PhD**, private practice, Olympia, Washington.

A CLINICAL HYPNOSIS PRIMER

Expanded and Updated

George J. Pratt, PhD

Dennis P. Wood, PhD

Brian M. Alman, PhD

Edited by

Naneene Van Gelder

WILEY

A WILEY INTERSCIENCE PUBLICATION

JOHN WILEY & SONS

New York • Chichester • Brisbane • Toronto • Singapore

ISBN 0-471-61384-3

Printed in the United States of America

10 9 8 7 6 5 4 3

To the present and future professionals who incorporate hypnotic techniques into their practices of medicine, dentistry, and psychology.

FOREWORD

It may seem contradictory to refer to a comprehensive primer. A primer is supposed to be elementary—a catechism, not a treatise—to use an analogy from theological studies. However, the authors of *A Clinical Hypnosis Primer* have accomplished what may seem a contradiction. They give us a text addressed primarily to professionals with little or no knowledge of hypnosis, and yet they present the clinical applications of hypnosis in some depth. Profound and practical, serious and easy to comprehend, scientifically objective and clear: These are some of the polarities that apply to this volume.

There are few comprehensive texts for the beginning professional student of hypnosis. *A Clinical Hypnosis Primer* will take its deserved place next to the classics by Cheek and LeCron, Crasilneck and Hall, and Kroger. But why another text when the ones just mentioned are superb? For one thing, this is a current book. Of the three listed, only Kroger's has been revised, and this already more than 6 years ago. Even more important, Pratt, Wood, and Alman have managed to provide in a lucid and direct style the essential basic information needed by the tyro, without burdening the reader with the finer and often controversial points of research.

I find it difficult to select specific aspects or chapters for praise, because the whole book is done with respect for data and evidence. But more important than the scientific accuracy, I sense that this book was written with caring and love. Reading it, I perceive the warmth of the authors for their clients, the enthusiasm for hypnosis as a glorious helping method, and the labor of love that writing this book was for all those concerned. The authors have succeeded in organizing the text so that the five contributors, while preserving their individual points of view and style, fit perfectly well into the body of this work.

Part III, Clinical Applications, offers a true overview of recent activity in the field of hypnosis, with sample induction models and wise suggestions for treatment, plus a valuable list of further readings for each subject area. Above all, the authors update the whole clinical hypnosis field by presenting the views of modern clinical hypnosis without falling into the Ericksonian cultist trap so many current authors in the field have placed themselves in.

The excellent chapter on history implicitly connects this book with the teachings of the New Nancy School, which in the 1920s took a firm stand on many views of hypnosis that have become widely accepted in the last decade. One of these views is that hypnosis is a natural, healthy state of mind. Another emphasized the work and function of the subject, rather than the ministrations or histrionics of the hypnotist, as being responsible for the hypnotic phenomenon. For reasons beyond the scope of this foreword, the prevailing views of hypnosis up until the first two decades of this century were those of Charcot, Janet, and other masters of the Salpêtrière school, who explained hypnosis in terms of psychopathology. The trend has been reversing in the last few years, and the authors of *A Clinical Hypnosis Primer* join the Nancy tradition.

Even though it is difficult to single out special portions of this volume for praise, I do want to mention several chapters that offer innovative and original ideas either in theory or in treatment methodology. The chapters on imagery, self-hypnosis, and the future of hypnosis are superb contributions, stimulating one's thinking with new ideas. For instance, that "suggestions work to the extent that they produce an image in the patient's mind," is a concept that can modify a clinician's entire approach to the use of hypnosis in general and to that of suggestions in particular. Other authors writing on hypnosis state that imagery prepares the mind to accept suggestions. That imagery is suggestion is especially important in view of what Watzlawick and his colleagues of the Mental Research Institute have taught us about the function of the right hemisphere and its activity in the process of human change. In clinical application, this equation will affect the language of clinicians as well as their perceptions of their role and therapeutic function.

The concept that imagery is suggestion transcends the consulting room and clinical work. There are tremendous implications here for the culture that through television and the movie industry has become so visually conditioned. Perhaps social justice can be accelerated by means of healing images, mental health can be helped by images of peace, and benign images can diminish violence. The ancient injunction to "think thoughts of peace and not of afflication," may find its psychological justification in current knowledge of self-suggestion.

Chapter 18, A Bona Fide Brave New World, is, in a sense, a detailed revolutionary proclamation of imagery and self-suggestion—what I have called the New Hypnosis. When are we not hypnotized? When are we not using imagery for self-suggestion? The responses to these questions are important to our understanding of much of human behavior, from interpersonal relations to immunological function, from human happiness to emotional pathology.

The last chapter of the book is an ingenious "written panel" on hypnosis that presents the statements of outstanding practitioners who responded to the authors' invitation to predict the future of hypnosis. Each one of these statements deserves careful attention.

I am honored to introduce this book to you, the reader. My hope is that it may reach a very wide circle of people, both professionals and generally curious, open-minded women and men in search of a richer, fuller life.

DANIEL L. ARAOZ

Professor, Long Island University
New York

PREFACE TO
THE EXPANDED,
UPDATED EDITION

There is so much activity in the field of clinical hypnosis, that any book published on the subject is outdated as soon as it rolls off the presses. We welcome this opportunity to issue an expanded and updated edition of *A Clinical Hypnosis Primer* and to add a new chapter on current trends in the field. We hope the reader will find that this overview of clinical hypnosis strikes a balance between the advanced texts in the field and popular simplifications. We hope, too, that the reader will share our enthusiasm for this exciting field and go on to pursue a more intensive course of study.

Overshadowing everything else that is happening in the field of clinical hypnosis today is the increased attention being given to psychosocial factors in healing. Less than a decade ago, practitioners such as Meares (1979) took a bold step by even suggesting that we should apply hypnotic techniques with the purpose of reversing the pathophysiology of such diseases as cancer.* Today, even though we cannot *prove* that the mind affects health and healing, it is difficult for even the most confirmed skeptic to ignore the significant body of scientific evidence suggesting that it does. In the growing field of behavioral medicine, hypnosis represents an extremely effective way of activating the healing forces within each person.

Amidst the complexity of the past several years, we have also become more aware of some simple truths: that the unconscious is a powerful ally, the depth and strength of which we have only begun to explore, and that most human interactions, from the medical setting to schools and families, contain hypnotic elements that are unconsciously being used for good or ill. As we continue to explore the phenomenon of hypnosis, in the lab, in the clinic, and in everyday life, we must be both well-informed and open-minded. By the year 2000, hypnosis may well be seen, not merely as an adjunct to medicine and psychology, but as an essential element in our everyday lives and in our approach to mental and physical health.

GEORGE PRATT
DENNIS WOOD
BRIAN ALMAN

---

*Meares, A. (1979) Meditation: A psychological approach to cancer treatment. *The Practitioner*, 222, 119–122.

INTRODUCTION

Hypnosis is both an ancient practice and a new frontier. The phenomenon has inspired speculation, wonder, and belief; it has provoked fear, scorn, and hostility; and since the late eighteenth century, it has been a subject of scientific debate.

The past decade has witnessed a tremendous burgeoning of interest in clinical hypnosis. As researchers try to pin down the whats and whys of the phenomenon, practitioners are finding new, expanded, and more effective ways of using hypnosis in medicine, psychology, and dentistry. And even now, with our rapidly increasing understanding of the theory and practice of clinical hypnosis, it remains a field with more questions than answers.

For the interested practitioner or student of medicine, psychology, and dentistry, the literature on hypnosis is vast and varied. In fact, there is almost too much information for someone who is not prepared to launch an exhaustive study of the subject. There are several excellent and comprehensive texts of clinical hypnosis as well as important books on special fields. There are two professional journals devoted exclusively to the subject and hundreds of articles on hypnosis published in other professional journals.

The intent of *A Clinical Hypnosis Primer* is to provide the professional, the student, and the interested layperson with an introduction to the fascinating and rapidly growing field of clinical hypnosis. The book provides a summary of current research and thinking, illustrations of specific clinical uses of hypnosis, sample induction and treatment verbalizations, and suggestions for further reading in each subject area.

The reader can use this book to gain an overview of the field, and perhaps, to develop an increased awareness of the hypnotic elements in the health care professions. The authors hope that some readers will use this text as a starting point for more in-depth study.

Parts I and II of the book provide an orientation to the field of clinical hypnosis, and these chapters should be read in sequence. Part III focuses on specific clinical applications of hypnosis, and with the first part of the book as background, each stands alone and can be read according to the interests of the reader. Part IV offers a glimpse into the future of hypnosis as seen by some of the field's outstanding practitioners.

A Clinical Hypnosis Primer will not turn the reader into a practitioner of clinical hypnosis. Present-day techniques of hypnosis are far more sophisticated than those of the past. One cannot become proficient at hypnosis by reading about it and practicing on a friend. The skills required for the clinical application of hypnotic techniques are acquired only through long-term training and study. Each of the two hypnosis societies conducts beginning and advanced training workshops for the professional, and many approved medical and graduate schools incorporate hypnosis training into their curricula.

Because the field is expanding so rapidly, any text on hypnosis is outdated before it rolls from the presses, and this book is no exception. New research into the unconscious by Anthony Marcel of Cambridge University, as well as brain wave studies by researchers such as Benjamin Libet of the University of California, promise to have a tremendous impact on the theory and application of clinical hypnosis. In fact, there is very little research occurring in medicine and psychology today that does not relate to hypnosis. The authors hope that some of the readers of *A Clinical Hypnosis Primer* will be the authors of books relating to the exciting and as yet unknown future of hypnosis.

CONTENTS

A
CLINICAL
HYPNOSIS
PRIMER

PART I

OUT OF THE SHADOWS

This discussion will begin by taking hypnosis out of the shadows of myth and mystery and looking at it in the light of modern clinical practice. Chapter 1 provides an overview of hypnosis as it is now practiced. Chapter 2 reviews the history of hypnosis and acknowledges the pioneers whose work has contributed to our present understanding. Much of what we know about hypnosis has not changed in the past 150 years. On the other hand, modern practice and research have expanded the clinical applications of hypnosis and given it the credibility it often has lacked in its long history.

Hypnosis has always been an enigma. The more it is subjected to the light of modern empirical scrutiny, the more it eludes definition. Like the blind men in the fable who attempt to describe an elephant, researchers know a great deal about hypnosis but remain unable to fit the parts into a single concept of the whole.

It may be that not enough is yet known. On the other hand, it may be that hypnotic phenomena are so pervasive—permeate so much of our existence—that trying to explain them is like trying to explain life itself. Although a great deal can be said about hypnosis and its practical application for the clinician, the data are not all in. In fact, with the merging of many disciplines and fields of study, we appear to be on the verge of new breakthroughs in our understanding of human potential. Studies on neurolinguistic programming, biofeedback, the placebo effect, right and left brain functions, and such altered states of consciousness as meditation are providing a wealth of information. Many of the distinctions between these areas of study may eventually prove to be primarily semantic

To borrow from the popular "Star Trek" series, "the human adventure is just beginning"—not only to the stars, but within ourselves. Hypnosis, however defined, will surely play a part in that adventure.

1
Myths and Realities

*[Hypnosis] is a universal agent, there is nothing
new in it but the name; and it is a paradox only
to those who are disposed to ridicule everything
and who ascribe to the influence of Satan all
those phenomena which they cannot explain.*

—Jan Baptist van Helmont
De Magneticum Vulneratum Curatione

The word "hypnosis" has many connotations. For some people, it
conjures up visions of a stage entertainer who uses hypnosis to
make volunteers behave foolishly for the audience's amusement. At the
other extreme are those who, in our self-help era, see hypnosis as a
quick and easy cure-all for their problems, from smoking to chronic
back pain.

Hypnosis is neither a tool to control other minds nor a panacea. It
is, rather, a natural phenomenon that helps people harness their inner
resources to improve their physical, emotional, and mental well-being.
The ability to hypnotize or to be hypnotized is latent in everyone.
Hypnosis can be induced without a formal induction procedure and is
part of everyday existence. When we become so absorbed in a book or
a film that we are oblivious to external stimuli, we have put ourselves in
a light hypnotic trance. When a mother kisses a child's hurt to "make it
better," she is using the principle of hypnotic suggestion. In a clinical
setting, these principles are applied in such a way that their effects are
heightened and directed to specific problems.

We are being hypnotized—allowing ourselves to change states of
consciousness—to some degree all the time. Many "miraculous" cures
can be attributed to the physician's (or faith healer's or shaman's) power

of suggestion—the ability to convince the patient that a particular treatment will bring the desired results. People in advertising have long understood the power of suggestion to influence the consumer. We are bombarded with both direct and indirect suggestions about what we should eat, drink, own, and do; what we should look like, read, and believe. Many evangelists use hypnotic techniques intuitively.

On the basis of studying the communication patterns of highly effective therapists, including Milton Erickson, the grand master of modern clinical hypnosis, Bandler and Grinder (1975, 1976) developed a neurolinguistic programming model that can be used to enhance the communication skills of other therapists. Moine (1982) found that successful salespeople in a variety of fields, from insurance to jet airplanes, used the same communication patterns, and he concluded that "superior sellers use the techniques of the clinical hypnotist; mediocre ones do not" (p. 52). The pervasiveness of hypnotic phenomena has been summarized by Muses (1974), who expressed the view that all acculturation is essentially slow hypnosis.

Clinical hypnosis is entering a modern renaissance, dovetailing with a growing interest in biofeedback, natural approaches to healing, neurolinguistic programming, and nonpharmacological paths to altered states of consciousness. In 1955, the British Medical Association formally approved hypnosis as a valid and supported therapeutic technique. In 1958, the American Medical Association and the American Dental Association sanctioned its use in treatment. Today, the number of medical schools, dental schools, and graduate schools in psychology that offer courses in hypnotic techniques is steadily increasing.

Historically considered to be "unscientific" or faddish, hypnosis is gradually being applied in most medical specialties. Hypnotic techniques also are being popularized under many names—including visualization, mental rehearsal, and guided imagery—for the purpose of self-improvement. *Mind-Play* (Singer and Switzer, 1980), the *Inner Athlete* (Nideffer, 1976), and *Visualization: Directing the Movies of Your Mind* (Bry, 1978) are a few of many such publications in recent literature. The use of hypnosis to improve human life is more widespread than ever. As interest in hypnosis increases, research continues to extend its applications to a variety of approaches to physical and psychological change.

MISCONCEPTIONS

Hypnosis has not yet been completely demystified. In most bookstores, books on the subject of hypnosis are still shelved under "Occult." Stage hypnotists and sensational stories in the media often perpetuate false ideas about hypnosis that are unrelated to clinical use and that can make the use of hypnosis in a clinical situation more difficult.

The following common fears are often mentioned by patients who are considering hypnosis for the first time. Any practitioner must address these misconceptions before using hypnosis with a patient.

Hypnosis is a state of sleep or unconsciousness.   The word "hypnosis," from the Greek *hypnos* (to sleep), is a misnomer. Under hypnosis, a patient is not asleep, but in a state of relaxed attention— alert, able to hear, speak, move around, and think. The electroencephalogram (EEG) of a hypnotized person is that of someone who is awake rather than asleep. Reflexes, such as the knee jerk, which are absent during sleep, are present under hypnosis. It is common for persons who have achieved a light trance to argue that they haven't been hypnotized at all.

Only gullible, weak-willed, or passive people can be hypnotized.   The reverse is true. More intelligent, strong-willed, creative people tend to be the most responsive to hypnosis because their powers of concentration are better. The role of the practitioner using hypnosis is to direct this concentration as an orchestra conductor directs the orchestra. In any case, strong motivation is the most important factor in the ability to participate in the hypnotic experience.

Hypnosis allows someone else to control your mind.   Stage hypnotists sometimes give the impression that they are exercising power over a subject, that they can make people act any way that they want them to act. In fact, people cannot be hypnotized against their will and, once under hypnosis, cannot be forced to do something they find objectionable. A hypnotic suggestion is only effective to the extent that it is accepted by the patient. (See Conn, 1981, for a further discussion of this myth.) Clinical hypnosis is a means of giving people more, not less, control over their lives and behavior.

A hypnotized person might be unable to come out of a trance.   It is more difficult to induce and maintain a trance state than it is to slip out of one. If a hypnotherapist stops talking or leaves the room, a patient will either come out of the trance or drift into slumber and awaken naturally.

A hypnotized person will give away secrets.   Only in film or fiction can hypnosis be used to extract secrets from an unwilling subject. In life, a hypnotized person is aware of everything that happens both during and after hypnosis unless the person accepts and follows a specific suggestion for amnesia. While hypnosis can help patients to express what they want or need to express, it cannot force them to reveal secrets unwillingly.

I probably cannot be hypnotized.   Although some people are more responsive to hypnosis than others, nearly everyone can achieve at least a light trance. Factors that may interfere with patients' responsiveness to hypnosis include trying too hard, maintaining fears or misconceptions about hypnosis, or desiring unconsciously to retain the problem for which treatment has been sought. An experienced practitioner can help the patient to overcome such resistance.

Hypnosis is a quick, easy cure-all.   This misconception is at the opposite extreme from the notion that hypnosis is a mysterious and dangerous phenomenon. Hypnosis loses more credibility by such extravagant and inaccurate claims than it does from arguments voiced against it. In a clinical setting, hypnosis is a vehicle for change, often used in conjunction with psychotherapy or medical treatment. In some cases, dramatic results can be achieved in a few sessions. However, treatment for habits or symptoms that have developed over years can be very complex and may take much longer.

People seeking therapy or medical treatment are not the only ones with these misconceptions. Similar misunderstandings about hypnosis may have kept many physicians, dentists, and psychologists from incorporating hypnotic principles into their professional practices.

DANGERS

To dispel the myths about hypnosis is not to say that there are no dangers associated with it. Like any tool or technique, it can be misused. The biggest problem is the use of hypnosis outside of a clinical setting, especially for entertainment. Stage hypnotists are adept at direct, rapid inductions and at choosing responsive subjects from an audience. Their expertise usually ends there.

Hartland (1971) recounts the incident of a secretary who was given the post-hypnotic suggestion by a stage hypnotist that she would fall asleep every time she heard the tune "I'm So Tired." When the orchestra played the tune from time to time, she did fall asleep, much to the amusement of the audience. Unfortunately, the performer neglected to remove the suggestion. Two days later, when the secretary heard an office boy whistling the tune, she immediately fell asleep at her desk.

Forgetting to remove a suggestion is only one of the potential problems caused by the untrained hypnotist. The amateur might underestimate a subject's physiological reaction to a suggestion of physical activity, for example, possibly producing disastrous effects in someone with a heart condition. It also is possible to awaken accidentally a traumatic memory in a subject (Kleinhauz, Dreyfuss, Berna, Goldberg, and Azikiri, 1979), stimulating reactions the entertainer is not equipped to handle. For these reasons, the American Society of Clinical Hypnosis (ASCH), the Society for Clinical and Experimental Hypnosis (SCEH), and trained practitioners everywhere overwhelmingly oppose the use of hypnosis as entertainment.

Unfortunately, there are no federal laws governing the use of hypnosis, and few states have licensing procedures. In most states, anyone can adopt the title of "hypnotist" and advertise in the yellow pages. Clinical hypnosis, as discussed in this book, refers only to the use of hypnosis by a professional who is qualified to treat a patient in other ways as well and who chooses to use hypnosis as an adjunct to clinical practice. Like any treatment modality, hypnosis can be misused, even in a clinical setting. In such instances, however, it is not hypnosis per se that is the problem, but rather the practitioner's misdiagnosis or mismanagement of the psychotherapeutic situation.

Some traditional therapists express the concern that, if hypnosis is used to remove a symptom such as compulsive overeating or phobia, another, possibly worse, symptom will take its place. This issue has been addressed by many authors (Cheek and LeCron, 1968; Hartland, 1971; Hershman, 1980; Kroger, 1977; Wolberg, 1945), who agree that there is no evidence that unless the cause is treated another ailment will appear. If a patient has a strong need to retain a symptom, hypnosis usually will not be effective in removing it. As stated above, suggestions are only effective when they are accepted by the patient. By wording suggestions permissively and teaching the patient self-hypnosis (see Chapters 4 and 6), the practitioner can reduce if not eliminate the likelihood of symptom substitution. Furthermore, the authors have found that the improvement in well-being resulting from the removal of a distressing symptom is often generalized to other areas of a patient's life.

Kroger (1977) summarized the situation:

> The incontrovertible fact is that it is doubtful if, when properly used, there is another modality *less* dangerous in medicine than hypnosis. Yet there is no medical technic which makes a better "whipping boy" than hypnosis! (p. 104)

Conn (1972) came to the same conclusion: "There are no significant or specific dangers associated with hypnosis per se" (p. 61). In a combined 40 years of experience with clinical hypnosis, the authors of this book have observed no dangerous side effects resulting from the use of hypnosis in a clinical setting.

DEFINITIONS AND THEORIES OF HYPNOSIS

Hypnosis is difficult to define because no one knows exactly how it works or why. According to the ASCH (1973), "none of the definitions of hypnosis satisfies the criteria for a good scientific theory" (p. 1). As in many fields, practical application has far outdistanced scientific comprehension. For example, the fact that the mechanisms through which chemoanesthetics operate upon the body are not clearly understood has not prevented their widespread use in medicine. Similarly, many practitioners find hypnosis an effective treatment modality for a wide variety of problems, even though researchers have not yet provided a comprehensive scientific explanation for its effectiveness.

Hypnosis lends itself easily to laboratory study, and considerable research has been conducted on the physiological, behavioral, and phenomenological indices of the trance state. The results of research have raised as many questions as they have answered. No single set of physiological correlates has been identified with hypnosis; certain behaviors closely associated with hypnosis also have been observed to occur in nonhypnotic states; and self-reports of the hypnotic experience do not necessarily correlate with other measures.

In the eighteenth century, Franz Mesmer hypothesized the physiological basis for hypnosis as a magnetic fluid that flowed inside all animate and inanimate bodies. Although his theory has long since been discounted, researchers have continued to search for the physiological foundations of hypnosis. In the nineteenth century, behavioral manifestations of the hypnotic trance led James Braid to coin the word "neurohypnotism," or nervous sleep. In the twentieth century, Ivan Pavlov still believed that hypnosis was a "partial sleep" that involved inhibition of some brain functions.

To his credit, Braid soon realized that hypnosis bore no resemblance to actual sleep (a fact that research has long since corroborated) and tried to substitute the word "monoideism," or single idea, because he found that trance induction relies on fixation of attention. But "hypnosis" had caught on. Nearly 140 years later, we are still trying to explain hypnosis exactly.

The complexity of hypnosis is indicated by the sheer number of theories advanced to explain it over the past two centuries. The following include a sampling of theories that at one time or another have enjoyed some degree of popularity.

Psychoanalytic theories claim that the hypnotized person regresses to childhood and associates the hypnotist with a parent he or she then strives to obey. Although age regression is one of the phenomena associated with hypnosis, childhood regression theories run counter to modern clinical practice, which understands the power of hypnosis to reside in the patient, and not in the practitioner.

Dissociation theories contend that the hypnotized person is dissociated from the conscious mind or external events. Dissociation is characteristic of the hypnotic state, but like many hypnotic phenomena, it is also characteristic of other states, such as dreaming. A lowered sensory threshold, in which colors seem more vivid and hearing is more acute, also is common in hypnosis.

The role-playing theory asserts that a hypnotized person behaves the way he or she believes a hypnotized person is supposed to behave. Although most patients do try to cooperate with and please the practitioner using hypnosis, this theory cannot encompass indirect methods of hypnosis, spontaneous hypnotic states, and the fact that young children with no concept of hypnosis can be hypnotized.

Atavistic theories describe hypnosis as a regression to a primitive mode of mental functioning like that exhibited by animals as a defense mechanism to ward off fear or danger. That some people will spontaneously put themselves into a trance when they are undergoing medical or dental procedures suggests that this ability may have developed as a phylogenetic adaptive response mechanism.

The theory of hypersuggestibility postulates that hypnosis merely focuses the patient's attention on the words of the hypnotist to the exclusion of everything else. Again, this theory explains one aspect of hypnosis—increased suggestibility—but fails to include other hypnotic phenomenon. It also emphasizes the role of the practitioner and underplays the choices of the patient.

The altered state of consciousness theory views hypnosis as an altered state similar to that achieved through meditation, biofeedback, and autogenic training. (See Chapter 3 for a detailed dicussion of this approach to understanding hypnosis.)

One of the most respected practitioners in the field, Erickson (Erickson, Rossi, and Rossi, 1976) never formulated a theory of hypnosis and maintained a pragmatic approach to its discussion and application. The authors of this book agree with Fromm (1972) that "as interest in the subjective aspects of hypnosis increases . . . the search for physiological and neuroelectric substrata of hypnosis as proof of the existence of a hypnotic state will fade into the background" (p. 583).

There remains a need, however, to clarify the term hypnosis, which can refer either to a state of mental functioning or to the process by which that state is achieved. Although most authors agree that hypnosis involves a focus or concentration of attention away from the external environment and towards a set of ideas suggested by oneself (self-hypnosis) or another (hetero-hypnosis), there is no single generally accepted definition of this condition. There are as many definitions as there are authors; in a sample of definitions, hypnosis is, variously:

> . . . a complex of two fundamental processes. The first is the construction of a special, temporary orientation to a small range of preoccupations and the second is the relative fading of the generalized reality-orientation into nonfunctional awareness. (Shor, 1959, p. 592)

> . . . not a sharply delineated state, but a process along the broad, fluctuating continuum of what is loosely referred to as awareness. . . . (Kroger, 1977, p. 312)

> . . . an altered state of consciousness usually involving relaxation, in which a person develops heightened concentration on a particular idea or image for the purpose of maximizing potential in one or more areas. (Olness and Gardner, 1978, p. 228)

> . . . a state in which the critical mental faculties are temorarily suspended and the person uses mainly imagination or primary process thinking. (Araoz, 1982, p. 9)

It is generally accepted among researchers and practitioners that suggestibility is closely connected to hypnosis. In the opinion of Gindes (1973), for example, "the entire procedure of hypnosis, from induction to awakening, is founded upon suggestion" (p. 175). The Russians call hypnosis "suggestology," highlighting their view of the important role suggestion plays in hypnotic induction and treatment. However, as Erickson (Erickson et al., 1976) has pointed out, the trance state does not guarantee that suggestions will be accepted.

There still is controversy over whether hypnosis is a sharply delineated state for which researchers will be able to develop objective indices or merely a shift from one form of consciousness to another, from an external to an internal reality somewhere along a continuum of awareness. Is goal-directed daydreaming the same thing as hypnosis, or do we need signs, such as eye closure or limb rigidity, to guarantee that a person has been hypnotized? The authors agree with Erickson et al. (1976), who refer to the hypnotic trance as an extension of common, everyday processes of living, and who believe that the experience of trance can vary from one person to another. For the moment, however, definitions and theories are of less concern than function in modern clinical practice.

TRENDS IN CLINICAL HYPNOSIS

The use of hypnosis in medicine, dentistry, and psychotherapy has greatly increased over the past 20 years. Articles on the use of hypnosis are regularly contributed to the *American Journal of Clinical Hypnosis* and the *International Journal of Clinical and Experimental Hypnosis*, by physicians, psychotherapists, dentists, and other clinicians and researchers. Since ASCH was organized in 1957, its membership has increased from 20 to approximately 4,300 members. ASCH members must have a doctoral degree in psychology, dentistry, or medicine; they must have training and experience in clinical hypnosis, as well as meet additional criteria.

As a treatment methodology, hypnosis is unique in the wide variety of problems to which it can be applied. The rapidly growing body of research demonstrating that the mind has a direct influence on bodily processes has paved the way for increasing use of hypnosis in medical treatment and therapy. Biofeedback studies have shown that people can bring autonomic functions, such as heart rate and temperature, under conscious control. Yogis able to perform amazing feats of self-regulation have come under Western scientific scrutiny. Throughout history, the placebo has been found to have a variety of positive physiological effects, depending on which drug the patient believes he or she is receiving.

In the past, hypnosis has been associated with dramatic or impressive cures. Since the 1950s, its use has been extended to routine procedures as well. Hypnosis can help to alter perceptions of pain, eliminate warts, and control bleeding and inflammation. It is being used before, during, and after surgery to help the patient relax, feel comfortable, and heal quickly. Hypnosis for pain management is used in a variety of contexts, from brief medical or dental procedures to terminal illnesses. Recently there has been increasing interest in the ability of patients to increase immune function through hypnosis; both clinical and research evidence have supported that hypothesis (see Hall, Longo, and Dixon, 1981).

Hypnosis also is used to treat organic conditions with a psychogenic component. There is no longer any doubt that strong emotional states or unconscious psychological conflicts can in time cause organic symptoms or exacerbate existing organic pathology. By current estimates, 50%–80% of all illness is psychosomatic rather than organic. Hans Selye (1974), an authority in the physiology of stress, believes that stress plays a role in all diseases because it reduces the ability of the immunological system to function properly. Hypnosis helps people deal with stress or anxiety without relying on external sources. Although as Kroger (1977) pointed out, a patient is not treated *by* hypnosis, but *in* hypnosis, there is considerable evidence that for many problems the relaxation that accompanies the hypnotic state is beneficial in itself (see Chapter 3).

Hypnosis in combination with psychotherapy can help patients understand the cause of symptoms and ameliorate or eliminate them. Under hypnosis, someone can be trained to relive an experience, modify disturbing mental images, and initiate new defenses or patterns that are healthier and more functional. As a technique for reaching the unconscious, hypnosis is an effective treatment methodology for many problems, from phobias to sexual dysfunction and obesity.

A more recent use of hypnosis has been its application to nonpathological populations. Practitioners work with athletes to enhance athletic performance and with students to increase concentration and optimize test-taking ability. Both professional and recreational athletes are using hypnosis to reduce performance anxiety, build confidence, and promote concentration.

Recent years have seen not only new applications of hypnosis, but a shift in our approach to clinical hypnosis. The realization that all hypnosis is essentially self-hypnosis is basic to modern clinical practice.

Understanding of the patient's innate ability to experience a change in consciousness, and even more importantly, the patient's willingness to experience that change, is replacing the traditional conception of the "hypnotist" as one who does something to the patient. As a result, the practitioner's role is now one of teacher or facilitator of change. This attitude is consistent with the larger trend toward holistic approaches to health, in which responsibility for well-being is returned to the individual, who has the inner resources for growth and change.

More and more, hypnosis is seen as a process of learning on a new level rather than just obedience to suggestions formulated by the practitioner. The trend is away from formal, authoritarian inductions and toward the indirect, permissive techniques introduced by Erickson. The indirect approach gives the patient more freedom to create personally meaningful images and suggestions. Self-hypnosis is also becoming a greater part of clinical practice, as patients are asked to reinforce therapy or treatment by practicing self-hypnosis at home.

Finally, the gap between experimental and clinical hypnosis seems to be widening to the extent that concepts that are useful for one are not always applicable to the other. For example, such issues as "hypnotizability" and depth of hypnosis are of less concern to many practitioners who have found that nearly everyone can be hypnotized. When hypnotic techniques facilitate desired change, the issue of whether or not the patient has actually been "hypnotized" becomes moot. As clinical work with hypnosis becomes more creative and more individualized with our current medical and psychological techniques, it becomes more difficult to offer empirical proof how and why hypnosis works.

THE HYPNOTIC SESSION

A typical session in a therapeutic situation begins with a discussion of the patient's history (including likes and dislikes, current situation, and past experiences), the patient's understanding of his or her problems, and the nature and purpose of treatment using hypnosis. This preliminary work is necessary if the practitioner is to tailor the induction procedure and suggestions to each patient's needs and strengths. In other situations, such as emergency rooms or operating rooms, surgeons, anesthesiologists, or psychologists sometimes work with people they are seeing for the first time and must rely on brief conversations and external cues to personalize inductions and suggestions to the extent possible.

An induction is a method of achieving a trance, moving from a usual state of consciousness into the hypnotic state. Because successful induction of hypnosis depends on concentration and relaxation, patients are asked to relax and make themselves comfortable; sometimes the practitioner will take a patient through specific techniques for muscle relaxation.

In inducing hypnosis, the main concern is to quiet the conscious mind, the source of our judgmental, evaluative, and critical abilities, and to make the unconscious more accessible. The relationship of the unconscious mind, the seat of all of our memories, all our past experiences, all our associations, and all that we have ever learned, may be seen in perspective by analogy: If the conscious mind is a beach in San Diego, then the unconscious is the Pacific Ocean. Speculating on the power of hypnotic suggestion, Lewis Thomas (1979) talked about "a kind of superintelligence that exists in each of us, infinitely smarter and possessed of technical know-how far beyond our present understanding" (p. 65). When suggestions penetrate the unconscious mind, which exercises very little critical faculty, they are realized more completely and effectively than if they were given in a normal waking state.

Using the technique of misdirected attention is an excellent way of bypassing the conscious mind. A mother trying to feed a recalcitrant child will dangle a toy in front of his eyes, and, once he is engrossed, put a spoon in his mouth. Similarly, the practitioner may have a patient focus attention on a target, such as an external object or the patient's own breathing, and when the patient "isn't paying any attention," make suggestions for comfort and relaxation.

Although there are as many kinds of inductions as there are practitioners, there are several common denominators. Ideally, the physical environment should be as distraction-free as possible, although hypnosis can be achieved under even the most chaotic conditions. The effect of any method of induction depends largely on the patient's belief in the validity of the hypnotic phenomenon and in the practitioner's integrity. Therefore, the practitioner must develop a good rapport with the patient and dispel any misconceptions about hypnosis.

Closely related to belief, expectation is another powerful force at work. The person who expects to respond to hypnosis usually does so. The potency of expectation may be seen in an apprehensive patient who can feel the pain of the dentist's drill before it touches him—or in the young girl waiting in anticipation, who hears the doorbell ring several times before her date arrives. This same principle is at work in faith healing, in which a certain ritual or suggestion has the expected effect on the physical organism.

The induction process usually takes from a few minutes to an hour in a clinical setting. The resulting trance state has traditionally been characterized as light, medium, or deep, although these are not distinct states but rather points on a continuum. Studies using self-report scales to measure hypnotic depth have shown that trance depth fluctuates during any given session (Tart, 1972). Research also has shown that 90% of people can achieve what is considered to be a light trance; 70% can achieve a medium trance; and 10%–20% can enter a deep trance or somnambulistic state. For the most part, hypnotic depth is not related to the outcome of treatment. However, a deep state is required in some instances, such as when hypnosis is used as the sole anesthetic for major surgery. The type and length of induction varies according to the preference of the practitioner, the situation, the personality of the patient, and the goals of therapy or treatment.

In general, inductions have moved away from traditional, direct, lock-step authoritarian approaches that use gadgetry such as spinning discs or pendulums, toward more permissive, indirect approaches that are more individualized, make greater use of symbol and metaphor in phrasing suggestions, and emphasize the patient's responsibility and power of choice. The indirect method is often clinically more effective because patients feel more in control and have the sense that they are doing something for themselves rather than having something done to them. Chapter 4 provides a more specific discussion of the many approaches to hypnotic induction and treatment.

Once a patient is in a relaxed state of attention, the practitioner makes positive, functional, and constructive suggestions. If the patient has no strong objections to the suggestions, they will be accepted uncritically without the interference of the conscious mind, which may intellectualize or rationalize. Suggestions may be phrased in many ways: permissive or commanding, direct or indirect, positive or negative. Research has shown that the way in which suggestions are phrased has a great influence on their effectiveness and outcome.

After the specific suggestions have been made, the practitioner asks the patient to return to full waking or normal consciousness, usually incorporating the suggestion that he or she will feel refreshed and relaxed. Before ending the session, the practitioner discusses the patient's experiences to gain insight for further sessions.

HYPNOTIC PHENOMENA

People who have been hypnotized usually recognize the experience as distinctly different from their usual waking or sleeping states, but beyond that realization, words often fail them. Most describe it as a relaxed, pleasant experience in which they feel detached, very reluctant to move, and have a lowered or increased sensory threshold, depending on the goals of the session.

The outward signs of hypnosis may vary from person to person and from one time to another. In a neutral trance state, before the introduction of suggestions, most people show signs of lethargy and muscular relaxation. Breathing is heavier and slower, arms are limp, and the head may fall to one side or onto the chest. In this relaxed state, the heartbeat slows; blood pressure and heart rate decrease. With the introduction of suggestions, physiological reactions may vary according to the nature of the suggestions.

Several kinds of behavior occur in a hypnotic trance, although not all occur every time. Some are routinely present even in a light trance; others are most often manifested in a medium to deep trance state; and still others are demonstrated as the result of specific suggestions. The phenomena associated with a light to medium trance depth are usually effective in cases where a practitioner would employ hypnosis as an adjunct to psychotherapeutic, medical, and dental treatment. Since these phenomena overlap one another, it is best to view them on a continuum rather than as a series of distinct occurrences.

Release of inhibitions. (Light to deep trance.)   Inhibitions normally present in the waking state partially disappear in a trance state, making it easier to express emotions, thoughts, and opinions concerning behaviors. Demonstrating to patients in trance that they can relax makes the next step—behavioral conditioning or insight-oriented psychotherapy—easier.

Changes in capacity for volitional activity. (Light to deep trance.)   In a trance state, people become reluctant to initiate actions arising from their own will. For example, when a telephone rings, a person normally jumps up to answer it. Under hypnosis, the same person hears the phone but has less interest in answering it because attention is focused elsewhere. This phenomenon can be used to increase trance depth through suggestions that external sounds become cues for entering a progressively deeper and deeper level of relaxation.

Suggestibility. (Light to deep trance.) The ability to respond positively to ideas, whether given by oneself or another, heightened suggestibility is the sine qua non of hypnosis. Increased receptivity to suggestion is associated with decreased activity of the critical ego and increased activity of what might be called the observing ego, making the unconscious more accessible.

Detachment. (Light to deep trance.)   This phenomenon is a splitting process in which the perception of the body's position in space and time is altered. People who have been hypnotized report, for example, that their arms or legs seemed to be very long or that they seemed to be watching themselves from a distance. Detachment can be used to facilitate the deepening phase of induction through suggestions that, as patients feel themselves moving away from their bodies, they can allow themselves to experience an increased sense of relaxation. This phenomenon also has obvious implications for pain control.

Dissociation. (Medium to deep trance.)   The ability to view oneself from a safe and comfortable distance, which is primarily a cognitive phenomenon, theoretically allows the process of emotional dissociation to occur. In hypnosis, a person can relive a negative experience without its discomfort or become dissociated from a present context that may be unhappy or painful. For example, through age regression, one can return to the death of a parent, see the event from a distant perspective, and leave behind or "disrupt" a representative portion of the old emotion associated with the event.

Catalepsy. (Medium to deep trance.)   With this form of muscular rigidity, a limb will remain in almost any position, such as an arm raised in the air or extended to the front or side. This phenomenon is sometimes used to demonstrate the ability of the unconscious to control muscular activity and also is useful as a deepening technique.

Age regression. (Medium to deep trance.)   Reliving past experiences in all five senses in a present context can occur in two forms: total regression and partial regression. In total regression, a person returns experientially to an earlier state of development and may write or behave in a way that is appropriate to that age, with no recall of subsequent events. Referred to as revivification, this type of regression usually requires a deep trance. In a partial regression, a person relives a childhood experience but retains recall of later events and a point of view appropriate to present age.

Amnesia. (Medium to deep trance.)   A dissociation from the ability to remember, amnesia sometimes occurs naturally during medium to deep hypnosis. It is often produced through posthypnotic suggestion that a painful memory, for example, may best be left in the unconscious.

Ideomotor activity. (Medium to deep trance.)   The involuntary capacity of muscles and the nervous system to respond to thoughts, feelings, and ideas is useful to therapists, who employ ideomotor question techniques (see Cheek and LeCron, 1968) as a means of communicating with the unconscious mind. Different fingers are designated to signify "yes," "no," "I don't know," or "I don't wish to respond"; the appropriate finger lifts in response to questions posed by the practitioner.

Hallucination, positive and negative. (Medium to deep trance.)   The ability to delete sensory information in the immediate physical environment or to experience stimuli that are not present can be used as a deepening technique. Hallucination also has a range of other therapeutic uses, from hallucinating a balloon, putting old grief in it and letting it float away, to hallucinating a television or movie screen and watching something happen on it.

Hypermnesia. (Medium to deep trance).   With this vivid recall of past memories to an extent not possible in the waking state, a patient can alter conscious negative memories by remembering and re-experiencing past positive ones.

Time disorientation. (Medium to deep trance.)   Time may be accelerated or slowed down in the hypnotic state, and the boundaries between past, present, and future can be blurred. Suggestions for time disorientation may be used to aid a patient in tolerating uncomfortable appliances or positions following surgery or to reduce the time between meals experienced by people in a weight reduction program. From a psychotherapeutic perspective, this phenomenon can enable patients to see themselves at a future time, when treatment goals have been accomplished. This process helps patients to realize the degree of control they have over their own recovery.

These phenomena are not exclusive to the hypnotic trance. Many occur in other states as well. For example, most of us experience momentary amnesia when we forget the name of a close friend in the midst of an introduction. The sight of an oasis to a thirsty desert traveller is a classic hallucination. Ideomotor activity is manifested when a passenger in a car reflexively slams on an imaginary brake to avoid a collision. And for all of us, our sense of time varies according to our circumstances. Time can crawl by for a parent awaiting the birth of a child or a student sitting in a boring class. For lovers, an entire day can rush by in what seems like only a few moments. Such occurrences remind us again that hypnosis is not an otherworldly phenomenon, but a natural, fascinating, and valuable resource available to each of us.

FURTHER READING

Araoz, D. L. (1982). *Hypnosis and sex therapy* (Chapt. 1). New York: Brunner/Mazel.

Cheek, D. B., & LeCron, L. M. (1968). *Clinical hypnotherapy*. New York: Grune & Stratton.

Crasilneck, H. B., & Hall, J. B. (1974). *Clinical hypnosis: Principles and applications*. New York: Grune & Stratton.

Erickson, M. H., Rossi, E. L., & Rossi, S. I. (1976). *Hypnotic realities*. New York: Irvington Publishers.

Hartland, J. (1971). *Medical and dental hypnosis*. London: Bailliere Tindall.

Kroger, W. S. (1977). *Clinical and experimental hypnosis* (2nd ed.). Philadelphia: Lippincott.

REFERENCES

American Society of Clinical Hypnosis ASCH (1973). *A syllabus on hypnosis and a handbook of therapeutic suggestions*. Des Plaines, IL: Author.

Araoz, D. L. (1982). *Hypnosis and sex therapy*. New York: Brunner/Mazel.

Bandler, R., & Grinder, J. (1975). *The structure of magic, I*. Palo Alto, CA: Science and Behavior Books.

Bandler, R., & Grinder, J. (1976). *The structure of magic, II*. Palo Alto, CA; Science and Behavior Books.

Bry, A. (1978). *Visualization: Directing the movies of your mind*. New York: Harper and Row.

Cheek, D. B., & LeCron, L. M. (1968). *Clinical hypnotherapy*. New York: Grune & Stratton.

Conn, J. H. (1972). Is hypnosis really dangerous? *International Journal of Clinical and Experimental Hypnosis, 20*, 61–79.

Conn, J. H. (1981). The myth of coercion through hypnosis. *International Journal of Clinical and Experimental Hypnosis, 29*, 95–100.

Erickson, M. H., Rossi, E. L., & Rossi, S. I. (1976). *Hypnotic realities*. New York: Irvington Publishers.

Fromm, E. (1972) *Quo vadis* hypnosis? Predictions of future trends in hypnosis research. In E. Fromm & R. Shor (Eds.), *Hypnosis: Research developments and perspectives*. Chicago: Aldine·Atherton, Inc.

Gindes, B. C. (1973). *New concepts of hypnosis*. Hollywood, CA: Wilshire.

Hall, H., Longo, S., & Dixon, R. (1981, October). *Hypnosis and the immune system: The effect of hypnosis on T and B cell function*. Paper presented to the Society for Clinical and Experimental Hypnosis, 33rd Annual Workshop and Scientific Meeting, Portland, OR.

Hartland, J. (1971). *Medical and dental hypnosis*. London: Bailliere Tindall.

Hershman, S. (1980). Methods for habit disruption. In H. J. Wain (Ed.), *Clinical hypnosis in medicine*. Miami, FL: Symposia Specialists.

Kleinhauz, M., Dreyfuss, D. A., Berna, B., Goldberg, T., & Azikiri, D. (1979). Some after-effects of stage hypnosis: A study of psychopathological manifestations. *International Journal of Clinical and Experimental Hypnosis, 27*, 219–226.

Kroger, W. S. (1977). *Clinical and experimental hypnosis* (2nd ed.). Philadelphia: Lippincott.

Moine, D. J. (1982, August). To trust, perchance to buy. *Psychology Today*, pp. 51–54.

Muses, C. M. (1974). Introduction. In C. Muses & A. M. Young (Eds.), *Consciousness and reality*. New York: Avon Books.

Nideffer, R. M. (1976). *The inner athlete*. New York: Crowell.

Olness, K., & Gardner, G. G. (1978). Some guidelines for uses of hypnotherapy in pediatrics. *Pediatrics, 62*, 228–233.

Selye, H. (1974). *Stress without distress*. New York: New American Library.

Shor, R. E. (1959). Hypnosis and the concept of the generalized reality-orientation. *American Journal of Psychotherapy, 13*, 582–602.

Singer, J. L., & Switzer, E. (1980). *Mind-play: The creative uses of fantasy*. Englewood Cliffs, NJ: Prentice-Hall.

Tart, C. (1972). Measuring the depth of an altered state of consciousness, with particular reference to self-report scales of hypnotic depth. In E. Fromm & R. E. Shor (Eds.), *Hypnosis: Research developments and perspectives*. Chicago: Aldine·Atherton.

Thomas L. (1979). *The medusa and the snail*. New York: Viking Press.

Van Helmont, J. B. (1661). *De magneticum vulneratum curatione*. Paris.

Wolberg, L. R. (1945). *Hypnoanalysis*. New York: Grune & Stratton.

2
Historical Roots

*If my work is not accepted today, it will be
tomorrow when there will be a new turn in
fashion's wheel which will bring back hypnotism
as surely as our grandmother's styles.*

—Pierre Janet
Psychological Healing

The historical pathway leading to the present understanding of
hypnosis is long and uneven, with apparent dead-ends and switch-
back trails along the way. It is a path people have created over an
extended period of time out of quite different philosophies, beliefs, and
scientific orientations, coming from diverse national backgrounds, and
with varied motives.

Early accounts of phenomena that may have been what we now
call hypnotic can be found in such sources as the Bible, the Talmud, and
a 3000-year-old Egyptian stone stele. A technique using a lighted lamp
in what seems to have been a self-hypnosis procedure is described in a
document referred to as the Demotic Magical Papyrus which is now in
museums in London and Leiden (British Museum Manuscript 10070 and
Leiden Museum Manuscript 1.383). Descriptions of trance states and of
miraculous healing among the ancient Greek oracles, Persian magi,
Hindu fakirs, and Indian yogi indicate that all of these early peoples
practiced forms of hypnosis. Similarly, the healing powers attributed
for many centuries to the "royal touch" of kings and princes may be
viewed as having a basis in hypnosis and hypnotic suggestion, as can
the achievements of healers who used their hands, religious or mystical
objects, or exorcism and prayer to cure the sick.

During the sixteenth century in Europe, some attempts were made
to provide scientific explanations for the existence and the cure of dis-

21

ease, which had until then largely been accepted as explainable only in supernatural or metaphysical ways. One of the earliest to attempt a more scientific explanation was Paracelsus (1493–1541), a Swiss-born alchemist and physician who theorized that magnets and the heavenly bodies had healing effects on human disease. During the next two centuries, similar ideas influenced the work of various astronomers, healers, physicists, and physicians. In 1679, a Scottish physician, Gul Maxwell, proposed that a universal and vital spirit affects all humans. Isaac Newton's attempts to identify the natural laws underlying all living systems led English physician Richard Mead (1673–1754) to investigate the universality of life. And around 1771, a Viennese Jesuit, Maximilian Hehl, became famous for cures obtained by applying steel plates to the bodies of the ill.

MESMERISM

These experiments and hypotheses inspired Franz Anton Mesmer (1734–1815), an Austrian physician, to write his medical dissertation about the influence of the planets on the human body. Mesmer developed the theory of animal magnetism, postulating a universal fluid present in all objects that produced disease when it was out of balance in the human body. Mesmer also developed techniques that he believed could restore the balance of the magnetic fluid and thus cure the diseases of his patients. His techniques included making "passes" over the bodies of his sick patients to draw the fluid with his own "magnetic influence" and cure such problems as urine retention, toothache, earache, depression, and paralysis. However, Mesmer's claims for animal magnetism were not accepted by his Viennese colleagues, and he left for Paris in 1778.

In Paris he practiced even more theatrical techniques, in which groups of patients joined hands and applied to their bodies iron rods protruding from a large oak tub containing water, iron filings, and powdered glass. Accompanied by piano music, Mesmer himself would appear, dressed in a lilac silk robe and passing a long iron rod over the patients. These dramatic activities resulted in hysterical outbursts by those being treated—and, astonishingly, most were apparently cured after two or three such sessions. Mesmer was unable to formulate any convincing scientific explanation for these cures. He was again denounced as a quack by his colleagues, denied acknowledgment by scientific societies, and forced to leave the city.

But "mesmerism," as it came to be called, had gained disciples and such wide interest in France that Louis XVI appointed a royal commission in 1784 to investigate and test mesmeric treatment. Benjamin Franklin, who was serving as United States Ambassador to France, joined the famous chemist Antoine Lavoisier, the physician Joseph Guillotin (now remembered for his advocacy of the machine named for him) and other scientists and physicians on the commission. After careful observation, the members agreed that some patients were indeed cured through mesmerism, but they doubted the existence of Mesmer's universal magnetic fluid that could be transferred from him to inanimate objects and then to his patients. The commission finally concluded that "the imagination is the true cause of the effects attributed to the magnetism" (Tinterow, 1970, p. 114).

Despite the findings of the commission, mesmerism continued to capture the interest of many, leading to experimentation and related discoveries: Pététin observed and discovered catalepsy; the Marquis de Puységur described "artificial somnambulism," in which the ideas and actions of the "magnetized" patient could be directed by the "magnetizer"; and Barbarin discovered that he could "magnetize" without the use of paraphernalia.

Thus, new variations, theories, and uses were formulated out of the practice of mesmerism. José Custodi di Faria, an abbot who had lived in Portuguese Goa, a colony in India, gave public exhibitions of animal magnetism in Paris in 1814 and 1815, using neither the manipulations nor the elaborate equipment of Mesmer. Faria, who could induce somnambulism in his subjects with a simple command, felt that the resulting cures were not due to magnetism but rather to the expectations and the cooperation of the patients—elements now considered to be crucial to hypnotic induction.

French and American surgeons who were interestd in mesmerism began performing major operations using hypnoanesthesia and claiming good results. In England, John Elliotson (1791–1868), a professor of theology and medicine at London University, became an enthusiastic experimenter with mesmerism. Despite his distinguished status in the medical community (he was responsible for the introduction of the stethoscope in England) his lecture on magnetism before the Royal College of Physicians caused him to be denounced, criticized, and finally asked to resign his post. He continued his strong interest in the subject, however, and between 1842 and 1856 he published 13 volumes of a journal, *The Zoist*, concerning mesmerism and cerebral physiology. Elliotson also published a book in 1843, *Numerous Cases of Surgical Operations Without Pain in the Mesmeric State*, in which he concluded that the positive results he and his colleagues had observed were due to mesmeric passes, and that imagination had no role in the cures of his patient.

HYPNOSIS IN MEDICAL PRACTICE

Braid (1795–1860), a Scottish surgeon and a contemporary of Elliotson, was one of many distinguished contributors to our present knowledge who began as skeptics and later became ardent proponents of hypnosis. He was so skeptical about the claims of mesmerism that in 1841 he tried to expose it as a fake during a public demonstration by La Fontaine, a Swiss mesmerist on tour in Manchester. Instead, Braid became convinced that the girl on stage was in a genuine trance. His subsequent investigations of mesmerism left us with a new term—"hypnosis"— which he later tried to change to "monoideism," and provided the basis for much of our present understanding.

Experimenting with friends and relatives, Braid found that he was able to produce a trance by having his subjects fix their eyes on a bright object, such as his lancet case. He also recognized that some people could enter a trance without a formal induction. In his investigations, he searched at first for a physiological basis for mesmerism but finally concluded that the French commission had been correct in rejecting the idea of a universal magnetic fluid or forces flowing from the operator's body. Instead, Braid formulated a theory of hypnosis that included the contributing factors of expectation, imagination, and fixed attention by the subject. His observation led him to recognize the power of the mind over the body and conclude that hypnotic phenomena are the result of suggestion and that the power of hypnosis resides within each person.

As others before him, Braid met with opposition and ostracism. He was criticized for his conclusions, not only by the mesmerists, but by the British Medical Association, which refused to allow him to present a paper and give a demonstration in 1842. However, he continued to use hypnosis for anesthesia during surgery, as well as self-hypnosis to ease his own arthritic pain. In *Neurypnology; or the Rationale of Nervous Sleep* (1843), Braid elucidated his theories and techniques. He also had early insight with an idea that he called "double consciousness," which foreshadowed the investigations of Pierre Janet and Morton Prince into the phenomena of multiple personalities 50 years later.

PSYCHOLOGICAL CHARACTER OF HYPNOSIS

While Braid is sometimes called the father of modern hypnosis for bringing hypnosis within the sphere of science, two Frenchmen who were working at about the same time have been considered the founders of modern psychotherapy. Ambroise-Auguste Liébeault (1823–1904) was a country doctor in Nancy who offered to treat his poor patients without fee if they would accept hypnotic treatment instead of more conventional approaches. His use of hypnosis in the treatment of illnesses was the subject of a book he published in 1889, *Le sommeil provoqué*. It received little notice.

However, Liébeault's work came to the attention of Hippolyte Bernheim (1840–1919), a professor of medicine at Strasbourg and a famous neurologist, when Liébeault cured a chronic case of sciatica in one of Bernheim's patients. Hoping to expose Liébeault and his country clinic as fraudulent, Bernheim traveled to the clinic and was, instead, amazed. Within a short period of time, Bernheim went on to become an authority on the subject of hypnosis, and because he was known and respected in the medical profession throughout Europe, his theories could not be easily dismissed. Together, Bernheim and Liébeault clarified Braid's theories by recognizing the importance of imagination and the key role played by suggestion. They also viewed hypnosis as a function of normal behavior and recognized individual differences in response to suggestions. Bernheim published his now-famous book, *De la suggestion et de ses applications à la thérapeutique*, in 1884. A milestone in the history of hypnosis, it called attention to the importance of Liébeault's earlier work and cited many examples of cures to support the idea that hypnotic treatment is psychological rather than physical in nature. In his book, Bernheim claimed cures for such problems as hysterical hemiphlegia and aphonia, gastric difficulties, "depression of the spirit," pains, tremors, and sleepwalking.

Liébeault and Bernheim were not unopposed in France. The great French neurologist, Jean-Martin Charcot (1825–1893) also studied hypnosis but reached quite different conclusions. Working with a limited numer of patients at the Salpêtrière Hospital in Paris, he concluded that hypnosis was a pathological state and a form of hysteria. Nevertheless, the serious attention and experimentation given hypnosis by one of France's greatest medical teachers fueled new interest in the scientific and medical communities. Sigmund Freud's interest in the psychological source of neurosis was stimulated by his study of hysteria with Charcot in 1885. After Charcot's investigations, entire journals devoted to hypnosis appeared in France and Germany; articles on hypnosis were printed in both medical journals and popular publications.

Although hypnosis had moved away from the dramatics of Mesmer and into modern scientific scrutiny by the 1800s, misconceptions and misinterpretations of this ancient phenomenon were still to occur during the next hundred years. Once Bernheim's work had established the therapeutic possibilities of hypnosis, many experimenters began to apply hypnotic treatment to an assortment of ills. The list of such practitioners and the diseases they claimed to cure through hypnosis is a long one (Wolberg, 1948, p. 5-6). Success was claimed for such problems as hysteria, agoraphobia, satyriasis, nymphomania, homosexuality, drug addition, epilepsy, depression, skin diseases, and alcoholism. Children were treated for such disorders as incontinence, untruthfulness, and nail-biting.

In recent times, Ronald Shor (1972) pointed out an inherent ambivalence in hypnosis research: A researcher must maintain a disciplined, scientific skepticism, and yet maintain a confident persuasiveness to be a "positive catalyst" as a hypnotist (p. 15). In considering the list of ills and cures claimed by nineteenth-century practitioners, it becomes evident that they must have felt this difficulty and that their enthusiasm for "cures" overshadowed the necessary scientific skepticism. Follow-up studies were seldom done on presumably cured patients, and there was little understanding of the problems, often psychological, that lay behind the complaints.

Eventually, a few of those who were observing and studying the therapeutic methods of hypnosis began to look into the etiology of symptoms. French psychologist Janet, Prince in the United States, and others began to formulate hypotheses that proposed multiple systems of consciousness and underlying causes for manifest symptoms. But the research and observations of Josef Breuer (1842-1925) and Sigmund Freud (1856-1939) had the greatest impact on the subsequent study of causes hidden under symptoms. Although Freud finally took a position that rejected hypnosis as a therapeutic method, many of his contributions in charting the human psyche and in developing the process of psychoanalysis grew from his 1889 observations of Liébeault's clinic in Nancy (Chertok, 1968). Watching Liébeault and Bernheim perform their "astonishing experiments," Freud wrote later that he received "the profoundest impression of the possibility that there could be powerful mental processes which nevertheless remained hidden from the consciousness of men" (Freud, 1925/1953-1966, p.17).

Freud collaborated with Breuer, his colleague, in studying hypnosis and using it to encourage patients with hysterical symptoms to talk freely, often evoking revelations of long-repressed experiences that seemed in some way to cause the symptoms. Furthermore, the venting or catharsis provided by this spontaneous verbalization often led to the elimination of symptoms. Breuer and Freud published their studies together, *Studien über Hysterie* (*Studies in Hysteria*, 1895/1957), but for Freud this was only a starting point for his further explorations into the unconscious mind.

By observing that many memories were inaccessible even while a patient was under hypnosis, Freud was able to hypothesize other forces that were keeping certain memories from consciousness. When he was unable to induce a somnambulistic trance in "Lucie R.," Freud tried placing his hand on her forehead and encouraging her to repeat whatever came to mind. This was the beginning of the "free association" method, which would become a significant part of the psychoanalytic process. As Freud collected more evidence from his observations of the purposeful nature of symptoms in his patients, he concluded that the observed symptoms served an economic function in the psychic life of the patient and that symptom removal through hypnosis was not an adequate treatment.

Years later, in 1919, Freud would modify his rejection of hypnosis. In light of its usefulness in the treatment of war neuroses and with large numbers of people, he would speak of the need to blend "the pure gold of analysis plentifully with the copper of direct suggestion" (Freud, 1946, p. 402). But his early rejection of hypnosis slowed the development and understanding of hypnotic treatment. Despite its unpopularity, which was largely due to increased interest in Freudian psychoanalysis, hypnosis was still the subject of study by Janet (1859–1947), a contemporary of Freud. This great French psychologist and neurologist had begun in opposition to hypnosis but became a strong advocate after his investigations on relaxation.

POSTWAR RESEARCH

Interest in psychoanalytic theory and the increasing use of chemical agents to produce surgical anesthesia caused a temporary decline in the use of hypnosis in medicine, as well. By the early 1900s, except for the studies of a small number of investigators like Janet, hypnosis was visible mainly in occult practices or in demonstrations meant for entertainment. But the need to treat men suffering from battle neuroses during World War I, and later during World War II and the Korean War, greatly increased interest in hypnotherapy. The hypnotic trance was used to remove symptoms directly and to treat soldiers who had repressed the emotions of traumatic battle situations. Under hypnosis, the soldiers were able to recall those situations and thus release the tension relating to their experiences. As a result of wartime use, techniques of hypnosis became more acceptable in the field of psychiatry and created a wave of enthusiasm for hypnotherapy.

After World War I, American psychologist Clark Hull (1884–1952) carried out experiments at Yale using more precise scientific and statistical methods than had been previously applied to research in hypnosis. He used control groups, for example, in experiments designed to determine the nature of hypnosis. Both unhypnotized and hypnotized subjects were exposed to the same experimental conditions so that investigators could observe the differences caused by the hypnotic induction process. In 1933, Hull reported his findings in *Hypnosis and Suggestibility*, in which he observed that "the essence of hypnosis lies in the fact of change in suggestibility" (Shor and Orne, 1965, p. 179). His meticulous methods of experimentation were important as precedent for further studies and for the development of standardized, objective procedures for research in hypnosis.

Near the turn of the century, Janet had predicted that hypnosis would return to fashion just as surely as outmoded styles of dress (Janet, 1925). After World War II, this prediction was well on its way to fulfillment. Practitioners in the fields of medicine, dentistry, and psychology showed increasing interest in the techniques of hypnosis, and the number of publications, both books and articles, reflected this growing interest. In 1945, a practicing psychiatrist, Louis Wolberg, published *Hypnoanalysis*, which included a detailed case history of a patient treated with hypnoanalytical techniques. This book has been called a landmark in the developing history of hypnosis because the author was willing to attempt some combination of his classical Freudian orientation with the use of hypnosis.

In 1949, SCEH was founded in the United States, becoming an international society in 1959, when a second society, ASCH, was formed. The British Medical Association added new stature to the study and use of hypnosis when it passed a formal resolution in 1955 to approve hypnosis as a valid therapeutic technique for treating psychoneuroses and for relieving pain in surgery and childbirth. In 1958, the American Medical Association and the American Dental Association made policy statements recognizing hypnosis as a legitimate form of treatment in medicine and dentistry, and they encouraged training in hypnosis for students in those fields. In 1960, the American Board of Hypnosis in Dentistry was established to certify practitioners trained in the use of hypnotic suggestion. The American Psychological Association has also created a section for psychologists who are primarily concerned with hypnosis.

This chapter began with the observation that the historical pathway to the present understanding of hypnosis has been long and uneven. It is not yet clear just where the trail may lead, but it is certain that the subject of hypnosis—especially its neurophysiological and psychological aspects—is open for serious research, and that the availability and interchange of information among various fields of research has greatly increased.

FURTHER READING

MacHovec, F. J. (1975). Hypnosis before Mesmer. *American Journal of Clinical Hypnosis, 17,* 215–220.

Tinterow, M. M. (1970). *Foundations of hypnosis: From Mesmer to Freud.* Springfield, IL: Charles C Thomas.

REFERENCES

Bernheim, H. M. (1884). *De la suggestion et de ses applications à la thérapeutique* [Hypnosis and suggestion in psychotherapy] (2nd ed.). Paris. (English trans. 1888, reprinted 1964)

Braid, J. (1843). *Neurypnology; or the rationale of nervous sleep.* Revised as *Braid on hypnotism, 1889.* New York: Julian Press, 1960.

Breuer, J., & Freud, S. (1957). *Studies in hysteria.* New York: Basic Books. (Original work, *Studien über hysterie,* published 1895)

Chertok, L. (1968). From Liébeault to Freud. *American Journal of Psychotherapy, 22,* 96–101.

Elliotson, J. (1843). *Numerous cases of surgical operations without pain in the mesmeric state.* Philadelphia: Lea and Blanchard.

Freud, S. (1953–1966). An autobiographical study. In *Standard edition* (Vol. 20, pp. 7–70). London: Hogarth Press. (Original work published 1925)

Freud, S. (1946). Turnings in the ways of psychoanalytic therapy. In E. Jones (Ed.), *Collected papers by Sigmund Freud* (Vol. 2). London: Hogarth Press.

Hull, C. L. (1933). *Hypnosis and suggestibility: An experimental approach.* New York: Appleton-Century-Crofts.

Janet, P. (1925). *Psychological healing* (2 vols., E. Paul & C. Paul, Trans.). New York: Macmillan. (Original work published 1919)

Shor, R. E. (1972). The fundamental problem in hypnosis research as viewed from historic perspectives. In E. Fromm & R. E. Shor (Eds.), *Hypnosis: Research developments and perspectives.* Chicago: Aldine·Atherton.

Shor, R. E., & Orne, M. T. (Eds.). (1965). *The nature of hypnosis: Selected basic readings.* New York: Holt, Rinehart & Winston.

Tinterow, M. M. (1970). *Foundations of hypnosis: From Mesmer to Freud.* Springfield, IL: Charles C Thomas.

Wolberg, L. R. (1945). *Hypnoanalysis.* New York: Grune & Stratton.

Wolberg, L. R. (1948). *Medical hypnosis* (2 vols.). New York: Grune & Stratton.

PART II

MODERN PERSPECTIVES ON HYPNOSIS

A s we have seen, hypnosis is both an ancient practice and a new frontier, both an art and a science, a phenomenon amenable to both rational analysis and creative speculation. The word "hypnosis" has multiple connotations. It refers to the trance state itself, to the process by which that state is achieved, and to the way in which the hypnotic trance is used for clinical purposes.

In viewing hypnosis from each of these perspectives, the following chapters review pertinent research as well as offer individual points of view. In Chapter 3, Errol Korn discusses hypnosis in relation to other altered states of consciousness and provides insight into the nature and power of suggestion. Chapter 4, on the induction process, explores the many procedures for helping a patient to access a trance state, and Chapter 5 introduces the therapeutic uses of imagery. Chapter 6 describes self-hypnosis, presenting available evidence on the difference between hetero- and self-hypnosis, and outlining a method for teaching self-hypnosis to patients. Taken together, these chapters provide a theoretical framework for the practical applications of hypnosis described in Part III.

Picasso once said that the artist's chore is "to first master the rules, and then overcome them. The rules exist, but they can all be circumvented." This advice applies as well to the practitioner learning to use hypnosis. Only after the basic techniques have been mastered does the real challenge begin: to use, combine, and adapt hypnotic techniques to meet the individual needs of each patient.

3

Altered States of Consciousness

Errol R. Korn, MD

Formal psychology in this century simply has not dealt with ASCs, especially positive ASCs, to any reasonable extent, considering their potential importance.

—Charles Tart
Altered States of Consciousness

Many theories have been developed to explain the polymorphous phenomenon called hypnosis. As summarized in Chapter 2, these theories variously view hypnosis as a dissociation from the mainstream of awareness; a state or trance with definable characteristics; role-playing at an unconscious level; a regression with the hypnotist playing the role of parent; or a condition of hypersuggestibility. Researchers have also tried to understand hypnosis using a brain-computer analogy, in which the brain functions as a special-purpose computer (Kroger, 1977, chapt. 32).

While all of these theories explain certain phenomena that take place in hypnosis, none explains hypnosis itself. The most comprehensive approach to explaining hypnosis is to include it in the paradigm of altered states of consciousness (ASCs). This chapter will provide a broad definition of ASCs and explore the similarities between hypnosis and the other states commonly considered to be ASCs.

STATES OF CONSCIOUSNESS

In order to discuss ASCs, we have to be able to distinguish them from other states of consciousness (SCs). This task in itself is difficult, because our current scientific instruments are not sensitive enough to measure differences in subjective awareness with any precision. Physiological measures, such as variations in brain-wave patterns, galvanic skin response, blood pressure, and heartbeat, are too gross to pinpoint states specifically. Experiential and intuitive explanations from persons who have experienced altered states can shed some light on these phenomena, but these reports do not correlate well with physiological measures. It is possible, for example, for someone to display all the characteristics of a waking state and yet respond to suggestions as if in an hypnotic state.

Cultural and semantic problems also figure into the attempt to describe SCs. In Sanskrit, there are 20 nouns for consciousness, while in English there are only a few. As a culture, we appear less able to differentiate between SCs than are those cultures more practiced in attaining ASCs (Spiegelberg, Fadiman, and Tart, 1964).

Furthermore, what may be considered a usual or normal SC in one culture may be abnormal or altered in the context of another culture. For example, members of some primitive tribes have specific periods during the day when they practice techniques that induce meditative SCs. These states, which are part of everyday life in some cultures, are considered out of the ordinary in Western cultures.

An SC can be understood as a distinct physiological and psychological condition of awareness. Different SCs are not, however, discrete, but are located on a continuum stretching from alert waking to deep dreaming, with a gradual overlap of characteristics.

Charles Tart (1977), a pioneer in the exploration of SCs and ASCs, developed a model for studying SCs. He called variations within each state, "subsystems." These subsystems are actually psychological structures and consist of the following variables:

1. Exteroceptors (sensory organs for perceiving the external world).

2. Interoceptors (sensory organs for perceiving internal body conditions).

3. Input processing (selective attention).

4. Memory.

5. Sense of identity (associated with the ego).

6. Evaluation and decision-making processes.

7. The subconscious.

8. Emotions.

9. Feeling for the flow of space and time.

10. Internal and external motor states that are responses to the other modalities.

We remain in SCs as long as they are stable. Tart (1977) noted four means of stabilizing an SC:

1. Performing appropriate activities so that no energy is left over to disrupt the system.

2. Continually correcting deviations from the norm.

3. Rewarding acceptable activities.

4. Limiting the ability of any destabilizing influences of a subsystem.

Tart (1972) defined a normal or usual state of consciousness (USC) as the one in which a person "spends the major part of his waking hours" (p. 1). In the opinion of this author, however, USCs should not be limited to the waking state. Using a broader definition, a USC can be understood as any state that we experience regularly, including sleeping, waking, or dreaming.

There are a number of variations even within our waking consciousness, and we usually glide from one substate to another, quite unaware of the transitions. For example, we might lapse into a daydream while reading a book, be so totally absorbed in solving a problem that we shut out the external world, rake leaves in a pleasant semitrance, and sink into apathy in front of the television—all within a single day. There obviously are wide variations within what we consider to be USCs. Tart (1977) explained these variations by pointing out that the subsystems do not change the general characteristics of an SC, and that shifts in the subsystems do not necessarily signal a shift into another SC.

A statement by Muses (1974) further highlights the difficulty of trying to distinguish between USCs and ASCs. He suggested that:

> . . . there is really no such thing as an "ordinary state of consciousness." Everyone to the degree governed by his or her acculturation, upbringing and value system development and entrenchment, is in a state of waking trance to some degree. Accul-

turation is slow hypnosis, as is all conditioning and behavioristic manipulation. (p. 4)

The reader interested in a more comprehensive study of SCs should refer to the books listed in Further Reading, at the end of this chapter.

ALTERED STATES

As might be expected, if it is difficult to define a USC, it is equally difficult to define an ASC. Altered states cannot be defined according to their method of induction, physiological correlates, or purposes, although explorations of ASCs from each of these perspectives have helped enlarge our understanding. Benson (1975) defined an ASC as one that does not occur spontaneously and that we do not experience regularly. An ASC can be more broadly defined as any SC that is different from our USC, that is, any state that differs from sleeping, waking, or dreaming.

While naming some ASCs does not solve the problem of classification, it does help to clarify it. The following are usually associated with ASCs: meditation, hypnotic trance, fugue states, dreams, EEG states (alpha and theta), hypnagogic and hypnopompic states, extrasensory awareness, dissociation, deep relaxation, ecstasy, psychotic states, and psychedelic states.

To be of value, an ASC should enable someone to realize his or her full potential and to take command of mind-body processes. ASCs that lend themselves to these purposes share several characteristics: relaxation, inward focusing of attention, slower flow of attention than ordinary SCs, being inherently safe, and being controllable by the individual. Some ASCs, such as psychotic and hallucinatory states, are maladaptive and do not fit these criteria.

Another characteristic of ASCs is that they are active states, in the sense that a person chooses to enter them, rather than passive states, in which the person loses autonomy. According to Erika Fromm's (1977) ego-psychological theory of ASCs, the prevailing state in many healthy manifestations of ASCs is ego receptivity, in which a person allows unconscious and preconscious material to float into the mind. In an ASC, we relinquish some of the control functions of the left hemisphere of the brain and draw more on the holistic and spatial functions of the right cerebral hemisphere.

Inducing Altered States

As described in Tart's (1977) systems approach to SCs, an ASC is established when a USC is disrupted, thereby interfering with the stabilizing forces. There are several ways of disrupting an SC. Overload of stimuli, such as that resulting from the multiple traumas of an accident or the auditory overload of a rock concert, can put someone spontaneously into an ASC. Subjects in research studies who are placed in sensory deprivation chambers that block out all stimuli develop ASCs spontaneously. The introduction of stimuli so strange to the system that they cannot be processed can induce altered states. For example, going into the hospital for the first time alters the everyday sensations with which patients are familiar. As a result, a patient sometimes spontaneously enters an ASC. Withdrawing attention from a subsystem also may affect the stability of an SC enough to cause the formation of an ASC. For example, if exteroceptors were a major variable in stabilizing the system of the waking state, and we withdrew our attention from these processes, we would be more likely to change into an ASC.

"Patterning forces," such as the monotonous repetition of a sound, may be applied to form a new system or ASC (Tart, 1977). The greater the stability of this ASC, the more it will persist, but because an ASC usually is more disorganized than the USC, the latter usually returns. For this reason, ASCs are difficult to maintain. However, if the patterning forces in the new stabilizing systems are fortified by techniques such as hypnosis, the ASC can persist for longer periods of time and become more powerful.

A given ASC may be reached through different methods. Hypnosis, for example, is attained by using a number of techniques, from the traditional pendulum swing of a watch on a chain, to various spoken forms of induction, to self-induction. Similarly, one method of induction may bring about a variety of states. Consider, for example, the array of responses elicited by tetrahydrocannabinol (THC), the active ingredient in marijuana, which range from drowsiness, to pleasant euphoria, to paranoia or hallucination. Even people who practice hypnosis or meditation will achieve different levels of trance, depending on their goals and level of expertise.

Physiological Correlates

There are several formal systems for altering consciousness with the purposes of enabling people to monitor body processes, overcome stress, develop optimal health and wellness, and ameliorate disease processes. These systems include, among others, various forms of meditation, autogenic training, progressive relaxation, hypnosis, and biofeedback. Just as there is overlap among different SCs, so there are broad areas of similarity among these systems for inducing ASCs, many of which lead to states producing similar responses. A major incentive for keeping many of these disciplines separate in the public mind is profit. If a system can be advertised as unique, then only those trained in that system are able to administer therapy or instruction. The actual differences among these systems and the resulting ASC are often more semantic than real. A comparison of the major methods of inducing ASCs highlights the physiological similarities of the various altered states.

Meditation. Meditation systems fall into two broad categories: concentrative or "one-pointed" meditation, in which attention is narrowed to block out the external world; and expansive or "opening out" meditation, in which attention takes in a wide field. Founded by Maharishi Mahesh Yogi, transcendental meditation (TM) is a type of meditation based on yoga. The major components of this system are a quiet environment, repeated mental device (mantram), receptive attitude, and comfortable position (Benson, 1975). Using these same four requirements but changing the Sanskrit mantram to the English word "one," Benson (1975) developed what he called the relaxation response, which brings about the same physiological changes that occur during the practice of TM. There are many other varieties of meditation, and each meditative system has variations that depend on the level of practice.

Autogenic training. Originated in the early part of this century by J. H. Schultz, a German psychologist, autogenic training has been popularized more recently by Luthe (1969). Its goal is to use autohypnosis to reduce stress, control pain, and treat maladies caused by tension. Standard exercises, such as those that produce a feeling of heaviness or warmth and regulate the heartbeat and breathing, are used to induce relaxation and other physiological changes. Using a set of meditative exercises, the patient forms images of concepts and asks questions of the unconscious.

Progressive relaxation. Popularized through the work of Jacobson (1938), progressive relaxation consists of alternately contracting and releasing tension in the body's muscle groups.

Biofeedback training. Physiologic monitoring devices provide immediate feedback to patients seeking to control their physiological responses. By controlling their physiology, patients can experience relaxation and tranquility as well as lowered blood pressure, controlled heartbeat, and stabilized skin temperature, among numerous other phenomena.

Hypnosis. As a system of induction, hypnosis is more difficult to categorize than the others. Hypnosis can be a self-induced phenomenon similar to meditation, or it can be induced with the guidance of others. It can be directed toward a specific goal, such as the management of lower back pain, or used for general purposes, such as relaxation. It is more difficult to view hypnosis as a separate phenomenon than to see its similarities with other states. As Kroger (1977) stated, the practitioners of various methods of attaining ASCs:

> . . . who are not familiar with modern and sophisticated technics of hypnosis, which do not require an induction technic, will naturally not believe they are using task motivation instruction in a hypnotic manner. Likewise, those using various forms of meditation and A.S.C. are seldom aware that they are resorting to self-hypnosis. (p. 144)

Studies of physiological changes produced by the different systems for inducing ASCs have identified many similarities. The most complete analysis of the physiology of ASCs has been performed on practitioners of TM, which is characterized by a predominance of alpha in EEG; a decrease in heart rate, blood pressure, respiratory rate, muscle tension, and blood lactate; and an increased blood flow to the brain. All of these changes, which are the antithesis of the stress response, are compatible with Benson's relaxation response (Orme-Johnson and Farrow, 1977; Jevning, Wilson, Smith, and Morton, 1978; Wallace, 1970). Benson, in turn, has concluded that the physiological state of neutral hypnosis is comparable to the relaxation response (Benson, Arns, and Hoffman, 1981).

Autogenic training and yogic meditation produce similar changes, including decreased respiratory and heart rates, predominance of alpha, and a decrease in muscle tension. Progressive relaxation also produces a decrease in respiratory rate, heart rate, blood pressure, and muscle tension (Bagchi and Wenger, 1959; Borkovec and Fowles, 1973; Jacobson, 1938).

The physiological changes occurring within hypnosis are more varied than those found within the other ASCs. Whereas induction methods for the other disciplines are fairly standardized, hypnotic inductions vary considerably. Some inductions are similar, if not identical, to those of autogenic training and progressive relaxation, while some relaxation techniques used in hypnosis are similar to meditation practices.

The difference between hypnosis and other ASCs is in the method and content of the hypnotic suggestion rather than the mode of induction, whether it be self-induced or hetero-induced. Crasilneck and Hall (1959) distinguished between "neutral" hypnosis, in which the patient has achieved the trance state, and hypnosis after specific suggestions are given. It appears that the physiological changes accompanying hypnosis reflect the milieu suggested by the hypnotist or, in the case of self-hypnosis, directed by the patient (Wallace and Benson, 1972). For example, if the hypnotist introduces images conducive to relaxation, heartbeat and respiration will decrease. Conversely, these measures will increase during task performance or suggestions causing excitement.

A study by Morse, Martin, Funst, and Dubin (1977) compared the physiological effects of an alert waking state, meditation using TM and simple word meditation, relaxed hypnosis, task performance hypnosis, and relaxation. This study overcame the methodological errors of earlier studies, which failed to study the disciplines in the same protocol and did not take into account differences in the content of hypnotic suggestions. As might be expected, Morse found relaxed hypnosis and the meditative states to be physiologically similar, whereas the two hypnotic states (relaxed hypnosis and task performance hypnosis) were significantly different. (See Barmark and Junitz, 1979, Edmonston, 1979, Paul, 1969, and Walrath and Hamilton, 1975, for studies documenting the similarities among ASCs.)

We can conclude from these findings that to attain the benefits of an ASC, any of the methods discussed here is satisfactory. This conclusion is undoubtedly true, as well, for many similar methods that have not yet been studied physiologically. Meditation techniques, autogenic training, biofeedback, and other systems enable people to monitor their body processes, overcome stress, develop optimal health and wellness, manage pain, and ameliorate disease processes. So does hypnosis. Meditative and other states of consciousness lead to self-actualization, improved learning, enhanced creative ability, task motivation, and alteration of habit patterns. So does hypnosis.

Because all of the ASCs discussed above produce beneficial effects, a patient's needs can in many instances be met simply by learning to induce an ASC. A technique that works for one person may not work for another. Therefore, a practitioner familiar with many approaches and methods will be able to benefit the greatest number of patients. Suggestions of imagery (see Chapter 5) should be introduced only after the patient is practiced in attaining an ASC.

SUMMARY

Hypnosis represents an ASC that is similar to other ASCs, which are beneficial in themselves. ASCs promote physiological changes that are the opposite of the stress response and may in fact be our innate way of preventing the detrimental effects of this response, which is biologically programmed into all of us. ASCs also increase the effectiveness of suggestions and imagery.

Tart (1977) believed that entering into an ASC allows shifts in perspective that facilitate a different view of the universe. He envisioned a science of ASCs that would parallel our present science associated with the waking, alert state. As people become proficient at moving from one state into another, perhaps the USC will expand to include more of what we now think of as ASCs, making us richer both in personality and in understanding.

FURTHER READING

Korn, E. R., & Johnson, K. (1983). *Visualization: The uses of imagery in the health professions.* Homewood, IL: Dow-Jones-Irwin.

Tart, C. T. (Ed.). (1972). *Altered states of consciousness.* New York: Anchor Books.

Tart, C. T. (1975). *States of consciousness.* New York: E. P. Dutton.

Zinberg, N.E. (Ed.). (1977). *Alternate states of consciousness.* New York: Free Press.

REFERENCES

Bagchi, B. K., & Wenger, M. A. (1959). Electrophysiological correlates of some yogi exercises. In L.Van Bagaert & J. Radermecker (Eds.), *Electroencephalography, clinical neurophysiology and epilepsy,* Vol. 3 of First International Congress of Neurological Sciences. London: Pergamon.

Barmark, S. M., & Junitz, S. C. B. (1979). Transcendental meditation and hetero-hypnosis as altered states of consciousness. *International Journal of Clinical and Experimental Hypnosis, 27,* 227–239.

Benson, H. (1975). *The relaxation response.* New York: Morrow.

Benson, H., Aɪns, P. A., & Hoffman, J. W. (1981). The relaxation response and hypnosis. *International Journal of Clinical and Experimental Hypnosis, 29,* 259–270.

Borkovec, R., & Fowles, D. (1973). A controlled investigation of the effects of progressive and hypnotic relaxation on insomnia. *Journal of Abnormal Psychology, 82*, 153–158.

Crasilneck, H. B., & Hall, J. A. (1959). Physiological changes associated with hypnosis: A review of the literature since 1948. *International Journal of Clinical and Experimental Hypnosis, 7*, 9–50.

Edmonston, W. E. (1979). The effects of neutral hypnosis on conditioned responses: Implications for hypnosis as relaxation. In E. Fromm & R. E. Shor (Eds.), *Hypnosis: Developments in research and new prospectives* (2nd ed.). New York: Aldine Publishing.

Fromm, E. (1977). An ego-psychological theory of altered states of consciousness. *International Journal of Clinical and Experimental Hypnosis, 25*, 372–387.

Jacobson, E. (1938). *Progressive relaxation.* Chicago: University of Chicago Press.

Jevning, R., Wilson, A. F., Smith, W. R., & Morton, M. E. (1978). Redistribution of blood flow in acute metabolic behavior. *American Journal of Physiology, 235*, R89–R92.

Kroger, W. S. (1977). *Clinical and experimental hypnosis* (2nd ed.). Philadelphia: J. B. Lippincott.

Luthe, W. (Ed.). (1969). *Autogenic therapy* (Vols. 1–5). New York: Grune & Stratton.

Morse, D. R., Martin J. S., Funst, M. L., & Dubin, L. L. (1977). The physiological and subjective evaluation of meditation, hypnosis and relaxation. *Psychosomatic Medicine, 39*, 304–324.

Muses, C. M. (1974). Introduction. In C. Muses & A. M. Young (Eds.), *Consciousness and reality.* New York: Avon Books.

Orme-Johnson, D., & Farrow, J. T. (Eds.). (1977). *Scientific research on transcendental meditation programs. Collected papers* (Vol. 1). Livingstone Manor, NY: Maharishi European Research University Press.

Paul, G. L. (1969). Physiological effects of relaxation training and hypnotic suggestion. *Journal of Abnormal Psychology, 74*, 425–537.

Spiegelberg, F., Fadiman, F., & Tart, C. (1964, June). *The concept of the subtle body.* Lectures at the Esalen Institute, Big Sur, CA.

Tart, C. (1972). Introduction. In C. Tart (Ed.), *Altered states of consciousness* (pp. 1–6). New York: Anchor Books.

Tart, C. T. (1977). Putting the pieces together; a conceptual framework for understanding discrete states of consciousness. In N. E. Zinberg (Ed.), *Alternate states of consciousness* (pp. 158–219). New York: Free Press.

Wallace, R. K. (1970). Physiological effects of transcendental meditation. *Science, 167*, 175–195.

Wallace, R. K., & Benson, H. (1972). The physiology of meditation. *Altered states of awareness: Readings from Scientific American.* San Francisco: Freeman.

Walrath, L. C., & Hamilton, D. W. (1975). Autonomic correlates of meditation and hypnosis. *American Journal of Clinical Hypnosis, 17*, 190–196.

4
Induction

*An incubator supplies a favorable environment
for the hatching of eggs, but the actual hatching
derives from the development of life processes
within the egg.*

—Milton Erickson
Deep Hypnosis and Its Induction

T he more we learn about the phenomenon we call hypnosis, the
more it eludes us. The induction process has always been the
aspect most shrouded in mystery—from Mesmer's robes and wands to
the stage entertainer's seemingly uncanny ability to induce a trance in
volunteers from the audience.

The process of hypnotic induction is neither mysterious nor difficult.
Anyone who can communicate with others can learn the technique of
trance induction within a relatively short time. However, knowing how
to induce a trance does not qualify someone as a practitioner of
hypnosis any more than knowing how to make an incision qualifies
someone to be a surgeon. The safe and effective use of hypnosis
requires knowledge of the many variables at work in the induction
process and of the nature and use of suggestion, as well as a sensitivity
to a patient's needs and responses.

This chapter provides basic information on the induction process,
the variables influencing induction, and the laws of suggestion. The
authors strongly recommend that actual induction techniques be
learned through the formal training programs sponsored by ASCH and
SCEH or through the graduate and postgraduate training programs
offered at medical schools, hospitals, and institutions providing
graduate training in psychology.

TYPES OF INDUCTION

Induction techniques can be discussed according to several broad categories or approaches. Although each category encompasses a wide range of procedures, these divisions are useful to introduce the subject of hypnotic induction.

Direct vs. Indirect

Perhaps the broadest distinction among the various types of induction is between the direct and the indirect approaches. An induction can be either direct or indirect or reflect qualities of both. The direct or authoritative technique, which is older and better understood, has been the focus of most of the research on hypnosis and has historically been the more widely used approach. The indirect or permissive technique is less easy to define because it tends to be more individualized and more dependent on the personal relationship between patient and practitioner.

Because the indirect approach has been less known, people with only a cursory knowledge of hypnosis sometimes assume that the direct technique is the only technique for inducing an hypnotic trance. Before the 1950s, direct induction did appear to be the only technique. In the 1950s, however, the indirect approach was discussed by such authors as Erickson, David Cheek, and Leslie LeCron. The idea caught on in the early 1960s, and it has since been rapidly gaining in popularity with practitioners. Studies of the indirect approach to induction are also becoming more widely represented in the scientific literature.

In a training program, the direct approach usually is taught first because it is the easiest and quickest to learn. Direct inductions are more specific, take more of a "cookbook" approach, and are more easily applied than indirect inductions. The direct induction "makes full use of ritual and expectancy of success," according to Kroger (1977, p. 65). The practitioner assumes an authoritative role and gives clear direction for what the patient is to experience. Direct induction methods usually rely upon eye fixation (which results in fatigue of the muscles) combined with specific suggestions for relaxation or sleep.

The following excerpt from an induction by Kroger (1977) exemplifies the direct approach:

> Notice now that your eyes are getting very, very heavy; your lids are getting very, very, very tired. Your lids are getting heavier and heavier, and the heavier that your lids get now, the better you will

relax your lids. The better you relax your eyelids, the better you
will follow all subsequent suggestions. (p. 65)

Another direct approach, described in some detail by Hartland (1971),
combines eye fixation with the task of counting backward from 300.
The counting distracts the conscious mind and makes the unconscious
more accessible to verbal suggestions of tiredness and heaviness. Some
patients are most comfortable with the direct approach, and some
actually expect it because it is consistent with their preconceptions
about hypnosis.

The realization that the direct approach is not effective with
everyone paved the way for an exploration of other methods of induction. Erickson, the master of the indirect approach, did considerable
work with subjects considered unhypnotizable. The assumption
underlying indirect methods of induction is that permissive or indirect
suggestions, which do not appear to be commands, are less likely to
arouse conscious attention, and therefore, resistance. Erickson believed
in the wisdom of the patient's unconscious and phrased his suggestions
to express what he wanted to accomplish but not the exact means for
going about it. This type of indirect approach often works for patients
who feel threatened by more authoritarian induction procedures.

The following portion of a hand levitation induction illustrates the
way in which suggestions can be phrased to permit the patient a degree
of choice:

> Shortly your right hand, or it may be your left hand, will begin to
> lift up, or it may press down, or it may not move at all, but we will
> wait to see just what happens. Maybe the thumb will be first, or
> you may feel something happening in your little finger, but the
> really important thing is not whether your hand lifts up or
> presses down or just remains still; rather, it is your ability to sense
> fully whatever feelings may develop in your hands. (Erickson,
> 1967, p. 20)

Erickson developed his indirect techniques to facilitate his utilization
approach to induction and treatment. He viewed hypnotic suggestion
as "the process of evoking and utilizing a patient's own mental processes
in ways that are outside his usual range of intentional or voluntary
control" (Erickson and Rossi, 1976, p. 170). The practitioner employing
the utilization approach uses a patient's feelings, thoughts, and experiences to induce and deepen trance and to work toward treatment goals.

No two inductions will ever be exactly alike because no two patients are exactly alike.

Because indirect approaches to induction have been so closely associated with Erickson, it is worthwhile to note the elements Erickson considered the cornerstones of his technique. The following elements are summarized from *Hypnotic Realities* (Erickson, Rossi, and Rossi, 1976).

The "Yes" set.   By asking a series of questions requiring an obvious "yes" response, the practitioner can evoke a set of positive associations that will facilitate acceptance of the trance experience. Is your name John? Do you live on State Street? and Are you seated in that chair? are examples of questions that can be used to develop a "yes set."

Truisms.   The simplest form of suggestion, truisms are obvious statements of fact that cannot be denied and that use a patient's past experiences and associations. Examples include reminding patients that they once learned to recognize the letters of the alphabet or that they already know how to experience certain sensations, such as the warmth of the sun on their skin.

Implication.   An indirect way of evoking desired behavior, an example of implication would be Erickson's statement, "I don't know what chair you are going to sit in," which implies that the patient will sit down. "Certainly your arm won't be numb before I count to five" implies that the arm will be numb sometime after the count of five.

Double-bind questions.   Useful for resistant patients, a double-bind is a question that cannot be answered with one's usual conscious processes, that requires patients to turn their attention inward, and that facilitates a desirable response regardless of which alternative is experienced. For example, Erickson might ask a patient, "Do you want to enter trance now or in a few minutes?" or "Will your right hand move or lift or shift to the side or press down first? Or will it be your left hand?"

Because indirect techniques are more a process than a prescription, they are more difficult to learn than direct techniques. While it may take a few weeks of instruction to become successful in applying direct induction techniques, it takes many years of practice to become expert in the use of purely indirect techniques. The indirect approach is most often used by practitioners for whom hypnosis is a large, rather than an occasional, part of their practice. However, many practitioners incorporate elements of the indirect approach, such as permissive, choice-oriented suggestions, in their inductions and do so with great success.

The issue is not so much which technique—direct or indirect—is better, but which is likely to produce the best results for a patient in a given situation. Take, for example, Alman's case of the Marine drill instructor who requested hypnosis to control chronic pain in the lower back. Earlier treatment, including two surgeries and numerous medications, had been ineffective. The man was obviously angry with "all these softy doctors who aren't worth anything." An indirect, permissive approach to induction would probably have fit into the patient's "softy doctor" preconceptions. Therefore, to meet the patient on his own ground, Alman took an authoritarian approach: "Sit down, take off your shoes. . . . These are orders. . . . Don't say another word until I ask you to leave. . . . So now shut your eyes, count backwards from 100 to 1 and go into trance so you will focus on your lower back. NOW . . . " The induction was successful.

As this case suggests, flexibility in the practitioner is important in any induction. Because it is sometimes necessary to change or modify the focus of an induction when it becomes apparent that the first approach is not producing the desired results, it is important for practitioners to have experience with both direct and indirect techniques. Regardless of the approach used, consideration should be given to each patient's unique experience so that the induction can be personalized.

Formal vs. Informal

Using indirect suggestions and the concept of relaxation, an hypnotic trance can be achieved without a formal induction. Although the distinction is abstract, varying considerably in practice, a formal induction is explicit, requiring the conscious consent of both practitioner and patient to follow a step-by-step induction process. Direct inductions, using eye fixation or other methods of focusing attention combined with suggestions for relaxation, are formal inductions.

During an informal induction, hypnosis as such is not discussed, and the process of achieving a state of relaxation or trance is less structured. Hypnotic techniques are applied in a more open-ended way. The practitioner watches the patient's physiological responses and paces suggestions accordingly. Timing the phrases to match the patient's breathing, for example, a practitioner might say, "Each time you inhale oxygen into your body, and as your body maximizes its use of the oxygen, and as you exhale carbon dioxide from your body along with tension and anxiety, your level of relaxation somehow and in some way naturally and progressively increases." For extended treatment, when time is not crucial, informal techniques can be integrated into the overall process of therapy.

Erickson's concept of utilization can be a valuable part of an informal induction process, or what Erickson (1958b) termed a "naturalistic approach." Andolesk and Novik (1980) cited several case studies in which they induced trance in young children facing minor surgery in an emergency room. Instead of denying the frightening aspects of the situation, the authors used them. For example, one child could watch the surgical instruments being unwrapped and imagine that they were her Christmas presents being unwrapped on Christmas morning. She became very relaxed and fell asleep while she was being sutured without anesthetic.

Another instance of utilization can be seen in Alman's induction of an extremely nervous, highly strung woman. It was clear that the patient would be unable to respond to suggestions to relax and make herself comfortable as a prelude to a formal induction procedure. Her arms were shaking and she was constantly shifting in her seat. Therefore, while talking with the patient, Alman requested her to shake her left arm in an exaggerated manner, then both arms, then both arms and one leg, then both arms and both legs, and then her entire body. Before long, she was "shaken out"; she relaxed completely and quickly entered trance.

Using informal induction techniques should not be construed as tricking a patient into hypnosis. Informal techniques are but one way of helping a patient experience the beneficial effects of an altered state of consciousness, and the results are the same, regardless of the label (hypnosis, relaxation, or mental imagery) on the procedure.

Rapid Inductions

One of the arguments against the use of hypnosis in general and the indirect technique in particular is that the induction process is too time-consuming for a busy therapist, dentist, or physician. The assumption is that all inductions take 20 to 30 minutes and must follow a step-by-step process. Although beginners usually are taught standard inductions requiring approximately 20 minutes to complete, rapid inductions are an alternative employed by many experienced practitioners.

In some instances, inductions are overdone and oververbalized due to the practitioner's desire to be certain that the patient enters a hypnotic trance. A successful rapid induction, on the other hand, is partly based on the practitioner's confidence that in a cooperative atmosphere, a motivated patient will be able to access a trance state. When a practitioner works with someone over a period of time, inductions become briefer because of the patient's increasing expertise and expectation of success.

Rapid inductions are employed in first-time situations as well. Matheson and Grehan (1979) published a rapid induction technique used routinely by Hartland (1971). A modification of Erickson's (1964b) catalepsy induction technique, it can induce a hypnotic trance in less than 60 seconds. The basis of this technique, as the authors describe it, is "the nonverbal establishment of behavior outside of consciousness":

> The patient's arm is picked up at the wrist by the therapist and held in a horizontal position. The therapist slowly releases contact until it seems apparent that the arm will remain elevated without any further physical support. Then it is suggested that the eyes may close and the body relax. (p. 298)

If catalepsy is not achieved, the practitioner responds by letting the arm drop into the patient's lap and congratulates the patient for relaxing so well.

Barber (1977) reported success with his rapid induction analgesic (RIA) technique in 99 out of 100 dental patients. These patients were able to complete a variety of dental treatments (root canals, crowns, and extractions) with no chemical anesthetic. Even though this technique took approximately 10 minutes, from Barber's introduction to the patient to the beginning of dental treatment, it earned the name "rapid" because induction procedures to achieve sufficient hypnotic depth for analgesia normally require 45 minutes or more, as well as continued maintenance of the trance throughout the dental procedure. Two keys to Barber's approach are his use of permissive suggestions and the fact that analgesic suggestions are framed in a posthypnotic context.

Cheek and LeCron (1968) reported a rapid induction method that employs a "startle effect." After producing eye fatigue and asking the patient to close his or her eyes, they proceed as follows:

> As soon as his eyes close, the operator places his left hand at the back of the subject's neck with his right hand or fingers pressing on

the forehead. He then suddenly moves the subject's head around sharply and rapidly in a clockwise circle, telling him to relax his neck and shoulder muscles and to let go completely. The tone should be positive and the words should be spoken rapidly. Having one's head seized unexpectedly and rotated in this way produces a mild startle effect. (p. 32)

The practitioner then pushes the patient back onto a chair or a couch and continues with deepening techniques.

Erickson was known for a handshake induction in which he loosened his grip so slowly that the other person's hand was left cataleptic. The procedure was so effective that some of Erickson's colleagues refused to shake hands with him unless he reassured them first that no induction was intended (see Erickson et al., 1976, for his description of this technique).

Although these rapid inductions are considered prestige inductions, requiring extensive experience and considerable expertise on the part of the practitioner, they are further evidence that hypnotic induction is not necessarily a lock-step process or a prescribed formula.

Hetero-Hypnosis vs. Self-Hypnosis

Another major distinction between different types of induction procedures is between hetero-hypnosis and self-hypnosis. As discussed in Chapter 1, a major realization in the history of hypnosis has been that the power of hypnosis resides within each person and that all hypnosis is essentially self-hypnosis. Daydreaming is a form of self-hypnosis, as is absorption in a book, a task, a film, or a religious ceremony. In a clinical setting, self-hypnosis can be an effective way of reinforcing hetero-hypnosis and assisting patients to gain greater mastery over themselves and their lives.

In self-hypnosis, individuals enter a relaxed, highly suggestible state and give suggestions to themselves. In her research on the differences between self-hypnosis and hetero-hypnosis, Fromm et al. (1981) found that in self-hypnosis one's attention is more free-floating and the imagery is richer, while in hetero-hypnosis, one's attention is more concentrated and one is more successful in producing certain phenomena, such as age regression and hallucination.

The belief that self-suggestion can be more meaningful and more easily accommodated than suggestions coming from an outside source is basic to the indirect approach to induction and partially explains the demonstrated effectiveness of self-hypnosis in facilitating changes in behavior patterns. Because self-hypnosis is such an important factor in modern clinical hypnosis, a separate chapter has been devoted to self-hypnosis and the methods by which a practitioner can teach it to patients (see Chapter 6).

GENERAL PRINCIPLES

Induction is primarily an attention-getting process designed to focus the conscious mind and make the unconscious more accessible. Deepening procedures, which increase the depth of the trance, are often incorporated into the induction. For example, having the patient imagine walking down a staircase, becoming more and more relaxed with each step, is a common approach to both inducing and deepening a trance. The following general principles apply to most types of induction. Some are specific to certain situations and some are redundant in others.

1. Relaxation is a necessary first step in most induction procedures. The patient should be comfortable, either sitting or reclining while the practitioner gives suggestions for relaxation and, often, instructions for relaxing various muscle groups.

2. Most inductions rely on the repetition of monotonous, rhythmical, sensory stimuli for fixation of attention:
   a. Visual stimuli for eye fixation, such as staring at a fixed point, or an object (a spinning disk; a low-wattage, colored light bulb; or a pendulum).
   b. Auditory stimuli, or imagery described in a monotonous, rhythmical manner. Soft, slow music or a metronome set for a slow beat can also facilitate induction.
   c. Tactile stimuli, such as pressure on the arm or shoulder to increase the feeling of heaviness, or a light touch on the eyelids to anchor them after they close.

   Some practitioners use a combination of these stimuli. Some recommend that the practitioner avoid startling patients by informing them in advance when tactile stimuli are to be used.

3. Support and encouragement should be provided by letting the patient know that whatever behavior he or she is manifesting—such as swallowing or shifting position—is a good sign and will contribute to relaxation.

4. Suggestions for relaxation should be based on what the patient is experiencing at the time (for the purpose of induction and

deepening). For example: "As your arm becomes stiffer, you will go deeper and deeper" (direct language), or "With every breath you take, you may be interested in sensing your increased relaxation" (indirect language).

5. External sounds may be used to induce and deepen the trance. This technique is particularly valuable in places such as noisy hospital wards, where an environment free of distraction is unobtainable. For example:

> Any noise outside of the sound of my voice will somehow and in some way help you to, perhaps, relax more and more; as you hear the sound of the conversation in the next room, that tone and even the content of that conversation will somehow and in some way help you to relax; or as the sound of the airplane overhead fades into the distance, perhaps you find yourself relaxing more and more.

6. Patients should be allowed to deepen the trance at their own pace. Watch for such external signs as changes in respiration, relaxation of muscles, eye closure, and movement of eyes under the eyelids. Some practitioners ask patients to signal when they are as deep as they want to be, so that suggestions can be timed accordingly.

7. Successful challenges often can demonstrate to patients that they have been hypnotized and tend to deepen the trance. However, some patients will respond to a direct challenge, such as "Your eyes are glued tightly together. You cannot open them. . . . Now try to open your eyes . . ." by doing just that.

    Traditionally, an unsuccessful challenge is viewed as a setback for both patient and practitioner. However, by rephrasing the challenge in a more permissive way, the practitioner enables patients to give themselves suggestions. For example:

> You know that you can open your eyes any time that you wish . . . but you know that opening your eyes will take tremendous energy, and since you are so relaxed and comfortable, you really do not want to move more muscles than those muscles absolutely necessary to keep yourself safe and comfortable. . . . You might even give yourself a suggestion that the harder you might try to open your eyes, the heavier your eyelids may become.

The challenge continues using a double-bind technique (Erickson et al., 1976) that ensures the appropriate outcome regardless of which course the patient chooses:

> The more and more relaxed you are finding yourself, the more you want to continue this state of relaxation . . . and not disturb it. . . . You know that opening your eyes may somehow and in some way disturb your state of relaxation at this time . . . so keeping your eyes closed and comfortable helps you to continue your level of increasing relaxation. . . . If you open your eyes, your level of relaxation deepens, and as you close your eyes, your level of relaxation deepens even more. . . . If you feel that your level of relaxation is as deep as you may want it at this time, go ahead and try to open your eyes.

Using this type of challenge, the practitioner sets up a no-lose situation by suggesting to patients that they don't want to open their eyes, but that if they do, their level of relaxation will deepen even more.

8. For extended treatment, suggest that the trance can be elicited by progressively shorter and shorter induction processes. This can be accomplished through a direct or indirect posthypnotic suggestion, which includes a reinduction signal—a word, phrase, or other signal. Later inductions usually require only 3 to 5 minutes.

Overcoming Resistance

According to Daniel Araoz (1982), "the art of hypnosis relies on not providing the client with grounds for resisting" (p. 106). The best insurance against resistance during a hypnotic induction is proper preparation of the patient. Establishing good rapport, dispelling any misconceptions about hypnosis, discussing the purpose and expectations of the hypnotic procedure, and making sure that the patient is comfortable are crucial preliminary steps. If the patient does not respond as expected, the practitioner needs to reevaluate each of them.

It is also important not to expect too much too soon. To a large extent, the practitioner is a predictive factor in the induction process, for a patient is sensitive to spoken and unspoken cues. The practitioner's conviction that hypnosis will work is the best insurance against failure. A patient who initially appears to be unresponsive may eventually become a good hypnotic subject.

In a review of failures in hypnosis and hypnotherapy, Lazar and Dempster (1981) concluded that "most failures result from a poor fit between patient variables on one hand and treatment variables including therapeutic strategy [and] choice of hypnotic modality . . . on the other" (p. 52). In other words, the practitioner must remain flexible. If a patient resists direct suggestions, try indirect. If a patient doesn't like to imagine walking down a staircase, suggest walking up. To avoid choosing for the patient, use neutral language, such as "walk along a staircase."

Cheek and LeCron (1968) estimated the following results for an operator of average skill at a first hypnotic session: 15% of patients will achieve a deep trance; 35% will reach a medium state; 45% will reach a light trance state; and 5% will not be hypnotized. Induction is not a matter of success or failure: there is always some degree of change, even for the initially unresponsive, whether it be increased relaxation, pleasure related to a daydream, or temporary detachment from a problem. Always discuss a hypnotic session in terms of degree of success, not failure, and reassure the patient that next time will be even more successful.

SPECIFIC TECHNIQUES

Clearly, there is no single way to help a patient gain access to a trance state. Most experienced practitioners use many different types and combinations of inductions, examples of which have been included in Part 3, Clinical Applications. Several specific induction techniques widely used in clinical hypnosis are briefly described below. The list is by no means inclusive, but it does provide an overview of the variety of approaches that have been effective.

Eye fixation method.   Used by Braid in the 1840s, this method is today the most popular direct approach to induction. It can also be part of an indirect approach through the use of indirect, permissive language. The patient sits comfortably in a chair and fixes attention on something slightly above eye level, so that the eyes roll up in their sockets. The focus can be an object, a spot on the wall, a coin, or some other object held by the practitioner. Eyes held in this position will become physically fatigued, a condition that the practitioner reinforces with suggestions that the eyelids are becoming tired and heavy and soon will close. Once the patient is relaxed, with eyes closed, the practitioner can proceed with suggestions for deepening the trance.

A variation of the eye fixation method is a technique that combines deep breathing with opening and closing the eyes. Patients open their eyes widely while inhaling and allow their eyes to relax completely while exhaling. After a short time, the eyes become fatigued, and the practitioner suggests that the patient may prefer to leave them closed.

Coin technique.   The patient sits upright in a chair and extends one arm directly in front with the palm up. The patient is asked to focus attention on a large coin, which the practitioner places on the ulnar edge of the hand. The practitioner suggests that as he or she starts counting, the hand will begin to turn, and when the coin falls off, the patient's eyes will close, the arm will relax and fall to the lap, and relaxation will spread throughout the body.

Chiasson's method.   This method, described in the ASCH syllabus (1973), was devised by Simon Chiasson, an Ohio Obstetrician. Like the eye fixation method, it associates normal physiological responses with induction suggestions. The patient's hand is placed directly in front of the face, palm outwards, about 12 inches from the nose. As the fingers begin to spread apart, which they naturally tend to do in this position, the practitioner suggests that the hand will move toward the face. When it touches the face, the eyes will close, the hand will fall to the lap, and the patient will become completely relaxed.

Hand or arm levitation method.   This technique includes many of the characteristics of the indirect approach: (a) the patient plays an active part in the induction, (b) the concept of relaxation is used instead of sleep, and (c) the patient enters and deepens the trance at his or her own pace.

Sitting in a chair with both hands resting on the thighs, the patient is asked to focus on the dominant hand and notice the texture of the clothing underneath, the warmth of the skin, perhaps a tingling sensation in the fingers, and any other sensations that may occur. The practitioner suggests that when one of the fingers moves slightly, the hand will begin to feel light and begin to move up from the thigh—as if a balloon were tied to the wrist—and toward the forehead. When the hand touches the forehead, the eyes close, the hand falls to the lap, and the patient is completely relaxed and at ease.

Other ideomotor techniques use arm catalepsy, hands extended in front and slowly being drawn together, and arm heaviness (or reverse arm levitation). These techniques have the advantage of demonstrating to a patient that the unconscious does have the ability to control physical responses.

Relaxation techniques.   The patient sits or lies in a position conducive to complete relaxation, takes a few deep breaths, and concentrates on the practitioner's voice. The practitioner suggests that the patient's eyelids will relax and, when they are ready, close. The entire body feels relaxed, free from all tension and tightness. Breathing becomes slower and easy. The discourse continues by having the patient focus on and relax specific parts of the body, beginning with the feet, continuing through the legs, thighs, and pelvis, and so up through the facial muscles. Or the practitioner may ask the patient to imagine a relaxing scene and experience it vividly in all five senses. The imagery will have the same effect as progressive muscle relaxation.

Television or movie method.   A visual imagery technique, this approach is popular with children. The child is asked to sit comfortably, close his or her eyes, and visualize a television set or movie screen. The practitioner suggests that the child imagine turning on the set, adjusting the sound and picture, and settling down to watch a favorite program. Once the child is involved in the program, the practitioner suggests that as the scene fades, the child will become very relaxed and comfortable. A child undergoing a painful medical procedure can be encouraged to remain tuned in to the program. Or the induction can merge with treatment as the practitioner integrates suggestions into the ongoing program. (See Gardner and Olness, 1981, for other induction techniques for children.)

Imagery can emphasize auditory or kinesthetic experience as well as visual. For example, instead of turning on the television, a patient can be asked to imagine a favorite place, to imagine participating in a favorite activity, or to imagine listening to a favorite piece of music.

Story-telling techniques.   This technique also can be effective with children. Although the story may be original or familiar, it should emphasize a subject of interest to the patient. Elkins and Carter (1981) developed a science fiction technique that uses imagery associated with movies such as *Star Wars* and *Battlestar Galactica.*

Confusion technique.   Developed by Erickson (1964a), this technique is appropriate for patients who resist other methods. The practitioner speaks rapidly, using a play on words, non sequiturs, or contradictory statements that force the patient to struggle to sort out the intended meaning but never allow time for a response. The patient becomes eager for something understandable, something to which he or she can respond successfully; that is the hypnotic trance. As suggestions for relaxation are introduced, the practitioner speaks more slowly and in a monotone. This technique is difficult to handle properly and requires extensive training and practice.

Clenched-fist technique.   Developed by Stein (1963), this technique is used for both induction and treatment. The patient is asked to concentrate on the first pleasant memory that comes to mind, and when the memory is there, to close the dominant hand into a tight fist as a symbol of confidence and determination. The practitioner suggests that the tighter the patient closes the fist, the stronger the sensations of happiness, confidence, and strength will be. With practice, the clenched fist becomes a self-induction procedure that patients can use as an antidote for their own tensions. In treatment, unhappy memories are transferred to the nondominant fist, the "happy" fist is used as an antidote, and the "unhappy" hand relaxes, letting tensions and unhappiness drop onto the floor.

Most of these techniques can be used interchangeably as induction or deepening procedures. For example, a practitioner might use eye fixation for induction and arm levitation for deepening, relaxation for induction and the clenched fist for deepening, or storytelling for both induction and deepening. These techniques are merely tools that must be adapted in content and language for each patient. The language used in an induction for a young child will differ from that used with an adolescent. Suggestions for eye closure or sleep may have positive associations for an adult but create a negative response in a child (Gardner and Olness, 1981).

To quote Erickson (1958a), a good technique is:

> . . . one that offers to the patient, whether child or adult, the opportunity to have his needs of the moment met adequately, the opportunity to respond to stimuli and to ideas, and also the opportunity to experience the satisfactions of new learning achievements. (p. 29)

In order to achieve this goal, all induction techniques must be adapted to meet the needs of the patient, and not vice versa.

USE OF SUGGESTION

Induction and deepening techniques assist the patient to reach a state in which suggestions acceptable to the unconscious will be acted on to produce positive change. Just as induction merges into deepening, deepening merges into treatment. Just as induction procedures must be tailored to the individual patient, treatment suggestions must be unique for each. Clinical experience, however, has provided some general guidelines for phrasing effective treatment suggestions.

Guidelines for Treatment

Emil Coué (1923), a provincial French pharmacist at the turn of the century, was a pioneer in the uses and effects of suggestion. Research and practice over the past 60 years has confirmed his observations, or laws, which are widely followed by practitioners of hypnosis.

Law of concentrated attention.   Any idea that occupies the mind tends to realize itself. Repetition of a suggestion is therefore valuable because it will imprint itself to a greater extent upon the mind. If it is overdone, however, repetition will provoke irritation and resistance. Advertising slogans, jingles, and television commercials are all applications of this law.

Law of reversed effect.   "If one thinks 'I should like to do this but I can't,' the harder he tries, the less he is able," said Coué (1923). He offered many other examples of this law, including:

- The insomniac, determined to fall asleep but unable to do so, who will drift off as soon as he has given up.

- The person who tries to remember a word or a name without success until she directs her attention to something else, whereupon the word pops into her mind.

- The person who can easily walk a plank 9 inches wide and placed on the ground, but who would assuredly fall if the board were placed between the towers of a cathedral.

The law of reversed effect highlights the difference between the imagination and the will. Will power is a function of the conscious mind—of the determination to "try" to do something. You cannot will yourself into salivating, for example. But if you imagine that you are tasting a lemon or sitting down to a favorite meal, you salivate. Hypnotic suggestion appeals to the imagination, a much more potent force than will.

Law of dominant effect.   A stronger emotion will take precedence over a weaker one; for example, fear will displace feelings of pleasure. In hypnosis, the attachment of a strong emotion to a suggestion will make the suggestion more effective. This principle is also used in progressive desensitization during the treatment of phobic individuals, following Wolpe's (1958) principle of reciprocal inhibition. Using this method, the patient arranges his or her fears in a hierarchy. Those on the lower end are deconditioned by attaching to them positive or pleasant emotions more dominant than the strength of the fears. As treatment progresses, the dominant emotions help the patient to displace the fears, which become progressively weaker.

In addition to these laws, there are several other guidelines to keep in mind when formulating and delivering suggestions for patients in both the waking and hypnotic state:

1. Express suggestions in a positive, rather than a negative, fashion. This advice may seem obvious, but in practice it is not always easy to avoid the words "won't," "not," "don't," and "can't." If one tells a young gymnast that she won't fall from the balance beam, or a student that he won't fail the test, they will be left wondering whether they will fall or fail. Suggestions of comfort, relaxation, confidence, or reminders of successful past performances are more easily accepted and acted on. Similarly, references to peace, calm, warmth, and relaxation will displace symptoms of tension, pain, or anxiety without calling attention to the negative states. `

2. Avoid ambiguity. A hypnotized patient will respond to a suggestion literally. A suggestion that requires conscious interpretation can have undesirable effects. Hartland (1971) gave the following example:

> A patient who was terrified to go into the street because of the traffic was once told by a hypnotist that when she left his rooms she would no longer bother about the traffic and would be able to cross the road without the slightest fear. She obeyed his instructions so literally that she ended up in a hospital. (p. 37)

3. Vary the verbal delivery of suggestions by:
   a. Alterations in the volume.
   b. Changes in pace.
   c. Stresses on key words.
   d. Changes in the inflections and modulation of the voice.

4. Give only one suggestion at a time. Too many suggestions given at once may burden the unconscious and cause confusion. Combining a suggestion that the patient readily accepts with one that the patient resists may diminish the effect of the former.

5. Make suggestions refer to the immediate future to allow time for them to be absorbed and acted on. Commands in the present may strike the patient as contrary to facts and prevent them from taking effect.

6. Personalize suggestions to fit a patient's inner representational system. It is easier to accept an idea that relates to one's own past experience, beliefs, or habits than it is to absorb something totally new. The use of commanding or permissive language should also depend on the personality and expectations of the patient.

7. Create suggestions that use as many senses as possible. Because some people are primarily visual, while others are auditory or kinesthetic, a suggestion that employs the senses of sight, hearing, touch, and taste will have a greater chance of striking a responsive chord. (See Chapter 5, Imagery, for a more complete discussion of this point.)

For the use of suggestions with specific problems, the authors recommend *A Syllabus on Hypnosis and a Handbook of Therapeutic Suggestions*, published by ASCH (1973). Other specific suggestions may be found in the sample inductions included in the chapters in Part 3 of this book, Clinical Applications.

Using Suggestion in Arousal

Termination of a trance is generally much easier than induction. As explained in Chapter 3, an altered state (ASC) is less stable than the usual states of consciousness (USC), waking and sleeping. Therefore, once a trance is induced, the practitioner must continue supplying input, or "patterning forces," to maintain the ASC. Left alone, patients will gradually return to a USC.

Suggestions for a slow return to the waking state will usually terminate a trance. Before arousal, however, the practitioner should be sure to remove all suggestions not intended for posthypnotic effect.

General well-being suggestions and suggestions for increased energy, vigor, comfort, and ego strength should be incorporated into the arousal suggestions.

The following is an example of an arousal procedure:

As this session ends, you can gradually rouse yourself, wide-awake, energetic, vigorous, feeling as though you are awakening from a long, deep, peaceful, and health-restoring slumber, ready to do what you need to do, have to do, and want to do today, tomorrow and the day after, and the positive feelings you are now aware of and will continue to become aware of will be staying with you today, tomorrow and the next day; or if you choose you can continue relaxing, providing yourself with appropriate suggestions regarding your relaxation process and important issues; or if you wish, you can give yourself a suggestion to enter a profound level of slumber and sleep until it is time for you to awaken.

In a private office setting, patients invariably rouse themselves, whereas in the hospital setting patients typically elect to follow the suggestions to continue relaxing or go to sleep.

At the conclusion of the session, some practitioners find it useful to gain insight for further sessions by discussing the patient's experiences. Whether hypnotic suggestions are made conscious is a matter of the practitioner's preference. Some practitioners, particularly those using the indirect approach, believe that suggestions are more effective if not made conscious; they take care not to discuss treatment suggestions made during hypnosis. Others answer any questions the patient might have concerning treatment suggestions. Practitioners who use hypnosis along with behavioral techniques sometimes prefer to review material with the patient to reinforce the hypnotic suggestions consciously. In any case, it is important to be positive, talk about progress made during the session, and suggest that the next session will be even more valuable.

HYPNOTIC RESPONSIVENESS

Ever since hypnosis came under scientific scrutiny, researchers as well as practitioners have wanted to know whether a patient was hypnotized and to what extent, as well as what factors were influencing an induction. The answers have not always been self-evident, because hypnotic induction is not a clear-cut mechanical process. The many interacting personal and situational variables make clinical hypnosis as much an art as a science.

Some people clearly are more responsive than others: They enter the trance state more easily and are more open to suggestion. In the 1840s, James Braid recognized that some persons enter trance states spontaneously, without an induction. Research today suggests that some patients who are highly responsive to hypnosis and enter trance states easily have been misdiagnosed as schizophrenic. Douglas Kahn, a psychiatrist, is currently evaluating the correlations between bipolar illness and "grade 5 syndrome," a term applied by Spiegel (1974) to persons with extremely high scores on the Hypnotic Induction Profile (1973). (D. G. Kahn, personal communication, January 20, 1983.)

A case treated by Pratt could easily have been misdiagnosed had not the practitioner been experienced with hypnosis:

A young musician sought psychotherapy for acute anxiety and frequently recurring thoughts that he might act out against his loved ones in a violent way. Mr. C. was an otherwise gentle person who had no history of such behavior, but even though he would never consider acting upon his thoughts, he would not dismiss them. He was frightened and afraid that he was losing his mind. To help control the anxiety, he was drinking heavily, which in turn was having an adverse effect on his profession and on his marriage.

The course of the patient's recurring violent thoughts was found to be a combination of two factors: his addiction to horror movies and his extremely high responsiveness to hypnosis. Using the eye roll technique for induction, he went into a deep trance almost instantaneously. The violence and fear of the horror movies had made an unusually strong impression on the patient as a result of his extreme responsiveness to suggestion. He was in effect hypnotized by these movies, setting up a battle between his unconscious impressions and his conscious desires.

The therapist used the standard image of a brilliant white light that soothes and protects to promote self-confidence and help Mr. C. reduce his anxiety. The day after the hypnotic procedure, which lasted less than 3 minutes from induction to awakening, Mr. C. reported that the violent thoughts were gone, that he had never before felt more relaxed and confident, and that he just had auditioned successfully for an important job. Mr. C. now uses the white light image in self-hypnosis to protect and distance himself when he is watching movies and to relax before auditioning and performing.

As this case indicates, brief psychotherapy combined with hypnosis can be extremely effective. While highly responsive patients have sometimes been misunderstood, those not easily hypnotized are often denied the benefits of that treatment modality. What makes people more or less responsive to hypnosis? Research in the past two decades has only begun to provide some tentative answers to this question.

Standardized Tests

In order to identify people who can benefit most from hypnosis, and to explore the characteristics of the hypnotic state, a number of measures of hypnotic responsiveness have been developed over the past 50 years. The value of these scales in a clinical setting is a matter of ongoing debate that raises some interesting issues concerning the clinical applications of hypnosis.

The scales currently in use draw on a variety of behaviors consistently associated with hypnosis, such as catalepsy, eye closure, amnesia, and posthypnotic response, to measure individual responsiveness. Tests are constantly being revised by their authors, and new tests are being developed all the time. The scales most commonly available to researchers and clinicians are briefly described in the following list:

Stanford Hypnotic Susceptibility Scales (SHSS), Forms A, B, and C (Weitzenhoffer and Hilgard, 1959, 1962). SHSS, Form A has become a standard against which other hypnotic responsiveness scales have been judged. Forms A and B, with 12 test items, are weighted heavily in the direction of motor functions. Scale C includes more items to measure fantasy and cognitive distortion.

Harvard Group Scale of Hypnotic Susceptibility, Form A (Shor and Orne, 1962). This scale is an adaptation for group administration with self-report scoring of the individually administered and objectively scored SHSS, Form A.

Stanford Profile Scales of Hypnotic Susceptibility (SPS), Forms I and II (Weitzenhoffer and Hilgard, 1963). Although more time-consuming than SHSS to administer, these scales discriminate better at the upper end of the scale (high susceptibles). The SPS also provides more diagnostic information for the researcher who wants to select moderate to high susceptibles with specific hypnotic talents.

Stanford Hypnotic Clinical Scales for Adults (Hilgard and Hilgard, 1975), and Stanford Hypnotic Clinical Scale for Children (Morgan and Hilgard, 1979). These scales have been standardized against the SHSS and shortened for clinical use. The adult scale contains five items and requires 20 minutes to administer. The children's scale is useful for children aged 6 to 16.

Children's Hypnotic Susceptibility Scale (London, 1963). This scale also measures the responsiveness of a child to hypnotic suggestions.

There are two forms, for younger (5–12 years) and older (13–16 years) chldren. The scale consists of 22 items and takes approximately an hour to administer.

Barber Suggestibility Scale (Barber and Glass, 1962). Intended primarily for experimental purposes, the scale includes eight standardized test suggestions and requires 10–12 minutes to administer.

Creative Imagination Scale (Wilson and Barber, 1978). Designed to meet the need for a standardized series of permissive test suggestions for experimental or clinical use, this scale can be administered to individuals or a group, with or without a prior hypnotic induction. The series of 10 permissively worded items requires approximately 23 minutes to administer and score.

Hypnotic Induction Profile (HIP) (Speigel, 1973). The HIP was the first scale designed specifically for the clinical situation. It is both an induction procedure, using the Speigel eye roll technique, and a six-item test of hypnotizability that can be administered in 5–10 minutes. The authors emphasize the value of the scale to predict therapeutic success using hypnosis. They also claim that induction scores and profile patterns on the HIP can help in identifying persons with relatively severe psychopathology.

Alman-Wexler Indirect Hypnotic Susceptibility Scale (Wexler, 1982). A recent addition to the study of hypnotic responsiveness and currently undergoing research and refinement, this new test is based on the Harvard Group Scale and has been found to correlate positively with it. The Alman-Wexler scale (see appendix) uses indirect language rather than the Harvard scale's direct language. Studies in Europe and the United States are comparing it, the SHSS, and the Harvard Group Scale to determine whether indirect and direct approaches to induction result in differences in hypnotic depth.

Several studies have attempted to correlate sex, age, and personality variables with responsiveness to hypnosis as measured by the standardized scales. Weitzenhoffer and Weitzenhoffer (1958) found no significant difference in responsiveness between women and men. However, normative studies on age differences have found that children are more responsive to hypnosis than are adults (London and Cooper, 1969). In a study of 1,232 subjects, Morgan and Hilgard (1973) found that responsiveness peaks between the ages of 9 and 12, with a gradual decline thereafter.

Hilgard (1979) found a high correlation between responsiveness to hypnosis and capacity for imaginative involvement, and Roberts and Tellegen (1973) reported a correlation between self-trust and hypnotizability in women. In analysis of a wide range of personality variables, no other strong correlations have been found with hypnotic responsiveness, making it impossible to predict responsiveness on the basis of personality type.

Laboratory studies have shown positive correlations between hypnotic responsiveness and the ability to diminish the perception of pain through hypnosis (Evans and Paul, 1970; Hilgard and Hilgard, 1975). Other authors reported significant correlations between responsiveness and successful treatment (Frankel et al., 1979; Mott, 1979). Thus, the scales of hypnotic susceptibility have been viewed as predictors of success in clinical situations.

Many clinicians question this assumption, however. One point of debate is the concept of hypnotizability as an inborn trait that varies greatly among people but that is constant within a particular person over time (Morgan, Johnson, and Hilgard, 1974). One implication of the trait theory is that if a patient is found to be "unhypnotizable," hypnosis should be avoided as a treatment method.

While it is clear that persons who score highly on the standardized scales are good candidates for treatment using hypnosis, persons with low scores should not necessarily be discounted for such treatment. Some authors view hypnosis as a skill, rather than a trait, and have conducted studies to show that there are many methods of modifying this skill, including imitation, instruction, and practice (Diamond, 1977; Kinney and Sachs, 1974; Reilley, Perisher, Corona, and Dobrovolsky, 1980). As pointed out by Gardner and Olness (1981, p. 25), a person's ability to experience hypnosis is increasingly being referred to as "responsiveness" rather than "susceptibility," reflecting the growing awareness that the locus of control resides within the patient rather than the practitioner. If responsiveness can be increased, then few patients can be labeled categorically as unhypnotizable.

It also is clear, as pointed out earlier in this chapter, that some people do not respond well to the direct approach to induction. However, because the majority of hypnotic responsiveness scales use the direct approach, one can conclude that a person who has a low score on the SHSS probably will not respond well to a direct, authoritarian method of induction. One should not conclude that this person will necessarily be unresponsive to a more indirect approach.

For example, Barber (1976) demonstrated that with Erickson's indirect induction technique there was no difference in the ability to reduce experimental pain between people of high susceptibility and those of low susceptibility. Alman and Carney (1980) conducted a study using four groups of 12 college students, matched for susceptibility score, age, and previous experience with hypnosis. They found that an indirect induction procedure produced significantly higher levels of response to a posthypnotic suggestion than did the direct induction methods. Alman and Carney also found that the success of posthypnotic behavior was significantly correlated with susceptibility scores only for students in the direct induction group.

In an experimental setting, the use of standardized measures of hypnotic responsiveness can contribute valuable information on the characteristics of hypnosis, identify the most responsive subjects, and suggest associated influences. This contribution will be even more valuable for the clinician as more research is done on hypnotic responsiveness and the indirect approach to hypnotic induction and treatment. Clinicians who use hypnosis infrequently may find such measures helpful in identifying patients at the high or low ends of the scale and, thus, in assessing the advisability of using hypnosis in treatment. However, a poor response on a scale of hypnotizability does not eliminate hypnosis as an effective treatment modality. The authors agree with Crasilneck and Hall (1975), who stated that "the only final reliable test for hypnotizability is a clinical attempt at induction, repeated several times" (p. 45).

Associated Variables

Several other issues need to be addressed concerning individual responsiveness to clinical hypnosis beyond what can be measured by standardized scales.

Responsiveness of infants and very young children.   Clinical scales do not test children below the age of 5, and formal induction methods only go down to age 4, leaving researchers and practitioners to speculate on the response to hypnosis of the very young.

Podoll (1981) and Gardner (1977) pointed out several instances of hypnotic behaviors in infants and young children. For example, universally accepted ways of quieting infants, such as patting, rocking, or crooning, contain the hypnotic elements of continuous soothing stimulation. These elements are also present in the ways small children stroke or rock themselves. The hypnotic technique of eye fixation may be seen in the way an infant stares at a slowly moving mobile. Gardner (1977) reported the case of "an 8-month-old who ignored a rather prolonged intravenous puncture when sucking vigorously on a bottle" (p. 159). For a young child, Gardner suggested that hypnosis can be determined by observing common hypnotic phenomena, such as a wakeful quiet behavior, (b) involvement in vivid imagery, (c) heightened attention to a narrow focus, and (d) behavior corresponding to posthypnotic suggestions.

Ultradian cycle. One variable that eventually may prove to be an important factor in hypnotic induction has been suggested by recent research on the ultradian cycle, a 90–120-minute cycle of activity and rest that can be measured physiologically and observed behaviorally. There is evidence (Kripke, 1982; Rossi, 1982) that during the rest phase of the cycle, in which right brain hemisphere processes are more dominant, a person is more receptive to trance. During his leisurely therapeutic sessions, which extended well beyond the usual 50 minutes, Erickson created an environment in which he could recognize and take advantage of signs of trance readiness, such as quietness of body, focused eye contact, and an attitude of expectation (Erickson et al., 1976).

According to Rossi (1982), research on the ultradian cycle has become too complex to see a one-to-one correspondence between the rest phase of the cycle and Erickson's concept of the "common everyday trance." However, Rossi stated that hypnosis, too, is an extremely complex phenomenon, and "it is precisely this correspondence in complexity that lends credence to the view that ultradian cycles could be one of the important psycho-neuro-physiological foundations for hypnotic phenomena" (p. 24). Rossi went on to suggest that these naturally occurring cycles could be used not only to facilitate trance but also to facilitate posthypnotic suggestions. The reader interested in pursuing this line of inquiry is referred to Rossi's article and to the work of Kripke (1982), a leading researcher in the field.

Situational variables. A study by Schafer and Hernandez (1978) suggested that situational elements may be more crucial to success in therapy for pain management than scores on susceptibility scales. Spontaneous trance is a common phenomenon in medical and dental situations, where a strange environment, combined with fear of pain or discomfort, disrupt a patient's usual state of consciousness and make it easier to slip into an altered state.

Motivation. An important variable in most situations in which hypnosis is used as a treatment modality, Perry, Gelfand, and Marcovitch (1979) found that patient motivation was the most crucial factor in the success of hypnotic intervention to reduce the smoking habit. Success is unlikely if for some reason (conscious or unconscious) a patient does not want to succeed.

Professional relationship. Induction can be facilitated or hindered by the relationship between practitioner and patient. In an unpleasant interpersonal situation, patients are unlikely to attend willingly to the practitioner's instructions. Uncertainty or misconceptions about hypnosis will also prevent a patient from relaxing and concentrating. The practitioner must accurately perceive these situations and take steps to alleviate them. A practitioner's expectations can also influence the success of a hypnotic session, as Erickson pointed out:

> The operator should know that the patient comes to him with full respect and will be entirely willing to develop a trance if the operator does not first suggest by manner, attitude, or bearing the idea that maybe he cannot. This realization is the most important part in learning any technique of hypnosis. (ASCH, 1973, p. 69)

SUMMARY

Given the number of recognized induction techniques and the wide variety of approaches to each technique, there is an almost infinite variety of ways to induce a hypnotic trance. Ideally, the practitioner develops several approaches with which he or she is comfortable and then modifies them to meet each patient's needs and personality. As in any psychotherapeutic situation, the relationship between the patient and practitioner can facilitate or hinder hypnotic induction and treatment. Flexibility and a positive attitude on the part of the practitioner are the best insurance against failure.

While the standardized susceptibility scales have their place in research and can identify highly responsive individuals, a low score on a scale does not mean that hypnosis is to be discounted in a clinical setting. With practice, even the least responsive patients may find hypnosis an extremely effective treatment modality.

The wording of hypnotic suggestions greatly influences the degree to which they are accepted and acted on by the patient. Suggestions that are most likely to succeed (a) are clearly worded, (b) employ imagery using all five sensory modalities, (c) fit into the patient's inner representational system, (d) are worded permissively, and (e) are expressed in a positive fashion. Throughout induction and treatment, it is important to remember that the locus of control is with the patient and that the role of the practitioner is to provide the environment in which a patient can mobilize the inner resources to achieve treatment goals.

FURTHER READING

American Society of Clinical Hypnosis (ASCH). (1973). *A syllabus on hypnosis and a handbook of therapeutic suggestions.* Des Plaines, IL: Author.

Haley, J. (Ed.). (1967). *Advanced techniques of hypnosis and therapy: Selected papers of Milton H. Erickson, M.D.* New York: Grune & Stratton.

Pratt, G., & Korn, E. (1983). *Clinical hypnosis: Techniques and applications* [Videotape]. San Diego: School of Medicine, University of California, San Diego, Office of Learning Resources.

REFERENCES

Alman, B. M., & Carney, R. E. (1980). Consequences of direct and indirect suggestions on success of posthypnotic behavior. *American Journal of Clinical Hypnosis, 23,* 112–118.

American Society of Clinical Hypnosis (ASCH), Education and Research Foundation. (1973). *A syllabus on hypnosis and a handbook of therapeutic suggestions.* Des Plaines, IL: Author.

Araoz, D. L. (1982). *Hypnosis and sex therapy.* New York: Brunner/Mazel.

Andolesk, K., & Novik, B. (1980). Use of hypnosis with children. *Journal of Family Practice, 10,* 503–507.

Barber, J. (1976). *The efficacy of hypnotic analgesia for dental pain in individuals of both high and low hypnotic susceptibility.* Unpublished doctoral dissertation, University of Southern California, Los Angeles.

Barber, J. (1977). Rapid induction analgesia: A clinical report. *American Journal of Clinical Hypnosis, 19,* 138–147.

Barber, T. X., & Glass, L. B. (1962). Significant factors in hypnotic behavior. *Journal of Abnormal and Social Psychology, 64,* 222–228.

Cheek, D. B., & LeCron, L. M. (1968). *Clinical Hypnotherapy.* New York: Grune & Stratton.

Coué, E. (1923). *How to practice suggestion and auto-suggestion.* New York: American Library Service.

Crasilneck, H. B., & Hall, J. A. (1975). *Clinical hypnosis: Principles and applications.* New York: Grune & Stratton.

Diamond, M. J. (1977). Modification of hypnotizability: An alternative approach. *International Journal of Clinical and Experimental Hypnosis, 25,* 147–166.

Elkins, G. R., & Carter, B. D. (1981). Use of a science fiction-based imagery technique in child hypnosis. *American Journal of Clinical Hypnosis, 23,* 274–277.

Erickson, M. H. (1952). Deep hypnosis and its induction. In L. M. LeCron (Ed.), *Experimental hypnosis.* New York: Macmillan, pp. 70–114.

Erickson, M. (1958a). Pediatric hypnotherapy. *American Journal of Clinical Hypnosis, 1,* 25–29.

Erickson, M. H. (1958b). Naturalistic techniques of hypnosis. *American Journal of Clinical Hypnosis, 1,* 3–8.

Erickson, M. H. (1964a). The confusion technique in hypnosis. *American Journal of Clinical Hypnosis, 6,* 183–207.

Erickson, M. H. (1964b). An hypnotic technique for resistant patients. *American Journal of Clinical Hypnosis, 7,* 8–32.

Erickson, M. H. (1967). Deep hypnosis and its induction. In J. Haley (Ed.), *Advanced techniques of hypnosis and therapy: Selected papers of Milton H. Erickson, M.D.* (pp. 7–31). New York: Grune & Stratton.

Erickson, M. H., & Rossi, E. L. (1976). Two level communication and the microdynamics of trance and suggestion. *American Journal of Clinical Hypnosis, 18,* 153–171.

Erickson, M. H., Rossi, E. L., & Rossi, S. I. (1976). *Hypnotic realities.* New York: Irvington Publishing.

Evans, M., & Paul, G. (1970). Effects of hypnotically suggested analgesia on physiological and subjective responses to cold stress. *Journal of Consulting and Clinical Psychology, 35,* 362–371.

Frankel, F. H., Apfel, R. J., Kelly, S. F., Benson, H., Quinn, T., Newmark, J., & Malmaud, R. (1979). The use of hypnotizability scales in the clinic: A review after six years. *International Journal of Clinical and Experimental Hypnosis, 27,* 63–73.

Fromm, E., Brown, D. P., Hurt, S. W., Oberlander, J. Z., Boxer, A. M., & Pfeiffer, G. (1981). The phenomena and characteristics of self-hypnosis. *International Journal of Clinical and Experimental Hypnosis, 29,* 189–246.

Gardner, G. G.(1977). Hypnosis with infants and preschool children. *American Journal of Clinical Hypnosis, 19,* 158–162.

Gardner, G. G., & Olness, K. (1981). *Hypnosis and hypnotherapy with children.* New York: Grune & Stratton.

Hartland, J. (1971). *Medical and dental hypnosis.* London: Bailliere Tindall.

Hilgard, E. R., & Hilgard, J. R. (1975). *Hypnosis in the relief of pain.* Los Altos, CA: William Kaufmann, Inc.

Hilgard, J. R. (1979). *Personality and hypnosis: A study of imaginative involvement* (2nd ed.). University of Chicago.

Kinney, J. M., & Sachs, L. B. (1974). Increasing hypnotic susceptibility. *Journal of Abnormal Psychology, 83,* 145–150.

Kripke, D. F. (1982). Ultradian rhythms in behavior and physiology. In F. M. Brown & R. C. Graeber (Eds.), *Rhythmic aspects of behavior*. New Jersey: Erlbaum Associates.

Kroger, W. S. (1977). *Clinical and experimental hypnosis* (2nd ed.). Philadelphia: Lippincott.

Lazar, B. S., & Dempster, C. R. (1981). Failure in hypnosis and hypnotherapy: A review. *American Journal of Clinical Hypnosis, 24*, 48–54.

London, P. (1963). *Children's hypnotic susceptibility scale*. Palo Alto, CA: Consulting Psychologists Press.

London, P., & Cooper, L. M. (1969). Norms of hypnosis susceptibility in children. *Developmental Psychology, 1*, 113–124.

Matheson, G., & Grehan, J. F. (1979). A rapid induction technique. *American Journal of Clinical Hypnosis, 21*, 297–299.

Morgan, A. H., & Hilgard, E. R. (1973). Age differences in susceptibility to hypnosis. *International Journal of Clinical and Experimental Hypnosis, 21*, 78–85.

Morgan, A. H., & Hilgard, J. R. (1979). The Stanford hypnotic clinical scale, adult. *American Journal of Clinical Hypnosis, 21*, 134–147.

Morgan, A. H., Johnson, D. L., & Hilgard, E. R. (1974). The stability of hypnotic susceptibility: A longitudinal study. *International Journal of Clinical and Experimental Hypnosis, 22*, 249–257.

Mott, T. (1979). The clinical importance of hypnotizability. *American Journal of Clinical Hypnosis, 21*, 263–269.

Perry, C., Gelfand, R., & Marcovitch, P. (1979). The relevance of hypnotic susceptibility in the clinical context. *Journal of Abnormal Psychology, 88*, 592–603.

Podoll, E. (1981). The use and misuse of hypnosis in children. *Journal of the American Society of Psychosomatic Dentistry and Medicine, 28*, 56–62.

Reilley, R. R., Perisher, D. W., Corona, A., & Dobrovolsky, N. W. (1980). Modifying hypnotic susceptibility by practice and instruction. *International Journal of Clinical and Experimental Hypnosis, 28*, 39–45.

Roberts, A. H., & Tellegen, A. (1973). Ratings of "trust" and hypnotic susceptibility. *International Journal of Clinical and Experimental Hypnosis, 21*, 289–297.

Rossi, E. L. (1982). Hypnosis and ultradian cycles: A new state(s) theory of hypnosis? *American Journal of Clinical Hypnosis, 25*, 21–32.

Schafer, D., & Hernandez, A. (1978). Hypnosis, pain and the context of therapy. *International Journal of Clinical and Experimental Hypnosis, 26*, 143–153.

Shor, R. E., & Orne, E. C. (1962). *Harvard group scale of hypnotic susceptibility*. Palo Alto, CA: Consulting Psychologists Press.

Spiegel, H. (1973). *Manual for hypnotic induction profile. Eye-roll levitation method* (revised). New York: Soni Medica.

Spiegel, H. (1974). The grade 5 syndrome; the highly hypnotizable person. *International Journal of Clinical and Experimental Hypnosis, 22*, 303–319.

Stein, C. (1963). The clenched-fist technique as a hypnotic procedure in clinical psychotherapy. *American Journal of Clinical Hypnosis, 6,* 112–119.

Weitzenhoffer, A. M., & Hilgard, E. R. (1959). *Stanford hypnotic susceptibility scales,* Forms A and B. Palo Alto, CA: Consulting Psychologists Press.

Weitzenhoffer, A. M., & Hilgard, E. R. (1962). *Stanford hypnotic susceptibility scale,* Form C. Palo Alto, CA: Consulting Psychologists Press.

Weitzenhoffer, A. M., & Hilgard, E. R. (1963). *Stanford profile scales of hypnotic susceptibility,* Forms I and II. Palo Alto, CA: Consulting Psychologists Press.

Weitzenhoffer, A. M., & Weitzenhoffer, G. B. (1958). Sex, transformance and susceptibility. *American Journal of Clinical Hypnosis, 1,* 15–24.

Wexler, D. B. (1982). Hypnotic susceptibility as measured by direct vs. indirect inductions and its relation to psychological differentiation. Unpublished doctoral dissertation, California School of Professional Psychology, San Diego.

Wilson, S. C., & Barber, T. X. (1978). The creative imagination scale as a measure of hypnotic responsiveness: Applications to experimental and clinical hypnosis. *American Journal of Clinical Hypnosis, 20,* 235–249.

Wolpe, J. (1958). *Psychotherapy by reciprocal inhibition.* Stanford, CA: Stanford University Press.

5

Imagery

Errol R. Korn, MD

The soul . . . never thinks without a picture.

—Aristotle
Organon

I magery has played a significant role in the development of the human species, both in its ontogeny and in its phylogeny. Studies of cognitive processes in children imply that human beings thought in images long before the development of language (Horowitz, 1967, 1972). Primary process thinking, the cognitive mode typical of pre-verbal childhood, relies on images. It precedes secondary process thinking, the dominant cognitive mode of the adult, which is abstract, goal-directed and verbal.

Internal images preserved in the form of art may be seen in cave paintings dating as far back as 60,000 B.C. Often used for healing and spiritual development, imagery appears in the early records of all ancient cultures (Doob, 1972). Aristotle believed that thought was composed of images, and Hermetic philosophy taught that imagery could affect the physical world. Today, shamans, faith healers, Christian Scientists, and esoteric and mystical groups, such as the Rosicrucians, use imagery for the purpose of diagnosis and healing.

Carl Jung (1933) believed that images are representations of deep inner experience and that similar images will surface in different cultures when they are needed to guide the way or solve a problem. One image basic to all societies is the mandala. Circular in shape, with spokes radiating from the center, the mandala is found in nature (the flower is a good example) as well as in cave paintings, the Aztec calendar, and the early art of most societies. In Hinduism, Buddhism, and Sufism, the mandala is used as an aid to meditation.

It appears that thoughts and ideas are encoded in images and that language was developed in response to a human need to make those thoughts and ideas known to others (Begg, Upfold, and Wilton, 1978). When one understands the image as the foundation of language, it is not surprising that the phrase "a failure to communicate" is so familiar. When one person communicates with another, the listener instantly changes the speaker's words into images, responds to those images, and translates that response back into words. Words, therefore, become a vehicle for communicating images, which represent patterns or symbols within each consciousness. When someone responds to words by means of their own images, those images may not be the ones that were intended. This chapter will explore the potency of images and the implications that the individualized nature of the imaging process has for the practitioner using hypnosis.

NATURE AND FUNCTIONS

Gordon (1972) defined an image as a sensory perception in the absence of the external object or stimulus that usually results in that perception. However, it is not so easy as Gordon's definition implies to distinguish between imagery as an internal event and perception as an external event. As demonstrated by Perky (1910) more than 70 years ago, a physical stimulus can be confused with an imagined image. In hallucinations, for example, internal images appear to have external loci. Quantum theory has revealed the connection between internal and external reality, demonstrating that the observer influences the phenomenon being observed. Instead of trying to separate external perceptions and mental images, it is more productive to envision both as part of a continuum, as suggested by Holt (1972).

There are large variations in the way in which people process imagery. Those of us who process external information primarily in the visual mode tend to think that imagery is strictly visual. Although visual imagery does provide about 85% of our subjective experience of the external world, imagery is not limited to the visual sense. Bandler and Grinder (1979) showed that, while many people are visual, others are primarily auditory (hearing) or kinesthetic (feeling, in both the internal sense of emotions and the external sense of touch or temperature).

Lay made this point in 1897 in his discussion of the difference between Socrates and Protagoras, who had different modes of imaging:

If one is auditory-linguistic, he should never enter into an argument with a motor-linguistic person, as in all topics except the most concrete facts, either will inevitably fail, completely, to understand the other. Words and their meanings are created and validated in a social context, while images and their meanings are personal creations . . .

Differences in modes of imaging frequently lead to misunderstandings in personal communication. For example, the author, who is primarily auditory, once waylaid a friend with the remark, "I'd like to run something through you," meaning, "I'd like you to listen to an idea I have." For the friend, who is equally visual and kinesthetic, those words elicited the image and feeling of having something run through him. It is important to remember that words are merely symbols and do not have intrinsic meaning. Practitioners must take into account the connotations of the words they use to communicate with their patients, whose mode of imaging may be different from their own.

All modalities of imagery depend on the brain as the apex of the perceptual hierarchy. It can be difficult to differentiate percepts from images because we see not with our eyes, but with our visual cortex. Muses (1974) stated that " . . . the objects we see *are* images, all made up of whirling, rapidly-moving constituents." The new physics, which sees matter as electrons moving rapidly in space, the positions of which are expressed in terms of mathematical probabilities, appears to corroborate Muses' statement. It seems that our brain organizes these patterns into recognizable images, and that this organization is consistent throughout the various societies on our planet.

The *functions* of imagery are the activities that take place whether or not people are aware of them. Imagery plays a functional role in many human processes. As mentioned earlier, imagery is the foundation of language and the cognitive mode for primary process thinking. When humans learn something through the verbal processes of reading, writing, or listening to a lecture, they change the verbal processes into images, which are stored in the brain. They also preserve experiences as images, using them to relate past to present, as well as to fix experiences for future use.

On the other hand, the *uses* of imagery need to be actively directed, at least in part, on a conscious level. Rehearsing future events and improving performance by imaging the desired result are common uses of imagery in the waking state. Evidence that experiences are recorded in all sensory modalities, along with the emotional equivalents that occurred at the same time, has led to the development of eidetic psychotherapy, which uses techniques for eliciting and manipulating mental imagery. All forms of meditation use imagery, and imagery as the expression of unconscious wishes is central to psychoanalysis. Imagery also is one of the most effective tools of hypnosis.

TYPES OF IMAGES

Although images, like most of life's experiences, do not fall easily into distinct categories, they can be classified for the purpose of explanation. One important distinction is between spontaneous and induced images. *Spontaneous images* enter one's conscious awareness without effort. These images probably come from deep levels of the psyche and relate to fundamental needs. Psychoanalysis is predicated on the belief that much can be learned about oneself and one's particular problems by paying attention to spontaneous images. *Induced images* are created with some element of conscious or preconscious activity. When used in hypnotherapy, these images are useful for problem-solving and can lead to changes in patients and their environments.

Induced images can be further divided into process images and end-result images. *Process images* delineate mechanisms (real or fantasized) by which desired effects can be achieved. The image of one's hands being enclosed in thick, warm gloves is a process image used to increase blood flow to the extremities. *End-result imagery*, which was popularized by Maltz (1966) in *Psycho-Cybernetics*, focuses on a desired result as already having taken place. For example, the end-result image in weight control is being thin. You are not planning to lose weight, you *are* thin.

An end-result image is the most powerful type of induced image. Similarly to feeding a command into a computer, we communicate what we want to accomplish and let the mind do the rest. A classic study reported by Richardson (1969) showed that basketball players who imagined making successful free throws, but did not practice, scored as well in performance as those who had practiced. Both groups scored better than a third control group. Several years earlier, studies by Jacobson (1942) showed that imagining an activity actually results in minute but measurable contractions of the muscles required to perform that activity. By focusing on an end-result image, we are not just thinking ourselves into doing (or not doing) something; we are, in essence, creating within ourselves the ability to do (or not do) it.

Images may be further described as general or specific. *General images* are used for an overall effect, such as relaxation, stress reduction, and ego strengthening. End-result and process images are both examples of *specific images*, which are directed toward an identified goal. Because general imagery is applicable to a variety of situations, it should be taught to patients before their instruction in specific imagery.

IMAGERY IN HYPNOSIS

There is a very close relationship between hypnosis and imagery (Sheikh, Richardson, and Moleski, 1979). Hypnotic suggestions usually evoke imagery, and imagery can be particularly vivid under hypnosis. Responsiveness to hypnosis appears to be related to the ability to fantasize and use the imagination (Sheehan, 1972). For an image to be effective, the patient must be in a receptive state of consciousness. Hypnosis is an excellent way of inducing that state and of focusing full attention on an image.

Although many of the great hypnotherapists use imagery in their work, few give credit to the imagery process. Hypnotic suggestions are most effective when they are conveyed in the form of images. In fact, suggestions work to the extent that they produce an image in the patient's mind. Open-ended imagery, which enables patients to draw upon their own imagery experiences, is consistent with the indirect, permissive approach to hypnosis. Personal images created by a patient tend to be more powerful than any created by a practitioner.

Even though imagery is humanity's innate way of processing information, there are people who feel they lack the ability to create mental images. These persons usually are referring to imagery in the visual sense and may be unaware that imagery can be experienced in the other sensory modalities as well. Patients' confidence in their ability to image can be increased simply by familiarizing them with the different modes of imaging.

Even limiting the definition of imagery to the visual sense, it can be demonstrated that all people do image. For example, everyone dreams, and the predominant sensory modality in dreams is visual. Furthermore, in the hypnagogic state (just before falling asleep), most people experience vivid visual imagery. We are not always aware of this imagery because we are daily exposed to so many sensory phenomena that the experience of these more subtle phenomena is inhibited (Richardson, 1969). Any system or ability that is not nurtured tends to atrophy. When we do not use our birthright of imagery experience, we eventually "forget" the experience entirely.

To prove to even the most recalcitrant patient that everyone has the ability to image, the practitioner can ask patients to count the windows in their homes. The only way this task can be performed accurately is to employ the visual mode of imagery to count the windows. This technique, an adaptation of Ahsen's (1977) work, demonstrates not only that visual imagery is possible, but also that we use it to solve many of the problems of daily life.

Even a reluctant imager can learn to develop imagery skills by following a simple sequence of exercises suggested by Samuels and Samuels (1975):

1. Look at a two-dimensional object such as a triangle, and then close your eyes and attempt to visualize it.

2. Repeat the exercise for a three-dimensional object.

3. Visualize a childhood room.

4. Image a large object, such as a house, and move around and through it.

5. Image a more complicated three-dimensional object, such as a tea kettle.

6. Go back to the room and actually do things in the room.

7. Image a person.

8. Image yourself as if looking in a mirror.

Imagery in hypnosis can be used to prevent or heal diseases and disorders, to alter negative habit patterns, to increase creativity, and to improve performance. There are a few basic guidelines for using imagery in hypnosis:

1. Before imagery is introduced, the patient should learn to enter the hypnotic state and should practice self-hypnosis daily.

2. Because end-result imagery is usually more powerful and long-lasting, it should be used first. However, experience demonstrates that it may take longer for end-result imagery to be effective. Therefore, in life or death situations, such as cancer therapy or accidents with multiple traumas, process images, which may hasten the onset of effective imagery, may be introduced earlier.

3. The patient must have confidence in the practitioner and the imaging process, because the initial changes may be subtle and difficult to recognize.

4. The patient must make a commitment to the process if the maximum benefits of the imagery techniques are to be realized. This commit-

ment will mean daily practice in addition to the sessions with a practitioner.

5. In any hypnotherapy session, the creation of an image in all five senses is bound to be more successful than verbal, linear suggestions. For example, a therapist who wants a patient to learn to warm his or her hands (excellent therapy for migraine headaches) should not simply say "You will feel your hands becoming warm." Instead, the therapist helps the patient to recall a situation, such as sitting by an open fireplace, in which the hands were warm. The patient should be helped to see the fire, feel the warmth, hear the crackling, and smell the aroma of the wood.

6. It is more important for the patient to be able to control the image than for the image to be lifelike. The image is the sensory method by which we "program" the brain to effect the multiple changes it will require to bring the image or idea to fruition. Therefore, the image, particularly if it is dynamic rather than static, must be controllable to the extent that it does what we wish it to do. Otherwise, we will program undesirable effects into the brain, and these effects, rather than the desired ones, will take place. The best way to develop control over an image is to rehearse it repeatedly in the mind.

Throughout the therapeutic process, the therapist must be aware of the differences between people, both in their ability to image and in their mode of imaging. To tie into the patient's imageric system, it is important that the therapist employ all sensory modalities.

SAMPLE IMAGES
The following pages present both general and specific images that have been used effectively by the author. These examples should not be used verbatim but should be adapted to suit each practitioner's style and the individual needs of patients.

General Relaxation
Move into as comfortable a position as you possibly can. The position can be a seated position with legs uncrossed and arms resting comfortably . . . or it can be lying down with feet uncrossed and toes pointed slightly to the sides . . . arms down comfortably by the sides. . . . Remove eyeglasses and loosen all constrictive clothing. . . . Now simply close your eyes. . . . This in itself is enough to produce a quietness . . . and rest . . . and relaxation. . . . Now to

experience even further comfort and relaxation, begin to breathe deeply . . . and as you do . . . pay particular attention to the sensations you experience as the air leaves the body. . . . Let yourself feel that with every breath you take out . . . you are breathing out tension . . . discomfort . . . stress . . . and strain. . . . When you do that you can feel the muscles in the body relax . . . most prominently in the chest, but also in other muscles that are particularly tense . . . such as the shoulders . . . and neck . . . and back. . . . It is just as though as you exhale the air . . . you are exhaling with it all of your troubles . . . all of your discomforts . . . and all of your anxieties. . . . You may hear noises and sounds in your environment . . . but you can use those to even deepen your state of relaxation. . . . In reality, when you breathe out you really *are* eliminating tension . . . discomfort . . . and stress. . . . Experience then what really does take place. . . . With the breath, we eliminate toxins and waste products. . . . The lungs are one of the most efficient eliminators of waste we have in the body. . . . So just let yourself feel that with every breath out you are becoming more comfortable. . . . With this process alone . . . you may be surprised . . . to find that you can eliminate almost all of the tension and discomfort . . . that you have accumulated. . . . However, if there are still residual areas of discomfort or tension . . . you can eliminate them in a progressive fashion. . . .

I'm going to ask you now to put your consciousness into your toes. . . . Now that may sound difficult to do, but realize that your consciousness doesn't have to be where most of us think it is, that is the head. . . . We only perceive our consciousness to be in our head because the brain, the most concentrated organ of consciousness, resides in the head. . . . You can place your consciousness anywhere in the body . . . you want to. . . . In fact, if you were to stub your toe . . . your consciousness would travel there instantly. . . . At this time, just place your awareness there . . . not because you have to . . . but because you . . . want to. . . . With your consciousness in your toes, simply let yourself experience whatever it is you experience when you think of the word . . . relax. . . . It may be a heaviness . . . or a lightness . . . or tingling . . . or numbness . . . or warmth . . . or coolness . . . or maybe something else . . . but even if you feel that there has been no change, rest assured that at some level of your being there is a change . . . a lessening of tension in that toe. It may be that its change is too subtle for you to perceive at this time . . . but no matter whether you perceive it . . . or not, it still takes place.

Now, let the relaxation spread to the toes of the other foot . . . and whatever it is you feel, just let it spread upward through the feet . . . through the lower portions of the legs . . . and in the knees . . . as though you were standing knee-deep in a swirling . . . warm . . . relaxing Jacuzzi. . . . Allow the comfort and relaxation to spread upward into the thighs . . . and into the groin area. . . . Let it spread through the pelvis and buttocks . . . into the abdomen and back all the way to the waist . . . as though you are now standing waist-deep in that warm . . . comfortable Jacuzzi . . . allowing the entire body from waist down to feel relaxed . . . comfortable . . . loose . . . and limp. . . . In fact . . . you may be surprised . . . to find parts of your body feeling so relaxed . . . that you lose awareness for those parts. . . . That's perfectly all right, those parts are still there and functioning just as your lungs and heart function when you are not aware of them. . . . You can regain the awareness whenever you wish to . . . but for now . . . let the comfort and relaxation spread upward into the upper abdomen and midback . . . and in the chest . . . both front and back, so that the breathing which has been . . . relaxed . . . to this point . . . becomes even more comfortable and relaxed. Now . . . let the soothing wave of relaxation go into the shoulders . . . an area in which we hold much of our tension. . . . Just let the shoulders . . . drop. . . . If you are sitting . . . feel them being pulled down by gravity and . . . if you are lying down . . . just feel your shoulders melting into the floor. . . . Let this looseness and warmth and comfort travel from the shoulders . . . all the way down the arms . . . past the elbows . . . into the wrists . . . hands . . . and fingers . . . feeling the arms just dangling without substance . . . loose and limp . . . like a rag doll. . . . Now allow the comfort to spread into another area in which we hold much tension . . . the neck. . . . Feel the neck become loose . . . and limp . . . comfortable . . . and feel that comfort spread into another area in which we hold much tension . . . and rarely realize it . . . and feel how good it will feel to let the tension go from this area . . . so good you'll not only feel it in the local area . . . but also in the rest of the face . . . head . . . and neck. . . . The area I am referring to is the . . . jaw. . . . And feel how good it feels to just let . . . the jaw drop. . . . And now let the comfort spread into the face . . . around the eyes . . . letting the eyes become relaxed . . . the area of the temples . . . the forehead . . . and the top of the head . . . letting the entire head and face become very comfortable and relaxed. . . . At this point, the entire body should be loose . . . and limp . . . and relaxed. . . .

If there is any residual discomfort present . . . take a few more deep breaths . . . and concentrating on that area of discomfort . . . feel each breath remove more . . . and more of that discomfort until that part of the body is as comfortable and relaxed . . . as the remainder of the body. . . .

Remember that in this relaxed state, you are still totally . . . in control . . . of the situation. . . . If any emergency were to arise, you would be able to come out of the state . . . and respond to it . . . rapidly and efficiently. . . . If at any time you feel apprehensive . . . it is only necessary to open your eyes and you can emerge from this relaxed state . . . feeling calm and comfortable . . . alert and relaxed. . . . Remember, in this relaxed state you are still . . . fully in control. . . . At some level, your mind will perceive everything . . . but your mind is discriminating . . . and will choose only those things that are appropriate to your growth and development . . . only the things that you are able to tolerate . . . at the present time. . . .

Now begin to take a few deep breaths again . . . and become aware of what it feels like when you . . . inhale. . . . Remember the importance of the substances that you take in with the breath. . . . We take in food . . . but we can survive for long periods of time without food. . . . We take in water . . . but we can survive several days without water. . . . However, we can only survive . . . a few minutes . . . without that which we take in through the breath. . . . So feel the energy coming back into the body . . . entering a body that is fully relaxed . . . and feel it not just in the lungs . . . but feel it spread from the lungs into . . . every single cell . . . of the body. . . . Feel the energy, and remember that you can feel energetic and vigorous . . . at the same time that you remain . . . comfortable and relaxed. . . . And as you feel the energy coming in, become more aware of the room that you are in . . . the time and place you are experiencing . . . and become more aware of your body . . . and especially any body parts that you may have lost awareness of . . . and whenever you are fully ready . . . you can open your eyes . . . feeling the benefits of all that you have just experienced.

General and specific images should be inserted after relaxation has been achieved and before the dehypnotizing procedure in the last paragraph.

Safe Place

The safe place is a general image used to attain the benefits of ASCs: overcoming the detrimental effects of the stress response, actualizing, enhancing the creative process, and promoting health and well-being..

Think of the words peace . . . safety . . . comfort . . . and happiness . . . peace . . . comfort . . . and happiness. . . . Now . . . let your mind spontaneously take you to a place . . . that means as many of those things as possible to you. . . . It may be a place that you go to frequently . . . or one that you have visited only in the distant past . . . or maybe one that's totally imaginary. . . . But *stay with the first place that comes to your mind.* . . . If you find yourself going from place to place . . . those are tricks being played on you by the conscious part of your mind . . . the part of your mind that says that you can't do something or puts judgments on things . . .

or that leads you to an external rather than an internal experience. . . . The first place, . . . the one that appeared spontaneously . . . is the place to stay with because that place appeared to you from deep down . . . inside . . . and is associated at some level of your being . . . with comfort . . . with relaxation . . . with peace . . . and with safety. . . .

Appreciate this scene with all of your senses. . . . See or imagine it . . . as vividly as you can. . . . Hear the sounds . . . appreciate the aromas . . . touch and feel the environment . . . and objects therein . . . and appreciate the tastes. . . . Perceive above you . . . beneath you . . . and all around you . . . exploring in fine detail all of the ingredients of this scene . . . whether it be outside . . . or inside. . . .

As you practice this image . . . this place becomes associated in the important . . . deep . . .parts . . . of your mind . . . with the concepts of peace . . . safety . . . comfort . . . happiness . . . and relaxation. . . . Over time, the associations will strengthen . . . to the point where you could go to this place mentally . . . and dissociate completely from what was happening to you in waking consciousness. . . . You could feel relaxed . . . when you normally would be unrelaxed. . . . You could feel comfort . . . when usually you would feel pain, and later . . . as your practice increases . . . even in your waking state . . . simply thinking about this place . . . could institute all of the feelings of comfort . . . peace . . . safety . . . relaxation . . . and quietness . . . that you experience now. . . . In addition, you could practice this image by just thinking . . . of it . . . several times . . . a day in your usual waking state. . . . Remember, every time you practice . . . going to this safe place . . . it becomes imprinted in your mind . . . so that as time goes by it will become . . . easier . . . to achieve the benefits of this image. . . . Even more important is that each time the concepts and images become . . . more permanently fixed . . . in your mind, and when they are there, they become . . . active . . . creating changes in your life that are . . . beneficial . . . to you and leading toward a . . . realization of those changes. . . .

Pain as Object

This image is used to give a more concrete representation to abstract sensations, such as pain and discomfort. We can then work with the image to change the subjective feelings of discomfort that it represents.

Most of us at one time or another . . . experience sensations . . . that we would regard as unpleasant, such as pain, discomfort, tension, stress, and strain. . . . Just by relaxing and concentrating on the . . . exhalation phase . . . of respiration, we have already learned one method . . . of alleviating . . . these uncomfortable sensations. . . . These sensations are all subjective phenomena. . . . We feel them . . . but as we know only too well . . . it is very difficult to consciously . . . modify these . . . feelings. . . . We usually find it easier to modify concrete objects . . . so the purpose of this image is to . . . change our unpleasant sensation . . . into an object . . . that is a . . . symbol . . . of this sensation. . . . If you now have a pain . . . discomfort . . . or tension . . . or even if you don't, going through the procedure anyway at this time will enable you to use it later . . . when these problems do develop. . . . Take that pain . . . tension . . . stress . . . or anxiety . . . and . . . give it a shape . . . by imagining or visualizing the first shape . . . that comes to mind. . . . The shape may be . . . abstract . . . or concrete. . . . It can be an object . . . an animate form . . . or a geometric design. . . . It can also be amorphous. . . . The first shape that comes into your mind is the . . . appropriate one . . . to work with. . . . Anything else tends to be conscious . . . judgmental effort. . . . Next . . . give the shape a color. . . . Now . . . give it a size. . . . You can establish the size by just knowing it . . . or by picturing next to it . . . an object of known size. . . . Realize that this shape is a symbol . . . of your tension or discomfort . . . and the larger it is, the more vibrantly and vividly colored it is . . . the more intense the discomfort it represents will be . . . and conversely . . . the smaller . . . and less vividly colored it is . . . the less severe . . . and less significant . . . the discomfort will be. . . . So practice . . . by changing the size of the object. . . . Because we usually are able to increase discomfort much more easily than decrease it, . . . make the object larger. . . . Make it as large as you need to make it . . . to feel somewhat more uncomfortable . . . and when it is as large as it needs to be . . . make it . . . smaller. . . . If you have any difficulty in making it smaller just by . . . wanting it . . . to be smaller . . . then . . . you can attempt to kick it . . . or throw it away . . . place it on a boat . . . or truck . . . or tie it to an airplane . . . and let it fly away . . . or if it is a balloon . . . you can put a needle into it . . . and deflate it. . . . Realize that as the symbol becomes smaller . . . the feelings associated with it become . . . less intense. . . . You can make it as small as it is comfortable for you to do so. . . . And practice making it larger and smaller because these are skills and, as with any skill . . . the more you practice . . . the more . . . powerful . . . the skill becomes. . . .

Picture Gallery

This is a three-part image that allows a person to obtain a true perspective of his or her self-perception. The parts can be used together or separately for specific purposes. The third part of the image elicits an end-result image—the image of what one desires to take place. Other methods for end-result imagery are to imagine oneself on a television or movie screen or in an imaginary mirror.

Imagine now that you are in a very large, private . . . comfortable . . . room of an art gallery. . . . All of the walls are empty except for one . . . and on that wall there are three empty frames of identical size and structure . . . placed side . . . by side . . . by side. . . . Approach the first frame . . . and as your attention focuses on that blank space . . . let there appear an image, an image of you . . . as you perceive yourself to be. . . . As you have previously learned . . . allow whatever image appears spontaneously . . . to be the one that you study. . . . And even if it is indistinct . . . just appreciate whatever of its essence that you are able to perceive. . . . And appreciate not only the visual image . . . but the feeling . . . that you get as you study it . . . and any other sensations that pervade your consciousness. . . . Study the image intensively and if you can, even . . . allow the image to move . . . so that you can see it from various sides and so that you can . . . appreciate . . . not just the static qualities but the . . . movement qualities as well. . . . All of these will add to the sense . . . of what this image really conveys. . . . And spend a few moments studying the image . . . in all its fine detail. . . .

Move your attention now to the second frame . . . and allow an image spontaneously to appear there . . . of you . . . as you really are. . . . Take a few moments now . . . to fully perceive . . . this image . . . in the manner that you perceived image number 1. . . . And now compare . . . and contrast . . . images 1 and 2. . . . In most people there are differences . . . and these differences . . . represent the fact that our own . . . perceptions of ourselves . . . are very rarely the same . . . as we really are. . . . From time to time . . . by going back to these two images . . . you may be able to judge . . . progress . . . in becoming more aware of yourself . . . as you really are. . . .

Now become aware of the third frame . . . and allow spontaneously to appear there . . . an image of . . . how you wish yourself to be. . . . And as you previously have done with numbers 1 and 2 . . . allow yourself to . . . fully study and appreciate . . . the image of how you . . . wish to be. . . . Then compare and contrast the second and third images . . . how you really are with . . . how you wish yourself to be . . . and become keenly aware of the . . . similarities . . . and . . . differences. . . . By periodically . . . reevaluating . . . these images . . . you will be able to perceive . . . changes . . . that have been made. . . . You will be able . . . to appreciate . . . the progress. . . . The method of instituting these changes is by . . . identifying clearly . . . with the third image . . . not just by looking at it but by . . . feeling it . . . merging with it . . . actually feeling your consciousness . . . become that image. . . . Remember, the language of the brain is pictures . . . and by using this particular picture . . . the one in the third frame . . . you send the message to the brain . . . of what you desire. . . . The brain controls . . . all bodily functions . . . and has the ability to translate these desires . . . into the changes in habits . . . life style . . . actvity . . . and so on . . . that will lead to the attainment . . . of your goal.

Healing White Light

The following image will allow the patient to consciously direct and channel the forces in the body that lead to health and healing. By translating desires into images, people can begin to direct forces of the central nervous system that are usually beyond their conscious control.

Allow yourself to concentrate . . . on an area in the midportion of your forehead . . . so that you may even begin to feel . . . a tingling sensation there. . . . As you do so . . . you are bringing all your attention . . . all of your consciousness . . . to this area. . . . By centering your consciousness . . . you can bring the . . . full power . . . of it to . . . enhance . . . the establishment of . . . wellness . . . in the body-mind axis. . . . Now allow this spot of attention . . . to become as small as you possibly can . . . so that all of your consciousness is . . . concentrated . . . in a very small area. . . . Now project this point . . . to an area about a foot above your head . . . and let it expand . . . to the size of a baseball. . . . Let this sphere obtain the appearance . . . of a glowing sphere . . . of radiant . . . fiery . . . white . . . light. . . . Perceive the glowing and fiery nature . . . feel the warmth . . . and maybe even hear . . . the vibratory qualities of this object. . . . And now let it begin to slowly . . . expand . . . until it achieves the size of a moderately sized melon, still radiantly . . . fiery . . . glowing . . . white. . . . Allow the bottom to open . . . as though the top were hinged . . . and as it does . . . begin to see a downpour of fiery . . . white . . . radiant . . . light energy. . . . Feel and see the energy entering the body through the top of the head . . . and flowing downward . . . through the entire body . . . from the head . . . into the neck . . . down the arms to the hands . . . back up the arms . . . down the chest . . . both front and back . . . the remainder of the trunk . . . front and back . . . down into the legs . . . and feet . . . and out the feet . . . into the ground. . . . Permit yourself not only to see this energy pour through the body . . . but feel it . . . and also hear it. . . . True health and wellness would be exemplified by a . . . free flow . . . of this fiery . . . radiant . . . white . . . light . . . energy through the body. . . . If there are problems in the body such as disease or discomfort . . . whether they be consciously realized or not . . . they can be manifested by some impedance . . . or even a complete blockage . . . of the flow of this fiery . . . radiant . . . white . . . light . . . energy . . . through that particular area or areas of the body . . . . When these areas are perceived . . . you may be able to feel and see these areas being fragmented . . . and consumed . . . by this fiery . . . radiant . . . white . . . light . . . energy. . . . It is as though the debris and garbage of the body . . . were being incinerated . . . by this . . . healing force. . . . When the discomfort . . . disorder . . . or disease has been fragmented . . . and consumed . . . by this fiery . . . radiant . . . white . . . light . . . energy . . . the result will be . . . free flow . . . of energy through this area. . . . Continue to feel . . . and perceive . . . this downpour . . . coming from that sphere . . . above the head through the entire body . . . and out the feet . . . into the floor . . . until free flow . . .of this fiery . . . radiant . . . white . . . light . . . energy . . . has been established through the body . . . so when this free flow has been established . . . it will represent the elimination of all toxins . . . wastes . . . and debris . . . that interfere with the . . . maintenance of health. . . .

When this free flow has been established . . . allow the sphere to close . . . and the downpour to cease. . . . Then allow the sphere . . . to get larger . . . approximately 3 feet in diameter . . . and allow it to descend . . . very slowly . . . so that it descends . . . around . . . the entire body . . . from head . . . to toes. . . . The function of the sphere at this time . . . is to absorb any accumulated debris . . . that has been left behind by the radiant . . . light . . . downpour. . . . When it reaches the feet . . . the entire body should be cleansed of all debris detrimental to maintenance of physical . . . and emotional . . . wellness. . . .

Now let the sphere begin to . . . slowly . . . rotate . . . in the opposite . . . direction around its vertical axis . . . and let it slowly begin to ascend . . . the body. . . . The function . . . of the sphere . . . at this time is to . . . instill . . . new . . . vitalizing . . . energy . . . into the body. . . . Not only is this energy being instilled into the body . . . but it is being instilled . . . into a body . . . that has been completely freed . . . of all forces that would hinder the . . . complete assimilation and utilization . . . of this energy. . . . When the sphere reaches the top of the head . . . and then ascends . . . above the head . . . the entire . . . body-mind axis . . . can be free . . . of all debris . . . and filled with a vitality . . . and energy . . . heretofore rarely, if ever, experienced. . . .

The sphere can now . . . stop rotating . . . and begin to . . . shrink . . . in size and eventually . . . return to the body as a point of . . . concentrated consciousness . . . in the forehead region. . . . Then, with a few deep breaths . . . this consciousness can travel throughout the body . . . and you can return slowly to the waking state . . . as you have done . . . in the previous exercises.

SUMMARY

Imagery is the basis of human thought processes, and is therefore the appropriate language for communicating with the human biocomputer. By accessing the imaging processes, the practitioner can rapidly reach deep levels of a patient's perception.

The internal world of imagery is just as real, emotionally and physiologically, as the external world. During hypnosis, images can be very vivid, increasing their potency as change agents. End-result imagery, or an image of a desired result rather than the process leading to that result, is the most effective type of image for inducing change.

When using imagery in hypnosis, the practitioner must be cognizant of the differences among people—both in their ability to image and in their primary mode of imaging. Some people are visual, while others are primarily auditory or kinesthetic. In order to tie into the patient's system of imaging, the practitioner should employ all sensory modalities in the creation of an image. Furthermore, instead of painting a definite image for a patient, it is more effective to take an indirect approach by helping patients draw on their own experiences to create images that will have personal meaning.

FURTHER READING

Korn, E. R., & Johnson, K. (1983). *Visualization: The uses of imagery in the health professions.* Homewood, IL: Dow-Jones-Irwin.

Sheehan, P. W. (Ed.). (1972). *The nature and function of imagery.* New York: Academic Press.

Samuels, M., & Samuels, N. (1975). *Seeing with the mind's eye.* New York: Random House.

REFERENCES

Ahsen, A. (1977). Eidetics: An overview. *Journal of Mental Imagery, 1,* 5–38.

Bandler, R., & Grinder, J. (1979). *Frogs into princes: Neurolinguistic programming.* Moab, UT: Real People Press.

Begg, I., Upfold, D., & Wilton, T. D. (1978). Imagery and verbal communication. *Journal of Mental Imagery, 2,* 165–186.

Doob, O. W. (1972). The ubiquitous appearance of images. In P. W. Sheehan (Ed.), *The nature and function of imagery* (pp. 311–333). New York: Academic Press.

Gordon, R. (1972). A very private world. In P. W. Sheehan (Ed.), *The nature and function of imagery* (pp. 63–80). New York: Academic Press.

Holt, P. R. (1972). On the nature of generality of mental imagery. In P. W. Sheehan (Ed.), *The nature and function of imagery* (pp. 6–33). New York: Academic Press.

Horowitz, M. J. (1967). Visual imagery and cognitive organization. *American Journal of Psychiatry, 123*, 938–946.

Horowitz, M. J. (1972). Image formation: Clinical observations of cognitive model. In P. W. Sheehan (Ed.). *The nature and function of imagery* (pp. 281–309). New York: Academic Press.

Jacobson, E. (1942). *Progressive relaxation*. Chicago: University of Chicago Press.

Jung, C. G. (1933). *Modern man in search of a soul*. New York: Harcourt, Brace & World.

Lay, W. (1897). Mental imagery. *Psychology Reviews, Monographs and Supplements, 92*, 1–59.

Maltz, M. (1966) *Psycho-cybernetics*. New York: Pocket Books.

Muses, C. M. (1974). The exploration of consciousness. In C. M. Muses & A. M. Young (Eds.), *Consciousness and reality* (pp. 102–131). New York: Avon Books.

Perky, C. W. (1910). An experimental study of imagination. *American Journal of Psychology, 21*, 422–452.

Richardson, A. (1969). *Mental imagery*. New York: Springer Publishing.

Samuels, M., & Samuels, N. (1975). *Seeing with the mind's eye*. New York: Random House.

Sheehan, P. W. (1972). Hypnosis and the manifestations of "imagination." In E. Fromm & R. E. Shor (Eds.), *Hypnosis: Research developments and perspectives*. Chicago: Aldine·Atherton.

Sheikh, A. A., & Richardson, P., & Moleski, L. M. (1979). Psychosomatics and mental imagery: A brief review. In A. A. Sheikh & J. T. Schaeffer (Eds.), *The potential of fantasy and imagination* (pp. 106–118). New York: Brandon House.

6
Self-Hypnosis

*. . . patients can throw themselves into the
nervous sleep and manifest all the usual
phenomena of mesmerism, through their own
unaided efforts.*

—James Braid
The Power of the Mind over the Body

A natural phenomenon, self-hypnosis is part of our everyday lives. Daydreaming is a form of self-hypnosis, as is absorption in a book, a task, or a religious ceremony. Unlike daydreaming, however, self-hypnosis in a clinical setting is practiced systematically and applied toward clearly defined goals. Patients using self-hypnosis under the guidance of a practitioner learn how to enter a state of deep relaxation and to give themselves constructive and positive suggestions.

The use of clinical self-hypnosis has been increasing in proportion to the growing use of indirect and permissive forms of hetero-hypnotic induction. Both have as an underlying principle the idea that the power of hypnosis resides in the patient rather than in the practitioner. In hetero-hypnosis, the practitioner offers suggestions, and the patient selects those that are acceptable to his or her unconscious. In self-hypnosis, each person can create self-suggestions that may be more meaningful and therefore more easily accommodated than suggestions coming from an outside source.

In general, self-hypnosis is appropriate whenever hetero-hypnosis is appropriate. It has been used effectively with adults of all ages and with children as young as 5 years. Self-hypnosis has proved to be an effective tool to alter habit patterns, such as smoking or thumb-sucking, as well as to decrease anxiety and increase self-confidence. It is used by athletes in many sports to increase concentration and improve performance. It also is used for controlling chronic pain, for reducing migraine attacks, for controlling the symptoms associated with diseases such as asthma, and for managing the pain of childbirth. A patient's successful use of self-hypnosis may increase the intervals between clinical appointments and may reduce overall treatment time. In all cases, self-hypnosis can give a patient the confidence or self-mastery and the ability to control a problem rather than be controlled by it.

The purpose of this chapter is to provide an overview of the recent research on self-hypnosis and to present guidelines for practitioners who wish to teach self-hypnosis to their patients. The application of self-hypnosis to a wide variety of treatment goals will be discussed in Part 3, Clinical Applications. For the use of self-hypnosis with children for cancer, functional megacolon, enuresis, and habit disorders, the reader is referred specifically to the work of Gardner (1976, 1978), LaBaw, Holten, Tewell, and Eccles (1975), and Olness (1975, 1976). For examples of the use of self-hypnosis with adults, see LaBaw (1975) on hemophilia, Sacerdote (1978b) on chronic pain, and Wakeman and Kaplan (1978) on burn therapy. For self-hypnosis in childbirth, see Chapter 10.

RESEARCH

The phenomenon of self-hypnosis was recognized over a century ago. Braid noted it in his writings on hypnosis and found it a useful tool for his own problems. As an area of empirical study, however, self-hypnosis is still in its infancy. Until recently, research on hypnosis has been confined to research on hetero-hypnosis. The traditional view was that hetero-hypnosis and self-hypnosis were essentially the same, distinguishable primarily because in self-hypnosis the patient both gives and receives suggestions.

In 1972, Fromm predicted that "there will be a great upsurge of scientific interest in self-hypnosis in the next decade" (p. 579). Since then, several researchers have begun the scientific study of self-hypnosis, Fromm and her research group outstanding among them. In one important, frequently cited study, Ruch (1975) identified self-hypnosis as the primary phenomenon in hypnosis and hetero-hypnosis as "guided self-hypnosis." From this point of view, it is assumed that the suggestions given by the practitioner are translated into autosuggestions by the patient. Many modern practitioners now reassure their patients that "all hypnosis is self-hypnosis."

Several authors have attempted to define self-hypnosis and to make behavioral and phenomenological distinctions between hetero- and self-hypnosis (Fromm et al., 1981; Johnson, 1979; Johnson and Weight, 1976; Ruch, 1975; Shor and Easton, 1973). Although the results of this research, discussed in the following pages, are tentative and need further replication and confirmation, they have validated clinical experiences, answered some questions, and raised many others.

Definitions

Researchers studying self-hypnosis have implicitly defined the phenomenon in different ways through different research methodologies. Ruch's (1975) operational definition of self-hypnosis as "any hypnotic behavior intentionally performed by the subject without substantial real-time guidance or intervention by a hypnotist, particularly in terms of the induction procedure" (p. 284), is representative. Within this broad definition, there are several ways of looking at self-hypnosis from a procedural point of view:

1. A spontaneous, unaided self-hypnotic experience by someone with no previous hetero-hypnotic experience. Gardner (1981) termed this phenomenon "autohypnosis" (a term commonly used interchangeably with self-hypnosis). Fromm et al. (1981) referred to it as "self-defined hypnosis," as opposed to laboratory or clinically defined hypnosis, where some form of instruction provides a framework for experiencing hypnosis. Sacerdote (1981) called this type of unaided trance experience "pure" self-hypnosis. As Gardner (1981) suggested, this kind of self-hypnosis is frequently evidenced in infants and children and supports the position that hypnosis is an inherent ability. Spontaneous trance by a naive person does not lend itself easily to laboratory investigation. However, an awareness of this kind of experience may facilitate hypnosis for patients in a clinical setting.

2. Self-hypnosis learned through some form of instruction but without previous hetero-hypnotic experience. For experimental purposes, this instruction has ranged from a very brief description of a possible induction technique (Ruch, 1975) to a full induction which subjects were asked to read to themselves (Shor and Easton, 1973). Outside of a clinical setting, instruction in self-hypnosis can be obtained through one of the many books or audio tapes on the subject. In the clinic, practitioners sometimes teach self-hypnosis to patients who

are resistant to hetero-hypnosis. Forms of self-hypnosis in this sense appear in many other therapeutic and self-help techniques, such as visualization and Benson's (1975) relaxation response.

3. Self-hypnosis that has been preceded by hetero-hypnosis. Most practitioners use hetero-hypnosis to familiarize a patient with the hypnotic experience and then proceed to teach self-hypnotic skills. In Gardner's (1981) words, "The therapist or E facilitates the use of hypnotic talent by S who then takes over as his own guide" (p. 301). Practice varies even within this general category, however. For example, the practitioner can teach self-hypnosis with or without posthypnotic suggestions that the patient will be able to enter self-hypnosis at a later time according to a prearranged cue. Self-hypnosis can be further influenced by the presence or absence of the practitioner and by the extent to which the practitioner, if present, initiates suggestions.

There is no consensus on the value of hetero-hypnosis in teaching or facilitating self-hypnosis. Although their research was not addressed to this question, Fromm et al. (1981) believed the hetero-hypnotic experience to be beneficial for those learning self-hypnosis. Ruch (1975) found that hetero-hypnosis was unnecessary and in some cases inhibited subsequent self-hypnosis. Johnson and Weight (1976) agreed that prior hetero-hypnosis was unnecessary but found no evidence that it was detrimental to later self-hypnosis.

At one extreme, therefore, we have spontaneous self-hypnosis by someone who may never have heard of hypnosis or identified the experience as hypnotic. At the other extreme, self-hypnosis is learned through previous hetero-hypnosis and self-hypnotic suggestions are initiated by the practitioner, as in the studies by Johnson and Weight (1976) and Shor and Easton (1973). These authors defined self-hypnosis primarily as self-directed response to suggestions and did not include the criterion that suggestions be self-initiated. These distinctions were drawn by Fromm and her research group (1981).

In this chapter, self-hypnosis will refer to a hypnotic experience that occurs outside of the presence of the practitioner (with the exception of the initial learning period in which the patient may practice with the practitioner), and in which the patient "takes full responsibility for achieving the trance state and selecting ideas or suggestions on which he will focus for his own benefit" (Gardner, 1981, p. 302). Hetero-hypnosis is an effective means of introducing a patient to the hypnotic experience, and as such, it is a valuable tool in the overall process of teaching self-hypnosis.

Characteristics

In a comprehensive study, Fromm et al. (1981) "looked for the state, content, and context variables which might provide a unique definition of self-hypnosis" (p. 235). They found that self-hypnosis is not a unitary phenomenon, but one that is influenced by the interplay of these variables. Many of their findings, based on the experiences of 33 volunteer subjects (58 began the study) with high scores on susceptibility tests, relatively little knowledge of hypnosis, and no evidence of psychopathology, are of general interest to the practitioner teaching self-hypnosis to patients. The participants in Fromm's study were required to practice self-hypnosis 1 hour each day for 4 weeks. They were given three hetero-hypnotic experiences (in the form of standardized scales) before the self-hypnosis program, and one hetero-hypnotic experience midway through the experiment. (See the *International Journal of Clinical and Experimental Hypnosis*, 1981, *29* (3), for the complete article and for responses to this study by several other authors.) The findings may be summarized as follows:

1. Fromm's group of researchers studied four characteristics of hypnotic trance: absorption, relinquishment of the generalized reality orientation, depth, and attention. They found that an inner absorption and a relinquishing of the generalized reality orientation are common to both hetero- and self-hypnosis. Self-hypnosis, however, is characterized by a greater fluctuation of trance depth and more expansive attention. In self-hypnosis, a person is more receptive to internal images and sensations. In hetero-hypnosis, attention is more focused and people are more performance-oriented.

2. With continued practice, changes occurred in the intensity of phenomena as well as in the interaction between trance-related and personal variables. The authors concluded that "one of the hallmarks of self-hypnosis may be its changeability. The interplay between S [subject] and state is constantly changing" (p. 217).

3. Imagery plays a greater role and images are more vivid in self-hypnosis than in hetero-hypnosis. Thematic content varies according to individual needs and wishes, making imagery in self-hypnosis more idiosyncratic than it is in hetero-hypnosis.

4. The phenomena of positive and negative hallucinations, hypermnesia, and age regression are more successful in hetero-hypnosis.

5. There is some evidence that personality factors may affect one's success with and experience of self-hypnosis. Two participants in the study had difficulty in achieving a satisfactory state of self-hypnosis, even though they had achieved high scores on hetero-hypnotic scales.

6. At the beginning of the study, participants experienced a period of anxiety and doubt about their ability to enter self-hypnosis. With practice, the process became "automatized," they felt more confident, and they were able to enter and deepen trance more quickly.

Other studies (Johnson, 1979; Johnson and Weight, 1976; Ruch, 1975; and Shor and Easton, 1973) emphasized behavioral rather than phenomenological comparisons between self-hypnosis and hetero-hypnosis. Johnson (1981) reviewed the findings of these studies in light of the study by Fromm et al. (1981). For example, Fromm's group wanted to "chart the essential landmarks of self-hypnosis"; therefore, they chose participants who were highly responsive to hypnosis and, according to a pilot study, who were best able to distinguish between the two states. Studies in which participants were not screened for hypnotic responsiveness, and which used different research methodologies, have had different findings. Subjects in the study by Johnson and Weight (1976) felt more active and self-controlling in self-hypnosis than in hetero-hypnosis. Both this research and Ruch's (1975) study stressed the similarities rather than differences between the two states.

Interest in self-hypnosis is high, and preliminary data have piqued that interest. All of the current researchers in the field agree that present lines of research show great promise and that much remains to be done. Fromm et al. (1981) would like to see investigations of personality type and self-hypnosis; the extent to which rhythmic fluctuations in arousal (such as the ultradian cycle) influence self-hypnosis; "alert self-hypnosis," such as that cultivated by athletes; and different methods of learning and practicing self-hypnosis. Gardner (1981), who works with children, sees a need for comparing the value of self-hypnosis for different age groups, for different problems, and with different approaches. To facilitate future research, Orne and McConky (1981) encourage the development and refinement of performance scales for assessing behavioral response and phenomenological awareness in people experiencing self-hypnosis.

TEACHING SELF-HYPNOSIS TO PATIENTS

Most practitioners can do much more than they are to help their patients assume greater responsibility for their own well-being. Self-hypnosis, an excellent means of facilitating therapy or medical treatment and of reducing a patient's dependency on the practitioner, is also a treatment modality with positive side effects, such as reduced tension or improved sleep. Most patients find that self-hypnosis for one problem has a positive effect on other areas of their lives as well.

"The methods of teaching self-hypnosis are as varied as the experience, creativity, involvement, and expectations of the teachers and the receptivity of the learners" (Sacerdote, 1981, p. 286). The approach outlined in this section has been developed over a period of 9 years by Alman, based on Erickson's work. This approach uses hetero-hypnosis as an important tool in developing the techniques of self-hypnosis. The following discussion includes a four-session overview of the steps to follow in teaching self-hypnosis; an outline for patients to use when practicing self-hypnosis; and some general guidelines for helping a patient to overcome difficulties and realize success in using self-hypnosis.

Four-Session Overview

This general approach to teaching self-hypnosis is appropriate for either an individual or a group. Four sessions, of approximately 1 hour each, are necessary to allow time for the practitioner to obtain feedback from the patient and to use that feedback to enhance motivation and to adjust subsequent sessions. The time required to reach a satisfactory level of expertise may vary slightly, depending on a patient's history and motivation. In general, however, by the end of the fourth session, the patient is able to recognize, induce, and feel comfortable with the hypnotic state. These four sessions do not include treatment time using self-hypnosis. Work on specific problems or goals begins after a patient has learned the techniques of self-hypnosis.

Session 1. The major purpose of the initial session is to create a trusting, comfortable atmosphere in which the patient can learn self-hypnosis as a technique for permanent positive change. The preliminary discussion is an opportunity for the practitioner to assess the patient's strengths, problems, and degree of self-confidence, to listen for key words or expressions, and to observe body language, all of which are crucial for developing an individualized approach to induction for facilitating self-hypnosis.

1. Discuss the myths and misconceptions pertaining to hypnosis and self-hypnosis (see Chapter 1).

2. Clarify the patient's treatment goals and make sure they are realistic, healthy, and suitable for self-hypnosis. For example, self-hypnosis for recurring headaches should not be done in the absence of a medical examination. Self-hypnosis for weight loss needs to address the issues of exercise and nutrition.

3. Discuss estimated length of treatment, fees, and what is expected of both patient and practitioner. Stress the need for active involvement on the part of the patient, which will include practicing 10–20 minutes, twice a day.

4. Discuss the patient's work, home situation, and hobbies for the purpose of understanding family relations, lifestyle, routines, and existing conflicts.

5. Explain the nature of the change experience. For example:

> Everywhere around us we see motion, momentum, and change. Day becomes night, tides ebb and flow, and winter becomes spring. Similarly, you can use your inner changes to maximize your potential, your performance, and your ability to keep growing and changing.

6. Introduce hypnosis as a learning experience and a naturalistic approach to change, and at the same time initiate a contemplative process by talking about something in which the patient is interested. By asking questions such as "If we were sitting on the edge of the lake, do you think we would be looking at ducks or birds?" lead the patient into thinking in new ways:

> If you watched the ducks more closely and noticed how they paddle with their feet, you might be surprised at how much movement they make . . . and how much movement you can make beginning right now.

Patients sometimes will go into a light trance without realizing it. This conversational induction can be taped for the patient to use for practicing throughout the week.

7. Teach the patient two induction techniques, such as eye fixation, arm levitation, or reverse arm levitation (see Chapter 4). Take the patient in and out of trance using these techniques so that the patient

knows what to expect when practicing. Encourage the patient to experiment with these techniques during the week.

8. Explain that it is best to get up and do something else immediately after practicing self-hypnosis. Conscious analysis of the session may interfere with the unconscious integration of new material. Discussion and analysis at a later time are perfectly appropriate.

9. Observe any changes in the patient, briefly answer any questions, and conclude the session on a positive note.

Session 2.   This session is used to learn more about the patient, to work with the patient's practice experiences, and to teach additional self-hypnosis techniques.

1. Assess the week's experience in practice and the techniques that the patient found most useful.

2. Begin an induction, using the approach the patient reported as successful.

3. Facilitate the patient's learning both in and about the trance. Some patients need an outline for practicing self-hypnosis (included later in this chapter). Others require less guidance and are more comfortable experimenting on their own.

4. Present alternative induction techniques. Emphasize the importance of exploring different techniques in practice to discover the most effective ones, and then practicing them until confidence in them is developed. Alternatives include: imagery and progressive relaxation (see Chapters 4 and 5), dream induction (in which you relax and suggest to yourself that you will have a pleasant dream), and the conversational induction (silently talking to yourself to facilitate trance). Stress that the patient can work out most problems through practice.

5. Review and discuss the session and answer any questions.

Session 3.   By this time, the practitioner has done 2 or 3 hours of homework on the patient, the patient's goals, the inductions and suggestions that are working best. This session continues the ongoing process of obtaining feedback on the patient's experiences in self-hypnosis, providing encouragement, supporting successes, and answering questions. At this point, the practitioner also begins to talk about ways of wording suggestions.

1. Using an individualized induction, take the patient into and out of trance three times in a row. This process results in increasingly deeper trances and increases the patient's awareness of the differences between the waking, sleeping, and trance states.

2. Have the patient demonstrate his or her self-hypnosis technique.

3. Discuss with the patient ways of wording suggestions, using imagery, and constructing metaphors. Stress that motivation and an understanding of specific goals are more important than the exact wording of suggestions. In other words, relieve patients of the burden of believing that they have to be hypnotherapists to phrase effective suggestions. The unconscious will hear the positive messages, regardless of how they are worded.

4. Explain how patients can use clues in their environment for posthypnotic suggestion. For example, a businesswoman may suggest to herself that as she comes home in the evening and her hand touches the doorknob on the front door, she will leave all of the tensions and cares of the day behind.

5. Suggest that patients use other opportunities, such as jogging, daydreaming, or listening to music, to give themselves positive suggestions.

6. Review the session, encourage continuing practice, and plan for the final meeting.

Session 4. In this concluding session, the practitioner draws on experience and information from preceding sessions to assist the patient in practicing and refining hypnotic techniques.

1. Review the patient's practice experiences, changes, and comfort with hypnosis. Set a positive tone by reinforcing present experiences and encouraging future ones.

2. Practice with specific suggestions, such as glove anesthesia or lightness of limbs.

3. Work with the patient on formulating individualized, goal-oriented suggestions. This step amounts to a creative brainstorming session.

4. Do a final induction, taking into consideration all previous

inductions. Give suggestions about practicing and reinforcing natural abilities and positive changes.

5. Leave open the possibility of a follow-up session in 2 or 3 months and further contact by telephone or mail.

Self-Hypnosis Outline for Patients

The following is a step-by-step self-hypnosis guide developed by Alman and Lambrou (1983) for patients who are just beginning to practice or patients who may feel more comfortable having some instructions for reference. Encourage patients to use this outline only as a starting point for experimentation to find techniques that work best for them.

   I. Preparing and relaxing.
     A. Assume a relaxed position, either sitting or reclining.
     B. Close your eyes and take several deep breaths.
     C. Feel the calming sensations of becoming more and more relaxed.
     D. Ask yourself, "How relaxed can I feel right now?"
     E. If your mind insists on thinking about something, pursue that train of thought for a minute or two, and then return to relaxing.

  II. Generalizing.
     A. Generalize your relaxation to your entire body, beginning with the toes and working up to the head.
     B. Travel in your mind to a relaxing scene, such as the ocean or a meadow, and experience yourself in that place as you feel more and more relaxed.
     C. Tell yourself that your conscious mind will be doing nothing of importance for now.
     D. Integrate any outside distractions into your experience: "As I hear the airplane flying into the distance, I know that I am becoming more and more relaxed."
     E. If you have some problems that are bothering you, imagine attaching them to a great big red balloon and then releasing that balloon and watching them float away.
     F. Pay attention to any feelings and thoughts you may have, and use them. If you are worried about work, for example, talk to your boss and co-workers in your mind, noticing how as you finish talking to each person, you feel more and more relaxed.

 III. Working. Give yourself suggestions in one or more of the following ways:
     A. Repeat direct suggestions, or clear statements of what you wish to achieve, several times.

    B. Make indirect suggestions. Begin by telling yourself, "I don't know what suggestions will be most effective, but I know that I will benefit from some of them. . . . " Give yourself a choice by phrasing one or two different suggestions in several different ways, realizing that your unconscious will act on some of them.

    C. Use imagery to elicit the response you desire. For example, if you are tense or anxious, visualize a scene in which you feel secure, comfortable, and relaxed. It might be a beach scene, a mountain cabin, or your own home.

    D. Find a parallel experience for what you wish to achieve. Tension, for example, can be experienced as a tightly wound spring or stretched elastic that you are able to unwind or relax.

IV. Reinforcing and summarizing.

    A. Review the self-hypnotic session: "I know I have given myself suggestions of *(whatever you worked on this session)*."

    B. Reinforce the experience: "As I leave this experience behind, I know I will feel more and more comfortable."

    C. Prepare for the next session: "I know that as I come out of trance I will be able to return to this state with greater and greater ease."

    D. Leave the experience and go to something else. If you start analyzing too soon, you can undo what you have accomplished.

Guidelines for the Practitioner

After the first week of practicing self-hypnosis, many patients report some anxiety, self-doubt, difficulty entering trance, or difficulty choosing or formulating suggestions. The practitioner can reassure those patients that their experiences are perfectly normal. The subjects in the study by Fromm et al. (1981) experienced the same difficulties but with continued practice were able to move beyond them. Beyond reassurance, there are many ways of helping patients overcome their initial problems with self-hypnosis.

Some patients are afraid of or uncomfortable with the hypnotic state. For those who are afraid of losing control, the practitioner should explain that, although hypnosis is a state where you "let go" (or relinquish the generalized reality orientation), you do not go into oblivion. Instead, you "let go" into a heightened and focused state where you do important work. This state is similar to that experienced by a musician playing a piece of music or an athlete concentrating on an athletic event.

Some patients need time to adjust to the new experience. A useful analogy is to draw a parallel between learning self-hypnosis and going into the ocean:

During your first experience with the ocean, you probably only went in up to your ankles. The next time, you might have gotten your knees wet before coming back out. Eventually, step by step, you learned to trust yourself in the ocean, just as you will in self-hypnosis. Once you become more familiar with the trance state, you will realize that it is a powerful, natural state that we experience all of the time.

Erickson believed that the more the therapist learns about a patient's unconscious, the more he or she can help that person. In hetero-hypnosis, the practitioner needs to know the patient in order to individualize the inductions and suggestions. In self-hypnosis, people need to know themselves. Patients should be encouraged to respect the unconscious and to learn about it. People can find clues for self-hypnosis by observing themselves and by paying attention to feelings and thoughts.

Some patients worry that they are not achieving a trance state deep enough to be effective. The practitioner should reassure these patients by explaining that in self-hypnosis, the most significant factor is not the depth of trance but the kinds of suggestions that are given. Depth will vary from person to person and from session to session. Trance depth also fluctuates within each self-hypnosis session. If a patient is making some progress, the trance depth is sufficient.

Patients who secretly hope that self-hypnosis will prove to be a cure-all for their problems may be distressed to find that they are not achieving the miraculous results that they desired. Here the practitioner needs to emphasize the importance of practice. With continued practice there will be progress, although the gains may be imperceptible at first.

Patients also should be aware of how clever people can be in maintaining old patterns. Sometimes the harder we try to change a habit, the more we find ourselves adhering to it. Patients can use variations on the following suggestion to acknowledge the problem and to begin finding a solution: "I know how clever I can be in continuing to" . . . (describe the pattern to be changed). "And I also know that I can cleverly design a way to look at this pattern differently."

Self-hypnotic dreams can be used to find solutions to problems. After relaxing, the patient gives an autosuggestion to have a pleasant dream. The dream is a place where individuals can be more in touch with themselves (Sacerdote, 1978a). The patient should be given the following steps to use after the dream:

1. Clarify the problem and state your goal.

2. Be aware of blockages that are preventing you from reaching the goal.

3. Begin identifying ways of making specific changes.

4. Become aware of your potential for positive change. For example, at first you didn't think you could achieve a trance state, and here you are using it.

In some cases, without realizing it, patients will undermine their own progress by doubting, or by allowing negative thoughts to enter their suggestions. As in hetero-hypnosis, images should be individualized and realized in all five senses, and special emphasis should be placed on controlling the image (see Chapter 5). Some patients need considerably more help than others to create suggestions that will have a desired effect.

An anxious and depressed patient who has a background in music and who feels best when she is playing the piano has found this suggestion to be effective:

I know that the piano is made up of many different parts . . . 52 keys, both black and white . . . and of strings of different lengths and thicknesses. . . . And there are different varieties of pianos, with different tones. . . . Just as I can anticipate notes in music I am playing . . . I can sense when an emotional note is about to make itself heard . . . and if it is depressive or anxious . . . I can control it. . . . I can play loud, strong pieces . . . and experience a release of tension and anger . . . and through the different kinds of music . . . played in different ways . . . I can experience more and more of myself . . . my enjoyment . . . my potential. . . . And as I practice the music in my mind . . . soon I will have only to hear the first notes . . . or think of the name . . . and I will be able to have the experiences associated with playing the whole piece.

A patient who enjoys backpacking and hiking formulated this suggestion to facilitate change:

I have noticed how nature is always changing. . . . At one time the earth was covered with ice . . . and now there are tropical places . . . where it is warm and rich in color . . . and I can search out and find these places. . . . As I walk from one place to another when I am hiking . . . I can make progress. . . . As long as I am moving, I am progressing . . . and controlling my direction . . . without thinking about it . . . just one foot following another.

Sample Inductions

The following are examples of inductions a practitioner might use with a patient during the first few sessions of the four-step process of teaching self-hypnosis. The inductions are open to alteration, depending on the experiences of the patient.

The purpose of these inductions is to give the patient an hypnotic experience and to help the patient become comfortable with that experience. The inductions begin with a contemplative process that emphasizes concentration or absorption in the words and becomes absorption in the hypnotic process itself.

Induction 1.   I understand that you've had some doubts about coming in here today. I understand that you doubt . . . that a lot is even going to happen . . . with what we're calling hypnosis. But whether you know very much about hypnosis or not, you probably know it's just a term to describe a very natural state. Somehow through the years . . . as far back as the 1800s . . . there have been labels . . . and descriptions that have clearly defined what hypnosis isn't . . . as much as what it is. So if we can just assume . . . that this experience will be a comfortable . . . 10-minute . . . relaxing session . . . that may or may not fit into your doubts about how much will happen, you can enjoy cooperating with yourself in a way that is natural . . . and relaxing. So at your own pace, when you feel ready to relax . . . when you feel ready to feel more comfortable . . . you may want to first give up . . . or even slow up . . . some of the conflicts and hesitancies that got you in here. But it's curious that what got you in here may have been your own doubts, but now that you are here . . . all you need to do is take your time . . . and listen to my words . . . naturally . . . and positively. It's helpful sometimes to take a couple of deep . . . satisfying breaths . . . and other times you may want to take as many as six or ten. But there are no guidelines as to how many you have to take. . . . You can take as many as you think you'll need. Once you've done this . . . you know that you'll naturally move on past . . . and what you may move on past to is an opportunity, . . . that's right, . . . to make your body more comfortable, and that may simply mean just letting yourself sink back into the chair, . . . feel some heaviness, . . . feel some limpness, . . . and rather than tell you what's going to happen . . . I can allow you to experience whatever does happen and know that this is solely your experience . . . something you're capable . . . of perhaps . . . enjoying. Now, I'd like to explain to you how tensions and conflicts, concerns and worries that may have been lingering and concerning you . . . can be minimized in a natural way. You can allow yourself now . . . as you're feeling more comfortable than you were a few minutes ago . . . and already having taken a few deep . . . satisfying breaths . . . you can again . . . enjoy your natural . . . personal experience. . . . That's right. Changing is as natural as nature. If you've ever seen the seasons of the year you certainly know the changes . . . that are present in nature. If you've seen the rainbow after the rain . . . the sun shining on the ocean . . . or on a lake . . . you just know . . . that blue skies often follow gray. But when you think . . . of the birds you may hear in the distance . . . or even the sounds you may hear that resemble birds . . . or just the picture of one in your mind, . . . you'll know that the flight from one place to another looks easy to some . . . and yet your own flight . . . may be naturally changing and becoming easier . . . becoming more comfortable. . . . That's right. So in all the moving around you may find yourself doing . . . you'll find that any moving you do will just be to find more and more of your own niche in this kind of experience. So you may be more surprised than curious or you may be more curious than surprised . . . to find that you . . . are naturally available to nature's changes. And your own nature, of course, desires some changes . . . and as you realize . . . more and more within yourself . . . you can surprise . . . even some of the most curious parts of you. . . . You can resolve even the most significant doubts you've had . . . as to what an impact you can have on your environment. . . . In using this kind of opportunity, you can feel more and more in control of where you . . . are following yourself. As you follow . . . as you continue . . . you'll naturally feel . . . more and more . . . of that shift, . . . of that comfort, . . . and of that control that you know is more available to you than perhaps you ever thought was even possible. That's right, . . . that's fine.

Induction 2.   The first thing I want you to do . . . is get yourself as comfortable as you can. Take your shoes off, loosen your tie, loosen your button, take off your watch. . . . Just make sure you're as comfortable as you can. You might want to shift around into the position that will make you feel most comfortable. . . . That's right. And as you do this, take a few deep, satisfying breaths . . . a couple of relaxing breaths, just to blow off some tension and frustrations . . . and maybe with an amusing thought at the same time. There is no need to try and think of anything; in fact, there is no need to do anything at all. After you have taken a few deep, satisfying breaths you'll naturally feel more comfortable . . . and begin to feel as relaxed . . . and at ease as you'd like. You do know when you take this kind of time out . . . that it's a centering time . . . a focusing time . . . a chance to let your conscious mind be elsewhere . . . perhaps get busy on the sounds from inside the room or outside the room and just give yourself the opportunity to use your own resources . . .

to use your own natural abilities . . . to make change . . . whether it be very subtle or dramatic. . . . You know that change is a natural function of nature . . . and your own nature can allow you to use untapped resources and begin to open doors that give you some of the solutions to some of the questions that your unconscious is aware of. So there is nothing your conscious mind will be doing . . . of any importance. . . . There's nothing to think about . . . and no need to try . . . to allow your unconscious to be present. . . . All you need to do . . . is allow this to happen. You know full well that whenever you take this kind of time out . . . whether now . . . or when you use a tape, . . . in my office or in privacy, . . . there is no one to bother you, . . . there is no one to disturb you, . . . and there is no one to take care of. So as you feel yourself becoming even more and more comfortable . . . you can create a more tranquil sense . . . of self. If you've been active or busy, even nervous about things . . . you can acknowledge this, even pay attention to it . . . and when you feel you've given it adequate attention for this kind of experience, which may be as long as a full minute, but just as much as you need . . . you can move on . . . to a more relaxed and a more comfortable state . . . very naturally . . . at your own pace. And now it may be helpful to you to count backward . . . from 30 to 1. You may feel as if you're going down a flight of stairs . . . and of course the closer you get to the bottom . . . the deeper and more relaxed you can feel. You may feel you need to pay attention to my voice, but there's no need to pay attention. . . . You may feel that as you get deeper and feel more comfortable you may fall asleep or your body may feel deeply relaxed . . . and yet your mind may feel heightened . . . focused. . . . That's right. And even more clear than perhaps it has felt in quite awhile. You know what it's like to feel your physical body responding to change. . . . And now you may notice some heaviness in your legs . . . some heaviness in your arms . . . and at the same time be able to experience a more true sense of how you can feel lightness and heaviness at the same time . . . warmth and even coolness as well. Certainly how much better you can take care of yourself . . . by having this kind of opportunity . . . and taking this kind of time . . . out for yourself. No one to bother you . . . and no one to disturb you. And as you're entering this natural state . . . this quite relaxed state . . . you're able to begin the work that is so important.

(At this point the practitioner makes suggestions related to the goal of learning and practicing self-hypnosis.)

And now that you've taken this kind of time out . . . you can naturally feel a renewed sense of having tapped some resources and used some natural abilities that enter . . . into your realm of personal control. Whether you understand what's conscious or unconscious is unimportant. . . . You may even feel more able . . . naturally from the result of this tape. You can remember some things and forget other things. . . . You can remember to forget as you may remember what you had for lunch yesterday yet forget what you had a month ago yesterday. Of course the information is there if you really need it . . . but there's no need . . . so you can allow it to happen. So you may remember some things later in the week and some things earlier . . . some things you may associate with months or even years from now. . . . So whenever you'd like . . . you may want to count up to 30 by yourself. . . . You may only need to count up to 10. And you can understand from this time on . . . you can feel a profound change in your abilities to relax . . . that will follow into each future experience . . . as well as your abilities to take care of yourself in this natural . . . and positive way. So when you're ready . . . at your own pace. . . . That's right. Deep breath, more refreshed, and more alert . . . very naturally . . . fine.

Induction 3.   Are you in a trance right now? You may be in trance right now. . . . Then . . . you're not sure if you're in a trance. . . . Perhaps you could be and haven't even known it. But whether you wonder more or you're curious more . . . being in a trance is a very natural state. . . . You don't have to try and make it happen, it can just happen as easily . . . and comfortably . . . just like this. So as you wonder and are curious, you can also find . . . that your own body may be feeling differently in just a few moments than it had been. But being in trance is as natural . . . as awakening and sleeping. It's a state you may find yourself in as often as every 15 minutes or so . . . in what you may call a daydream. Also being in a trance now makes available the opportunity . . . to make changes and give yourself certain suggestions . . . that will be long-lasting in effectiveness. But of course the question of what trance can do or even what trance is . . . may be a more interesting question to ask yourself in a trance state than in any other state. . . . So when you're ready to further your own experience . . . your own growth and your own knowledge . . . you can take a few deep breaths. . . . You can begin to move into a more fluid state . . . a more flowing state. . . . That's right. Where you enter into some of the more resourceful . . . reservoirs . . . than perhaps you would have even thought were available. But if you've ever walked down a path . . . and found a stream or a lake . . . you know what it's like to find the unexpected. Even if you expected to see it, somehow when you find it . . . there's a moment with the unexpected. Because it always appears different . . .even if you've seen it . . . many times before. If you do . . . you'll be able to enjoy some of your own natural surprises . . . that you can feel a pleasant . . . refreshment with.

Now you know . . . what trance can offer just in a few short minutes. So you can wonder what trance could offer over a longer period of time. . . . That's right. And when you may wonder if something disturbing in thought or even in sound may come your way . . . you can allow it to pass through . . . as though it's moving down the stream. . . . That's right . . . very naturally. Perhaps it's getting easier to understand how using some techniques that you've probably been using for many years . . . can enhance change and even enhance your own positive abilities to make some changes, whether small or large, whether noticeable now . . . or noticeable when completed. . . . The week to follow can be a week where many of these suggestions filter through . . . and even have an impact on your daily experiences . . . and even your nightly experiences. . . . That's right.

(Note: This is the point at which suggestions for specific changes are given. Careful attention should be paid to individualizing the approach to each patient.)

SUMMARY

Self-hypnosis is a natural state, many forms of which occur frequently in everyday life. In a clinical setting, self-hypnosis is a technique that can reinforce work done in hetero-hypnosis, thus imparting a greater degree of responsibility and control to the patient. Research has identified some phenomenological differences between the two states. In self-hypnosis, attention is more expansive, there is a greater fluctuation of trance depth, and imagery plays a greater role. The phenomena of positive and negative hallucinations, hypermnesia, and age regression are more successful in hetero-hypnosis.

Hetero-hypnosis is an excellent means of introducing the hypnotic experience to a patient who wishes to learn self-hypnosis. Most patients can learn to recognize, induce, and feel comfortable with the hypnotic state within four 1-hour sessions, held weekly. During these sessions, the practitioner introduces a variety of induction techniques, refines techniques based on patient feedback, helps the patient phrase effective suggestions, and provides needed support and encouragement. Between sessions, the patient is expected to practice self-hypnosis daily for two 10–20-minute periods.

Initial problems, such as fear of the trance state, difficulty inducing trance, and insecurity about forming suggestions easily, can be overcome with daily practice and weekly hetero-hypnotic sessions. Gains realized through self-hypnosis often generalize to other parts of a patient's life.

FURTHER READING

Alman, B., & Lambrou, P. (1983). *Self-hypnosis: A complete manual for health and self-change.* San Diego: International Health Publications.

Gardner, G. C. (1981). Teaching self-hypnosis to children. *International Journal of Clinical and Experimental Hypnosis, 29,* 300–312.

Sacerdote, P. (1981). Teaching self-hypnosis to adults. *International Journal of Clinical and Experimental Hypnosis, 19,* 282–297.

REFERENCES

Alman, B., & Lambrou, P. (1983). *Self-hypnosis: A complete manual for health and self-change.* San Diego: International Health Publications.

Benson, H. (1975). *The relaxation response.* New York: Morrow.

Fromm, E. (1972) *Quo vadis hypnosis?* Predictions of future trends in hypnosis research. In E. Fromm & R. E. Shor (Eds.), *Hypnosis: Research developments and perspectives.* Chicago: Aldine·Atherton.

Fromm, E., Brown, D. P., Hurt, S. W., Oberlander, J. Z., Boxer, A. M., & Pfeiffer, G. (1981). The phenomena and characteristics of self-hypnosis. *International Journal of Clinical and Experimental Hypnosis, 29,* 189–246.

Gardner, G. G. (1976). Childhood, death and human dignity: Hypnotherapy for David. *International Journal of Clinical and Experimental Hypnosis, 24,* 122–139.

Gardner, G. G. (1978). Hypnotherapy in the management of childhood habit disorders. *Journal of Pediatrics, 92,* 838–840.

Gardner, G. G. (1981). Teaching self-hypnosis to children. *International Journal of Clinical and Experimental Hypnosis, 29,* 300–312.

Johnson, L. S. (1979). Self-hypnosis: Behavioral and phenomenological comparisons with hetero-hypnosis. *International Journal of Clinical and Experimental Hypnosis, 27,* 240–264.

Johnson, L. S. (1981). Self-hypnosis: The Chicago paradigm. *International Journal of Clinical and Experimental Hypnosis, 29,* 247–258.

Johnson, L. S., & Weight, D. G. (1976). Self-hypnosis vs. hetero-hypnosis. Experimental and behavioral comparisons. *Journal of Abnormal Psychology, 85,* 522–526.

LaBaw, W. L. (1975). Auto-hypnosis in haemophilia. *Haematologia, 9,* 103–110.

LaBaw, W. L., Holten, C., Tewell, K., & Eccles, D. (1975). The use of self-hypnosis by children with cancer. *American Journal of Clinical Hypnosis, 17,* 233–238.

Olness, K. (1975). The use of self-hypnosis in the treatment of childhood nocturnal enuresis. *Clinical Pediatrics, 14,* 273–279.

Olness, K. (1976). Auto-hypnosis in functional megacolon in children. *American Journal of Clinical Hypnosis, 19,* 28–32.

Orne, M. T., & McConkey, K. M. (1981). Toward convergent inquiry into self-hypnosis. *International Journal of Clinical and Experimental Hypnosis, 29,* 313–323.

Ruch, J. C. (1975). Self-hypnosis: The result of hetero-hypnosis or vice versa? *International Journal of Clinical and Experimental Hypnosis, 22*, 282–304.

Sacerdote, P. (1978a). *Induced dreams: About the theory and therapeutic applications of dreams hypnotically induced.* New York: Gaus.

Sacerdote, P. (1978b). Teaching self-hypnosis to patients with chronic pain. *Journal of Human Stress, 4*, 18–21.

Sacerdote, P. (1981). Teaching self-hypnosis to adults. *International Journal of Clinical and Experimental Hypnosis, 19*, 282–297.

Shor, R. E., & Easton, R. D. (1973). A preliminary report on research comparing self- and hetero-hypnosis. *American Journal of Clinical Hypnosis, 16*, 37–44.

Wakeman, J. R., & Kaplan, J. Z. (1978). An experimental study of hypnosis in painful burns. *American Journal of Clinical Hypnosis, 21*, 3–11.

PART III

CLINICAL APPLICATIONS

T he variety of problems for which it can be used makes hypnosis a unique therapeutic tool. Part 3 describes some of the major clinical applications of hypnosis, but the discussion is by no means comprehensive. For example, modification of habits is only touched upon. Excluded entirely is hypnosis for personal creativity or to enhance athletic performance. The many uses of hypnosis described in these chapters have a common denominator, their positive side effects. Hypnosis as a therapeutic modality is itself reinforcing as a means of developing self-mastery and facilitating relaxation.

In these chapters, the reader will discern not only the variety of ways in which hypnosis can be used as a clinical tool, but also the major controversies surrounding its use. The issue of the nature and definition of hypnosis recurs in most discussions of its applications. For example, when an anesthesiologist makes suggestions for comfort to a patient who is being wheeled into an operating room, the patient may become extremely relaxed and detached and require less than the usual amount of anesthesia. Can one conclude that the patient is in a trance state and that the anesthesiologist facilitated that state? Or when a physician tells a patient, with great conviction, that a placebo will ameliorate a presenting symptom, and the desired effect is achieved, can the result be attributed to something like an hypnotic interaction between doctor and patient? Similarly, when a volunteer subject in a weight reduction study is "hypnotized" through a formal induction, given direct suggestions for weight loss, and is less successful than nonhypnotized controls, should one conclude that hypnosis is not effective for weight reduction, that hypnosis was not achieved, or that some other variable not identified in the study was responsible for the results?

The problems in reducing the hypnotic phemonenon to terms that can be described and controlled arise partly because "clinical hypnosis" does not refer to a clearly defined state, but to the systematic use of certain techniques that bypass the conscious mind and focus attention on specific issues. Therapeutic results achieved under the rubric of covert techniques, autogenic training, or one of many other procedures, may well be similar to, or identical with, those achieved through hypnosis.

Another major issue that will surface frequently in these chapters is the extent to which experimental results are applicable to the clinical setting. Lieberman (1977) stated the problem as follows: "There seems to be a very large question of whether we have any right to generalize conclusions from laboratory experiments with a recorded standard induction on college students to all hypnotic inductions in all situations" (p. 64).

The greater freedom of the clinic, where induction variables need not be controlled, may well account for the absence of laboratory data to support reported clinical success. For now, it appears that the effectiveness of hypnosis cannot be proven. The scientific community's desire for hard evidence to support the choice of one therapeutic modality over another will continue to conflict with the views of clinicians who, based on their professional experience, advocate the use of hypnotic techniques tailored to the needs of each patient for an ever-increasing variety of physical and psychological disorders.

Each chapter in this section is meant as a starting point for the reader pursuing the specific applications of hypnosis in greater depth. Although the references to the literature in each field are not comprehensive, they provide a wealth of resources for further study. The wording of sample inductions and treatment suggestions demonstrates both the common principles and the individual approaches taken by different practitioners. Taken together, these chapters suggest both the limitations and the potentialities of modern clinical hypnosis.

REFERENCES

Lieberman, L. R. (1977). Hypnosis research and the limitations of the experimental method. *Annals of the New York Academy of Sciences, 296,* 60–68.

7

Medicine

The mind may produce diseases—and cure them.
—Paracelsus
Libri De Virtute Imaginativa

I n a 1976 issue of the *New England Journal of Medicine*, Norman
Cousins published an account of his now-celebrated battle with a
degenerative collagen disease. Fighting odds set by specialists at 500 to
1, Cousins recovered sufficiently to resume a vigorous life, despite (or,
Cousins argues, because of) his defiance of traditional medical thinking
by stopping all medication (primarily pain-killing and anti-
inflammatory drugs) and removing himself from the hospital. Whether
his recovery should be attributed to his self-prescribed treatment of
massive doses of vitamin C combined with laughter therapy, or to "a
mammoth venture in self-administered placebos" (p. 45), as some doctors have hypothesized, makes little difference to Cousins.

In *Anatomy of an Illness*, his book expanded from the original
journal article, Cousins (1979) explained what he considered a key to
his success:

> Since I didn't accept the verdict, I wasn't trapped in the cycle of
> fear, depression and pain that frequently accompanies a suppos-
> edly incurable illness. . . . I knew I had a good chance and relished
> the idea of bucking the odds. (p. 45)

His highest praise goes to his physician, who, Cousins believes,
encouraged his will to live and helped him mobilize his body's natural
defense mechanisms.

In his book, Cousins quoted Albert Schweitzer: "Each patient car-
ries his own doctor inside him. . . . We are at our best when we give

the doctor who resides within each patient a chance to go to work" (p. 69). Modern medical hypnosis is predicated on the belief reflected in Schweitzer's statement. Erickson saw hypnosis as a means of helping the patient do what was necessary to achieve health—in other words, allowing the doctor who resides within to go to work.

This chapter will provide an overview of the role hypnosis can play in all facets of medicine, from the management of routine medical procedures to improving the prognosis for patients with life-threatening diseases. The field is so vast that we can touch briefly on only a few important areas. The reader interested in pursuing the subject in greater depth is referred to the Further Reading section and to the many references cited in this chapter.

MIND AND BODY

Increasing numbers of physicians now are methodically using hypnotic techniques that many successful healers over the ages used intuitively with excellent results. Thomas (1979) recounted a story told by an associate of William Osler (known as the father of modern medicine) about that renowned doctor's method for removing warts. He would "paint gentian violet over a wart and then assure the patient firmly that it would be gone in a week, and he never saw it fail" (p. 77). Since then several studies have demonstrated the effectiveness of the placebo in eliminating warts (see Barber, 1970, pp. 170–171, for a summary).

The history of medicine is replete with routine "cures" that from today's vantage point seem more miraculous than the removal of warts through the application of tinted water. For patients who were subjected to such once-popular medical treatments as bloodletting or purging with emetics, the miracle from a physiological standpoint is that some of the seriously ill patients survived at all. The success of such treatments must at least partly be ascribed to the patient's belief in their efficacy. Their confidence in the fact that the physician was administering the right treatment enabled them first to overcome the cure and then to master the disease.

Shapiro (1959) called the placebo the unwritten therapeutic agent in almost every prescription. Kroger (1977) termed it "the one constant in medicine" (p. 136). Cousins' (1979) research and personal experience led him to believe that "the doctor himself is the most powerful placebo of all" (p. 57).

One of the most dramatic and often-quoted examples of the placebo effect was reported by Klopfer (1957). A patient with advanced lymphosarcoma begged his doctor to treat him with the drug

Krebiozen, which was being acclaimed in the media as a cure for cancer, and which was later demonstrated to be ineffective. Once on the drug, the patient made a dramatic recovery, his huge tumor masses shrinking to the point where he could resume normal activities. However, when the American Medical Association and the U.S. Food and Drug Administration reported negative results in testing Krebiozen, the patient started failing.

As an emergency measure, the doctor told his patient that he had developed a new, refined, and doubly strong form of the drug. The injections that he administered were only distilled water, yet the patient once again recovered and remained symptom-free for more than 2 months. Then further negative news about the drug appeared in the press: "Nationwide tests show Krebiozen to be a worthless drug in the treatment of cancer." Within a few days of the appearance of those headlines, the patient was dead.

While the placebo is gaining a new respectability in medicine, research in many other fields is continuing to invalidate the Cartesian separation of mind and body upon which much of modern medicine is based. Biofeedback studies, for example (Schwartz and Beatty, 1977), have demonstrated the human ability to alter physiological processes at will. The stress response, which releases corticosteroids that inhibit immune system function, has long been associated with the onset and prognosis of disease (see Blumberg, West, and Ellis, 1954; Rahe and Arthur, 1978; Selye, 1956). The emerging field of psychoneuroimmunology (Ader, 1981), which is exploring the relationship between the immune system and the mind, demonstrates the medical establishment's increasing recognition of the role played by psychological factors in the onset and progress of disease.

Scientific research is increasing our understanding of the process by which the mind mediates physiological processes. According to Hall (1983), hypnosis may make a significant contribution to our understanding of the mind-body relationship by providing "a model for studying how psychological and cognitive factors contribute to recovery from medical disorders" (p. 101). The scientific community has long recognized the role of psychological factors in the cause of certain diseases. We are now beginning to explore the ways in which the mind can heal the body.

USES OF MEDICAL HYPNOSIS

Historically, medical hypnosis has been primarily identified with symptom removal and anesthesia for surgery. Mesmer's mass cures and

Braid's success during the 1840s in using hypnoanesthesia for major surgical procedures are good examples. Today, hypnosis plays a wider role in medicine and is used more often for routine procedures than for dramatic cures.

General Categories

The following categories provide an overview of the many ways hypnosis can contribute to medical practice:

1. To contribute to overall patient management. Hypnosis is a means of motivating and encouraging the patient, reducing fear and anxiety, exploring the etiology of an illness, and even communicating with unconscious patients.

2. To control habits or behaviors that interfere with treatment. For example, hypnosis can be used to help patients with emphysema stop smoking or to help hypertensive patients manage stress and reduce their high blood pressure.

3. To contribute to a multimodal approach to treating a variety of problems, as in Crasilneck and Hall's (1975) work with burn patients. They reported the effective use of hypnosis to manage the pain of the burn as well as that associated with skin grafting and dressing changes, and to increase the patient's food intake, which is essential to the regeneration of tissue.

   The Hypnosis and Psychosomatic Medicine Clinic described by Sheehan and Surman (1978) demonstrates one way in which hypnosis can be effectively integrated into an ongoing medical program. The clinic was established in response to an increased need for an outpatient counterpart to the psychiatric consultation and psychosomatic service at Massachusetts General Hospital. Staffed by four psychiatrists and two psychologists, the clinic provides short-term, multimodal treatment on an outpatient basis. Hypnosis is employed extensively in combination with behavior therapy, biofeedback training, and short-term psychotherapy for diagnosis and treatment of many illnesses and for habit control. Patients are given instruction in self-hypnosis and are provided with tapes for home use.

4. To eliminate or ameliorate symptoms. The removal of warts through hypnotic suggestion is a good example of the use of hypnosis in direct treatment.

5. To assist patients in recovering from life-threatening diseases, such as cancer. This is the newest frontier in the use of medical hypnosis, and although researchers are cautious in their claims, there is considerable evidence that hypnosis can enhance immune system functioning (Hall, 1983).

6. To control pain. Hypnosis is also becoming an important therapeutic component in pain clinics around the nation. Wain (1980a) reported that 50% of the pain patients referred to the Walter Reed Army Center received some form of hypnotic intervention and that hypnosis had become an integral part of the treatment program.

Symptom removal.   As hypnosis has gained wider acceptance among the medical community, its original use—that of symptom removal—has been called into question. Some practitioners are concerned that the removal of a symptom without treatment of its underlying cause will lead to the formation of a substitute symptom or recurrence of the original symptom.

Most practitioners today have found that those fears are not born out by clinical experience. Kroger (1977) and Cheek and LeCron (1968) pointed out that most medical treatment is directed toward the removal of symptoms, whether it be aspirin for a headache or prochlorperazine (Compazine) for nausea. Hartland (1971) and Cheek and LeCron (1968) stated that patients using hypnosis would abandon their symptoms only when they were psychologically prepared to do without them. As discussed in the first chapter of this book, hypnotic suggestions can be effective only when they are acceptable to the patient. There is no such thing as a forced removal of a symptom through hypnosis.

The term "symptom removal" is itself somewhat misleading, because it implies that a symptom is simply banished outright. In practice symptoms can be addressed in a number of ways through hypnosis. Spiegel (1967) preferred the term "symptom alteration," in which the practitioner "veers the patient's attention away from his symptoms and concomitantly reminds him that more resourceful and effective means are available for his use in coping with problems of adaptation" (p. 10).

When a patient has some emotional investment in a symptom, one symptom can be substituted for another that is less troublesome. Suggestions also can be made that a symptom will diminish to a manageable level but not disappear entirely. Most practitioners use ego-strengthening procedures to pave the way for the reduction or removal of symptoms. Finally, any risk associated with symptom removal can be further reduced through the use of permissive language and the absence of a specific time frame, so that the patient, and not the practitioner, determines the pace at which a symptom will recede.

Pediatrics. There is evidence that children as a group are more responsive to hypnosis than are adults (Morgan and Hilgard, 1973, 1979), and that infants and young children frequently experience hypnosis as a natural part of their lives (Gardner, 1977a). According to Olness and Gardner (1978), however, hypnosis is generally underused in pediatric practice.

The feasibility of incorporating an active hypnosis program into the work of hematology care teams treating pediatric cancer patients has been demonstrated by the Childhood Adaptation Project in San Diego (Hartman, 1981). In the mid-1970s, this project offered physicians, nurses, and social workers from three San Diego hospitals a series of seminars on the use of hypnotic techniques with pediatric cancer patients. In the 135 sessions using these techniques, the primary care team found that 90% of the patients were easily hypnotized and that the majority experienced positive benefits.

In general, the uses of medical hypnosis discussed in this chapter apply to children as well as to adults. There are, however, special considerations that distinguish pediatric hypnosis as a subspecialty. For example, a child is growing and a practitioner must frequently adapt hypnotic techniques to new developmental stages. The family unit also plays a larger role in pediatric hypnosis. In some cases parent involvement in the hypnotic process is advisable, while in others it is best to minimize the parent's role. These and other issues are thoroughly covered by Gardner and Olness (1981) in their comprehensive text on hypnosis with children. Readers interested in pediatric hypnosis are referred to this text and to Gardner's (1980) bibliography of 114 references on hypnosis with children, spanning the years from 1959 to 1979.

PATIENT MANAGEMENT

Because the thoughts, body, and emotions are interdependent, factors that influence one influence the others, as well. The role of the mind and emotions in functional or psychophysiological (psychosomatic) illness is widely recognized, but in the case of organic illness, their importance is often underestimated.

There are physical and psychological components to all illness, regardless of etiology. Emotional states that continue over extended periods can produce physiological changes (refer to Chapter 16 for a further discussion of the effects of stress on the body). The fear, anxiety, resentment, or depression that often accompany illness may prolong or exacerbate it and interfere with a patient's willingness or ability to participate in treatment. Addressing these issues through hypnosis can greatly improve the overall medical management of a patient, from the initial diagnosis through all forms of treatment, including treatment of unconscious and critically ill patients.

Diagnosis

The authors of this book agree with Hartland (1971) that every case should be examined in the context of the patient as a whole before any medical or therapeutic intervention is undertaken. Hippocrates stated this principle clearly: "It is more important to know what kind of a person has a disease than to know what kind of disease a person has." Personality variables can account for noncompliance with treatment. A patient who dislikes or disagrees with certain treatment procedures may not carry them out properly, thus diminishing their effectiveness. Similarly, someone who is convinced that a given prescription will not work may unconsciously negate its effects just to prove the point.

One advantage of modern clinical hypnosis is that it requires the practitioner to approach the patient as a whole person rather than as a collection of parts, one or more of which may be diseased. For the physician using hypnosis, a medical history goes beyond a list of past illnesses, allergies, and hospitalizations. When time and circumstances permit, a more comprehensive picture is developed to include an understanding of a patient's personality and present state of mind, life history, and the positive aspects as well as the stresses and strains of the patient's present environment. For example, a patient for whom the secondary gains from an illness (such as increased attention and sympathy) outweigh the discomforts may not want to be cured. This conflict needs resolution before treatment can be effective.

Motivation and Adjustment

There are both specific and nonspecific elements involved in all treatment situations, as Kroger (1977) pointed out. Certain drugs or medical procedures are intended to produce specific effects, such as reducing inflammation or lowering blood pressure. Other elements, such as emotional and psychological responses, are common to most treatment situations. Addressing the nonspecific factors can have an effect on the specific ones as well.

The personal communication and support intrinsic to clinical hypnosis make it a valuable tool for supporting and motivating a patient. This interaction can take the form of either a formal induction or an interaction similar to hypnosis between physician and patient. A physician's reassurance and encouragement alone can alleviate a patient's symptoms and improve the prognosis. In illnesses such as asthma, where fear of an attack is a pronounced if sometimes concealed factor, "the physician's most powerful weapon is explanation" (Brown, 1965). In other cases, simple relaxation techniques can help a patient to reduce the experience of pain and to facilitate his or her own recovery.

Hypnosis also has the advantage of being able to effect a change in attitude at the unconscious level—something no amount of verbal persuasion can accomplish. Hartland (1971) developed an ego-strengthening technique that consists of suggestions designed to increase patients' confidence in themselves and their ability to cope with problems. The importance of this approach to accompany hypnosis as an adjunct to treatment or for symptom removal is supported by other authors, including Cheek and LeCron (1968), Conn (1961), Kroger (1971), and Spiegel (1967).

In working with patients referred by physicians, an ego-strengthening routine may be routinely used to increase the patients' faith in their ability to recover, to help them to adjust to their situations, and to motivate them to carry out the procedures necessary for their recovery. The following example of ego-strengthening suggestions uses more permissive, indirect language than that used by Hartland:

Every day . . . you are looking forward to becoming physically stronger and fitter. . . . You may also be looking forward to becoming more alert . . . more wide awake . . . more energetic . . . more encouraged. Every day your determination can become stronger and steadier. . . . You are looking forward to becoming more deeply interested in whatever you are doing . . . so deeply interested in whatever is going on . . . that your mind can become much less preoccupied with yourself . . . and you can become and may find yourself becoming much less conscious of yourself . . . and your own feelings. . . . Every day . . . your mind can become much calmer and clearer . . . more composed . . . more placid . . . more tranquil. You are, perhaps, becoming progressively more and more settled . . . more relaxed. . . . You are looking forward to being able to think progressively more and more clearly . . . and you are looking forward to being able to concentrate more easily. . . . Your memory can continue to improve . . . and you can see things in their true perspective with more and more ease . . . without magnifying them . . . without allowing them to get out of proportion. . . . Every day . . . you are looking forward to continuing to become much calmer . . . much more settled . . . much more in control. . . . And every day . . . you can and perhaps are feeling a greater feeling of personal well-being . . . a greater feeling of personal safety and security . . . than you may have felt for some time. . . . Every day . . . you can continue to suggest to yourself that you are becoming and you are remaining . . . more and more completely relaxed . . . both mentally and physically. . . . And as you continue to become . . . and as you remain . . . more relaxed . . . you can continue to develop much more confidence in yourself. . . . Much more confidence in your ability to do . . . not only what you have to do each day . . . but also . . . much more confidence in your ability to do whatever you ought to be able to do. . . . Because of your ability to relax and provide yourself with more and more positive suggestions . . . every day . . . you can feel more and more independent . . . more and more able to "stick up for yourself" . . . to continue to stand . . . and to progressively "stand upon your own feet" . . . to continue . . . and to more and more progressively . . . "hold your own" . . . no matter how difficult or trying things may be. . . . And because all these things can happen . . . and perhaps are already continuing to happen . . . perhaps exactly as I suggest them to you and as you suggest them to yourself . . . you are looking forward to feeling much happier. . . . Progressively more optimistic . . . progressively more and more relaxed and comfortable.

Using hypnosis to increase a patient's confidence and motivation helps to reduce dependence on the physician as an external authority. As the patient regains a sense of control, recovery becomes a cooperative venture in which the practitioner helps the patient to mobilize his or her own emotional, mental, and physical resources.

Uncovering Causes of Resistance

Physicians sometimes encounter patients whose conditions or illnesses do not respond to medical treatment. Cheek and LeCron (1968) identified seven causative factors, one or more of which often are involved in illnesses with a strong psychosomatic component. When time allows, these seven keys can be explored to determine the genesis of an illness and whether or not a symptom is serving an unconscious purpose that is resistant to treatment:

1. Conflict: A situation where we want to have to do something that is prevented by our moral code or the taboos of society can produce either conscious or unconscious conflict. A common example is guilt feelings about sexual desires.

2. Motivation: An illness or a symptom can serve a hidden purpose, such as attraction of attention, escape from an unpleasant situation, or defense against unacceptable feelings. Hysterical blindness, for example, could be motivated by the desire to escape from seeing something painful. Motivation to retain a symptom can obviously interfere with a patient's adherence to a treatment regime.

3. Identification: Childhood identification with parents or other influential people can be carried over into adulthood. Such identification may contribute to hereditary tendencies: The man who develops heart problems at exactly the same age that his father and grandfather did is one example.

4. Masochism: Self-punishment due to strong guilt feelings can be a factor in illness and in damaging behaviors leading to illness. Accident-prone people often are unconsciously punishing themselves.

5. Imprints: An idea can become fixed in the unconscious and carried out as if it were a posthypnotic suggestion or a conditioned reflex. The imprinting occurs during times of extreme emotion, when people naturally slip into an ASC. Cheek and LeCron (1968) cited the case of a woman with a chronic cough, who under hypnosis recalled that at the age of 4, when she was critically ill with whooping cough, a physician told her parents, "She'll never get over this." Although the woman did fully recover, the idea, and the cough, stayed with her.

6. Organ language: Actual physical difficulties can result from the ideas expressed in such phrases as, "That makes me sick," and "I can't swallow that." The gastrointestinal tract in particular seems susceptible to psychosomatic problems, such as globus hystericus, nausea, and ulcers.

7. Past experiences: Traumatic experiences in one's past may be responsible for the development of phobias or for other effects, such as stuttering. These experiences may also be associated with one of the other six keys.

Ideomotor questioning techniques, described in detail by Cheek and LeCron (1968), provide a reliable and relatively easy method of uncovering emotional and psychological factors in an illness that may exist at the unconscious level. Using this technique, the practitioner poses questions that require a yes or no response from the patient. Because the unconscious interprets things literally, questions must be worded carefully. Responses are given by the unconscious through a prearranged code, such as the movement of a pendulum or the lifting of a finger.

With the finger method, the patient will designate different fingers on one hand to mean "yes," "no," "I don't know," or "I don't want to answer," in response to the questions posed by the practitioner. The last response option is consistent with a permissive approach to hypnosis. It is not necessary for the practitioner to know the cause of the illness, as long as the patient is able to identify the source of the problem at the unconscious level.

Ideomotor responses can be obtained from a patient in either the waking or trance state. Cheek and LeCron (1968) stressed the importance of explaining to the patients that their responses do not represent a voluntary effort. Neither are they magic. Just as the unconscious controls the movement of muscles for such functions as breathing and walking, so it can signal a response to questions without the patient's conscious effort. A true ideomotor response will usually be slow, and the finger may tremble slightly. In some cases, the finger may jerk upwards. By contrast, a voluntary movement of the fingers will be more rapid and smooth.

The following case study provides an example of the use of ideomotor questioning in a case of pain with an hysterical component.

LT was a 17-year-old male who had been in the Navy approximately 3 days when he was brought into a physician's office clutching his left hand in extreme pain. He would withdraw the hand with the slightest touch, making examination difficult. Examination and x-rays were negative for any physical defects. History revealed that 3 months earlier, LT had been in a car accident during which his hand had been forced into a position of extreme dorsiflexion. He had claimed to have pain since that period.

Ideomotor testing revealed that (a) the pain was legitimate, (b) LT did not believe that the hand was broken, (c) he did not want to get rid of the pain, (d) he was a very nervous person who was having family problems at home, (e) he would not answer as to whether his physical problem was related to his family problems. After being told that he did not need the pain to get his secondary gain, LT consented to relaxation therapy, during which he confirmed his previous answers through ideomotor response. He was given suggestions for pain transference and relaxation and told that he could keep as much of the pain as he needed for his body's own protection.

Once out of the altered state of consciousness, LT reported that 95% of the pain was gone, and he was able to submit to an examination without flinching. His strength and range of motion had increased three-fold. The next day there was hardly any pain with almost full return of strength and range of motion, and by the third day there was no difference between the two hands.

Cheek and LeCron (1968) claimed a 95% success rate using the finger or pendulum method of ideomotor questioning. It is also possible for people to question their own unconscious using this technique.

Insight into Needs of Critically Ill Patients

Clinical observations of practitioners employing hypnosis have provided crucial insight into the needs of the critically ill. Many physicians familiar with hypnosis have noted that patients will automatically slip into an ASC when faced with a medical situation they find frightening. At such times, hypnotic techniques are easily employed without an induction. Cheek (1969) believed critically ill patients to be in an altered state in which the unconscious is easily accessible. Even though they may be outwardly apathetic or even unconscious, such patients will be very responsive to helpful suggestions, equally vulnerable to harmful ones, or depressed by what may appear to be ominous silence. Careless conversation around the critically ill can have a devastating effect, for they not only hear what is being said, but also interpret the remarks literally.

Crasilneck and Hall (1975) noted additional evidence that psychological processes may continue in patients who are unconscious or show no signs of ordinary social responsiveness. Their findings are consistent with additional cases summarized by Cheek (1964) and Cheek and LeCron (1968), which indicate that anesthetized patients hear, and under the hypnosis can recall, comments by operating room staff.

Following is a summary of Cheek's (1969) recommendations for interacting with critically ill patients:

1. Consider the critically ill to be already in hypnosis.

2. Avoid negative suggestions and convey hope and optimism to the extent possible without being insincere.

3. Since the physician's tone of voice and actions will affect the patient's confidence, approach the patient calmly and confidently.

4. Keep the patient informed about the nature and purpose of treatment procedures to help put the patient in the role of assistant rather than victim.

5. Outline simple sequential goals for the future, thus providing a tacit suggestion that there will be a future.

6. If possible, give medication for pain as a way of showing you are interested and taking positive action. Tell the patient what you are giving and for what purpose.

7. If possible, talk with the patient about family, work, or hobbies to distract the mind from pain and fear.

Johnson and Korn (1980) reported a case in which hypnosis was used to facilitate the rehabilitation of a comatose patient. In their positive approach to treatment using hypnosis and imagery, Johnson and Korn applied many of Cheek's recommendations:

A 16-year-old female had sustained a hemolytic contusion of the right frontoparietal lobe, extensive lacerations of the liver, and a fracture of the left clavicle. Following surgery, there were many indications (including unstable vital signs, intractable tachycardia, and continued loss of consciousness) that her undifferentiated anxiety response to the situation was interfering with her recovery.

Hypnotic techniques were first used with the unconscious patient to reduce anxiety and foster relaxation. They consisted of acknowledgment of her predicament and assurances that the care being provided to her was nurturing rather than an attempt to remove control further from her.

Once the patient learned to relax and began to be more responsive to her environment, traditional hypnotic induction and deepening techniques were used as part of a holistic approach to rehabilitation following damage to the central nervous system. Thirteen weeks following the injury, the patient had achieved age-appropriate motor skills and verbal skills, was able to perform personal care activities, and had returned to her previous social and emotional status.

Relationship with Terminally Ill Patients

The terminally ill suffer from many kinds of pain. They suffer physical pain caused by the disease, by lab procedures, and by the side effects of treatment. Equally distressing is the emotional and psychological pain of facing the issues of death and dying. Patients can begin to feel isolated from family and friends and abandoned by health professionals who withdraw emotionally and assume an air of forced cheerfulness.

There is a growing body of literature related to the use of hypnosis in support of terminally ill patients. The effectiveness of hypnosis in managing pain and countering the side effects of radical treatment will be addressed extensively in Chapter 9. Several authors (Crasilneck and Hall, 1975; Dempster, Balson, and Whalen, 1976; Gardner and Olness, 1981) focused on the value of hypnosis as a tool for reducing anxiety and providing much-needed emotional support for the patient who is dying.

Dempster et al. (1976) stressed the importance of the therapeutic relationship between the hypnotherapist and the patient as a way of overcoming a dying patient's increasing sense of isolation. These authors recommended the following:

> It is useful for the therapist and his patient to conclude a contract which recognizes that the issue of when the patient will die is beyond them. The manner of the patient's living is not. The hypnotherapist can help ensure that, while the disease may order the time and manner of the patient's death, it need not control his living. (p. 4)

Case reports by Gardner and Olness (1981) demonstrated the extent to which hetero-hypnosis and self-hypnosis may be used to reduce the fear and anxiety of dying children as well as increase the family's ability to understand the child. Gardner (1977b) discussed the way in which hypnosis facilitates the process through which dying children exercise their rights as individuals.

All of these authors acknowledged the cost to the practitioner who makes the kind of commitment to a dying patient that is fostered by hypnotic interaction. As stated by Gardner and Olness (1981), "The practitioner must be able to deal with his or her own reactions to loss" (p. 269). However, the difference between a lonely and fearful patient who focuses on dying and a relaxed and hopeful patient who concentrates on living is so great that some practitioners are willing to make the investment.

TREATMENT OF SPECIFIC CONDITIONS

The use of hypnosis in most if not all medical specialties has been documented in the literature. A detailed study of the role of hypnosis in the treatment of medical disorders could fill volumes. The purpose here is to provide the reader with a general orientation and overview, including a few illustrative examples. Additional information on the various medical specialties may be found through the Further Reading section at the end of this chapter. For the use of hypnosis in surgery and childbirth, see Chapters 8 and 10.

Several general areas in which hypnosis can be most useful for the physician have been identified by Olness and Gardner (1978). Although these authors referred specifically to pediatrics, their categories apply equally to adults.

Habit Disorders

Hypnosis can be used alone or in combination with other approaches to overcome a variety of habit disorders. While some problems, such as thumb-sucking, can be resolved rather quickly, others, such as overeating, sometimes require extended treatment or a multidimensional approach. Smoking and enuresis are two examples of habit disorders that can be managed through hypnosis.

Smoking. Hypnosis can play a useful role in the treatment of a multifaceted problem such as smoking, which can not only lead to illness but also interfere with medical treatment. Hypnosis has been used to stop the smoking habit in a variety of ways and with varying success, as may be seen in Johnston and Donoghue's (1971) review of the literature on hypnosis and smoking. The *International Journal of Clinical and Experimental Hypnosis,* 1970, *18,* samples the different approaches, from Kline's (1970) extended group hypnotherapy sessions to Spiegel's (1970) single-treatment method.

Hall and Crasilneck (1970) studied 75 consecutively treated adult male cigarette smokers who had smoked an averge of two packs per day for 27 years. Over 90% of the subjects had tried to stop smoking before; most were referred for treatment because of a serious medical problem such as emphysema or asthma. As a group, these patients were strongly motivated to stop smoking.

After an initial screening interview, patients were seen for three hypnotic sessions on consecutive days and for one session a month later. Telephone contact was maintained between the third and fourth sessions. Hypnotic suggestions emphasized that the patient would cease to crave a habit that had affected his life negatively, and that he would be relaxed and pleased with himself for giving up the habit.

Of the total group, 64% stopped smoking without substituting another oral habit, 18% switched to cigars, pipes, or chewing gum, and 18% continued smoking at the pretreatment rate.

Watkins (1976) presented an individualized five-session approach designed specifically for college students. The term hypnosis was avoided, and "concentration relaxation technique" was used in its place. The key to Watkins' approach was a detailed smoking history, including information on the past use of cigarettes, other attempts at stopping, reasons for wanting to stop, feelings about smoking, and associations with it. Using this history, Watkins customized suggestions for each subject to reinforce reasons for wanting to stop, to attack rationalizations, and to undermine motivations for continuing to smoke. Supportive therapy, telephone contact, and self-hypnosis (referred to as "self-induction of the relaxation state") were also included in the five-session approach. Of the 36 students who completed the program, 67% were not smoking cigarettes at the end of 6 months.

A case treated by Wood demonstrates a similar approach:

MF was a 72-year-old male who was diagnosed in 1965 as having emphysema. Since that time he had been treated with a combination of the medications typically prescribed for chronic obstructive pulmonary disease.

MF began smoking in early adolescence and by 1982, he had been smoking three packs a day for 20 years. He was aware that he was further compromising his health by continuing to smoke and reported that he had tried to stop smoking twice since his emphysema was diagnosed. Both times, he had started to smoke again because he felt that cigarettes "calmed his nerves."

At the time of treatment, MF was taking 100 mg of amitriptyline hydrochloride (Elavil) at bedtime for depression. During the first session he acknowledged a relationship between his smoking habit, his depression, and his decreased level of activity. With the help of the therapist, he developed a plan to increase his activity level gradually as he reduced his smoking habit.

Treatment extended over 12 sessions and consisted of hetero-hypnosis as well as training in progressive relaxation and self-hypnosis. Through posthypnotic suggestions and self-hypnosis, MF learned to associate relaxation with a variety of daily activities, such as watching television, taking a shower, or drinking a beverage. In this way, he was able to "calm his nerves" without reaching for a cigarette. He also learned to associate relaxation with a reduced urge to smoke.

The therapist also advised MF to use cigarette filters manufactured by Water-Pik as an adjunct to hypnotherapy. Each filter in the set removes an *increasing percentage of tar and nicotine, with the fourth and last filter removing 90%.*

By the fifth treatment session, MF had reduced his cigarette consumption to 15–20 per day. By session 8, he was using the fourth Water-Pik filter and smoking 10–12 cigarettes daily. By session 9, he was smoking the 10–12 cigarettes only half way and then putting them out. By the 12th and final session, he was smoking 2 or 3 cigarettes a day and extinguishing them early. At a 2-month follow-up, his consumption had increased slightly but had stabilized at 5 or 6 cigarettes, which he continued to extinguish after smoking only half of each.

Pederson, Scrimgeour, and Lecoe (1979) tried to identify the variables of hypnosis related to success in a smoking withdrawal program. Habitual smokers were assigned to four treatment groups: (a) live hypnosis and counseling, (b) videotaped hypnosis and counseling, (c) relaxation hypnosis (to control for the placebo effect of hypnosis) and counseling, and (d) counseling alone. Hypnosis occurred at the third of six weekly sessions.

Six months after treatment, the live hypnosis and counseling group reported a 53% abstinence rate, compared to 13%–18% for the other groups. This study suggests that the presence of the hypnotherapist is an important variable in treatment using hypnosis.

It is difficult to draw any conclusions at this point about how hypnosis can be used most effectively to eliminate the smoking habit. It is possible to assert, however, that because suggestion is more powerful under hypnosis than at ordinary waking levels of consciousness, hypnosis can help patients to replace harmful habits with new and more positive patterns.

Enuresis. Enuresis is one of the most common and often one of the more vexing problems seen by the pediatrician. Because childhood enuresis can have a negative effect on the family environment, the physician is under pressure to find a solution to the problem. Burke and Stickler (1980) cautioned against overtreatment, citing the high rate of spontaneous remission and the prevalence of the problem in all cultures, as well as studies indicating that enuresis represents an inadequate neuromuscular maturation of the bladder. They recommended that physicians either "reassure parents with a thorough and adequate explanation of the physiology as we understand it or utilize a conditioning treatment program" (p. 119).

For the practitioner using hypnosis, reassurance can take the form of positive suggestions for both parents and child: The child has a weak bladder that will become stronger as the child matures, or the child will soon stop wetting the bed without urging. When direct treatment seems warranted, hypnosis is a viable treatment alternative. Gardner and Olness (1981) reported that approximately 75% of the children in studies by Olness (1975), Kohen, Olness, Colwell, and Heimel (1980), and Stanton (1979) were completely cured or achieved significant improvement within two or three sessions.

Gardner and Olness (1981) described a comprehensive approach to the evelation and management of enuresis. The following discussion is summarized from their text, to which the reader is referred for further information.

There are many factors to consider before hypnotic treatment for enuresis. A physical examination should be conducted to rule out organic causes. The problem should also be assessed in the context of the family unit: For a child under 5 years of age, the problem may be in the parents' unrealistic expectations for a dry bed before the child is developmentally ready. The practitioner also should interview the family to identify emotional problems or stressful events, such as the death of a family member or moving to a new neighborhood, that may have preceded the bed-wetting. Gardner and Olness (1981) developed a model questionnaire for assessing enuresis that takes into consideration these and other factors.

The approach taken by these authors emphasizes the child's involvement in treatment and responsibility for managing the problem. The practitioner and child come to an agreement on the best time for the child to practice self-hypnosis, and the parents are asked not to remind the child or to interfere in any way. The practitioner also explains to the child that the bladder is a muscle that can be controlled like any other muscle.

Hypnosis is induced using an individualized induction based on the child's likes and dislikes. Ideomotor questioning is used to determine whether the child would like to have a dry bed and is ready to work on the problem. A negative response may indicate that the child is receiving secondary gains from the bed-wetting or is simply not ready to work on the problem. In such cases, it is best to postpone treatment.

Children who are motivated to have dry beds are told in hypnosis to give instructions to their bladders to send a message to the brain when it is full of urine. Ego-strengthening suggestions and suggestions for enjoying the dry bed are also given. The child is told to practice self-hypnosis daily and to give instructions to his or her bladder in both the hypnotic and waking state. Younger children are asked to keep calendars and graphs of their successes.

Psychophysiological (Psychosomatic) Problems

Hypnosis has been used effectively as an adjunct to the treatment of numerous problems with autonomic nervous system components. The following discussion summarizes the uses of hypnotherapy with several such conditions:

Asthma. There have been many controlled studies and successful case reports on the use of hypnosis in the treatment of asthma, which is the most common of the psychophysiological respiratory disorders. Through hypnosis, a patient can be helped to break the vicious cycle in which anxiety and emotional upsets can trigger an acute asthma attack, which in turn produces anxiety and fear of other attacks.

Arnoff, Arnoff, and Peck (1975) reported a study on the use of hypnotherapy to abort acute asthmatic attacks in 17 children ranging in age from 6 to 17. The average improvement in pulmonary function during the posthypnotic period was 50% above the baseline measurement. The authors concluded that "in some, if not most, severe asthmatic attacks in children, hypnotherapy may be an important tool in ameliorating symptoms, improving ventilatory capacity and promoting relaxation" (p. 361).

In two controlled studies, Maher-Loughnan (1970) compared a treatment approach using hypnosis and self-hypnosis with two other approaches: a bronchodilator, and progressive relaxation followed by special breathing exercises. In both cases, hypnosis supported by self-hypnosis was significantly more effective in reducing the symptoms of asthma than were control procedures. The author also found that patients whose asthma was triggered by allergic responses or infections progressed as well using hypnosis as those whose asthma flared when they were emotionally upset. It is important to note that there appeared to be no correlation between trance depth and clinical response.

A recent study (Hobby-Burns, Clinton, Danziger, and Wood, 1983) found that a program of education and relaxation training significantly reduced the frequency of asthma symptoms in a group of asthmatic children. Children in a control group did not experience the same reduction in symptoms.

Although hypnosis is usually not the treatment of choice in status asthmaticus, emergency measures may occasionally be called for: Crasilneck and Hall (1975) reported a case of a young woman who achieved relief from an acute 3-day attack within 10 minutes using hypnosis. Sinclair-Grieben (1960) reported a similar response to hypnosis in a 60-year-old man in status asthmaticus.

Migraine. Migraine headaches are believed to be triggered by an initial vasoconstriction of cranial arteries followed by dilation and distention that cause the pain. In a study of three migraine patients, Daniels (1976) found that a taped induction with suggestions for relaxation, warming the hands, and cooling the forehead, resulted in considerable relief and diminution of the headache.

Stambaugh and House (1977) presented a case study that assessed the relative effects of drugs, biofeedback, relaxation, autogenic training, and hypnosis in migraine treatment. Only self-hypnosis, through which the patient produced posthypnotic anesthesia of the left hand (glove anesthesia) with transfer to the temple, was successful in maintaining significant symptom remission and a decrease in analgesic consumption over 1-month and 8-month follow-up periods.

Yarnell (1980) reported complete remission of migraines in 78% of 36 women who participated in a treatment program that used hypnosis for ego-strengthening, handwarming, and assertiveness training. The combination of these three components was more successful than any of the components alone.

Raynaud's syndrome. Suggestions for warmth that result in increased blood flow to the fingers have also proved helpful with this cardiovascular disorder characterized by chronic poor circulation. Jacobsen, Hackett, Surman, and Silverberg (1973) treated a patient with Raynaud's disease by increasing the temperature in his hands using a combination of hypnosis and biofeedback. Crasilneck and Hall (1975) reported a success rate of about 60% in the treatment of this disorder by improving blood flow to the fingers through hypnosis.

High blood pressure. Nearly all hypertensive patients (90%-95%) suffer from essential hypertension, or hypertension of unknown cause. Although it appears to be related to the increased sympathetic nervous system activity of the stress response, the relationship between stress and hypertension has been assumed rather than proved.

Research by Deabler, Fidel, Dillenkoffer, and Elder (1973) used muscular relaxation and hypnosis to lower systolic pressure 14%-17% and diastolic pressure 17%-19% in both medicated and nonmedicated hypertensive patients. All patients were trained to continue the process through self-hypnosis.

Use of the relaxation response (Benson, 1975) has also been successful in significantly lowering blood pressure in hypertensive patients (Benson, Rosner, Marzetta, and Klemchuk, 1974a,b) and reducing end-organ responsivity to sympathetic nervous system stimulation (Hoffman et al., 1982). The components necessary to elicit the relaxation response are a quiet environment, a relaxed position, a passive attitude, and a repeated mental device. The benefits of the relaxation response are maintained only with continued daily practice. Thus, it is not a cure for hypertension, but a way of managing the disease, either as a sole therapy for mild forms of the disease or as an adjunct to pharmacological treatment for more severe forms.

Benson, Arns, and Hoffman (1981) noted the similarities between hypnosis and the relaxation response, both in their induction procedures and in their physiological correlates. Both hypnosis and the relaxation response are characterized by decreased heart rate, respiratory rate, and oxygen consumption, as well as increased frequency and intensity of alpha waves.

These findings provide a strong argument for teaching self-hypnosis, the relaxation response, or similar techniques to hypertensive patients who wish to use nonpharmacologic means of reducing blood pressure, either alone or as an adjunct to other treatment.

Hiccoughs.   Wood and Allen (1979) reported employing a combined behavioral and pharmacologic approach in the successful management of a patient with intractable hiccoughs. The hiccoughs of the 18-year-old male patient had no organic etiology and treatment with chlorpromazine (Thorazine) had been unsuccessful.

Through hetero-hypnosis sessions and self-hypnosis, the patient was able to achieve hiccough-free periods but was unable to attain complete symptom control. Because clinical data suggested a possible phobic-like response to stress, amitriptyline was introduced at the ninth treatment session. The patient subsequently reported that he was hiccough-free at night and was able to use self-hypnosis to control episodes following meals and upon waking in the morning.

This case demonstrates the effectiveness of hypnosis as an adjunct to pharmacologic treatment and as a means of giving a patient control over symptoms.

Chronic Conditions

In addition to hypertension, hypnosis has been used to provide symptomatic relief of other chronic conditions such as musculoskeletal disorders and hemophilia.

Musculoskeletal disorders.   Lehew (1970) reported hypnosis to be a valuable adjunct to treatment for the majority of patients with musculoskeletal disorders, such as rheumatoid arthritis, myositis, osteoarthritis, as well as fractures, neuritis, neuralgia, and bursitis. In a study involving 74 patients, Lehew used hypnosis to improve patients' muscular relaxation, analgesia, motivation to follow through with exercises, reduction in the use of medications, and maintenance of limbs in a desired position for healing. Kroger (1970) also found hypnosis to be a valuable adjunct in the rehabilitation of patients with neuromuscular disorders.

Cioppa and Thal (1975) used hypnotherapy with a 10-year-old girl who had been diagnosed as having juvenile rheumatoid arthritis and who was not responding to treatment. During the first session, the girl was extremely depressed and confined to a wheelchair. By the second session, a month later, her mobility was still extremely limited. Ideomotor questioning had previously revealed that, although the girl understood the source of her problem at the subconscious level, she was unwilling to communicate it. During the second session, she was given the suggestion that the problem would resolve itself quickly if she wanted it to.

Four hours after this session, the patient rode her bicycle and was free of pain. Her depression began to lift; by the end of the fourth and last session she was active and cheerful and making good progress in school. Progress was maintained over a 31-month follow-up period. Cioppa and Thal attributed the remission to an alteration in the patient's attitude at an unconscious level in response to positive suggestions.

Hemophilia.   LaBaw (1975) conducted a study to determine the use of adjunctive trance therapy in the treatment of hemophiliacs ranging in age from 5 to 48 years. The emphasis was on enabling patients to tap their own dormant trance capability to reduce anxiety and increase autonomy and control over their disease, in which emotional stress has been found to increase hemorrhage. LaBaw found that trance therapy had a significant effect on the patients in the experimental group, who used significantly fewer units of blood over three 10-month periods than did patients in a control group. The practice of self-hypnosis also resulted in positive changes in the patients' outlook.

Diabetes.   Hypnosis can be a valuable tool to enhance mastery in diabetic patients who may resent their routine of urine tests, prescribed diets, and insulin injections. Kroger (1977) reported that in some cases "hypnotherapy can reduce the quantity of insulin needed to keep the urine sugar-free" (p. 201).

The following case treated by Wood illustrates the way in which hypnosis can help a child master a fear of blood tests. A similar approach could be used with a child for whom daily insulin injections have become an ordeal:

J is a 10-year-old male with a history of juvenile onset diabetes mellitus. At age 10 he was noted to have an enlarged thyroid gland, and the presence of antithyroid antibodies in his serum gave credence to the likely diagnosis of Hashimoto's thyroiditis. He subsequently was placed on a daily replacement regimen of thyroxine (L-Thyroxine), taken orally. Serial blood tests were required to aid in the adjustment of his thyroid medication.

J reported that during his regular blood tests he did not have a problem with insertion of the needle into his vein, but that he felt that he was going to faint and get sick when he "felt the needle being moved around." He also said that during his first blood test he experienced blurry vision, a racing heart, sweaty hands, and crying. Later, he began to experience these symptoms on the way to the hospital for his blood tests and was so upset that he had to be physically restrained by the laboratory technicians during the procedure.

During the initial consultation, the therapist explained to J that he was getting upset before and during his blood tests because his personal alarm system was working overtime. J then expressed interest in learning how to turn off his alarm system so that his blood tests would be more comfortable and not cause a panic reaction. He also was pleased to learn that he could use the same self-hypnosis skills when he was playing baseball.

J responded well to a permissive induction technique and to suggestions that he could control his sensations by visualizing a control center and turning off or adjusting the appropriate dials and switches to increase his comfort. The therapist also included ego-strengthening suggestions and suggestions that J could use his control center to increase his skill while playing baseball. J agreed to practice during the week by listening to a tape recording of the session and by remembering the suggestions on his own.

During the next two sessions, the therapist used J's feedback concerning his self-hypnosis experiences to expand and improve the induction used in the initial session. By the third session, J could enter a medium state of hypnosis within 2 or 3 minutes and signal by ideomotor finger response that he had adjusted the dials and switches and was ready for his blood test.

After his blood test a week later, during which he employed his self-hypnosis skills, he reported that he "did not feel a thing," surprising the laboratory staff who had witnessed his previous discomfort. J went home that afternoon and played in a Little League baseball game.

Pain

The relief of pain always has been a major purposes of medicine. The ability to reduce pain to a manageable level, and in some cases, to eliminate pain entirely, is one of the most important and enduring uses of hypnosis.

Because pain is experienced psychologically as well as physiologically, hypnosis can help people alter the perception of pain. While actively engaged in hetero- or self-hypnosis, a patient can block pain to specific areas of the body, lessen the sensation of pain, or move pain from one area of the body to another. This ability is useful in the management of many types of pain, including chronic back pain, postoperative pain, and the pain associated with illness, migraine headache, burns, childbirth, and medical procedures.

Erickson (1967) identified 11 categories of hypnotic procedures that could be used in pain control. These include direct abolition of pain, indirect permissive abolition of pain, amnesia, hypnoanalgesia, hypnoanesthesia, replacement or substitution of symptoms, displacement of pain, dissociation, reinterpretation, time distortion, and diminution of pain. These approaches are not mutually exclusive and are most often used in combination.

Using substitution, for example, the practitioner can help the patient to replace one type of discomfort, such as the pain of a burn, with another sensation, such as tingling, that is easier to endure. Time distortion is used to alter the proportion of painful to pain-free periods. Vivid mental scenes, such as a walk through a forest of pine trees, can be developed in hypnosis. Such scenes are incompatible with the sensation of pain and direct the mind away from it. Using the techniques of glove anesthesia, numbness is produced in the hand and then transferred to the area where pain is felt.

The literature on using hypnosis to reduce both clinical and experimental pain is extensive. Hilgard and Hilgard (1975) compiled an impressive body of research on hypnosis and the reduction of experimental pain and explored its applicability in a clinic setting. Sacerdote (1966, 1970) has written extensively on the use of hypnosis for pain control in cancer patients.

Sachs, Feuerstein, and Vitale (1977) reported a treatment program in which eight patients with severe intractable chronic pain were trained in hypnotic self-regulation procedures (self-hypnosis) to modify pain. The hypnotic treatment program resulted in significant reduction in (a) daily pain intensity, (b) the degree to which pain interfered with general functioning, (c) life dissatisfaction and suffering, (d) personality characteristics commonly associated with chronic pain, and (e) amount of self-administered pain medication.

Wakeman and Kaplan (1978) reported a study that demonstrated the usefulness of hypnosis in controlling acute pain in burn patients, aged 7–70. As a result of individualized inductions and suggestions of hypnoanalgesia, anesthesia, dissociation, and reduction of anxiety and fear, the experimental groups were able significantly to reduce their medication compared to control groups.

Wakeman and Kaplan (1978) found that the 7–18-year-old patients were able to achieve greater pain relief through hypnosis than were the older patients. LaBaw (1973) also reported on the use of hypnotic techniques to alleviate distress and reduce pain in severely burned children. Gardner and Olness (1981) commented that "children's reactions to pain are often influenced by the context of their expectations concerning adult response as much as by the response itself" (p. 174). They therefore advised all adults, parents as well as practitioners, to choose words related to pain very carefully when speaking to children.

As Wain (1980b) stated, "no single treatment modality appears to be effective for every patient and for all pain problems" (p. 2). Therefore, in a clinical setting, "the physician's creativity, his ability to listen and understand the patient and, at the same time, the patient's ability to communicate with him" (p. 6) play a crucial role in the management of pain through hypnosis. For further discussion of hypnosis and pain management, refer to Chapter 9.

Cellular Growth

Hypnosis plays a dual role in the treatment of burn patients, to manage pain and to accelerate healing. In 1955, Crasilneck, Stirman, Wilson, McCranie, and Fogelman demonstrated the effectiveness of hypnotic suggestions to increase burn patients' relaxation, comfort, food intake, and exercise. Several authors since then (e.g., Bernstein, 1965; Schafer, 1975; Wakeman and Kaplan, 1978) have found similar success.

The elimination of warts is an example of a more direct use of hypnosis to influence cellular growth. Recent research, although not yet conclusive, provides evidence that hypnosis may be effective in retarding the growth of cancerous tumors. Alteration of the disease process is the new frontier in medical hypnosis and, thus, a fitting subject with which to conclude this chapter.

Warts.   The successful treatment of warts through hypnosis provides one of the more spectacular manifestations of the power of mind over body. A common dermatological disorder caused by a virus, warts are perversely resistant to traditional treatment. They can be painted with a variety of remedies, curetted, cauterized, and yet reappear and proliferate.

In a frequently cited study by Sinclair-Gieben and Chalmers (1959), 14 patients were hypnotized and given the suggestion that all the warts on one side of the body would go away. Within 5 weeks to 3 months, 9 patients showed wart regression on the "treated" side while the warts on the other side remained unchanged.

Another carefully controlled study by Surman, Gotlieb, Hackett, and Silverberg (1973) showed significant improvement in 9 of 17 patients who were given the hypnotic suggestion that they would experience a tingling sensation in the warts on one side of the body, and that these warts would soon disappear. Unlike the earlier experiment, however, this research did not succeed in producing a selective reduction of the warts. Either the warts did not disappear at all, or they disappeared from both sides of the body. The warts of an untreated control group showed no reduction.

One interesting result of the Surman study was that patients responded in different ways to the suggestions: Four experienced a sudden loss of all lesions; four showed a gradual fading of the warts; and one experienced successive sudden loss of individual lesions.

Thomas (1979) considered the fact that warts can be "ordered off the skin" by hypnotic suggestion to be "one of the great mystifications of science" (p. 77). There are two basic hypotheses about the way hypnotic suggestion, acting on the autonomic nervous system, results in the disappearance of warts: (a) by altering the blood flow to the warts, thus influencing them directly, and (b) by influencing the body's immune response, thus acting upon the warts indirectly.

Case reports indicate that hypnotic suggestions based on each of these hypotheses can be equally effective in eliminating warts. Clawson and Swade (1975) reported three case studies in which suggestions to stop the blood supply to each wart produced a cure within 2–3 months. Ewin (1974) successfully treated four cases of venereal warts (condyloma acuminatum) with suggestions of warmth and the dilation of blood vessels to bring in more antibodies and white blood cells. Dreaper (1978) cured a case of recalcitrant warts with suggestions that they would gradually shrivel up. The fact that the body can eliminate warts in response to a placebo (see Barber, 1978 for a summary of several cases) as well as to a variety of hypnotic suggestions indicates that the key factor may be the patient's intention or expectations rather than the precise wording of suggestions.

Cancer.   The effectiveness of hypnosis in elminating warts has caused some speculation that hypnosis might be useful in the eradication of cancerous tumors as well. Clawson and Swade (1975), for example, saw the ability of hypnosis to destroy warts as a model for metastasizing tumors:

> Warts metastasize, although by way of viruses presumably, and not by cells. They may be numerous, and they may be spread over the whole body, or they may be limited to certain areas. Furthermore, they are nourished by capillaries, and we think that stopping blood flow to them brings about their destruction. If suggestion can destroy such a distribution of warts, we think likewise tumors can be destroyed. (p. 165)

Clawson and Swade (1975) also speculated that the control of blood flow through hypnosis can produce a local concentration or retention of drugs used in chemotherapy and that hypnosis can assist radiation therapy by controlling oxygen distribution from the blood into tumors. Barber (1978) also reviewed a number of experimental studies that provide convincing evidence of hypnotic suggestion influencing blood flow to localized areas of the skin.

Immune system functioning has been the focus of much recent research. Studies on the effects of stress on immune system functioning are lending scientific support to anecdotal reports that indicate hypnosis can be effective in altering the disease process in cancer patients.

Research with mice has shown that stress can increase tumor growth and decrease life span (Riley, 1981), while the ability to cope with stress can modify its ill effects and increase survival time (Sklar, 1979). Studies of cancer patients have found that the inability to relieve anxiety and depression (Blumberg et al., 1954) and the inability to express anger (Abeloff and Derogatis, 1977) correlate with a poor prognosis. On the other hand, patients with a positive outlook and a "fighting spirit" have a far better prognosis than those who respond with "stoic acceptance of feelings of helplessness and hopelessness" (Greer, Morris, and Pettingale, 1979).

Borysenko (1982) concluded that "behavioral interventions that reduce stress and enhance coping skills may prevent compromise of those cell-mediated immune mechanisms which can eliminate small foci of residual cancer cells" (p. 72). She advocated eliciting the relaxation response to intervene in the downward cycle of fear, anxiety, and depression that inhibits immune function and permits the growth of cancer cells. Meares (1983) used a form of intensive meditation to produce a "profound and prolonged" reduction in the anxiety level of cancer patients and reported a number of cases of tumor regression.

Over the past several years, the Simontons (Simonton, Matthews-Simonton, and Creighton, 1978) have based their cancer treatment program on the premise that unless the mind, body, and emotions are all striving toward health, a purely physical intervention (radiation therapy, in this case) will not be effective. Their relaxation and mental imagery procedure embodies the techniques of modern clinical hypnosis. The building blocks of the Simontons' approach are progressive muscle relaxation, followed by imagining oneself in a pleasant, quiet place, and then visualizing the cancer, the treatment destroying it, and the body's defenses mobilizing to enhance recovery.

In a clinical test of this approach with 159 patients who had medically incurable cancer and were given a year to live, 63 patients were still living after 2 years. Of those, 22% were in remission, 19% showed tumor regression, and 27% had stabilized.

In a more controlled study to examine the effects of hypnosis on immune system function, Hall, Longo, and Dixon (1981) used a composite of the images described by the Simontons (white blood cells as powerful sharks attacking the weak germ cells) in hypnosis and self-hypnosis to raise the number of T-cells in the blood of 20 healthy volunteers. The T-lymphocytes are the part of the body's immune system that protect it from abnormal "non-self" cells, such as cancerous ones.

Lymphocyte function in the blood was measured 1 hour before hypnosis, 1 hour after, and 1 week following practice in self-hypnosis. The study found that hypnosis did significantly increase the immune function in younger subjects (below the age of 50) and in subjects most responsive to hypnosis.

For the past 8 years, Newton (1983) has used hypnosis, imagery, and psychotherapy to treat cancer patients at a private treatment center in Los Angeles. He reported that nearly all of the 105 patients seen for a minimum of ten 1-hour sessions experienced significant improvement in their quality of life. The treated patients also demonstrated a significantly greater duration of life, compared to the national median survival rates for persons with the same cancers at the same stage of development; in some instances these treated patients were able to achieve full remission of the disease. Newton (1983) also reported a survival rate for patients with advanced metastatic lung, bowel, and breast cancer 7.5–19 months longer than the survival rate reported by Simonton et al. (1978).

These results indicate that patient hopes and expectations may be a newly discovered and potentially powerful weapon to add to physicians' treatment arsenal in the battle against one of our century's most frightening and devastating diseases.

The uses of hypnosis in medical treatment are many and varied. Additional research is required to isolate key hypnotic variables in treatment situations. Even that information, however, will never translate into a cookbook approach to medical hypnosis. As in all other areas, the use of hypnosis in medicine will vary with the needs of the patient and the orientation of the practitioner.

Techniques such as hypnosis, which can assist people to counter anxiety, foster hope, and enhance the will to live, deserve greater attention from the medical profession. It is time for the physician without and the physician within to combine forces. As hypnotic principles are conciously applied by an increasing number of practitioners, we see a corresponding increase in the number of "medical miracles."

SAMPLE INDUCTIONS

Group Induction

The following induction and treatment suggestions are part of an education and stress reduction program offered diabetic children and their families at the Naval Regional Medical Center in San Diego. In three 90-minute training sessions, the participants learn the basics of self-hypnosis, discuss the relationship between stress and the management of diabetes, and review specific stressful situations encountered by the diabetic children or their families.

The program helps participants develop increased stress-coping skills and gradually strengthen their belief that they can have control over their lives. A research project is currently underway to test hypotheses about the positive benefits of this stress reduction program to help diabetic children and their families better manage the direct and indirect aspects of diabetes. The following induction and treatment suggestions were provided to a group of diabetic children who were 9–12 years old.

Induction suggestions. I would like each of you to start off by letting yourself become as comfortable as you want to become . . . think about how it is that you let yourself rest and relax before or while you have been at home . . . or at school . . . or at a friend's house . . . or at work . . . wherever it is that you might have been . . . and know that you can let yourself rest and relax very, very quickly and very . . . very easily. . . . I would like you to let yourself continue relaxing. . . . I would like you to think about having a daydream or an image of relaxing. . . . You might think about or remember the last time you went to the beach and you were lying on the warm sand relaxing . . . or playing in the ocean . . . or swimming in the ocean. . . . In your mind I would like to create an image of what you might look like while you are relaxing . . . or what you might feel . . . or what you might be thinking when you are relaxing. . . . As you take one or two very gentle breaths . . . inhaling cool and refreshing oxygen into your lungs and exhaling tensions or anxieties . . . think about letting yourself relax. . . . You might even let your eyes close at this point if you have not done so already, so that you can see your daydream more clearly. . . . Think about letting yourself relax. . . . Any noise outside of my voice or any outside noise other than the suggestions that you give yourself will somehow and in some way help you to relax more and more. . . . If you hear a baby cry down the hall . . . or the ringing of a phone . . . or the noise of a plane overhead landing at the airport . . . any and all of these noises can somehow and in some way help you to relax more and more . . . can help you daydream better and better. . . . You know that as soon as you close your eyes you can have that as a signal to turn on your relaxation. . . . Closing your eyes is one of your signals to turn on your daydreaming and relaxing responses. . . . Each time you move to make yourself more comfortable you think about becoming more and more relaxed. . . . Each time you breathe you are inhaling oxygen into your lungs that your body needs and then your lungs are transferring this oxygen to your blood so that the oxygen can be available throughout your body to help keep you healthy and strong, and it is important that you give your body the tools it needs to keep you healthy and strong. . . . It is important that you follow proper meal programming . . . obtain proper rest and exercise . . . and continue to take the correct amount of insulin.

Treatment suggestions. Your mind and body know what they need to do to keep themselves balanced. . . . Your mind and body regulate your body temperature, . . . they regulate your digestion process, . . . they regulate the process of sleep, . . . all automatically. . . . You do not necessarily have to know how your mind and body perform these regulation processes, but maybe it is not important that you know how all this occurs because your mind and body know how to take care of you. . . . You can help your mind and body take better care of you by resting and relaxing and by doing the other activities you know are important for someone with diabetes. . . . One of the beliefs you have that it is important for you to know about is your sense and belief in control. . . . Just as you decide what clothes you put on each day and just as you decide whom it is you wish to play with and just as you may decide what to read or what to watch on TV, you can also decide many other things in your life. . . . Some of the decisions that you make are easy to make and some of these decisions are more difficult. . . . Somehow and in some way you can, and look forward to becoming better and better at making these decisions . . . becoming more confident . . . more energetic . . . taking better and better care of yourself. . . .

Note: the remaining suggestions focused on ego-strengthening and associating relaxation with everyday activities such as getting dressed, picking up a book, drinking a beverage, opening or closing a door, or going to sleep. Almost anything that people do can become a cue to access a relaxation process.

Individualized Induction

The following induction and treatment suggestions were provided to a 56-year-old man with multiple medical problems, including degenerative disc disease, hiatal hernia, recurrent esophageal spasms, and diverticulosis. He had frequent pain and suffered from insomnia.

His treatment with hypnosis and adjunctive psychotherapy was designed to augment his ongoing medical care and focused on increasing his general relaxation, facilitating his sleep onset, increasing his pain threshold, reducing his pain perception, and reducing his gastrointestinal hyperactivity.

Induction suggestions.   All right, Bill: What I'd like you to do is to continue your process of relaxation. . . . You know, as soon as you close your eyes . . . as soon as you take one, two, or three easy breaths . . . you're well on your road to relaxation . . . breathing in and out slowly and deeply . . . relaxing your whole body by that method that you've designed that works best for you.

As you're relaxing, you know that you can be very much aware of letting any of your ideas of discomfort, pain, stress, anxiety, depression become like bubbles in your consciousness. . . . You can imagine that these bubbles are being blown out of your mind, out of your body, out of your consciousness by a breeze that draws them away from you far into the distance until you no longer see them or feel them . . . or need to see them or need to feel them. . . . You know that you can watch these bubbles disappear in the distance as the sound of the jet overhead disappears into the distance.

One, two, or three easy, gentle breaths, and as I, with your permission, pick up your left hand and arm, the muscles in your left hand and arm and the muscles in your right hand and arm can become progressively as loose and as limp as the chain links in the necklace that you're wearing. . . . Pick your necklace up and let it go; it falls down to your chest. . . . As I pick your arm up in just a moment and let it go, it falls down toward your side, perhaps as heavy as lead . . . perhaps as heavy as your eyelids . . . perhaps as heavy as any heavy substance you will ever come across. . . . Your arm can be and is becoming progressively loose, limp, relaxed, and very, very comfortable. . . . All the muscles in your body are relaxing completely and profoundly . . . and when I let your arm go, your arm falls down to your lap.

Treatment suggestions.   You know that an aspect of your process of relaxation, Bill, can be like taking a ride down into a building representing your level of consciousness. . . . Take a ride down to the first . . . second . . . or third basement or even lower, to wherever the engineering spaces in this building are located. . . . In this engineering space or in these engineering spaces as you go down, taking an elevator or stairs or an escalator or some other means or mechanism, are located computers, dials, meters, and switches that control all the resources available to you. There can also be any additional resources that you need available . . . gastrointestinal neutralizers . . . antispasmodic agents . . . substances similar to tryptophan or Dalmane in terms of sleep agents . . . and natural substances produced by your body to help your system be as balanced as possible. . . . In this engineering space you can imagine that the area around you is filled with a bright . . . clear light so you can see anything and everything. . . . And this light can go wherever you need the light to illuminate whatever process it is you need or wish to be involved in. . . . And you can allow that light to flow into your body, Bill, . . . making you brighter and filling you with the energy of health. You enjoy basking in this light, as well as using this light with the processes that you need or wish to use it with. . . . As you focus on this light and as you focus on the engineering space that you're in, you can direct your resources to whatever areas of your body you need or wish to direct the resources to . . . whether it's to your esophagus area, whether it's to your lower back, whether it's to your abdominal intestinal area, or whether it's to a sleep area in your brain. . . . And as you go through each one of these systems, making sure the program on the computer is right and it is operational for your program, working with yourself in terms of these particular areas that we have been focusing on . . . and as you make sure that the meters . . . the switches . . . the dials . . . and the resources respond and go in the directions you want and need them to go, you can let your fingers rise up indicating each one of these systems that you have activated and checked out and trouble-shot. . . . And as your fingers go up, one finger for a system . . . you obtain a kinesthetic cue that you have checked these programs . . . trouble-shot these programs . . . debugged these programs . . . and these programs are working just perfectly. And you know that you can adjust the rheostat . . . the switches . . . or dials . . . of your computer based on the feedback that you're getting through the meters . . . or based on the feedback that you're getting through any other monitoring system or systems . . . as you make sure that your computer is working the way it's designed to work.

Note: After these suggestions, each one of Bill's systems or symptom target areas was reviewed individually, using the ideomotor questioning techniques outlined by Cheek and LeCron (1968).

SUMMARY

In an essay on warts, Thomas (1979) captured the mystery and the wonder of the phenomenon we call hypnosis:

> Some intelligence or other knows how to get rid of warts, and this is a disquieting thought. It is also a wonderful problem, in need of solving. Just think what we would know, if we had anything like a clear understanding of what goes on when a wart is hypnotized away. We would know the identity of the cellular and chemical participants in tissue rejection, conceivably with some added information about the ways that viruses create foreignness in cells. We would know how the traffic of these reactants is directed, and perhaps then be able to understand the nature of certain diseases in which the traffic is being conducted in wrong directions, aimed at the wrong cells. *Best of all, we would be finding out about a kind of superintelligence that exists in each of us, infinitely smarter and possessed of technical know-how far beyond our present understanding.* (p. 81. Italics added.)

Because mind, body, and emotions are interdependent, a physician can influence the course of an illness by using hypnosis to address nonspecific factors such as a patient's anxiety, depression, and fear. The use of hypnotic techniques can help patients to regain a sense of control and responsibility for their own recovery, to increase confidence in their ability to recover, to uncover causes of an illness that does not respond as expected to treatment, and to improve their quality of life.

In addition to patient management, hypnosis has been found effective in controlling habit disorders, managing both acute and chronic pain, treating psychophysiological disorders, and reducing the morbidity of patients with chronic conditions. Recent research is opening up a new frontier for medical hypnosis: the use of hypnosis to strengthen the immune system, reduce tumor size, and increase the life span of cancer patients.

While scientists pursue these lines of research, it is hoped that more and more practitioners will take advantage of the "superintelligence," or the doctor within each patient, by using the versatile tool of hypnosis.

FURTHER READING

Benson, H. (1979). *The mind/body effect.* New York: Berkeley Books.

Cheek, D. B., & LeCron, L. M. (1968) *Clinical hypnotherapy.* New York: Grune & Stratton.

Cousins, N. (1979). *Anatomy of an illness.* New York: W. W. Norton.

Crasilneck, H. G., & Hall, J. A. (1975). *Clinical hypnosis: principles and applications.* New York: Grune & Stratton.

Hartland, J. (1971). *Medical and dental hypnosis.* London: Bailliere Tindall.

Kroger, W. S. (1977). *Clinical and experimental hypnosis.* Philadelphia: J. B. Lippincott.

Simonton, C. O., Matthews-Simonton, S., & Creighton, J. (1978). *Getting well again.* Los Angeles, J. P. Tarcher.

REFERENCES

Abeloff, M. D., & Derogatis, L. R. (1977). Psychologic aspects of the management of primary and metastic breast cancer. *Progress in Clinical and Biological Research, 12,* 505–516.

Ader, R. (Ed.) (1981). *Psychoneuroimmunology.* New York: Academic Press.

Arnoff, M., Arnoff, S., & Peck, L. W. (1975). Hypnotherapy in the treatment of bronchial asthma. *Annals of Allergy, 34,* 356–362.

Barber, T. X. (1970). *LSD, marijuana, yoga, and hypnosis.* Chicago: Aldine.

Barber, T. X. (1978). Hypnosis, suggestions, and psychosomatic phenomena: A new look from the standpoint of recent experimental studies. *American Journal of Clinical Hypnosis, 21,* 13–27.

Benson, H. (1975). *The relaxation response.* New York: Morrow.

Benson, H., Arns, P., & Hoffman, J. W. (1981). The relaxation response and hypnosis. *International Journal of Clinical and Experimental Hypnosis, 29*, 259–270.

Benson, H., Rosner, B. A., Marzetta, B. R., & Klemchuk, H. M. (1974a). Decreased blood pressure in borderline hypertensive subjects who practiced meditation. *Journal of Chronic Diseases, 27*, 163–169.

Benson, H., Rosner, B. A., Marzetta, B. R., & Klemchuk, H. M. (1974b). Decreased blood pressure in pharmacologically treated hypertensive patients who regularly elicited the relaxation response. *Lancet, 1*, 289–291.

Bernstein, N. R. (1965). Observations of the use of hypnosis with burned children in a pediatric ward. *International Journal of Clinical and Experimental Hypnosis, 13*, 1–10.

Blumberg, E. M., West, P. M., & Ellis, F. W. (1954). A possible relationship between psychological factors and human cancer. *Psychosomatic Medicine, 16*, 276–286.

Borysenko, J. (1982). Behavioral-physiological factors in the development and management of cancer. *General Hospital Psychiatry, 4*, 69–74.

Brown, E. A. (1965). The treatment of bronchial asthma by means of hypnosis. *Journal of Asthma Research, 13*, 1–10.

Burke, E. C., & Stickler, G. B. (1980). Enuresis—is it being overtreated? *Mayo Clinic Proceedings, 55*, 118–119.

Cheek, D. B. (1964). Further evidence of persistence of hearing under chemoanesthesia: Detailed case reports. *American Journal of Clinical Hypnosis, 7*, 55–59.

Cheek, D. B. (1969). Communication with the critically ill. *American Journal of Clinical Hypnosis, 12*, 75–85.

Cheek, D. G., & LeCron, L. M. (1968). *Clinical hypnotherapy.* New York: Grune & Stratton.

Cioppa, F. J., & Thal, A. D. (1975). Hypnotherapy in a case of juvenile rheumatoid arthritis. *American Journal of Clinical Hypnosis, 18*, 105–111.

Clawson, T. A., & Swade, R. H. (1975). The hypnotic control of blood flood and pain: The cure of warts and the potential for the use of hypnosis in the treatment of cancer. *American Journal of Clinical Hypnosis, 12*, 75–85.

Conn, J. H. (1961). Preparing for hypnosis in general practice. *Roche Report, 3*, 3.

Cousins, N. (1976). Anatomy of an illness (as perceied by the patient). *New England Journal of Medicine, 295*, 1458–1463.

Cousins, N. (1979). *Anatomy of an illness.* New York: W. W. Norton.

Crasilneck, H. B., & Hall, J. A. (1975). *Clinical hypnosis: Principles and Applications.* New York: Grune & Stratton.

Crasilneck, H. B., Stirman, J. B., Wilson, B. J., McCranie, E. J., & Fogelman, M. J. (1955). Use of hypnosis in the management of patients with burns. *Journal of the American Medical Association, 158*, 103–106.

Daniels, L. K. (1976). The effects of automated hypnosis and hand warming on migraine: A pilot study. *American Journal of Clinical Hypnosis, 19*, 91–94.

Deabler, H. L., Fidel, E., Dillenkoffer, R. L., & Elder, T. S. (1973). The use of relaxation and hypnosis in lowering high blood pressure. *American Journal of Clinical Hypnosis, 16*, 15–82.

Dempster, C. R., Balson, P., & Whalen, B. T. (1976). Supportive hypnotherapy during the radical treatment of malignancies. *International Journal of Clinical and Experimental Hypnosis, 24,* 1–8.

Dreaper, R. (1978). Recalcitrant warts on the hand cured by hypnosis. *The Practitioner, 220,* 309–310.

Erickson, M. H. (1967). An introduction to the study and application of hypnosis for pain control. In J. Lassner (Ed.), *Hypnosis and psychosomatic medicine* (pp. 83–90). New York: Springer-Verlag, 83–90.

Ewin, D. M. (1974). Candyloma acuminatum: Successful treatment of four cases by hypnosis. *American Journal of Clinical Hypnosis, 17,* 73–78.

Gardner, G. G. (1977a). Hypnosis with infants and preschool children. *American Journal of Clinical Hypnosis, 19,* 158–162.

Gardner, G. G. (1977b). The rights of dying children: Some personal reflections. *Psychotherapy Bulletin, 10,* 20–23.

Gardner, G. G. (1980). Hypnosis with children: Selected readings. *International Journal of Clinical and Experimental Hypnosis, 28,* 289–293.

Gardner, G. G., & Olness, K. (1981). *Hypnosis and hypnotherapy with children.* New York: Grune & Stratton.

Greer, S., Morris, T., & Pettingale, K. W. (1979). Psychological response to breast cancer: Effect on outcome. *Lancet, 13,* 785–787.

Hall, H. R. (1983). Hypnosis and the immune system: A review with implications for cancer and the psychology of healing. *American Journal of Clinical Hypnosis, 25,* 92–103.

Hall, H. R., Longo, S., & Dixon, R. (1981, October). *Hypnosis and the immune system: The effect of hypnosis on T and B cell function.* Paper presented to the Society for Clinical and Experimental Hypnosis, 33rd Annual Workshops and Scientific Meeting, Portland.

Hall, J. A., & Crasilneck, H. B. (1970). Development of a hypnotic technique for treating chronic cigarette smoking. *International Journal of Clinical and Experimental Hypnosis, 18,* 283–289.

Hartland, J. (1971). *Medical and dental hypnosis.* London: Bailliere Tindall.

Hartman, G. A. (1981). Hypnosis as an adjuvant in the treatment of childhood cancer. In Spinetta, J. J. & Deasy-Spinetta, P. M. (Eds.), *Living with childhood cancer* (pp. 143–152). St. Louis: Mosby.

Hilgard, E. R., & Hilgard, J. R. (1975). *Hypnosis in the relief of pain.* Los Altos, CA: William Kaufmann.

Hobby-Burns, L., Clinton, B. K., Danziger, R., & Wood, D. (1983). *Who's in control: A family-oriented approach for the management of asthma.* Paper presented at the American Nursing Association Annual Convention, Denver, CO.

Hoffman, J. W., Benson, H., Arns, P. A., Stainbrook, G. L., Landesberg, L., Young, J. B., & Gill, A. (1982). Reduced sympathetic nervous system responsivity associated with the relaxation response. *Science, 215,* 190–192.

Jacobson, A. M., Hackett, T. P., Surman, O. S., & Silverberg, E. L. (1973). Raynaud phenomenon: Treatment with hypnotic and operant technique. *Journal of the American Medical Association, 225,* 139–140.

Johnson, K., & Korn, E. R. (1980). Hypnosis and imagery in the rehabilitation of a brain-damaged patient. *Journal of Mental Imagery, 4*, 35–39.

Johnston, E., & Donoghue, J. R. (1971). Hypnosis and smoking: A review of the literature. *American Journal of Clinical Hypnosis, 13*, 265–272.

Kline, M. V. (1970). The use of extended group hypnotherapy sessions in controlling cigarette habituation. *International Journal of Clinical and Experimental Hypnosis, 18*, 270–282.

Klopfer, B. (1957). Psychological variables in human cancer. *Journal of Projective Techniques, 21*, 331–340.

Kohen, D., Olness, K., Colwell, S., & Heimel, A. (1980, November). 500 pediatric behavioral problems treated with hypnotherapy. Paper presented at the annual meeting of the American Society of Clinical Hypnosis, Minneapolis.

Kroger, W. S. (1970). Hypnosis therapy in neuromuscular disorders. *OP/The Osteopathic Physician, 124*, 70–79.

Kroger, W. S. (1977). *Clinical and experimental hypnosis.* Philadelphia: J. B. Lippincott.

LaBaw, W. L. (1973). Adjunctive trance therapy with severely burned children. *International Journal of Child Psychotherapy, 2*, 80–92.

LaBaw, W. L. (1975). Auto-hypnosis in haemophilia. *Haematologia, 9*, 103–110.

Lehew, J. L. The use of hypnosis in the treatment of musculo-skeletal disorders. *American Journal of Clinical Hypnosis, 13*, 131–134.

Maher-Loughnan, G. P. (1970). Hypnosis and autohypnosis for the treatment of asthma. *International Journal of Clinical and Experimental Hypnosis, 18*, 1–4.

Meares, A. (1983). A form of intensive meditation associated with regression of cancer. *American Journal of Clinical Hypnosis, 25*, 114–121.

Morgan, A. H., & Hilgard, E. R. (1973). Age differences in susceptibility to hypnosis. *International Journal of Clinical and Experimental Hypnosis, 21*, 78–85.

Morgan, A. H., & Hilgard, E. R. (1979). The Stanford hypnotic scale for children. *American Journal of Clinical Hypnosis, 21*, 148–155.

Newton, B. W. (1983). The use of hypnosis in the treatment of cancer patients. *American Journal of Clinical Hypnosis, 25*, 104–113.

Olness, K. (1975). The use of self-hypnosis in the treatment of childhood nocturnal enuresis: A report on forty patients. *Clinical Pediatrics, 14*, 273–279.

Olness, K., & Gardner, G. (1978). Some guidelines for uses of hypnotherapy in pediatrics. *Pediatrics, 62*, 228–233.

Pederson, L. Scrimgeour, W. G., & Lecoe, N. M. (1979). Variables of hypnosis which are related to success in a smoking withdrawal program. *International Journal of Clinical and Experimental Hypnosis, 27*, 14–20.

Rahe, R. H., & Arthur, R. J. (1978). *Life change and illness studies: Past history and future directions* (Rep. No. 76-14). San Diego: Naval Health Research Center.

Riley, V. (1981). Psychoneuroendocrine influences on immunocompetence and neoplasia. *Science, 212*, 1100–1109.

Sacerdote, P. (1966). The uses of hypnosis in cancer patients. *Annals of the New York Academy of Science, 125*, 1011–1019.

Sacerdote, P. (1970). Theory and practice of pain control in malignancy and other protracted or recurring painful illness. *International Journal of Clinical and Experimental Hypnosis, 18, 160–180.*

Sachs, L. B., Feuerstein, M., & Vitale, J. H. (1977). Hypnotic self-regulation of chronic pain. *American Journal of Clinical Hypnosis, 20,* 106–113.

Schafer, D. W. (1975). Hypnosis use on a burn unit. *International Journal of Clinical and Experimental Hypnosis, 23,* 1–14.

Schwartz, G. E., & Beatty, J. (1977). *Biofeedback: Theory and research.* New York: Academic Press.

Selye, H. (1956). *The stress of life.* New York: McGraw-Hill.

Shapiro, A. K. (1959). A contribution to a history of the placebo effect. *Behavioral Science, 5,* 109.

Sheehan, D. V., & Surman, O. W. (1978). The hypnosis and psychosomatic medicine clinic. In T. P. Hackett & N. H. Cassem (Eds.), *Massachusetts general hospital handbook.* St. Louis: C. V. Mosby.

Simonton, C. O., Matthews-Simonton, S., & Creighton, J. (1978). *Getting Well again.* Los Angeles: J. P. Tarcher.

Sinclair-Gieben, A. H. C. (1960). Treatment of status asthmaticus by hypnosis. *British Medical Journal, 1651–1652.*

Sinclair-Geiban, A. H. C., & Chalmers, D. (1959). Evaluation of treatment of warts by suggestion. *Lancet, 2,* 480–482.

Sklar, L. S. (1979). Stress and coping factors influence tumor growth. *Science, 205,* 513–515.

Spiegel, H. (1967). Is symptom removal dangerous? *American Journal of Psychiatry, 123,* 1279–1283.

Spiegel, H. (1970). A single-treatment method to stop smoking using ancillary self-hypnosis. *International Journal of Clinical and Experimental Hypnosis, 18,* 235–250.

Stambaugh, E. E., & House, A. E. (1977). Multimodality treatment of migraine headache: A case study utilizing biofeedback, relaxation, autogenic and hypnotic treatments. *American Journal of Clinical Hypnosis, 19,* 235–240.

Stanton, H. E. (1979). Short-term treatment of enuresis. *American Journal of Clinical Hypnosis, 22,* 103–107.

Surman, O. S., Gotlieb, S. K., Hackett, T. P., & Silverberg, E. L. (1973). Hypnosis in the treatment of warts. *Archives of General Psychiatry, 28,* 439–441.

Thomas, L. (1979). *The medusa and the snail.* New York: Viking Press.

Wain, H. J. (1980a). Hypnosis in the treatment of chronic pain. In H. J. Wain (Ed.), *Clinical hypnosis in medicine.* Miami: Symposia Specialists, 1–10.

Wain, H. J. (1980b). Pain control through use of hypnosis. *American Journal of Clinical Hypnosis, 23,* 41–46.

Wakeman, J. R., & Kaplan, J. Z. (1978). An experimental study of hypnosis in painful burns. *American Journal of Clinical Hypnosis, 21,* 3–11.

Watkins, H. H. (1976). Hypnosis and smoking: a five-session approach. *International Journal of Clinical and Experimental Hypnosis, 24,* 381–389.

Wood, D. P., & Allen, J. (1979, April). *Treatment of intractable hiccups: A case report.* Paper presented at the California State Psychological Convention, Monterey, CA.

Yarnell, T. D. (1980). A comprehensive treatment of migraine headaches. In Wain, H. J. (Ed.), *Clinical hypnosis in medicine* (pp. 19–24). Miami: Symposia Specialists.

8

Surgery

*Nothing should be omitted in an art which
interests the whole world, one which may be
beneficial to suffering humanity, and which does
not risk human life or comfort.*

—Hippocrates
The Art of Medicine

The effectiveness of hypnosis in influencing perceptions and
inducing or accelerating physiological processes makes it a valuable tool for all phases of surgery. Before the discovery of chemical
anesthesia, hypnosis was the most effective means of managing pain
during surgery. There were several pioneers in the field, among them
Elliotson, the well-known London physician who introduced the stethoscope to England; Esdaile, a Scottish surgeon who practiced in India;
and Braid, who coined the term "hypnotism." All performed surgical
operations during the mid-1800s, using hypnosis as the sole means of
achieving anesthesia.

Esdaile in particular demonstrated spectacular success. During the
1830s in India, the mortality rate from surgery was nearly 50%. In the
course of several hundred surgical procedures, including 345 major
operations using hypnoanesthesia as the sole anesthetic, only 5% of
Esdaile's patients died (Kroger, 1977; Van Dyke, 1970). When chemical
anesthesia, in the form of nitrous oxide, ether, and chloroform, came
into vogue, interest in hypnosis waned. Two world wars reawakened
interest in hypnosis for pain management, anesthesia, and the treatment
of battle neuroses.

Research and clinical practice in the past two decades have confirmed what Braid, Esdaile, Elliotson and others demonstrated 150
years ago—that hypnosis can be effective during the preoperative,

intraoperative and postoperative phases of surgery. Due to the predictability of chemical anesthesia and the inability of most adults to enter a sufficiently deep trance to produce and maintain hypnoanesthesia during major surgical procedures, it is unlikely that hypnosis will become a substitute for chemoanesthesia. Hypnosis is, however, increasingly recognized by practitioners as an important adjunct to traditional medical methods of patient management. Hypnosis can facilitate pre- and postoperative procedures, reduce the need for chemoanesthesia, reduce pain and discomfort, and speed the healing process.

Although we talk about the reemergence of hypnosis in medicine and surgery, it has never been entirely absent. Most good physicians intuitively use hypnosis every day, even though the process of relaxing a patient and making positive suggestions may not be recognized as hypnosis. According to Joseph Reyher, the key ingredient is "the individual waiting silently for instructions in a situation that sanctions it" (Gunby, 1977, p. 938). As discussed previously in Chapter 7, most people faced with surgery or a painful medical procedure are in a receptive frame of mind and responsive to any suggestions that will reassure them. Some patients will spontaneously enter a light hypnotic trance as a way of coping with a medical or dental procedure. Many physicians today are recognizing the importance of consciously using tools, such as a patient's own coping mechanisms, that successful physicians of the past have used intuitively with excellent results.

The medical profession's growing interest in hypnosis parallels a growing concern for the patient as a whole person and not just a collection of "interesting pathological novelties," as Van Dyke (1970) described it. Some physicians, Van Dyke continued,

> . . . are so engrossed in the status of a peptic ulcer, an inflamed appendix, or an obstructing gallstone that all of our attention is concentrated on the somatic problems involved, to the exclusion of any awareness of the personality side of our patients. (p. 227)

As this chapter makes clear, by treating the whole person, the physician can achieve better results, both somatic and psychologic.

PREOPERATIVE USES OF HYPNOSIS

Most surgical patients experience anxiety due to their fear of death, postoperative pain, possible complications, or to their unfamiliarity with surgical procedures. Anxiety makes preoperative procedures more difficult and has a negative effect on the patient's psychological and physiological reaction to the stress of anesthesia and surgery. When one is anxious, muscles become tense, the perception of pain increases, and the body's ability to heal itself decreases.

In the mid-nineteenth century, before chemoanesthesia became commonplace, the fear of the excruciating pain associated with surgery was sometimes equal to the fear of death—and often contributed to it. Even now, as Hilgard and Hilgard (1975) expressed it, "it goes without saying that many patients are suffering from some degree of [psychological] pain prior to surgery, and that they anticipate pain after the operation is over" (p. 120). Preoperative fears are frequently calmed by tranquilizing medications. There are, however, several drawbacks to heavy preoperative medication. According to Scott (1976),

> . . . it may complicate anesthesia and recovery from it. More important, it does nothing to alleviate the weeks of terror such patients suffer while awaiting surgery, to modify the fear-provoking mechanism already established in the patient's subconscious mind or to create an improved outlook towards anesthesia and surgery in the future. (p. 796)

Meares (1960), Fredericks (1980), and Jones (1975, 1977) also noted the advantages of reducing or eliminating preoperative medication.

Hypnosis can be a key factor in an alternative approach to the preoperative preparation of patients for major surgery or for any other medical intervention. Before surgery, hypnosis can be induced either through a formal induction or a less structured method that uses suggestions to tie into the patient's own coping mechanisms. An empathic physician who establishes good rapport and makes positive suggestions can greatly assist a patient to reduce the physical and emotional stress of surgery or any medical procedure.

The preoperative use of hypnosis begins with one or more presurgical interviews. Depending on the situation and the needs of the patient, these can be conducted by a surgeon, anesthesiologist, psychologist, psychiatrist, or another member of the surgical team who is trained in hypnosis. The presurgical interview may include either a formal trance induction or the informal use of hypnotic principles to develop an hypnotic interaction with the patient.

There are several important areas to cover in a presurgical interview. The first is to dispel fears regarding surgery, because a patient's feelings and attitudes play an important role in recovery. In a "frank but always tactful" discussion, which Tiwari (1978) referred to as "the art of informing the patient" (p. 25), the surgeon should rehearse the entire process, including what to expect before, during, and after surgery. By allaying presurgical fears, this step in itself may reduce the need for medication before surgery.

When hypnosis is used, a light trance is induced and suggestions are made regarding relaxation and recovery. It is important that all statements be made in positive terms, without equivocation ("You can have the cast off in three months, *if* all goes well.") or negative implications ("You will be without *pain*."). The following suggestions are representative of those recommended by physicians experienced in the use of presurgical hypnosis (Cheek and LeCron, 1968; Fredericks, 1978; Van Dyke, 1970). The exact wording of suggestions should be adapted to patient needs and practitioner preferences:

- Relaxation.

  "Because you are relaxed, you may find yourself needing less anesthetic, although you will receive all that you need."

  "You are looking forward to sleeping well, both before and after the operation."

- Comfort during surgery.

  "You may find yourself becoming progressively more and more comfortable during surgery."

  "Because you are looking forward to being relaxed and comfortable during your surgery, you can look forward to your surgical wound being dry, which allows your surgeon to work quickly."

  "You need not notice hospital noises and operating room conversations during your procedure, unless you are addressed directly. And if you find yourself being aware of activity and conversation in the operating room during your procedure, somehow and in some way this stimulus may help you to relax more and more deeply."

- Postsurgical healing.

  "You are looking forward to awakening relaxed and comfortable, as if from a sound sleep."

"Your bowels and bladder will function promptly."*

"You may find yourself pleasantly hungry and thirsty upon awakening *(unless this suggestion is contraindicated by the surgery)*."

"You are looking forward to your wound healing quickly."

"You will be able to tolerate needles, tubes, catheters, or uncomfortable positions. You can consider appliances to be a temporary part of you that will be discarded as soon as the need for them no longer exists."

Before bringing the patient out of the trance, the practitioner should establish a reinduction signal, such as a touch on the shoulder, so that on the day of surgery the patient will be able to relax more quickly and deeply.

Fredericks (1978) reported the use of a dissociation technique to transfer a patient's attention away from painful stimuli to something pleasant. The patient is asked to visualize himself or herself on a beach or another favorite place. While enjoying himself or herself, he or she feels as if the surgery is being done to someone else. Cheek (1964) reported the similar device of a vacation trip to focus attention away from unpleasant procedures. The trip begins with the hypodermic injection in the morning and continues until the patient has been returned to the hospital room.

Studies by Hart (1980) and Field (1974) looked at the effectiveness of a tape-recorded surgical preparation that includes suggestions of relaxation and rapid postsurgical recovery. Hart (1980) found that open-heart surgery patients using the tapes required less blood post-surgically, felt less anxiety, and had greater feelings of self-control and self-direction than did patients in a control group. Field (1974) found that the taped hypnotic induction procedure was successful in reducing the stressfulness of the impending surgery but had little effect on postoperative pain, anorexia, or insomnia.

Physicians and anesthesiologists who use hypnosis to prepare patients for surgery report more impressive clinical results than the

---

*Cheek and LeCron (1968) took exception to this, arguing that urination is a natural process, and that a suggestion that it will be easy implies that the surgeon thinks the opposite might be the case.

experimental findings of Hart and Field. Some of the benefits of adding hypnotic preparation to the traditional preoperative preparation were summarized by Fredericks (1978) as follows:

1. Less premedication is needed to alleviate preoperative stress.
2. Less chemical anesthesia is needed and, therefore, the patient suffers fewer toxic effects.
3. There is less blood loss during surgery and, therefore, less need for replacement.
4. Patients experience less postoperative nausea and vomiting.
5. There is a prompt return of physiological functions, such as urination and defecation.
6. Wounds heal more rapidly, and patients have a smoother and shorter convalescence.

Beyond normal preoperative anxiety, there is another issue that should be addressed during the preoperative session. Some patients harbor a real fear of dying. In some cases, this fear is consciously expressed, and hypnosis can be used to discover its origin. In others, it remains subconscious, and, if gone untreated, may be responsible for complications or death, during surgery (Cheek, 1964).

Cheek (1964) uses the ideomotor question technique to identify potentially dangerous fears. The patient under hypnosis is asked to answer questions by lifting fingers designated to signify "yes," "no," or "I don't know" in response to a question similar to the following:

> After the sort of surgery I plan for you tomorrow, most of my patients are all well and ready to go home in five days. Does the subconscious part of your mind think you might do even better than that? (p. 57)

A "no" or "I don't know" response is a warning. There is a general consensus among practitioners that in cases where the patient either consciously or unconsciously believes he or she is going to die, the operation should be cancelled and not rescheduled until after the "death wish" has been resolved.

OPERATIVE USES OF HYPNOSIS

As an Adjunct to Chemoanesthesia

The types of suggestions begun before the operation should be continued while the patient is being prepared for surgery. While the intravenous solution is being started or the blood pressure cuff is being put on, it is important to talk to the patient in a calm and reassuring voice, whether or not a trance is induced. A patient who sees the physician as an ally will be more relaxed and will respond better to the stress of anesthesiology than a patient who feels frightened or alienated.

Intraoperatively, the anesthesiologist, whose main concern is the relief of pain, is in an ideal position to use hypnosis. Van Dyke (1970) pointed out that in the operating room, the physician can transfer rapport to the anesthesiologist who will continue with suggestions for relaxation and dissociation. Jones (1975) advocated the use of hypnosis as an important supplement to existing anesthetic techniques. Fredericks (1978, 1980) discussed the use of hypnosis by anesthesiologists and reported on a training program to teach hypnotic techniques to anesthesiology residents. Under this program, the anesthesiologist also conducts the preoperative interview.

The importance of the role that can be played by a hypnotically trained anesthesiologist becomes clearer in light of Cheek's (1962, 1964, 1965) findings that patients under anesthesia continue to hear sounds that are meaningful to them. Like a patient under hypnosis, an anesthetized patient interprets remarks literally. There are several examples of the persistence of hearing under chemoanesthesia.

Cheek (1964) reported the case of a 34-year-old patient undergoing a total vaginal hysterectomy. She was a good hypnotic subject and had extensive preoperative preparation. During surgery, the anesthesiologist casually remarked, "Oh, Dave, that unit of blood is all ready any time she needs it" (p. 58). After the operation, Cheek reinduced hypnosis to review the surgical experience with his patient. At one point, she became so agitated that she was unable to speak for some time. Cheek traced the agitation back to the anesthesiologist's remark. As the patient explained, "I didn't know I might have to get some blood, and I thought something more than you had told me must be wrong" (p. 59).

Levinson (1965) reported on a patient who underwent plastic surgery. During the operation, the surgeon found a lump on the patient's lip and remarked that it could be cancer. Although the patient was later informed the pathologist found the lump to be benign, she nonetheless became progressively more anxious and depressed over a period of 3 months. Under hypnosis, she identified the surgeon's remark as the source of her depression.

These and other cases have shown that although the anesthetized patient does not attend to all operating room sounds, he or she does remember remarks that are either threatening or reassuring. These remarks are interpreted literally and taken personally, regardless of to whom they are addressed. Therefore, a seemingly innocent remark can have traumatic consequences for a patient and interfere with what otherwise might have been a rapid and comfortable convalescence. On the other hand, carefully phrased suggestions, such as a suggestion of coldness to reduce bleeding and inflammation, can facilitate surgical procedures and reduce stress on the patient.

Cheek (1962) suggested and Fredericks (1978) concurred that the anesthesiologist "should talk to the patient during general anesthesia just as he would talk to a conscious patient under spinal anesthesia" (p. 227). This advice applies to all operating room personnel, who should conduct their conversations as if the patient were fully awake and conscious of the surroundings.

Cheek (1965) also found that fear is produced in some patients by unexplained movements or procedures, such as positioning or intubation. He recommended that the anesthesiologist or physician keep the patient informed of each new action during surgery. It is clear from these findings that important preoperative procedures, such as reviewing the operating room scene with the patient, need to be continued and reinforced during surgery as well.

In Special Surgical Techniques

Beyond its uses during general surgery, hypnosis can play an important role in special surgical techniques. A good example is the use of hypnosis in the management of scoliosis by Harrington rod fusion, as reported by Crawford, Jones, Perisho, and Herring (1976) and Jones (1975). During this operation, it is crucial that the physician be able to test whether the spinal cord has been compressed or the vascular supply has been reduced as a result of the rod's straightening action. If the patient can perform a series of intraoperative tests while still on the operating table, the physician can test for vascular compromise and take corrective measures.

In a series of sessions beginning a week or more before surgery, the anesthesiologist places the patient under hypnosis. The patient is familiarized with operating room procedures, taught the movements of the lower extremities designed to test for cord compression, and given suggestions for postoperative recovery. With 30 minutes' notice from the surgeon, the anesthesiologist-hypnotist awakens the patient and leads him or her through performance of the tests. Anesthesia is then reinduced and the surgery completed. The authors report 100% success with this technique in 18 cases, most of whom were teen-aged girls.

Bank and Kerber (1979) reported the use of hypnosis for patients undergoing therapeutic embolizations of the carotid and vertebral arteries. As explained by the authors,

> Our search for the wide awake patient who feels neither anxiety nor discomfort and remains immobile while a life threatening procedure is performed upon him led us to our clinical trials using medical hypnosis. (p. 250)

General endotracheal anesthesia, while satisfying most of these objectives, precludes the continuous evaluation of the patient's neurological state.

Trance is induced the night before the procedure and reinduced before an intravenous line is placed. The patient is taught to produce local anesthesia and given suggestions for relief of postprocedural pain. Bank and Kerber reported that only 4 of 45 procedures (performed on 27 patients) required supplemental narcotic during the procedure and the last 12 patients required no postprocedural narcotic.

A slightly different use of hypnosis was reported by Crasilneck and Hall (1975) in the surgical treatment of severely burned patients. Hypnosis was found to aid greatly in managing the pain of skin grafts and dressing changes that otherwise often required general anesthesia. It also was beneficial in increasing food intake, increasing exercise, and decreasing the use of narcotics for the constant and severe pain of the burn. Many more instances of the use of hypnosis in special surgical or medical procedures are cited in the literature. Suffice it to say here that hypnosis is a versatile medical tool, and that contemporary physicians are just beginning to explore its potential.

As the Sole Anesthetic

Although not the preferred approach by most surgeons, who consider it an adjunct to chemical anesthesia, hypnosis as the sole anesthetic agent does have advantages in certain situations and has been used in recent years for major surgery with great success. Hypnoanesthesia may be indicated (a) in older patients for whom chemical anesthesia would be risky, (b) for emergency cases where the patient has a full stomach and thus cannot receive a general anesthetic, (c) in cases of pulmonary infection, which increases the risks inherent in inhalation anesthesia, and (d) in neurosurgical procedures that require the patient's conscious cooperation.

Recent literature lists a number of successful major operations using hypnoanesthesia. For example, Kroger (1977) performed a Caesarean section using hypnosis as the sole anesthetic. Cheek and LeCron (1968) reported performance of a breast biopsy and referred to the success of a St. Louis physician, Lester Millikin, who used hypnosis for mastectomy, cholecystectomy, and gastrectomy with high-risk patients. The time required to induce and maintain anesthesia is considerably greater than that required when hypnosis is used as an adjunct to chemoanesthesia.

Emphasizing that perhaps the best use of hypnosis is for management of routine procedures, rather than for "dramatic and impressive conditions and cures," Andolesk and Novik (1980) reported four case studies in which they described the use of informal hypnotic techniques with 3- and 4-year-old children facing minor surgery in an emergency room. Through use of talking inductions and indirect suggestions, these authors helped the children use their own natural coping mechanisms to relax and undergo minor surgery without anesthetic: ". . . children are motivated by fear, pain, and curiosity, and are eager to grab onto suggestions that may relieve their fear" (p. 504).

Whether hypnosis is used as a sole anesthetic, an adjunct to chemical anesthesia, or simply as a technique for focusing attention away from a painful procedure, the results are impressive. The argument that hypnosis is too time-consuming for modern medical practice is easily countered by those who have used it successfully. Van Dyke (1970) pointed out that the use of a rapid induction method makes the time factor negligible. Andolesk and Novik (1980) felt that the time investment was well worth the enhanced pride and feeling of self-mastery experienced by the children they treated. Often, hypnosis saves time by avoiding prolonged battles with fearful children. Both surgeons and anesthesiologists are finding that when the hypnotic process is integrated into the traditional medical management of the patient, the real time spent on hypnosis alone is minimal.

POSTOPERATIVE USES OF HYPNOSIS

There are two major ways in which hypnosis is used postoperatively. First, pre- and intraoperative suggestions for relaxation, comfort, and healing can be reinforced following surgery while the patient is in the recovery room. Second, psychological problems arising from surgical procedures or poor patient management can be treated with hypnosis after the patient has been released from the hospital.

Most postoperative problems, including pain, nausea, fear of coughing, and the need to remain in an uncomfortable position to accommodate appliances, are addressed through posthypnotic suggestions made during the preoperative interview. As pointed out earlier, proper preparation of the patient can result in a shorter, more pain-free convalescence and a reduced need for narcotics.* Patients can also be taught pain management through self-hypnosis.

Nearly 20 years ago, Werbel (1964) reported on his use of hypnosis to control the violent physical reactions manifested by some patients as they awakened from a general anesthetic. The uncontrollable muscular activity was both frightening and dangerous for the patients, who sometimes dislodged tubes or appliances. Of 50 patients to whom Werbel gave the posthypnotic suggestion that they would awaken from the anesthetic as if from normal sleep, only one manifested any degree of muscular violence. C. W. Jones (personal communication, December 1983) also found that when hypnosis is used during arousal from general anesthesia, hypnosis patients experience less agitation.

While some adverse reactions can be prevented through careful patient management, others cannot always be foreseen. When problems surface while a patient is convalescing after leaving the hospital, they can be treated through hypnosis. For example, Deyoub (1980) cited two cases in which hypnosis was used to relieve hospital-induced stress. A 53-year-old man who began suffering from insomnia immediately after being discharged from the hospital following coronary bypass surgery was cured using a simple reconditioning procedure. A 30-year-old woman who refused postoperative radiotherapy following a mastectomy overcame her fears through hypnosis.

Bensen (1971) attempted to evaluate the effectiveness of postanesthetic communication with 100 surgical patients, including 30 children. He found that patients who received carefully phrased, positive sugges-

---

*Cheek (1968) recommended that the physician be certain that a hospital staff does not, as a matter of course, administer pain-relieving drugs to a patient using hypnosis.

tions during their recovery from anesthetic had an unusually rapid and comfortable convalescence. The author acknowledged the difficulty of separating the effects of postanesthetic suggestion from the other important phases of patient management, including the relationship between patient and surgeon, the validity of pre- and posthypnotic suggestion, and the atmosphere of faith and confidence created by the surgeon. All obviously play an important part in the overall management of the surgical patient. However, it seems clear that a consistent application of hypnotic principles, from presurgical interview to postsurgical follow-up, can have a cumulative beneficial effect on the patient.

CASE REPORTS

Case 1.   *A 17-year-old female was scheduled for retinal detachment repair. Her medical history documented a long history of child abuse and there was evidence of mild mental retardation. Her anesthesiologist rated this young woman's level of anxiety as being very high while she was in the holding area of the operation suite. Upon inquiry, she mentioned that she would like to be home in her own bed. Using this as a cue, the anesthesiologist employed a permissive hypnotic technique suggesting that the patient concentrate on various sensory inputs and images of feel, smell, temperature, hearing, and vision (various colors) associated with being in her own bed. Following these suggestions, there was a marked reduction in visible anxiety. A hypnotic state was maintained in the operating room before and during anesthesia and upon emergence from the general anesthesia in the recovery room. The operating room nurse who had observed the patient's early anxiety remarked on her transformation and was surprised to learn that the reduction in overt anxiety was the result of verbal guided imagery and not the administration of a pharmacologic parenteral agent. The total time involved in inducing and maintaining a state of hypnosis in this patient, apart from other tasks of medical management and supervision, was approximately 15 minutes.*

Case 2.   *BH was a 55-year-old female admitted to the cardiothoracic surgery service for debridement of a previously infected median sternotomy wound. The ward staff reported that she constantly complained, not only about the staff not paying attention to her, but also about her discomfort. Her dressing changes, which were required four times a day, were exceedingly difficult and caused her great discomfort.*

   Her surgeon presented hypnosis to BH as a therapeutic approach that would be useful in facilitating her relaxation and helping her to be more comfortable with the dressing changes, thus reducing her need for pain medication. During the test for responsiveness to hypnosis, BH spontaneously entered a somnambulistic state of hypnosis. She continued to respond exceedingly well to suggestions of relaxation and well-being. It was suggested to her that her recovery would progress rapidly, that she would require progressively less pain medication, that her dressing changes would progressively be more comfortable, that she would heal her wound well without further infections, and that she would be able to increase the blood supply to her wound, thereby helping her body to accept a skin graft.

Her surgeon also suggested that when he said "sleep, B (her first name)," she could immediately enter a deep state of self-hypnosis and would not require any premedication before her dressing changes. This induction process produced the desired results: During the first and subsequent dressing changes, BH rapidly entered self-hypnosis and required no premedication.

During the 2 weeks following BH's first session with hypnosis, her surgeon saw her two additional times and reinforced the earlier suggestions. BH also created techniques of her own designed to speed her hospital recovery.

BH's surgeon reported that after her first session with hypnosis, she no longer required pain medication before dressing changes or for general pain reduction and that she had become cheerful on the ward, responsive to the staff, and a pleasure to work with. She healed her wound well, including her skin graft, without any intercurrent infection. BH left the hospital 2½ weeks after her first hypnotic session.

Case 3. A 58-year-old man was admitted to the hospital for removal of a cancerous tumor in his throat, placement of a tracheostomy, and subsequent chemotherapy. While in the holding area, he indicated that he was somewhat anxious and apprehensive, due to the nature of the surgery and the uncertain outcome of chemotherapy. On inquiry, he related that since his retirement from the Navy, he had been a professional truck driver. His favorite and most relaxing activity was driving across country in his truck. Using this as a cue, the hypnotherapist who was assisting the surgeon induced a light trance using the Stein clenched-fist technique. The hypnotherapist asked the patient to see himself driving his truck on an interstate highway towards some destination and to report on what he saw and what he was doing when he reached this destination.

During this time, an intravenous line was started and secured with no visible discomfort to the patient. A few minutes later, after continued permissive indirect suggestion of relaxation and sensory images associated with driving his truck, the patient mentioned that he had arrived in Fort Lauderdale. He had just parked his truck and was walking into the Oasis Truck Stop, where it was his habit to buy a large hamburger and then go across the street to the Cloud 9 Bar where he would drink several cold beers. During this period, the patient's respiration slowed markedly, his arms demonstrated no tendon reflex, and his eyelids felt very heavy.

The patient was encouraged to focus on other sensory images of taste, smell, and texture while he was eating his hamburger and drinking his beer. It *was also suggested that he could anchor himself to these images if he wished by continuing to close his preferred hand, and that following his surgery, the images of driving his truck, eating the hamburger, and drinking the beer could facilitate his comfort. The patient was given further suggestions for relaxation, inattention to operating room conversation, and postoperative recovery. He was reminded that it was his day to rest and relax and the doctors' day to do all the work.*

The surgical procedure was completed with no complications, and upon arrival in the recovery room, the patient spontaneously commented that he had never tasted a beer as cold as that beer he had tasted before his surgery. The patient was seen three additional times while he was in the hospital; he reported that he continued to employ hypnosis to facilitate comfort in the surgical area, reduce his frustration about the removal of his larynx, and facilitate sleep.

The total time involved in inducing and maintaining hypnosis, apart from other medical procedures, was approximately 15 minutes.

SAMPLE INDUCTION

The following induction procedure was used by Jane Firth while she was a staff anesthesiologist at the Naval Regional Medical Center in San Diego. Although an anesthesiologist using hypnosis will ideally have the opportunity for a preoperative interview with the patient, Firth (personal communication, July 15, 1980) reported that she often saw the patient for the first time in the operating room. Even in this situation, however, hypnosis can be very effective if the anesthesiologist adjusts the procedure to the needs and responses of the patient. In only a moment or two, Firth was able to determine a patient's likes and dislikes and ask what he or she would like to be doing at that moment. This information provided an outline for induction and deepening suggestions that Firth modified as the case required. Her suggestions could also be modified for use with regional analgesia. While placing the intravenous catheter and completing the necessary paperwork, Firth would offer these suggestions:

Today is your day to relax completely where you are safe and all of your needs can be met. . . . Today is our day to do all of the work. . . . Make yourself comfortable. . . . We expect you will have a pleasant experience here today. . . . Let yourself relax. . . . You may be just as calm and quiet and comfortable as you want to be. . . . Here in the operating suite you may listen only to voices that speak directly to you. . . . You may pay no attention to any of the other sights or sounds or feelings in the room, . . . so you may pay no attention to bright lights, doctor talk, or people kicking the cart. . . . Rest back easily; breathe deeply, clearly, and easily. . . . You may let every muscle of your body be loose and relaxed and comfortable. . . . Let your eyes close, for when you do, you will become naturally calmer and quieter and more comfortable. . . . You may know we are performing parts of procedures, but you may be comfortable . . . just as calm and quiet and comfortable . . . as you want to be. . . . You will have good anesthetic and a good procedure, and you may feel good and healthy and comfortable.

Firth would sometimes increase relaxation by further suggesting that the patient move up or down a staircase or count backwards from 100, feeling more and more relaxed with each step or number. With the initiation of general anesthesia procedures, Firth would continue as follows:

You may feel your breathing. . . . You may hear your breathing. . . . You may think a beautiful thought or a specific image of your choosing. . . . If you would rather be drinking a bourbon-and-7 Up . . . or running in a particular locale . . . or minutely examining every detail of a flower garden . . . or listening to your favorite music . . . or resting at home in your own bed, . . . whatever you enjoy . . . focus on that image . . . thought . . . or idea.

All of the senses were employed to involve the patient as completely as possible in a chosen image, thought, or experience. Firth used ambient stimuli to increase relaxation and would suggest that:

Everything you experience today . . . somehow and in some way . . . will contribute to your increasing level of relaxation, comfort, well-being and health.

The overhead light might be the sun, the blue-gray linen might be the sea or the sky, the warm, tingly feeling of a conduction anesthetic might be warm sand on the beach, the mask of an inhalation anesthetic might be the mask of a pilot or a scuba diver. The possibilities were unlimited.

Firth would continue to make positive suggestions throughout the operation, even with patients under general anesthesia. At the end of the procedure, she would tell the patient:

Your procedure is finished. . . . You may feel alert, refreshed, good, healthy, and comfortable. . . . You will bleed very little. . . . You may heal very fast. . . . You won't become infected. . . . You may feel good and healthy and comfortable. . . . You know very well how to relax and increase your level of comfort . . . and in the same way that you were able to relax here in the operating room . . . you can let yourself relax during your recovery time . . . here in the hospital . . . or at home . . . progressively . . . more and more easily.

SUMMARY

The value of hypnosis in a surgical setting is primarily as an adjunct to the preoperative, intraoperative, and postoperative management of a surgery patient. Whether or not they are in a formal trance, most patients awaiting surgery or a painful medical procedure are receptive to any suggestions that bear upon their condition. Therefore, the impact of surgeons, anesthesiologists, nurses, and other hospital staff on the patient can be tremendous. A careless remark can compound the stress of an already anxious patient. Conversely, good rapport with the patient and carefully phrased suggestions for relaxation and recovery can facilitate preoperative procedures, reduce the need for chemo-anesthesia, reduce pain and discomfort, and speed the healing process.

Nearly 150 years ago, surgeons experienced great success using hypnoansthesia for major surgery. Today hypnosis is commonly used for major surgery only in cases where chemoanesthesia would be highly risky. However, hypnosis is playing an increasingly important role in special surgical procedures that require a patient's conscious coopera-tion. For minor surgical procedures, hypnoanesthesia is being used successfully on a more routine basis.

The evidence that patients hear remarks even under deep anesthe-sia, that they perceive as relevant to them, further emphasizes the need for a positive and supportive attitude on the part of the medical staff. Preoperative suggestions that are continued and reinforced during and after surgery have a cumulative effect, leading to a shorter and more comfortable convalescence. Hypnosis is a potent and versatile medical intervention, the uses of which have only begun to be explored by surgeons and anesthesiologists.

FURTHER READING

Bresler, D. E., & Trubo, R. (1979). *Free yourself from pain*. New York: Simon and Schuster.

Cheek, D. B., & LeCron, L. M. (1968) *Clinical hypnotherapy* (chapter 17). New York: Grune & Stratton.

Fredericks, L. E. (1978). Teaching of hypnosis in the overall approach to the surgical patient. *American Journal of Clinical Hypnosis, 20,* 175-183.

Jones, C. W. (1975). The use of hypnosis in anesthesiology. *Journal of National Medical Association, 67,* 122-125, 175.

REFERENCES

Andolesk, K. & Novik, B. (1980). Use of hypnosis with children. *Journal of Family Practice, 10,* 503-507.

Bank, W. O. & Kerber, C. W. (1979). Medical hypnosis during therapeutic embolizations of the carotid and vertebral arteries. *Neuroradiology, 17,* 249-252.

Bensen, V. B. (1971). One hundred cases of post-anesthetic suggestion in the recovery room. *American Journal of Clinical Hypnosis, 14,* 9-15.

Cheek, D. B. (1962). Importance of recognizing that surgical patients behave as though hypnotized. *American Journal of Clinical Hypnosis, 4,* 227.

Cheek, D. B. (1964). Further evidence of persistence of hearing under chemoanesthesia: Detailed case report. *American Journal of Clinical Hypnosis, 7,* 55-59.

Cheek, D.B. (1965, February). Can surgical patients react to what they hear under anesthesia? *Journal of the American Association of House Anesthesiologists,* 36-38.

Cheek, D. B., & LeCron, L. M. (1968). *Clinical hypnotherapy.* New York: Grune & Stratton.

Crasilneck, H. B. and Hall, J. A. (1975). *Clinical hypnosis: Principles and applications.* New York: Grune & Stratton.

Crawford, A. H., Jones, C. W., Perisho, J. A., & Herring, J. B. (1976). Hypnosis for monitoring intraoperative spinal cord function. *Anesthesia and Analgesia, 55,* 42-44.

Deyoub, P. L. (1980). Hypnosis for the relief of hospital-induced stress. *Journal of the American Society of Psychosomatic Dentistry and Medicine, 27,* 105-109.

Field, P. B. (1974). Effects of tape-recorded hypnotic preparation for surgery. *International Journal of Clinical and Experimental Hypnosis, 22,* 54-61.

Fredericks, L. E. (1978). Teaching of hypnosis in the overall approach to the surgical patient. *American Journal of Clinical Hypnosis, 20,* 175-183.

Fredericks, L. E. (1980). The value of teaching hypnosis in the practice of anesthesiology. *International Journal of Clinical and Experimental Hypnosis, 28,* 6-15.

Gunby, P. (1977). Hypnosis gains stature as serious modality of medical treatment. *Journal of the American Medical Association, 237,* 937-940.

Hart, R. R. (1980). The influence of a taped hypnotic induction treatment procedure on the recovery of surgery patients. *International Journal of Clinical and Experimental Hypnosis, 28,* 324-332.

Hilgard, E. R., & Hilgard, J. R. (1975). *Hypnosis in the relief of pain.* Palo Alto, CA: Kaufman.

Jones, C. W. (1975). The use of hypnosis in anesthesiology. *Journal of the National Medical Association, 67,* 122-125.

Jones, C. W. (1977). Hypnosis and spinal fusion by Harrington instrumentation. *American Journal of Clinical Hypnosis, 19,* 155–157.

Kroger, W. S. (1977). *Clinical and experimental hypnosis.* Philadelphia: J. B. Lippincott.

Levinson, B. (1965). States of awareness under general anesthesia. *British Journal of Anaesthesia, 37,* 544–546.

Meares, A. (1960). *A system of medical hypnosis.* Philadelphia: W. B. Saunders.

Scott, D. L. (1976). Hypnotic psychotherapy for pathological preoperative fear. *Anesthesia, 31,* 796–798.

Tiwari, R. (1978). Pain in the surgeon's practice. In *Current concepts in postoperative pain.* Report based on a symposium for the annual meeting of the American Society of Anesthesiologists, New Orleans.

Van Dyke, P. B. (1970). Some uses of hyposis in the management of the surgical patient. *American Journal of Clinical Hypnosis, 12,* 227–235.

Werbel, E. W. (1964). Use of hypnosis in certain surgical problems. *American Journal of Clinical Hypnosis, 7,* 81–85.

9

Pain Control

Robert L. Magnuson, MD

One of the most important of all considerations in inducing hypnosis is meeting adequately the patient as a personality and his needs as an individual.

—Milton Erickson
Naturalistic Techniques of Hypnosis

P ain control through hypnosis is often associated with phenomena that bear no relationship to its legitimate use in a clinical setting. For example, stage hypnotists who hold a flame beneath the hand of a "hypnotized" volunteer so that the flame licks the hand and leaves it blackened are merely performing a trick. As long as the flame is kept moving, the volunteer's hand will not become uncomfortably hot. Hypnosis has only been used to enable members of the audience to persuade themselves to participate in the demonstration.

Pain control has been one of the most important uses of hypnosis throughout its long history, and it continues to be an important use of modern clinical hypnosis. Despite advances in medical technology that have produced new chemicals, surgical procedures, and other treatments for pain, there is still a profound need for "expeditious, inexpensive, nonaddicting and safe" hypnosis (Wain, 1980). As the mechanisms of pain and its control through hypnosis have undergone scientific scrutiny, the irrefutable effectiveness of this safe modality has been begrudgingly accepted in the health field (Gorsky and Borsky, 1981).

THE PROBLEM OF PAIN
Pain is a common problem in our society. The two major types are acute pain and chronic pain. Although there is not a precise distinction

between the two, pain that causes significant alterations in functioning for more than 3–6 months will be referred to as chronic; pain of shorter duration is termed acute.

Low back pain is the second largest cause of missed workdays in the United States (National Safety Council, 1980). Approximately 8%–10% of the population suffers from some form of migraine headache (Waters, 1975). The Arthritis Association estimates that about 10% of the American population suffers from arthritis and places the cost at over $13 billion annually in lost productivity and medical expenses. Similar figures come from other sources (Feuerstein and Skjei, 1979). It is estimated that over $50 billion is spent annually on treatment costs and lost workdays as a result of chronic pain (Bonica, 1977). To our society, the cost of chronic pain is enormous. To the individual, its effects can be devastating.

PAIN THEORIES

Pain is not just a simple sensation; it is a very complex perception. Old theories of pain, such as the specific and pattern theories, have been inadequate. The specific theory posits pain receptors in the peripheral nervous system that, when stimulated, send impulses to the brain, thus producing the experience of pain. The pattern theory argues that peripheral stimulation alone is not enough, and that stimulus intensity and central summation are the critical determinants of pain (Melzack and Wall, 1965).

One of the most widely accepted contemporary theories of pain is the "gate control theory." Proposed in 1965 by Melzack and Wall, this theory postulates the existence of a "gate" in the dorsal horn portion of the spinal cord that can close under certain conditions to block out pain. Some portions of this theory have been supported by research, and others have undergone modifications (Dennis and Melzack, 1977). In the 1970s, other researchers (e.g., Hughes, 1975; Li and Chung, 1976; and Terenius and Wahlstrom, 1975) isolated opioid receptors and opioid peptides, such as endorphins, in the brain. Their presence appears to act as part of a natural pain suppression system. Threatening stress, exercise, and sexual activity have been thought to increase the release of endorphins and are being investigated.

If endogenous opioid peptides are needed to control comfort, it is not surprising that depression, which lowers endorphin levels, has a significant relationship to pain problems. The complexities of the pain perception processes have been the subject of ongoing research. Several authors have noted the effects of tricyclic antidepressants and stimulants to decrease pain perception and of depressants to increase pain behavior (Forrest et al., 1977; Lee and Spencer, 1977; Ward, Bloom, and Freidel, 1979). Hundreds of neuroactive peptides are being identified. With these discoveries, the new data on the behavior, depression, and sleep patterns of pain patients have a theoretical foundation.

There is some evidence that hypnotic analgesia is not mediated by the endorphin system (Goldstein and Hilgard, 1975; Barber and Mayer, 1977), but any definitive conclusions are premature at this point. While it is certain that other mechanisms will be found in the future, pain perception can be explained by presently known mechanisms: The impulse, which arises from physical stimulation of the peripheral nerve, synapses in the dorsal horn of the spinal cord, traverses the spinothalamic tract and the neospinothalamic tract to the brainstem and thalamus, and finally interacts with the hypothalamus and limbic forebrain structures.

PLACEBO EFFECT

The placebo effect, which is the action of the patient's imagination augmented by the practitioner's expectation, has impressive potency. Studies to test the effectiveness of new drugs require careful experimental design because the placebo effect can neutralize the pharmacologic effect of even the most powerful drugs. One study demonstrated that ipecac, an emetic that produces vomiting, could actually relieve nausea and vomiting when it was presented by a physician as a cure for these symptoms (Feuerstein and Skjei, 1979). A controversial drug, chymopapain, was injected into herniated lumbar discs in 100 patients and produced better relief than the traditional laminectomy or laminectomy-fusion in another group of 100 patients (Dabezies and Brunet, 1978). Even though another study of 97 subjects had demonstrated improvement of the nerve root function with electromyography in patients who had been injected with chymopapain (McNeil, Huncke, and Pesch, 1977), the release of this drug in the United States was delayed as a result of the double-blind studies that showed no significant difference between it and a placebo (Schetschenau, Ramirez, Johnston, Wiggs, and Martins, 1976).

While double-blind testing of surgical procedures, such as laminectomy, is difficult, double-blind experimental design to evaluate hypnotic effectiveness may be impossible. These difficulties were less apparent when a formal induction was thought to be an essential part of hypnosis. Now, there is a tremendous diversity of recognized induction techniques. If the placebo effect is an action of the imagination, and clinical hypnosis is the therapeutic use of the imagination and expectation, these ubiquitous elements of normal therapeutic relationships cannot be ignored in control groups.

The use of biofeedback is popular in the treatment of pain today. A study of patients with impaired circulation to their hands used high-quality temperature biofeedback with half the group and "paired-yolk" bogus biofeedback with the other half (R. S. Fowler, University of Washington, personal communication, December 1979). Both groups achieved the same improvement in circulation. One explanation for these results is that the process held the attention of both groups for a significant period, and both groups believed that they could improve blood flow to their hands. If hypnosis is considered a natural, frequently spontaneous phenomenon, and if the placebo effect is understood as a hypnotic phenomenon, we can argue that the participants in the biofeedback study received an informal induction, and that an informal hypnotic induction may be responsible for the success of other treatment modalities.

PRACTITIONER ATTITUDES

Because so much meaning is communicated by postures and nuances of expression, the practitioner should be conscious of what he or she presents to the patient's perception. If the practitioner believes that only imaginary pain can be treated by the imagination, that attitude will be detected by the patient. If, on the other hand, the practitioner believes that all pain is real, regardless of its source, and that the nervous system can control any pain with powerful mechanisms that can be harnessed by the imagination, this confidence will be communicated to the patient.

The literature on hypnosis and pain is filled with phrases such as "For subjects highly *susceptible* to hypnosis" (Hilgard and Hilgard, 1975). A common connotation of this term suggests that those who can use hypnosis for pain relief have a weakness in resisting influence. Although "capable of treatment of a specific kind" is a dictionary definition for "susceptible," the use of the word would be countertherapeutic for patients who accept the more popular connotation. As Alman and Carney (1981) noted, hypnotic susceptibility tests may measure responsiveness to direct induction procedures and bear little relevance when indirect procedures are employed.

The effective practitioner also will conceptualize the patient's goals in positive rather than negative terms. Because the unconscious mind does not register negatives, asking a patient not to think about pain will surely produce the opposite result. A positive approach helps the patient to focus on increasing degrees of comfort. Bressler and Trubo (1979) suggested that patients rate their condition on a scale of +10 (feeling great) to −10 (feeling terrible). A comfort scale (Listug, Damsbo, and Magnuson, 1980), where zero is as bad as one could possibly feel and 100 is as good as one could feel, is another positive approach that allows the patient to focus on positive or comfortable sensations. The goal is the presence of comfort, not the absence of pain.

Central to the practitioner's approach to treatment must be a basic respect for the patient and the patient's ability to control pain. By discussing the problem of pain and outlining treatment options, the practitioner can enable the patient to make an informed decision. Some patients have been so trained to submit passively to the doctor, who supposedly knows best and fixes all, that it is a struggle to persuade them to take an active part in the healing process. If all hypnosis is viewed as self-hypnosis, then the practitioner does not try to take control and responsibility away from the patient. The practitioner's role becomes one of a coach who teaches or guides a player but does not try to play the game for him or her. The effective practitioner helps the patient assume responsibility for pain management, and if necessary, deal with the reasons for failure.

IMPENDING ACUTE PAIN

Impending acute pain, including pain associated with diagnostic or treatment procedures, is generally easy to manage with positive suggestions and without a formal induction. There ordinarily are few psychological conflicts with turning off the pain. Usually, the alternative option is to hurt right then and there, and usually there is no reward for hurting. By explaining the procedure carefully with a selection of comfortable terms, avoiding negative suggestions ("This will not hurt."), and giving neutral instructions ("You will feel some pressure," or "you will be surprised how little this bothers you."), the practitioner can allow most patients to remain comfortable.

Many patients who have not been taught self-hypnosis will spontaneously put themselves into a trance state in order to tolerate an uncomfortable procedure. This phenomenon was observed in a 7-year-old boy who collided with a truck while he was riding his bicycle and who ended up in the emergency room. As the medical staff prepared to sew him up, he quietly read every detail of the x-ray report that he had been asked to hold. While he stared at the paper, the intern injected some lidocaine around the laceration over the pubis and noticed that there was no response to pain. The boy just kept looking at the piece of paper. So the intern started asking, "Do you feel this? Does this hurt?" as he poked around with the hypodermic needle. Finally the boy objected, "Are you doing that on purpose?" He was quite willing to tolerate the procedures necessary to sew him up, but he would not tolerate someone sticking him with a needle just to see if it hurt. This case also demonstrates the importance of the context and meaning of the sensation of pain.

If a formal induction is necessary or desired by the patient, the patient can easily be taught to achieve an appropriate level of hypnosis using the induction that will be presented later in this chapter. Any imagery with which the practitioner and the patient are comfortable can be used.

In some cases of impending pain, suffering can begin before the procedure. This suffering in anticipation of the event is common, for example, among cancer patients who develop nausea on the way to receive chemotherapy or among dental patients who feel the pain of the drill before the dentist has begun drilling. In such cases, the practitioner should address psychological factors, such as the memories of past experiences or expectations communicated by others, before using hypnosis for pain control. The patient may find a book on self-hypnosis helpful. *Self-Hypnotism: The Technique and Its Use in Daily Living* (LeCron, 1964) is recommended for its detailed discussion of the use of self-hypnosis in tension, pain, smoking, overweight, asthma, and emotional troubles. This book can expand on what is taught in therapy sessions. Other books may also complement the process. Occasionally, one can ask the patient to read the books before giving the instruction in self-hypnosis.

IMPEDIMENTS TO PAIN RELIEF

If a particular treatment does not work, the reason should be sought. If hypnosis, which is primarily a psychological process, does not work, the reason is usually a psychological one. As discussed earlier in this chapter, organic pain responds well to psychological approaches. An obstacle to relief, such as depression, may have nothing to do with the cause of the pain. Hypnotherapy can be used first to help resolve the depression and afterward to help the patient manage the pain by finding an acceptable alternative to hurting.

Since pain is not a mechanism of the conscious mind for dealing with problems, the practitioner can be most successful using approaches for dealing with the unconscious. Ideomotor questioning is a powerful technique for uncovering unconscious conflicts that are interfering with pain control. Questions put to the inner mind may be answered by pre-established, involuntary movements of the fingers as they are guided by the unconscious to signify: "yes," "no," "I don't know," or "I don't want to answer." It is almost always productive to review LeCron's seven keys (conflict, motivation, identification, masochism, imprinting, organ language, and past experiences) for identifying unconscious conflicts (see Cheek and LeCron, 1968, and Chapter 7). An alternative method is to ask the patient to visualize a chalkboard and write each "key" on the board while it is defined. Then the patient is asked to try to erase them and report which keys can't be erased, "as if they are painted on the chalkboard" (Cheek and LeCron, 1968).

Once the problem has been identified by the unconscious, the practitioner can use a variety of techniques to remove the impediment without dealing with it on a conscious level. These techniques may include the Stein clenched-fist displacement (Damsbo, 1979), Ericksonian resolutions (Haley, 1973), or subliminal therapy (Yager, 1980).

CHRONIC PAIN

Feuerstein and Skjei (1979) summarized the characteristics that typify the person with the chronic pain syndrome:

- Persistent pain despite multiple attempts by health professionals to relieve it.
- Sleep problems.
- Change in appetite.
- Fatigue.
- Depressed mood (pessimism about the future).
- Chronic anxiety.
- Hypochondriasis.
- Loss of interest in social activities.
- Breakdown of family relationships.
- Multiple drug use or abuse.
- Reduction in physical activity.
- Increased time spent in bed or lying down.
- Reduction in sexual activity.
- Changes in normal recreational pursuits.

The variety of these characteristics makes it reasonable to expect that when a patient fails to achieve adequate relief with the simple approach described for acute pain, a multifactoral, multidisciplinary approach may be needed. The treatment of chronic pain may require weeks of hospitalization in a special pain rehabilitation unit. Many authors have written extensively about the use of hypnosis to break the destructive cycle of chronic pain (Barber and Adrian, 1982; Sacerdote, 1970, 1982; Wain, 1980). For further information on hypnosis and pain management, see Chapter 7.

SAMPLE INDUCTION

That pain in which psychological factors play a minimal role will respond to simple hypnotherapy approaches. Of the many approaches described in the literature, the practitioner should choose the verbalization with which he or she is most comfortable. The one included below is a combination of concepts attributed to Elman (1970), Damsbo (1979), and LeCron (Cheek and LeCron, 1968), plus a simplified explanation of the gate theory. Following a preparatory discussion, the induction, deepening, and pain control verbalization can usually be delivered verbatim.

Preparation

Do you know anything about hypnosis? Here is my 30-second course on what hypnosis is and isn't. All hypnosis is really self-hypnosis. It is a natural phenomenon. Most of us go in and out of it several times a day. We call it daydreaming, concentrating, or trying to remember. Some people use it to prepare for athletic competition; some to get to sleep. On your first visit, if you want, I can teach you four things. One, I can guide you into the state. Two, I will show you how to turn off pain, anytime, anywhere, as much as you want for as long as you want. Three, I'll show you how to reenter the state very quickly and very easily anytime you wish. And four, I'll show you how to come out of the state feeling good. Do you have any questions?

(If there are many questions, they may reflect significant resistance that will need to be resolved.)

Induction and Deepening

I will ask you to play a little game. It is the kind of game you used to play when you were a little kid. I'm going to ask you to make believe, to pretend that your eyes just won't open, and while you're pretending, I'm going to ask you to try to open them. As soon as you experience the feeling that no matter how hard you try to open them, they just won't open, then you can relax those eyes and let that nice feeling in those eyes go all through your body. I would like you to really experience that. Really pull on those eyelids, and as soon as you experience the feeling that they just won't open, then relax those eyes and let that nice feeling in your eyes go all through your body, clear down to your toes.

In a moment, I will ask you to open your eyes and close them. As you do that, you can increase your relaxation tenfold over what it is right now. Now open your eyes . . . and close them. In a moment, I will ask you to do that again. This time you can double the relaxation that you have already achieved. So now open . . . and close them. That's right. . . .

I'm going to ask you to use your imagination again. I'm going to ask you to imagine a long stairway. Which way do you want your stairway to go? Up or down? (*Most patients choose up.*)

Very good. Imagine a long stairway. It might have lots of landings, lots of turns. It might even be deeply carpeted so that each step is nice and soft. Think back to a time when you could walk comfortably on the stairway. Imagine yourself walking comfortably on that stairway, letting each step increase your relaxation even further. I'm going to ask that you walk on that stairway of relaxation until you are relaxed enough. When you are relaxed enough, the stairway will open out onto a big panel of switches. Each switch will have a little light over it and some of those lights will be on. When you come to the panel of switches, let your right hand rise so that I will know that you are there. While you're walking on that stairway of relaxation, I will explain how you can use those switches to achieve your goal of comfort.

Pain Control Imagery

When you experience pain, it starts out as an impulse that comes into your spinal cord and there it stops on a neuron. If that neuron fires, it sends an impulse up to your brain where you perceive the pain. If that neuron fires, it can also send impulses to other neurons near it in your spinal cord. When they fire, some of those can send impulses to the muscles in that area of the body, causing them to tighten up. Others can send impulses to blood vessels in that area, causing them to tighten up and reduce the flow of blood to that area.

On that neuron where that impulse first comes into your spinal cord and stops, there are hundreds of other endings. When they fire, some of those endings make it easier for the neuron to fire. Others make it more difficult for that neuron to fire. So it is simply the balance of on and off impulses that determines whether that neuron fires. You can use the image of those switches to shift that balance as far as you wish.

Pause and wait for the hand to rise. If there is a long wait, ask if the patient is almost there. If not, ask what he or she is experiencing. There may be psychological factors blocking relief of the pain that need to be dealt with.

Very good! What color are the lights that are on?

The answer provides verbal feedback that the lights are visualized and reinforces the concept that the patient can speak while in hypnosis.

Very good! In a moment, I will ask you to start turning off those switches with the lights on. As you do that, almost immediately, you should feel relief coming into that area. As you turn off a few more, you should experience the muscles in that area relaxing even further. When you've turned off half the switches, you should experience a pleasant warmth come into that area as the blood flow returns to normal and the body speeds up its own healing processes. As you begin to experience the warmth, let your left hand rise so that I will know that that is what you are experiencing. If you notice your left hand wanting to rise before you have conscious awareness of the warmth, that's okay. It just means that the increased circulation has been perceived on a subconscious level and that you should have conscious awareness within a moment.

Again, wait for the feedback. If the delay is too long, ask the patient what he or she is experiencing.

Very good! Go ahead and turn off as many of the switches that are still on as you feel it is right to turn off at this time. If you turn them all off, you should be completely comfortable. If you choose not to turn them all off at this time, that's okay because you can go back any time you wish and turn off more. Turn off as many as you feel it is appropriate at this time, then let me know, and we will continue.

Again wait for the feedback. If the delay is too long, ask what the patient is experiencing.

Very good! Now take a moment and lock all those switches off that you turned off, so that they will not accidentally come back on, and so that you can remain this comfortable for as long as you wish.

You can use those switches anytime, anywhere, as much as you want, for as long as you want. If it is an acute pain like that of an appendicitis, you would not want to turn it all the way off until the medical evaluation was begun. Once that pain has served its useful purpose, then you can feel free to turn it all the way off if you wish.

Reinduction of Self-Hypnosis

In a moment, I will ask you to bring yourself out of this state. But before I do that, I want to explain how you can reenter this pleasant state very quickly and very easily anytime that you wish. All you have to do is play that little game. Pretend that your eyes just won't open. Then while you are pretending, try to open them, and as soon as you experience the feeling that those eyes just won't open, relax them and feel yourself glide back into this pleasant state.

Most of the things that you will want to achieve with self-hypnosis you can achieve at the very lightest level. If you need more relaxation, go to your stairway of relaxation and go on it as far as you need to go. Like most skills, the more you practice it, the better you should be able to use it. So I would encourage you to set aside a few moments each day to practice going into the state; if nothing else, just enjoy the relaxation.

Arousal

Now I am going to ask you to bring yourself out of the state. But just before you bring yourself out of the state, and I would encourage you to do this each time before you bring yourself out of the state, say to yourself a special word, such as "silver." It can be any word you choose. When you say that special word to yourself just before you bring yourself out of the state, you will feel relaxed and refreshed. Rested. That your body has responded to the relaxation by preparing all of its systems to function at the peak of their ability so that you can feel alert and alive all over, ready to do the things that you want to do. In other words, you can feel just great.

Now, at your own pace, bring yourself to a lighter level . . . say that special word to yourself . . . bring yourself out of the state, open your eyes and notice how good you feel. . . . How to you feel?

At this point, tell the patient that you would like to see him or her back after an appropriate interval to be sure that the patient is satisfied with the control of pain.

SUMMARY

Central to this discussion of pain control is the concept that the patient has control over his or her own comfort. The practitioner should examine carefully all hypnotherapeutic approaches to be certain that each part is consistent with an overall respect for the patient and the patient's responsibility for controlling pain. If a patient is not able to achieve a desired level of comfort, the practitioner should identify factors that may be blocking relief. There is almost always a better solution than hurting.

FURTHER READING

Barber, J., & Adrian, C. (Eds.) (1982). *Psychological approaches to the management of pain*. New York: Brunner/Mazel.

Feuerstein, M., & Skjei, E. (1974). *Mastering pain*. New York: Bantam.

REFERENCES

Alman, G. M., & Carney, R. E. (1980). Consequences of direct and indirect suggestions on success of posthypnotic behavior. *American Journal of Clinical Hypnosis, 23*, 112–118.

Barber J., & Adrian, C. (1981). *Psychological approaches to the management of pain*. New York: Brunner/Mazel.

Barber, J., & Mayer, D. (1977). Evaluation of the efficiency and neural mechanism of a hypnotic analgesia procedure in experimental and clinical pain. *Pain, 4*, 41–48.

Bonica, J. J. (1977). Introduction to the symposium on pain. *Archives of Surgery, 112*, 749.

Bressler, D. E., & Trubo, R. (1979). *Free yourself from pain*. New York: Simon and Schuster.

Cheek, D. B., & LeCron, L. M. (1968). *Clinical hypnotherapy*. New York: Grune and Stratton.

Dabezies, D. J., & Brunet, M. (1978). Chemonucleolysis vs. laminectomy. *Orthopedics, 1*, 26–29.

Damsbo, A. M. (1979). Tension headache treated with hypnosis. *Hypnosis 1979*. Amsterdam: Elsevier/North Holland Biomedical Press.

Dennis, S. G., & Melzack, R. (1977). Pain signaling systems in dorsal and ventral spinal cord. *Pain, 4*, 97.

Elman, D. (1970). *Explorations in hypnosis*. Los Angeles: Nash Publishing.

Feuerstein, M., & Skjei, E. (1979). *Mastering pain*. New York: Bantam Books.

Forrest, W. H., Brown, B. W., Brown, C. P., Defalque, R., Gold, M., Gordon, H. E., James, K. E., Katz, J., Mahler, D. L., Schroff, P., & Teutsch, G. (1977). Dexoamphetamine with morphine for the treatment of pain. *New England Journal of Medicine, 296*, 712–715.

Goldstein, A., & Hilgard, E. R. (1975). Lack of influence of the morphine antagonist naloxone on hypnotic analgesia. *Proceedings of the National Academy of Sciences, 72*, 2041–2043.

Gorsky, B. H., & Borsky, S. R. (1981). *Introduction to medical hypnosis*. New York: Medical Examination Publishing Co.

Haley, J. (1973). *Uncommon therapy, the psychiatric techniques of Milton H. Erickson, M.D.* New York: W. W. Norton.

Hilgard, E. R., & Hilgard, J. R. (1975). *Hypnosis in the relief of pain.* Los Altos, CA: Kaufmann.

Hughes, J. (1975). Isolation of an endogenous compound in the brain with pharmacological property similar to morphine. *Brain Research, 88,* 295.

LeCron, L. M. (1964). *Self-hypnotism: The technique and its use in daily living.* New York: New American Library.

Lee, R., & Spencer, P. S. U. (1977). Antidepressants and pain: A review of the pharmacologic data supporting the use of certain tricyclics in chronic pain. *Journal of International Medical Research, 5* (Supp. 1), 146–155.

Li, C. H., & Chung, D. (1976). Isolation and structure of an untriakontapeptide with opiate activity from camel pituitary glands. *Proceedings of the National Academy of Sciences,* Washington, DC: *73,* 1145.

Listug, C. A., Damsbo, A. M., & Magnuson, R. L. (1980). Chronic pain profiles of patients treated with imagery. Paper presented at the American Academy of Physical Medicine and Rehabilitation, Washington, DC.

McNeil, T., Huncke, B., & Pesch, R. N. (1977). Chemonucleolysis: An evaluation of effectiveness by electromyography. *Archives of Physical Medicine and Rehabilitation, 58,* 303.

Melzack, R., & Wall, P. D. (1965). Pain mechanisms: A new theory. *Science, 150,* 971.

National Safety Council. (1980). *Accidental facts.* Chicago: Author.

Sacerdote, P. (1970). Theory and practice of pain control in malignancy and other protracted or recurring painful illnesses. *International Journal of Clinical and Experimental Hypnosis, 18,* 160–180.

Sacerdote, P. (1982). Techniques of hypnotic intervention with pain patients. In J. Barber & C. Adrian (Eds.), *Psychological approaches to the management of pain* (pp. 60–83). New York: Brunner/Mazel.

Schetschenau, P. R., Ramirez, A., Johnston, J., Wiggs, C., & Martins, A. N. (1976). Double-blind evaluation of intradiscal chymopapain for herniated lumbar discs. *Journal of Neurosurgery, 45,* 622–627.

Terenius, L., & Wahlstrom, A. (1975). Search for an endogenous ligand for the opiate receptor. *Acta Physiologica Scandinavica, 94,* 74.

Wain, H. J. (1980). Pain control through use of hypnosis. *American Journal of Clinical Hypnosis, 23,* 41–46.

Ward, N. G., Bloom, U. L., & Friedel, R. O. (1979). The effectiveness of tricyclic antidepressants in the treatment of coexisting pain and depression. *Pain, 7,* 331–341.

Waters, W. E. (1975). Prevalence of migraine. *Journal of Neurology, Neurosurgery and Psychiatry, 38,* 613.

Yager, E. K. (1980). *Smoking control: A comparison of hypnosis and subliminal therapy.* Unpublished doctoral dissertation, University of Humanistic Studies, San Diego.

10

Childbirth

We are such stuff as dreams are made on . . .

—Shakespeare
The Tempest

In most cultures, the normal processes of pregnancy, labor, and childbirth are veiled by a mystique expressed in many different customs, expectations, and rituals. In some cultures, the husband of the woman in labor takes to his bed and behaves as if he were bearing the child. In other cultures, the woman in labor is assisted by her women relatives, who may keep vigil with her throughout labor and delivery. In Western cultures, especially during the twentieth century, the pregnant woman has been treated as a patient who gives birth in the sterile atmosphere of a hospital with the aid of a medical doctor and the benefits of modern medicine.

Among these different cultures, the standards for evaluating a "good" pregnancy, labor, and delivery vary a great deal. Indeed, even within our own culture, it is difficult to develop a valid scale for evaluating the kind of experiences women might have during pregnancy and childbirth. It is quite easy, however, to agree on what the successful outcome of the entire process should be—an infant and mother who are emotionally and physically healthy.

Related to this objective, especially in the West, is the attempt to relieve the mother from pain and unnecessary tension and anxiety during labor and delivery. Although hypnosis has been used to control the pain and anxiety of labor since at least the time of Mesmer, the emphasis on inhalation anesthesia during this century has overshadowed the use of hypnosis in obstetrics. As noted by Werner, Schauble, and Knudson (1982), little has been written about hypnosis in obstetrics during the past decade. In recent years, obstetricians and anesthesiologists have developed safer analgesia and anesthesia agents and methods of delivering them (Bremage, 1981; Cohen, 1981a; Devore, 1981; Shnider and Levinson, 1981; Shnider, Levinson, and Ralston, 1981). Evaluation of the neonate also has received increased attention: More sensitive methods have been developed to help assess the effects of iatrogenic influences on the newborn so that perinatal care can continue to be improved (Cohen, 1981b). Consistent with these advances, the techniques of hypnosis, especially when used in combination with methods of prepared childbirth, are being received with renewed interest.

In this chapter we will examine the ways that hypnosis can be used in combination with the Lamaze method of prepared childbirth to facilitate healthy pregnancies and satisfying birth experiences. A "good" pregnancy is defined here as one in which there is an absence of major complaints or problems, such as hyperemesis (excessive vomiting), premature labor, spontaneous abortion, heartburn, and the late toxemias of pregnancy (preclampsia and eclampsia). Similarly, a good labor and delivery would include a normal-length (or shorter) labor, some relief or control of pain and anxiety, and a nontraumatic delivery. Postpartum criteria would include the physical and emotional well-being of the mother, the health of the child according to standard measures, and the successful bonding of mother and child.

INFLUENCES ON PREGNANCY AND CHILDBIRTH

During the seventeenth century, the Frenchman Mauriceau (1668) wrote that pregnancy was an illness that lasted 9 months and that pregnant women were to be treated as patients. While we seem to have come a long way from Mauriceau's pronouncements, and while today there is a good deal of talk about the natural processes of pregnancy and childbirth, the emotional and psychological factors affecting these experiences remain complicated and difficult to define. The self-reports of women who have experienced normal childbirth run the gamut from exhilarating to agonizing. Many theories have been developed to account for this wide variation in an experience that, physiologically at least, is the same for women throughout the world.

Crasilneck and Hall (1975) emphasized the social and cultural effects on a woman's individual psychology but also took into account the pregnant woman's "deepest psychological level," which "touches on the archetype of the mother, with its fascinating and sometimes terrible affects and images" (p. 254). Those influences and feelings, as well as a woman's particular life circumstances—such as being unmarried, having had a previous unpleasant experience in childbirth, or not wanting the child—affect the woman's experience of pregnancy and childbirth.

Cheek and LeCron (1968) developed criteria for determining good risk and poor risk patients. Those identified as good risk are those with happy marriages, planned pregnancies, and uncomplicated previous pregnancies. Women in this group have less than a 5% chance of spontaneous abortion, less than a 5% chance of toxemia, less than a 4% chance of premature labor, and less than a 1% chance of serious hemorrhage. The criteria for poor risk patients range from such characteristics as several years of unexplained sterility to the patient's being the only child or the only surviving child of her family. Those identified as poor risk patients have significantly increased risks in all areas. Again, these criteria support the theory that an intricate network of psychological and social factors may affect the physiological state of the woman during pregnancy and childbirth.

At least since 1843, when Queen Victoria delivered her eighth child with the aid of anesthesia, childbirth has been anticipated in Western culture as a painful and disagreeable experience. As Kroger (1977) pointed out, "for generations women have been 'hypnotized' into thinking that they must have severe pain in childbirth" (p. 229).

Several studies support the view that maternal anxiety is directly related to physical or emotional difficulty in delivery. In a study of 48 women, Davids, DeVault, and Talmadge (1961a, b) found that those who experienced abnormalities or complications in childbirth had indicated considerably greater anxiety on psychological pretests than had women who experienced no unusual difficulties. Davenport-Slack and Boylan (1974) showed that, while pain itself was relatively constant among 75 private obstetrical patients, the subjective experience of childbirth varied widely. They concluded that women who play an active role in childbirth and whose husbands are present tend to have far more satisfying birth experiences than those who expect to rely on doctors and medications.

Also influencing the health and well-being of mother and newborn is the use of chemical anesthetics and analgesics during labor and delivery. While these agents may indeed relieve pain and anxiety, most have been shown to affect adversely to some degree both mother and child. Buxton (1962) observed that women whose deliveries are accompanied by chemical anesthesia routinely suffer 1–2 days postpartum depression. Several studies have shown that pharmacologic agents administered during labor and delivery affect the infant's general level of functioning, as measured by the Apgar instrument and other infant assessment tests (Apgar, 1953; Brackbill, Kane, Maniello, and Abramson, 1974; Cavenaught and Talisman, 1969). Since the Apgar score correlates strongly with later neuromuscular development, anesthesic drugs that cross the placenta and depress the infant have been considered undesirable. Anesthesia is also listed as the fourth leading cause of maternal death, following hemorrhage, infection, and toxemia, and preceding heart disease (Clark, 1973).

However, more recent research (summarized by Cohen, 1981b) has employed neurobehavioral testing techniques that are more sensitive than previous methods and has found "no evidence as yet of prolonged adverse effects being associated with neurobehavioral depression caused by maternal medication" (p. 383).

The greatest drawback of maternal medication appears to be the extent to which it interferes with bonding between mother and child. According to Cohen (1981b), excessive sleepiness in the mother may induce negative feelings toward the child, and infant drowsiness may interfere with the successful establishment of breast feeding. Other research has revealed a significant correlation between negative prenatal maternal attitudes and deviant behavior in the neonate (Ferreira, 1960; Ottinger and Simmons, 1964). Moss (1972) found a relationship between positive maternal attitudes and the responsiveness of mothers to the crying of their infants. Similarly, Newton (1973) found that women who felt that childbirth was a difficult experience were likely to be physically less nurturing mothers.

Within the context of all these social and cultural variables and contributing psychological factors, two methods of prepared childbirth may be considered as alternatives or supplements to sedative and analgesic drugs during labor and childbirth. Although there are several "natural" or "prepared" childbirth methods in common use today, this discussion will focus on only two: the psychoprophylactic relaxation training known as the Lamaze method, and hypnosis. Both Lamaze training and hypnosis can serve as safe means of facilitating relaxation that enhances the childbirth experience and contributes to the well-being of both mother and child.

LAMAZE TRAINING

The widely used Lamaze training is rooted in the hypnosuggestive method used in Russia by Platonov, a psychiatrist who conducted research into the concept of pain during the 1920s. Platonov's successful experimentation with hypnosis for the relief of pain during childbirth was soon put into use for the pregnant women of Russia by Velvovsky, who was in charge of promoting this program among the populace. Velvovsky (1972) stated that the fundamental objective of the system of psychoprophylaxis of labor pain was "not only individual labor pain relief but . . . an endeavor to do away with labor pain and the misgivings of women in childbirth as a mass phenomenon" (p. 318).

In the 1950s, a French obstetrician, Ferdinand Lamaze, visited Russia and was impressed by his observations of Velvovsky's method. Lamaze introduced this method in France and later promoted his own adaptation in England and the United States (Bing, 1969). Lamaze training assumes that women experience anticipated or psychological pain as well as physiological pain during childbirth, and that both of these can be reduced through specific training. While there is a "strong component of suggestion" in the Lamaze training, according to Hilgard and Hilgard (1975), the training is quite specific in its objectives and teachings. The Lamaze method includes instruction in what to expect during pregnancy and how to relieve pain by eliminating fear, as well as a series of respiratory and relaxation exercises and responses to facilitate labor and delivery.

Citing conflicting reports on the success of the Lamaze method, Hughey, McElin, and Young (1978) compared 500 consecutive Lamaze-prepared patients with a control group of 500 patients who were matched with the experimental group for age, race, parity, and educational level. The objective was to resolve the conflicts concerning the Lamaze method and to determine whether Lamaze childbirth preparation was harmless, harmful, or beneficial.

While the average labor time did not differ significantly between the two groups, the authors reported their Lamaze-prepared patients experienced a 50% higher level of spontaneous deliveries and a significantly lower incidence of cesarean section. They also found a significant increase in the incidence of fetal distress in the control patients. The Lamaze-prepared patients "had a significantly lower instance of both maternal morbidity and the use of antibiotics" (p. 646).

Furthermore, in every category of complication, including toxemia of pregnancy, the Lamaze-prepared patients fared better than the controls. Premature births occurred half as often in the prepared group as in the control group. The Apgar scores for infants delivered of prepared patients were better than the scores for control-group infants, although the differences were not statistically significant. "In virtually every obstetric performance category, the data suggest that the Lamaze method is beneficial" (Hughey et al., 1978, p. 646).

HYPNOSIS AND PREPARED CHILDBIRTH

Although the Lamaze prepared childbirth training can be traced to Velvovsky's methods and further to Platonov's use of hypnosis, the part played by hypnosis in prepared chilbirth methods is not widely recognized. Several proponents of the use of hypnosis in childbirth refer to an earlier statement by DeLee (1939), that "the only anesthetic without danger is hypnotism . . . I am irked when I see my colleagues neglect to avail themselves of this harmless and potent remedy" (p. 164).

Several authors have pointed out that hypnotic techniques often do play a part in successful childbirth experiences. Crasilneck and Hall (1975) noted that "a sympathetic, emotionally sensitive obstetrician who reassures and calms the woman in labor may actually be using hypnoidal influence, even if hypnosis is not employed" (p. 259). Kroger (1977) stated that "an experienced observer will recognize that successful natural childbirth patients have been hypnotized to a degree; some have reached at least a light stage, and others a medium stage of hypnosis" (p. 228).

Several authors have reported on the use of hypnosis and posthypnotic suggestion for pregnancy and childbirth. In a study of 442 women, August (1960) reported the successful use of hypnoanesthesia as the sole anesthetic agent for 93.5% of the deliveries. In a study of self-hypnosis as an adjunct in obstetrics, Ringrose (1967) concluded that hypnosis was useful, not only for shortening labor and reducing the incidence of toxemia, but also for enhancing the childbirth experience for the mothers. In a controlled study of 25 patients, Pascatto and Mead (1967) found that posthypnotic suggestion produced many positive results for both mother and infant, including reduced need for analgesics, increased composure in the mother, less insomnia, fewer headaches, and less postpartum breast discomfort.

Hilgard and Hilgard (1975) identified eight hypnotic procedures useful in relieving the pain of childbirth. These include:

1. Training rehearsals for actual labor.

2. Relaxation techniques.

3. Substitution of a minor symptom for pain.

4. Displacement of a symptom to another part of the body.

5. Direct suggestion of symptom relief.

6. Indirect suggestion of pain relief.

7. Practice of imaginative separation from the present scene.

8. Posthypnotic suggestions to reduce postoperative discomfort and set the stage for a positive attitude in the postpartum period.

Kroger (1977) similarly listed the advantages of the use of hypnosis for childbirth, stating that there are no ritualistic exercises and no elaborate education needed to achieve the kind of interpersonal relationship essential to the success of this method, and that the hypnotic rapport can be transferred to an associate, nurse, husband, or some other person who need only induce and maintain the hypnotic state by means of a prearranged cue. Kroger listed other advantages of hypnosis, such as reduced fear, tension, and pain, reduced need for chemoanalgesia and anesthesia, reduced physical and mental exhaustion after delivery, and decreased danger of fetal anoxia. Cheek and LeCron (1968) reported the successful use of hypnosis in managing the continuing problems of pregnancy and childbirth, including toxemia, placental separation, and fibrinolytic hemorrhage.

Several authors have noted that trance depth is not an important variable in the successful use of hypnosis in childbirth. After extensive experience with the use of hypnosis for relief of labor pain, Kroger and Freed (1956) offered the hypothesis that if a close relationship exists between the patient and obstetrician, approximately 10%–15% of nonmedicated patients will remain free of discomfort during labor without the formal induction of a trance.

Also deemphasizing the importance of a trance state, Winkelstein (1958) considered the following variables to be important: (a) the suggestions themselves, (b) the mental attitude of the patient toward pregnancy and delivery, (c) the will to succeed, (d) the confidence the patient has in the procedure as well as in the obstetrician, and (e) the patient-obstetrician rapport. Chlifer (1959) came to similar conclusions, finding that pain may be ameliorated by suggestions made to women in the waking state.

It appears, therefore, that when the parturient woman has a positive attitude towards childbirth and good rapport with the physician, hypnotic techniques can be effective in the absence of a formally induced trance. A more detailed analysis of many of the studies cited above has been provided by Werner et al. (1982) in a review and position paper on the obstetrical use of hypnosis.

A MODEL SELF-HYPNOSIS TRAINING PROGRAM

There are many similarities, both historically and in practice, between hypnosis and the Lamaze method for prepared childbirth. Several researchers have noted this similarity, not only as it exists between the conditioning phase of the Lamaze method and the induction and trance maintenance phases of hypnosis, but also as it exists among birth outcome variables (Clark, 1956; Kroger, 1977; Ringrose, 1967; Samuelly, 1972; Vellay, 1972; Velvovsky, 1972). Because both systems have achieved such success, a program that combines the principles and education of prepared training (Lamaze) with the empirically demonstrated benefits of hypnosis birth training should be very powerful. Using Malyska and Christensen's (1967) work on the combined use of natural childbirth and self-hypnosis as a precedent, the following model has been developed for an ongoing program of combined self-hypnosis and Lamaze training.

For the past 8 years, Wood has conducted self-hypnosis training as an adjunct to Lamaze training in a program conducted at Scripps Memorial Hospital in La Jolla, California. Both mothers and fathers are encouraged to participate in the Lamaze and self-hypnosis classes.

The Lamaze classes meet for 8–9 weekly sessions and follow the traditional method discussed by Bing (1969). In addition to the classes, physicians and nurses provide weekly lectures about labor and delivery, contraception, breast feeding, and bonding. Although Kroger (1977) stated that hypnotic conditioning should ideally begin during the 3rd or the 4th month of pregnancy, most couples participate in the self-hypnosis program at the end of the second trimester or the beginning of the third trimester because Lamaze training typically occurs then.

The self-hypnosis classes meet weekly for 5 weeks. Each session lasts 45 minutes and precedes the Lamaze class. The goals of the self-hypnosis workshop are:

1. To train expectant women in attaining light to medium levels of self-hypnosis so that they can relax quickly and easily, especially during labor and delivery (fathers also learn self-hypnosis).

2. To train the fathers (or labor coaches) in hetero-hypnosis so that they can facilitate a hypnotic trance in their wives during the remaining time of pregnancy and during labor and delivery.

3. To facilitate the increase of emotional and psychological support between the father and mother.

4. To facilitate the sense of increased participation by the expectant father in the pregnancy.

5. To discuss the similarities between Lamaze training and hypnosis and to demonstrate the ways they can jointly increase relaxation, comfort, and the expectant woman's ability to distract her attention away from a painful stimulus.

6. To increase the confidence of workshop participants through instruction in self-hypnosis as well as through the use of hypnotic suggestions for increased ego strength, relaxation, and feelings of well-being.

The participants in the self-hypnosis workshop are trained as a group. In only 4 hours of training, participants are able to attain useful levels of relaxation through hypnotic or self-hypnotic induction processes. By training the father or labor coach to help the mother, this program eliminates the need for a practitioner trained in hypnosis to be present throughout labor. Couples also are trained to ignore any inappropriate or negative remarks related to pregnancy and childbirth that might be expressed in their presence, either before or during labor and delivery.

Session 1
The goals of the self-hypnosis workshop are explained at the first session. Participants are encouraged to remember that self-hypnosis is an adjunct to Lamaze training and that neither hypnosis nor Lamaze training is considered a replacement for analgesia or anesthesia during labor and delivery. Participants are assured that the purpose of hypnosis and Lamaze is to minimize drug requirements, not necessarily to eliminate them, and that medication will be available on request during labor and delivery, should the women need it. However, many women in this program do forego the use of medication because they continue to maintain their useful levels of relaxation and comfort throughout childbirth.

During this first session, participants are provided with an introduction to hypnosis, including a brief history of hypnosis, a discussion of myths about it, and a brief presentation of current and appropriate uses of hypnosis in medicine, psychology, and psychiatry.

The participants are then invited to enter a hypnotic trance facilitated by a traditional eye-fixation technique, by suggestions about the depth of their increasing relaxation, and by exposure to a self-hypnosis conditioning technique similar to the Stein clenched-fist technique (Stein, 1969). Once in a light trance, participants are encouraged to employ the same procedures to arouse themselves and to reintroduce their state of relaxation. Following reinduction, suggestions are provided to facilitate the relaxation and to maintain or increase trance depth. It is important to note here that a permissive approach to teaching self-hypnosis is employed.

Post-hypnotic suggestions are given that encourage participants to associate increased relaxation with several daily activities related to their closing a hand, such as closing the hand around a door knob, a drinking glass, or a telephone receiver. These suggestions are an extension of a natural behavior and reinforce the Stein clenched-fist technique, which associates increased relaxation with closing the preferred hand and opening the nonpreferred hand to release tension, stress, and discomfort. Additionally, participants are encouraged to give themselves the suggestion developed by Coué (1923) that "every day and in every way, I am getting better and better."

Participants also are given the suggestion that they may find themselves employing the techniques of self-hypnosis to relax two or more times a day for 3–5 minutes. They are encouraged to give themselves positive suggestions and to use positive end-result images regarding labor and delivery while they are relaxing, going about their daily activities, getting ready for bed, and getting settled in bed to go to sleep. They are encouraged to set aside approximately 15–20 minutes, two or three times a week, to practice hypnosis for more extended periods. If they have tape-recorded the first training session, they are encouraged to use the recording to help them relax on these occasions. Finally, the group is once again led through an awakening and reinduction procedure with the suggestion that they will find themselves reentering hypnosis as they begin to awaken and that, although they may find themselves opening their eyes briefly and perhaps focusing their vision, when they close their eyes again they will return to their pleasant state of relaxation.

Session 2

During the second session, after questions have been answered and methods of self-hypnosis have been reviewed, participants are again encouraged to enter hypnosis. At this time, suggestions made during the first session are restated. Participants are encouraged to visualize walking, riding on a road, or riding an elevator or escalator in association with their increasing levels of relaxation. Participants also are encouraged to associate a pleasant thought, memory, idea, or experience with this process of relaxation, so that when they remember these thoughts and ideas, they not only have pleasant experiences but also find themselves thinking more and more of relaxation.

The "heavy eyelids" challenge test is introduced at the second session. This challenge is not employed so much as a test of trance depth, but rather as a technique for increasing the depth of hypnosis and demonstrating to the participants that they can let themselves be so relaxed that they do not want to move the muscles necessary to open their eyes. For those who let their eyes open during such a challenge, the suggestion is made that "if you want to open your eyes and do so, you might find yourself or allow yourself to double your level of relaxation." Two or three additional inductions are practiced at this session, including an adaptation of Benson's (1975) relaxation technique, and the suggestions presented earlier are restated.

Session 3

During the third session, after a question and answer period, attention is paid to other hypnotic techniques, such as rapid induction techniques and nonverbal induction and deepening techniques. For example, one nonverbal deepening technique is to apply gentle and steady downward pressure to the shoulder or to pick up the hand and arm and suggest that as it falls to the lap, the individual's level of relaxation may progressively deepen. Once these techniques are learned, accompanying verbal suggestions are not necessary. By the third session, the frequency of verbal suggestions is approximately half of what it was during the first session.

Sessions 4 and 5

During the fourth and fifth sessions, the relationship between self-hypnosis and Lamaze training is discussed, as are ways of combining hypnosis and Lamaze techniques during labor and delivery. Labor simulations, using pinching to simulate the uterine contractions, take place with the assistance of the labor coach and are mediated by hypnosis. Participants practice Lamaze techniques, and the labor coaches practice facilitating hypnosis in the mothers-to-be, helping them to maintain a beneficial level of relaxation (ASC) even during the pinching that simulates labor contractions. The mothers are also given the opportunity to help facilitate hypnosis in their coaches and to help them maintain this relaxation while being pinched during a labor simulation. Ego-strengthening suggestions and positive end-result images related to pregnancy, labor, delivery, and the postpartum periods are reviewed and provided to the participants while they are in hypnosis. Participants are encouraged to select or design and practice nonverbal suggestions for inducing and deepening their level of relaxation.

During these final sessions, the principles of glove anesthesia are also reviewed. Participants are taught to produce glove anesthesia and to transfer the anesthesia to other parts of the body, especially the abdomen, perineum, and lower back. Husbands and coaches are taught the suggestions for facilitating glove anesthesia, and these suggestions are employed during the labor simulation exercises. Again, couples are encouraged to practice brief hypnosis or self-hypnosis daily. In addition, they are encouraged to practice Lamaze exercises and labor simulation mediated by hypnosis and Lamaze techniques two or three times each week. The pregnant woman is encouraged to focus on positive end-result images while on her way to the hospital, during her admission to the hospital, and in the labor and delivery rooms.

By helping parents enhance their positive mental set concerning labor and delivery and increase their confidence in hypnosis and Lamaze techniques, this training program facilitates their active participation and helps them experience more fully the positive aspects of the birth process.

Research Findings

The validity of the approach described above is supported by an investigation conducted by Wood (1978). A sample of 28 women were divided into three groups: (a) 7 women who elected to have no birth preparation, (b) 8 women who chose Lamaze training, and (c) 13 women who chose both Lamaze and self-hypnosis training. Labor time and labor medication requested by women in each of the three groups were evaluated, as were the Apgar scores of the newborns. The results indicated that women from the combined training group requested significantly less labor medication before delivery than did women from the untrained group. The amount of labor medication requested correlated significantly with training, indicating that the more training a woman has for childbirth, the less medication she requests during labor. The study also indicated that the more education a woman has, the more she will involve herself with training for childbirth. The pretraining self-concept incongruence and inconsistency scores revealed that the combined-training group had significantly less self-concept incongruence and inconsistency than the untrained group. Lastly, the findings indicated that the more training a woman has, the less will be her need for epidural anesthesia for delivery.

SUMMARY

By focusing on the physical health of pregnant women, health-care professionals have sometimes neglected the emotional and psychological factors that can play a major role in the experience and outcome of pregnancy, labor, and delivery. Research suggests that maternal anxiety and negative expectations are correlated with birth abnormalities and complications, and that women's positive attitudes and active involvement correlate with satisfying birth experiences. Numerous studies also have provided evidence that chemical analgesics and anesthetics can have adverse effects on both mother and newborn by interfering with the bonding process. These findings make a strong argument for the judicious use of medication and for training programs that address emotional physical and psychological factors relating to childbirth.

Both Lamaze training and hypnosis can result in shorter labors, reduced medication, decreased perception of pain, and childbirth experiences that are perceived as satisfying and rewarding. There is some evidence that the more extensive the training (and therefore the commitment necessary to complete the training), the higher the degree of psychological adjustment. The model program described in this chapter combines a self-hypnosis workshop with Lamaze training for prepared childbirth. In only 4 hours of group instruction in hypnosis and self-hypnosis, plus frequent practice at home, most couples were able to increase their positive attitudes toward childbirth and to develop and maintain a level of relaxation and comfort that reduced or eliminated the need for medication during labor and delivery.

It is hoped that physicians, psychologists, and nurses will be alerted to the need to make such programs available to their patients and that they will be aware of the advantages of a comprehensive team approach to the management of the normal stresses of pregnancy and childbirth. The preliminary findings reported here indicate that more emphasis should be placed on finding ways of encouraging prospective parents who do not volunteer for training to take a more active role in their pregnancy, labor, and delivery. By doing so, they may increase their chances of obtaining the principal objective of that process, a healthy, happy mother and baby (DeVore, 1981, p. 74).

FURTHER READING

Bonica, J. J. (1980). *Obstetric analgesia and anesthesia* (2nd ed.). Amsterdam: World Federation of Societies of Anesthesiologists.

Shnider, S. M., & Levinson, G. (1981). *Anesthesia for obstetrics.* Baltimore: Williams & Wilkins.

REFERENCES

Apgar, V. (1953). A proposal for a new method of evaluation of the newborn infant. *Anesthesia and Analgesia, 32,* 260–267.

August, R. V. (1960, June). Obstetric hypnoanesthesia. *American Journal of Obstetrics and Gynecology, 79,* 1131–1138.

Benson, H. (1975). *The relaxation response.* New York: Morrow.

Bing, E. (1969). *Six practical lessons for an easier childbirth.* New York: Bantam Books.

Bowlby, J. (1958). The nature of the child's tie to his mother. *International Journal of Psycho-Analysis, 39,* 350–373.

Brackbill, Y., Kane, B. S., Maniello, R. L., & Abramson, D. (1974). Obstetric meperidine usage and assessment of neonatal status. *Anesthesiology, 40,* 116–120.

Bremage, P. R. (1981). Choice of local anesthetics in obstetrics. In S. M. Shnider & G. Levinson (Eds.), *Anesthesia for obstetrics.* Baltimore: Williams & Wilkins.

Buxton, C. L. (1962). *A study of psychophysical methods for the relief of childbirth pain.* Philadelphia: W. B. Saunders.

Cavenaught, D., & Talisman, M. (1969). *Prematurity and the obstetrician.* New York: Appleton-Century-Crofts.

Cheek, D. B., & LeCron, L. (1968). *Clinical hypnotherapy.* New York: Grune & Stratton.

Chlifer, R. I. (1959). Verbal analgesia in childbirth. In L. Chertok (Ed.), *Psychosomatic methods in painless childbirth.* New York: Pergamon.

Clark, R. N. (1956). A training method for childbirth utilizing hypnosis. *American Journal of Obstetrics and Gynecology, 72,* 1302–1304.

Clark, R. N. (1973). Anesthesia in obstetrics: General. *Postgraduate Medicine, 53,* 223–226.

Cohen, S. E. (1981a). Inhalation analgesia and anesthesia for vaginal delivery. In S. M. Shnider & G. Levinson (Eds.), *Anesthesia for obstetrics* (pp. 121–140). Baltimore: Williams & Wilkins.

Cohen, S. E. (1981b). Evaluation of the neonate. In S. M. Shnider & G. Levinson (Eds.), *Anesthesia for obstetrics* (pp. 370–384). Baltimore: Williams & Wilkins.

Coué, E. (1923). *How to practice suggestion and auto-suggestion.* New York: American Library Service.

Crasilneck, H. B., & Hall, J. A. (1975). *Clinical hypnosis: Principles and applications.* New York: Grune & Stratton.

Davenport-Slack, B., & Boylan, C. H. (1974). Psychological correlates of childbirth pain. *Psychosomatic Medicine, 36,* 215–223.

Davids, A., DeVault, S., & Talmadge, M. (1961a). Psychological study of emotional factors in pregnancy: A preliminary report. *Psychosomatic Medicine, 23*, 93–103.

Davids, A., DeVault, S., & Talmadge, M. (1961b). Anxiety, pregnancy, and childbirth abnormalities. *Journal of Consulting Psychology, 25*, 74–77.

DeLee, J. P. (1939). *Yearbook of obstetrics and gynecology.* Chicago: Yearbook Medical Publishers.

Devore, J. S. (1981). Psychological anesthesia for obstetrics. In S. M. Shnider & G. Levinson (Eds.), *Anesthesia for obstetrics* (pp. 65–74). Baltimore: Williams & Wilkins.

Ferreira, A. J. (1960). The pregnant woman's emotional attitude and its reflection on the newborn. *American Journal of Orothopsychiatry, 30*, 553–561.

Hilgard, E. R., & Hilgard, J. R. (1975). *Hypnosis in the relief of pain.* Los Altos, CA: William Kaufmann.

Hughey, M. J., McElin, T., & Young, T. (1978). Maternal and fetal outcome of Lamaze prepared patients. *Journal of Obstetrics and Gynecology, 51*, 643–647.

Kroger, W. S. (1977). *Clinical and experimental hypnosis.* Philadelphia: J. B. Lippincott.

Kroger, W. S., & Freed, S. C. (1956). *Psychosomatic gynecology.* Glencoe, IL: Free Press.

Malyska, W., & Christensen, J. (1967). Authohypnosis and the prenatal class. *American Journal of Clinical Hypnosis, 9*, 188–192.

Mauriceau, F. (1668). *Maladies de femmes grosses.* Paris: Henault.

Moss, H. A. (1972). Sex, age and state as determinants of mother-infant interaction. In I. B. Weiner & D. Elkind (Eds.), *Reading in child development.* New York: John Wiley and Sons.

Newton, N. (1973). *Maternal emotions.* New York: Paul Hoeber.

Ottinger, D., & Simmons, J. (1964). Behavior of human neonates and prenatal maternal anxiety. *Psychological Reports, 14*, 391–394.

Pascatto, R., & Mead, B. T. (1967, April). The use of posthypnotic suggestion in obstetrics. *American Journal of Clinical Hypnosis, 9*, 267–269.

Ringrose, C. A. D. (1967). Autohypnosis as an adjunct in obstetrics. In I. Goldstein & N. Flaxman (Eds.), *Medical Trial Technique Quarterly* (pp. 49–55). IL: Callaghan.

Samuelly, I. (1972). Lamaze childbirth. *American Journal of Clinical Hypnosis, 15*, 136–139.

Shnider, S. M., & Levinson, G. (Eds.). (1981). *Anesthesia for obstetrics.* Baltimore: Williams & Wilkins.

Shnider, S. M., Levinson, G., & Ralston, D. H. (1981). Regional anesthesia for labor and delivery. In S. M. Shnider & G. Levinson (Eds.), *Anesthesia for obstetrics.* Baltimore: Williams & Wilkins.

Stein, C. (1969). *Practical psychotherapy in nonpsychiatric specialties.* Springfield, IL: Charles C Thomas.

Vellay, P. (1972). Painless labor: A French method. In J. G. Howells (Ed.), *Modern perspectives in psycho-obstetrics* (vol. 5). New York: Brunner/Mazel.

Velvovsky, I. Z. (1972). Psychoprophylaxis in obstetrics: A Soviet method. In J. G. Howells (Ed.), *Modern perspectives in psycho-obstetrics* (vol. 5). New York: Brunner/Mazel.

Werner, W. E. F., Schauble, P. G., & Knudson, M. S. (1982, January). An argument for the review of hypnosis in obstetrics. *American Journal of Clinical Hypnosis, 24*, 149–171.

Winkelstein, L. B. (1958). Routine hypnosis for obstetrical delivery. *American Journal of Obstetrics and Gynecology, 76*, 152–160.

Wood, D. P. (1978). Self-hypnosis training as an adjunct to Lamaze training for childbirth (Doctoral dissertation, California School of Professional Psychology, San Diego). *Dissertation Abstracts International, 38*, 4494B.

11

Dentistry

Gerald L. McCracken, DDS

*Argue for your limitations and sure enough,
they're yours.*

—Richard Bach
Illusions

F ear of the dentist is almost epidemic in our society. It is estimated that 5%–6% of the American population (10–12 million people) manage to avoid dental care altogether, and in children of school age this figure may be closer to 16% (Horowitz, 1980). Fear of pain, embarrassment, ignorance of the procedures, and an exaggerated dread of "all those scary instruments and how they will be used" are just a few of the reasons that people stay away from the dentist. Surprisingly, there seems to be little correlation between fear of the dentist and socioeconomic status or educational background. Previous traumatic experiences and negative attitudes inherited from parents or communicated by siblings or peers apparently play equally important roles (Horowitz, 1980). Sadly, when people who have avoided dental care finally do seek attention, they often are found to have serious dental problems that require extensive and costly treatment (Pinkham and Schroeder, 1975). In the ensuing course of therapy, which can be painful and long due to the extent of the disease, people find further justification for their original fears.

As a result of this widespread fear of the dentist, many people in this country are caught in a corrective cycle that progresses roughly as follows:

1. A person experiences pain as result of a dental problem, such as a loose filling or a broken tooth.

2. The person eventually musters the courage to go to the dentist, usually because the pain has become so excruciating that there now is no alternative.

3. The actual treatment is often even more painful and expensive than it would have been had the person sought help at an earlier stage, either because acute infection has developed or because the fear itself has lowered the pain threshold.

4. The discomfort experienced during the corrective procedures reinforces the already negative associations with dental treatment, so that the patient will once again avoid the dental chair until a similar situation develops, forcing a repetition of the cycle.

People caught in the corrective cycle typically have poorer oral health than the rest of the population, along with general feelings of helplessness in regard to the care of their teeth. Restrained by their fears, they fail to learn the preventive measures that could reduce their corrective needs.

If we are to break this insidious cycle, we must first accept that we are dealing with habit patterns that, in many cases, developed as a result of earlier traumatic experiences at the dentist. These prior negative experiences appear to be the major cause of dental phobia (Horowitz, 1980). If we also recognize that habits are formed by repetition and that an undesirable habit can be eliminated simply by replacing it with a better, more constructive one, we begin to realize that hypnosis can be an invaluable asset to the dentist in establishing a more successful relationship with patients.

VARIABLES IN HYPNODONTIA

There are many variables to consider in the use of hypnosis in dentistry (hypnodontia). Tinkler (1971) described the problems of hypnotic induction as follows:

> The problems of hypnotic induction for dental purposes are rather different from those confronting the doctor or psychotherapist. In one sense, the dentist has a distinct advantage because the patient knows that hypnosis is only being used for a limited purpose, and consequently has the assurance that no exploration of his mind will be attempted. On the other hand, most dental patients suffer from the disadvantage that the fear and dread evoked by the prospect of dental treatment makes it more difficult for the patient to cooperate and relax. This can usually be overcome, however, pro-

vided that sufficient time and care are devoted to the preparation of the patient's mind before any attempt at induction is made. I cannot stress too strongly the importance of this step, which may well determine the difference between success and failure. (pp. 366–367)

Other important variables to take into account before using hypnosis are a patient's personality traits and attitudes and expectations about hypnosis and dentistry. These variables help determine what techniques and procedures will be used and to what extent the hypnotic experience will be successful.

Also important are the dentist's personality and the attitudes the dentist conveys to the patient, both verbally and nonverbally. These factors naturally affect the relationship that develops between doctor and patient and will influence the outcome of the procedure. The dentist who succeeds in gaining the trust and confidence of a patient will have a much better chance of producing the desired hypnotic state.

The office environment is an often-overlooked variable that contributes to the success of the hypnotic experience. "Environment" refers not only to the physical environment of the office, determined by decor, color schemes, furniture, and the type of music being played, but also to the degree of confidence inspired by the office staff. Is the office a comfortable place to be? Are the staff and doctor pleasant and friendly? Do they communicate a sense of competence and professionalism? All these aspects play a very important role in helping the patient relax and feel comfortable in the office setting.

ANXIETY-STRESS SYNDROME

Someone who feels threatened, with or without good reason, will probably exhibit symptoms of anxiety. Unchecked, these symptoms are quickly translated into stress, which in turn leads to more anxiety, thereby creating a self-perpetuating cycle. An extreme example of the way that the anxiety-stress syndrome manifests itself in the dental office can be found in the dental phobic. Dental phobics, although relatively rare phenomena, convert their anxiety into futile mechanisms that may take the form of uncontrollable crying or tremors, both of which are counterproductive to completing the appointment.

Dental patients typically fall into one of two categories or anxiety types. The first is the *normal reaction type*. Patients in this group may exhibit mild negative reactions to the syringe or hypodermic needle, but they do not manifest a reaction disproportionate to the situation. They are able to cope with their anxiety without resorting to repression or other neurotic mechanisms often used to withstand intrapsychic conflict. This type of patient represents the majority.

The second category is the *abnormal reaction type*. Patients of this type exhibit anxiety reactions that are greatly disproportionate to the actual threat involved. Such people tend to overreact to even the most benign dental procedures. A typical example is the patient who becomes hysterical at the mere sight or sound of the drill. Such overreactions obviously can produce stress in the doctor as well, particularly if he or she is unaware of the basic psychological mechanisms involved in this type of response. Patients such as these cannot only disrupt the office routine and schedule but also upset the morale of both doctor and staff. However, if handled skillfully and judiciously, such people can be helped to overcome their fears and eventually behave as model patients. Although patients in this category are in the minority, they do exist—and they require special care and attention.

HELPING PATIENTS OVERCOME FEAR

While rational fears are responses to a real danger, irrational fears are inappropriate responses to dangers that have no actual basis in reality. It is important that dentists, who must deal with the emotions of their patients every day, realize that emotion cannot be dispelled by logic. Dental phobics will seldom respond to reason because their actions clearly are beyond their control. A good rule of thumb is that logic will be of little use in curtailing the emotional storms of the problem patient. Failure to recognize this simple premise can lead to unnecessary frustrations for both the doctor and the office staff.

Of utmost importance in allaying patients' fears is establishing their trust in the doctor. To accomplish this goal, there are several things to consider. One is the patient's initial impression of the dental office. Typically, the patient's first contact is with a receptionist, secretary, or office manager. This very important person is, in essence, playing the role of host. As coordinator for the office, he or she is the first and last person the patient sees during a dental visit. Thus, it is crucial that this person exhibit a friendly and caring attitude toward the patient, whether face-to-face or over the telephone.

It should be made very clear to the patient, preferably in advance of the appointment, that the purpose of the first visit is to meet and talk with the doctor. During this first visit, a complete health history should be obtained, including information about previous dental problems, such as gagging, bruxing, temporal mandibular joint (TMJ) pain, or headaches. Any history of adverse reactions to anesthesia should also be noted. Health history questions are designed to draw out the patient and encourage an open expression of fears and concerns. The patient should be seated in the examination chair in a comfortable, upright position. To avoid all association with treatment, the discussion should be conducted without placing a napkin or turning on bright lights. At this point, the patient should be encouraged to relax as much as possible and to respond to the dentist's questions.

If, after the preliminary discussion, the patient is comfortable, the doctor may proceed with the examination. Using the preliminary discussion and the results of the examination, the dentist can assess the patient's need for hypnosis and determine the best techniques for dealing with the specific problem.

HYPNOTIC TECHNIQUES

Before attempting the first hypnotic procedure, the dentist should try to instill confidence in the patient by asking questions about his or her attitudes toward hypnosis. It is important to uncover and correct any fears or misconceptions the patient may have. Once this has been accomplished, the dentist can explain the objective of hypnosis and outline the session to follow. This explanation should include (a) describing the situation as the dentist sees it, acknowledging the patient's fears, wants, desires, (b) clearly stating what is to be accomplished, (c) briefly describing the particular technique the dentist plans to use, and (d) asking for questions before starting treatment.

Levels of Trance

There are various levels of trance associated with hypnosis. Although in the minority, some people readily achieve a deep trance with hypnosis and can undergo fairly extensive dental treatment without chemical anesthesia. After a number of sessions, the majority of patients can reach a medium or light trance state in which little or no anesthesia is needed.

More important than trance depth is that the dental experience itself becomes less stressful for such patients and that the pain threshold is raised. As a result, subsequent visits become more tolerable. As oral health, personal esteem, and trust in the dental office increase, the dentist can educate the patient preventively and reduce the need for future corrective care. In this way, the original corrective cycle is replaced with a constructive cycle. The goal is to teach the patient to view the dental experience as a means of ensuring optimal oral health.

Relaxation Techniques

Several relaxation techniques are particularly useful to the dentist because they do not require formal induction. These can be applied either on a daily basis or in special circumstances, such as emergencies, where the patient displays unexpected anxiety symptoms or fear.

The best way to counter anxiety is to stop the procedure and ask the patient to become very aware of his or her breathing. This shift in concentration will help the patient to become more relaxed and to release the anxiety. The following is an example of how this technique might be used:

> Mary, I would like for you to take a minute while I stop here. I would like you to become very aware of your breathing. Try to concentrate on feeling yourself breathing in nice, relaxing breaths of air and feeling the breaths going to your lungs and right on down to the tips of your toes. That's it, very good. As you breathe in, feel the relaxing breaths of air actually breaking down the tension in your toes and feet right out of your body, and as you exhale, feel all that tension being exhaled. Very good, you're doing just fine. Now move up to your ankles and calves. . . .

The relaxation procedure is continued until the patient's entire body, segment by segment, has been relaxed and the patient is breathing very rhythmically. A deeply relaxed patient will hesitate briefly before responding to a question or a request. This lack of spontaneity is a good indication that you have achieved your objective.

Once relaxation has been achieved, the patient may be asked to visualize a favorite environment, such as the beach, the mountains, or some other pleasant setting. Then the dentist can briefly describe a relaxing scene or experience that might occur in such a place. Should symptoms develop later on in the procedure, the patient can simply be asked to concentrate on breathing once again and recall the pleasant scene. Typically, the reinduction can be accomplished in less than a minute. This technique can be repeated several times during a procedure without interrupting the actual treatment.

A similar procedure can be used to relax the tight muscles of patients with TMJ symptoms, which can cause spasms and prevent full opening of the mouth. Once deep relaxation is achieved, as described above, the patient is asked to focus on inhaling deeply and directing the relaxing breaths of air to the involved muscles, which the dentist palpates. The dentist then suggests that, as the patient exhales, all tension will be allowed to escape with the outgoing air. With every breath of relaxing air, the patient can imagine the mouth opening wider and wider. This gentle cycle of relaxation is continued until the trismus is relieved. Once the problem muscles are licated, patients can use this technique at home.

Soothing music, delivered to the patient through a set of headphones, is an effective way of inducing relaxation by blocking out environmental noises that elicit fear responses. Occasional breaks for conversation are also reassuring to the patient and are subtle inducers of relaxation. Nitrous oxide, which can be used before hypnotic induction or to prepare the patient for anesthesia, has been found particularly helpful in treating the problem patient because the relaxation it produces makes the patient more responsive to induction techniques. As mentioned earlier, a good, caring staff can do wonders to calm anxious patients. Often a patient will more freely express fears to members of the staff than to the dentist, and so it is essential to have highly trained people working in the office.

Hypnotic Induction

Systematic desensitization and progressive relaxation are the most commonly used techniques in dealing with high dental anxiety, such as dental phobia. However, because these techniques are very time-consuming for the dentist, patients who require such special attention for extensive dental work are best referred in advance or concurrently with treatment to a licensed practitioner skilled in hypnosis. Similarly, imagery training and fear hierarchy determination, in which the patient undergoes sessions in desensitization to stressful situations, are best handled in advance of dental treatment by another practitioner experienced with hypnosis.

Modified progressive relaxation techniques are the favored induction methods in routine dentistry and are recommended in the treatment of the average dental patient. The focus in dentistry is on producing a light-to-medium hypnotic state that results in both deep muscle relaxation and analgesia. This procedure should require no more than 10 minutes.

Barber (1977) reported success with his Rapid Induction Analgesia (RIA) procedure in 99 of 100 dental patients. These patients had no previous experience with hypnosis and were undergoing a variety of routine dental procedures, such as fillings, root-canal treatments, extractions, and crown preparations. Barber's indirect and permissive induction procedure included suggestions for relaxation, comfort and amnesia, plus a posthypnotic suggestion to elicit analgesia during treatment. After the patients were aroused from the trance state, all but one were treated without a chemical anesthetic.

The following case study illustrates the treatment of a common dental problem using the RIA:

> Mr. C is a prominent businessman who had refrained from dental treatment because of his embarrassment over a gagging problem. Even routine x-rays or cleaning resulted in violent gagging and occasional vomiting. At the time of referral, Mr. C had a fractured restoration that his dentist had been unable to replace because of the gag reflex.
>
> On the initial visit, Mr. C discussed his embarrassment and his avoidance of dental treatment. He was greatly relieved to learn that the gag reflex is a perfectly normal and necessary response to keep foreign objects out of the airway. Therefore, the objective of hypnosis was to control the reflex, and not to eliminate it.
>
> Mr. C was afraid that he wouldn't be able to get a breath when his soft palate or tongue was touched by a foreign object, such as a dental mirror. Therefore, Mr. C was asked to take a very deep breath and hold it while the dentist placed a finger into the back of throat. To his amazement, he didn't gag. Using the RIA, the dentist induced anesthesia into the patient's soft palate and tongue and told him that whenever he felt the urge to gag, he would simply take a long, slow breath through his nose and exhale slowly. When he did this, all feeling would leave his soft palate and tongue and he would experience a calm, relaxed state that would be conducive to correcting his dental problem.
>
> Mr. C has since undergone crown and bridge work and multiple impressions with much more comfort than he ever imagined. A 5-minute reinduction is used when he returns to have his teeth cleaned during the year, and he is now a very successful dental patient.

SAMPLE INDUCTION

Barber's RIA, reprinted below, is useful for a variety of dental procedures. All suggestions are phrased to make it clear that the patient, and not the dentist, is in control. The entire procedure requires approximately 10 minutes to complete.*

> I'd like to talk with you for a moment to see if you'd like to feel more comfortable and relaxed than you might expect. Would you like to feel more comfortable than you do right now?
>
> I'm quite sure that it will seem to you that I have really done nothing, that nothing has happened at all. You may feel a bit more relaxed, in a moment,

---

*Copyright © 1975 by Joseph Barber. With permission of the author.

but I doubt that you'll notice any other changes. I'd like you to notice though, if you're surprised by anything else you might notice. OK, then. . . . The best way to begin feeling more comfortable is just to begin by sitting as comfortably as you can right now. Go ahead and adjust yourself to the most comfortable position you like. That's fine. Now, I'd like you to notice how much more comfortable you can feel by just taking one very big, satisfying deep breath. Go ahead . . . big, deep, satisfying breath. . . . That's fine. You may already notice how good that feels . . . how warm your neck and shoulders can feel. . . . Now, then . . . I'd like you to take four more very deep, very comfortable breaths . . . and, as you exhale, notice . . . just notice how comfortable your shoulders can become . . . and notice how comfortable your eyes can feel when they close . . . and when they close, just let them stay closed. . . . That's right, just notice that . . . and notice, too, how, when you exhale, you can just feel that relaxation beginning to sink in. . . . Good, that's fine. . . . Now, as you continue breathing, comfortably and deeply and rhythmically, all I'd like you to do is to picture in your mind . . . just imagine a staircase, any kind you like . . . with 20 steps, and you at the top. . . . Now, you don't need to see all 20 steps at once; you can see any or all of the staircase, any way you like. . . . That's fine. . . . Just notice yourself at the top of the staircase, and the step you're on, and any others you like. . . . However you see it is fine. . . . Now, in a moment, but not yet, I'm going to begin to count, out loud, from 1 to 20, and . . . as you may already have guessed . . . as I count each number I'd like you to take a step down that staircase . . . see yourself stepping down, feel yourself stepping down, one step for each number I count . . . and all you need to do is notice, just notice, how much more comfortable and relaxed you can feel at each step, as you go down the staircase . . . one step for each number that I count . . . the larger the number, the farther down the staircase . . . and the farther down the staircase, the more comfortable you can feel . . . one step for each number. . . . All right, you can begin to get ready. . . . Now, I'm going to begin . . . ONE . . . one step down the staircase . . . TWO . . . two steps down the staircase . . . that's fine . . . THREE . . . three steps down the staircase . . . and maybe you already notice how much more relaxed you can feel. . . . I wonder if there are places in your body that feel more relaxed than others. . . . Perhaps your shoulders feel more relaxed than your neck. . . . Perhaps your legs feel more relaxed than your arms. . . . I don't know, and it really doesn't matter. . . . All that matters is that you feel comfortable . . . that's all. . . . FOUR . . . four steps down the staircase, perhaps feeling already places in your body beginning to relax. . . . I wonder whether the deep relaxing, restful heaviness in your forehead is already beginning to spread and flow . . . down, across your eyes, down across your face, into your mouth and jaw . . . down through your neck, deep, restful, heavy. . . . FIVE . . . five steps down the staircase . . . a quarter of the way down, and already beginning, perhaps, to really, really enjoy your relaxation and comfort. . . . SIX . . . six steps down the staircase . . . Perhaps beginning to notice that the sounds that were distracting becomes less so . . . that all the sounds you can hear become a part of your experience of comfort and relaxation . . . anything you can notice becomes a part of your experience of comfort and relaxation. . . . SEVEN . . . seven steps down the staircase . . . that's fine. . . . Perhaps noticing the heavy, restful, comfortably relaxing feeling spreading down into your shoulders, into your arms. . . . I wonder whether you notice one arm feeling heavier than the other. . . . Perhaps your left arm feels a bit heavier than your right . . . perhaps your right arm feels heavier than your left. . . . I don't know, perhaps they both feel equally, uncomfortably heavy. . . . It really doesn't matter . . . just letting yourself become more and more aware of that comfortable heaviness . . . or is it a feeling of lightness? . . . I really don't know, and it really doesn't matter . . . EIGHT . . . eight steps down the staircase . . . perhaps noticing that, even as you relax, your heart seems to beat much faster and harder than you might expect, perhaps noticing the tingling in your fingers . . . perhaps wondering about the fluttering on your heavy eyelids. . . . NINE . . . nine steps down the staircase, breathing comfortably, slowly, and deeply . . . restfully, noticing that heaviness really is beginning to sink in, as you continue to notice the pleasant, restful, comfortable relaxation just spread through your body. . . . TEN . . . ten steps down the staircase . . . halfway to the bottom of the staircase, wondering perhaps what might be happening, perhaps wondering if anything at all is happening . . . and yet, knowing that it really doesn't matter, feeling so pleasantly restful, just continuing to notice the growing, spreading, comfortable relaxation. . . . ELEVEN . . . eleven steps down the staircase . . . noticing maybe that as you feel increasingly heavy, more and more comfortable, there's nothing to bother you, nothing to disturb you, as you become deeper and deeper relaxed. . . . TWELVE . . . twelve steps down the staircase. . . . I wonder whether you notice how easily you can hear the sound of my voice . . . how easily you can understand the words I say . . . with nothing to bother, nothing to disturb. . . . THIRTEEN . . . thirteen steps down the staircase, feeling more and more the real enjoyment of this relaxation and comfort. . . . FOURTEEN . . . fourteen steps down the staircase . . . noticing perhaps the sinking, restful pleasantness as your body seems to just sink down, deeper and deeper into the chair, with nothing to bother, nothing to disturb . . . as though the chair holds you, comfortably and warmly. . . . FIFTEEN . . . fifteen steps down the staircase . . . three quarters of the way down the staircase . . . deeper and deeper relaxed, absolutely nothing at all to do . . .

but just enjoy yourself. . . . SIXTEEN . . . sixteen steps down the staircase . . . wondering perhaps what to experience at the bottom of the staircase . . . and yet knowing how much more ready you already feel to become deeper and deeper relaxed . . . more and more comfortable, with nothing to bother, nothing to disturb. . . . SEVENTEEN . . . seventeen steps down the staircase . . . closer and closer to the bottom, perhaps feeling your heart beating harder and harder, perhaps feeling the heaviness in your arms and legs become even more clearly comfortable . . . knowing that nothing really matters except your enjoyment of your experience of comfortable relaxation, with nothing to bother, nothing to disturb. . . . EIGHTEEN . . . eighteen steps down the staircase . . . almost to the bottom, with nothing to bother, nothing to disturb, as you continue to go deeper and deeper . . . relaxed . . . heavy . . . comfortable . . . restful . . . relaxed . . . nothing really to do, no one to please, no one to satisfy . . . just to notice how very comfortable and heavy you can feel, and continue to feel as you continue to breathe, slowly and comfortably . . . restfully. . . . NINETEEN . . . nineteen steps down the staircase . . . almost to the bottom of the staircase . . . nothing to bother, nothing to disturb you as you continue to feel more and more comfortable, more and more relaxed, more and more rested . . . more and more comfortable . . . just noticing. . . . And now . . . TWENTY . . . bottom of the staircase . . . deeply, deeply relaxed . . . deeper with every breath you take . . . as I talk to you for a moment about something you already know a lot about . . . remembering and forgetting. . . . You know a lot about it, because we all do a lot of it . . . every moment of every day you remember . . . and then you forget, so you can remember something else. . . . You can't remember everything all at once, so you let some memories move quietly back in your mind. . . . I wonder, for instance, if you remember what you had for lunch yesterday. . . . I would guess that, with not too much effort, you can remember what you had for lunch yesterday . . . and yet . . . I wonder if you remember what you had for lunch a month ago today. . . . I would guess the effort is really too great to dig up that memory, although of course it is there . . . somewhere, deep in the back of your mind . . . no need to remember, so you don't. . . . And I wonder if you'll be pleased to notice that the things we talk about today, with your eyes closed, are things you'll remember tomorrow, or the next day . . . or next week. . . . I wonder if you'll decide to let the memory of these things rest quietly in the back of your mind . . . or if you'll remember gradually, a bit at a time . . . or perhaps all at once, to be again resting in the back of your mind. . . . Perhaps you'll be surprised to notice that the reception room is the place for memory to surface. . . . Perhaps not. . . . Perhaps you'll notice that it is more comfortable to remember on another day altogether. . . . It really doesn't matter at all. . . . Whatever you do, however you choose to

remember . . . is just fine . . . absolutely natural. . . . It doesn't matter at all
. . . whether you remember tomorrow or the next day, whether you remember all at once, or gradually . . . completely or only partially . . . whether
you let the memory rest quietly and comfortably in the back of your mind . . .
really doesn't matter at all. . . . And, too, I wonder if you'll notice that you'll
feel surprised that your visit here today is so much more pleasant and comfortable than you might have expected. . . . I wonder if you'll notice that surprise
. . . that there are no other feelings. . . . Perhaps you'll feel curious about that
surprise . . . surprise, curiosity. . . . I wonder if you'll be pleased to notice
that today . . . and any day . . . whenever you feel your head resting back
against the headrest . . . when you feel your head resting back like this . . .
you'll feel reminded of how very comfortable you are feeling right now . . .
even more comfortable that you feel even now . . . comfortable, relaxed . . .
nothing to bother, nothing to disturb. . . . I wonder if you'll be reminded of
this comfort, too, and relaxation, by just noticing the brightness of the light up
above . . . perhaps this comfort and relaxation will come flooding back,
quickly and automatically, whenever you find yourself beginning to sit down
in the dental chair. . . . I don't know exactly how it will seem. . . . I only
know, as perhaps you also know . . . that your experience will seem surprisingly more pleasant, surprisingly more comfortable, surprisingly more restful
than you might expect . . . with nothing to bother, nothing to disturb . . .
whatever you are able to notice . . . everything can be a part of your
experience of comfort, restfulness and relaxation . . . everything you notice
can be a part of being absolutely comfortable . . . and I want to remind you
that whenever (doctor's name) touches your right shoulder, like this . . . whenever it is appropriate, and only when it is appropriate . . . whenever (doctor's
name) touches your right shoulder, like this . . . or whenever I touch your
right shoulder, like this . . . you'll experience a feeling . . . a feeling of being
ready to do something. . . . Whenever I touch your right shoulder, like this
. . . or whenever (doctor's name) touches your right shoulder, like this . . .
you'll experience a feeling . . . a feeling of being ready to do something . . .
perhaps a feeling of being ready to close your eyes . . . perhaps a feeling of
being ready to be even more comfortable . . . perhaps ready to know even
more clearly that there's nothing to bother, nothing to disturb . . . perhaps
ready to become heavy and tired. . . . I don't know . . . but whenever I touch
your right shoulder, like this . . . you'll experience a feeling . . . a feeling of
being ready to do something. . . . It really doesn't matter . . . perhaps just a
feeling of being ready to be even more surprised . . . it doesn't really
matter. . . . Nothing really matters but your experience of comfort and
relaxation . . . absolutely deep comfort and relaxation . . . with nothing to
bother and nothing to disturb. . . . That's fine . . . and now, as you continue

to enjoy your comfortable relaxation, I'd like you to notice how very nice it feels to be this way . . . to really enjoy your experience, to really enjoy the feelings your body can give you . . . and in a moment, but not yet . . . not until we're ready . . . but in a moment, I'm going to count from 20 to 1 . . . and as you know, I'd like you to feel yourself going back up the steps . . . one step for each number . . . you'll have all the time you need. . . . After all, time is relative. . . . Feel yourself slowly and comfortably going back up the steps, one step for each number I count . . . more alert as you go back up the steps, one step for each number I count . . . when I reach three, your eyes will be almost ready to open . . . when I reach two, they will have opened . . . and when I reach one, you'll be alert, awake, refreshed . . . perhaps as though you'd had a nice nap . . . alert, refreshed, comfortable . . . and even though you'll still be very comfortable and relaxed, you'll be alert and feeling very well . . . perhaps surprised, but feeling very well . . . perhaps ready to be surprised. . . . No hurry, you'll have all the time you need, as you begin to go back up these restful steps. . . . TWENTY . . . NINETEEN . . . EIGHTEEN . . . that's right, feel yourself going back up the steps . . . ready to be surprised, knowing what you had for lunch yesterday, and yet . . . SEVENTEEN . . . SIXTEEN . . . FIFTEEN . . . a quarter of the way back up, more and more alert . . . no rush, plenty of time . . . feel yourself become more and more alert . . . FOURTEEN . . . THIRTEEN . . . TWELVE . . . ELEVEN . . . TEN . . . halfway back up the stairs . . . more and more alert . . . comfortable but more and more alert. . . . NINE . . . that's right, feel yourself becoming more and more alert. . . . EIGHT . . . SEVEN . . . SIX . . . FIVE . . . FOUR . . . THREE . . . That's right . . . TWO . . . and ONE. . . . That's right, wide awake, alert, relaxed, refreshed . . . that's fine. How do you feel? Relaxed? Comfortable?

SUMMARY

Hypnosis can be an invaluable asset to the dentist. The dental environment is a source of anxiety for most patients, and this anxiety creates a barrier both to treatment and preventive education.

It is important for the dentist to understand the causes of dental phobia and realize that fears cannot effectively be countered by logic. Taking the time to gain a patient's trust and providing a warm and relaxing office environment will establish the foundation for successful treatment.

In many instances, a formal induction is not necessary. The dentist can use simple hypnotic principles to relax the patient, alleviate fears, and raise the pain threshold. For more extensive procedures, the light-to-medium hypnotic state, resulting in both deep muscle relaxation and analgesia, is usually sufficient. These simple techniques and strategies can make the practice of dentistry more rewarding for both dentists and their patients.

FURTHER READING

Barber J., & Adrian, C. (Eds.) (1982). *Psychological approaches to the management of pain.* New York: Brunner/Mazel.

Hartland, J. (1971). *Medical and dental hypnosis.* London: Bailliere Tindall.

REFERENCES

Barber J. (1977). Rapid induction analgesia: A clinical report. *American Journal of Clinical Hypnosis, 19,* 138–148.

Horowitz, L. G. (1980). Use of progressive relaxation and imaginal flooding for the reduction of anxiety in the presurgical dental phobic. *Journal of Preventive Dentistry, 6,* 35–41.

Pinkham, J. R., & Schroeder, C. S. (1975). Dentist and psychologist: Practical considerations for a team approach to the intensely anxious dental patient. *Journal of the American Dental Association, 90,* 1022.

Tinkler, S. (1971). The use of hypnosis in dental surgery. In J. Hartland, *Medical and Dental Hypnosis.* London: Bailliere Tindall, 360–373.

12

Psychotherapy

Jesse James Thomas, PhD

The cure of soul has to be effected by the life of certain charms . . . and these charms are fair words.

—Socrates

The greatest difficulty in relating hypnosis to psychotherapy is in providing basic definitions. It is not clear what hypnosis is, as distinguished from other ASCs. It is not clear what psychotherapy is, or what role the unconscious plays in the psychotherapeutic process. And it is certainly not clear whether there is such a thing as hypnotherapy.

There is no universally accepted definition of hypnosis, although most authors agree with Shor (1959) that hypnosis involves a shift in attention away from the external environment and toward "a small range of preoccupations" and "the relative fading of the generalized reality orientation into nonfunctional awareness" (p. 592).

Most definitions of hypnosis (see Chapter 1 for a representative sample) distinguish hypnosis from ordinary states of consciousness, but do not distinguish hypnosis from other ASCs. Korn (1983) found advantage in describing the therapeutic uses of imagery, a common characteristic of all ASCs, and saw the choice of a particular ASC as somewhat arbitrary. He suggested that training in imagery can take place with or without specific training in hypnosis. The images that Korn described (see Chapter 3) borrow from a variety of historical traditions and are used in conjunction with many different ASCs, hypnosis among them.

Certainly, hypnosis has been more closely linked with psychotherapy than have other ASCs. It was hypnosis that provided the original incentive for much of Freud's work. After his own unsuccessful attempts to induce trance, Freud adapted hypnosis to psychotherapeutic use in his own method of free association, which he saw as superior in effectiveness and less dangerous in terms of transference problems. Hypnosis was thus instrumental in opening up the world of the unconscious to the therapeutic process. But this point brings us to another serious problem in definition. Just what is the unconscious?

Even after a half century of Freudian tradition, Cheek and LeCron (1968) declared that "for psychotherapy to be successful, we need to know much more than we do about the unconscious mind and how it functions" (p. 82). The most recent work in hypnosis, especially that of Erickson (Erickson, Rossi, and Rossi, 1976), suggests that the unconscious is not a cauldron of chaotic, surging desires so much as the locus of much of our most important learning, far more of which takes place below the level of consciousness than we realize. However, Erickson's discussion of the learning ability of the unconscious mind is more practical than theoretical, and much remains to be done in clarifying his definition and relating it to existing notions of the unconscious. In any case, a clearer concept of the unconscious is crucial to an increased understanding of the relationship between hypnosis and psychotherapy.

COMMON FACTORS IN PSYCHOTHERAPY AND HYPNOSIS

While much remains to be clarified concerning the nature of the unconscious, much has been done to clarify the nature of psychotherapy as a process. A number of writers have recently tried to demonstrate that no matter what style of psychotherapy is employed, all styles, from the most behavioristic to the most humanistic, have a number of common characteristics (Frank, 1973; Halleck, 1980; Marmour, 1980). Mott (1982) provided an excellent distillation of the characteristics common to different psychotherapeutic styles and emphasized the way in which hypnosis facilitates or enhances these characteristics. The following list summarizes Mott's points:

1. Good patient-therapist relationship with faith and hope in the power of the healer. Mott quoted a number of sources that stress the importance of this characteristic in nearly all styles of psychotherapy. In terms of hypnosis, he noted the statement by Erickson et al. (1976), that if a patient does not believe that he or she is in trance, further work is limited, because it is necessary to demonstrate that trance is

different from ordinary waking states. Faith in the power of the healer is, therefore, essential.

2. A belief held in common by the patient and the therapist as to the rationale or myth that explains the patient's illness and the treatment required. In discussing this characteristic, Mott relied especially on Spiegel and Spiegel's (1978) description of the way in which highly hypnotized subjects will abandon a current myth-belief constellation in favor of a new formulation that is forcefully and appropriately presented to them. Although Erickson insisted that conscious interpretations of our actions may be of little use in therapy, he nevertheless spent a great deal of time and energy building up the patient's confidence in the powers of the unconscious mind.

3. Cognitive learning and insight into the basis for the patient's difficulties. Mott's elaboration of this characteristic is sketchy, but he emphasized the way in which the hypnotic context encourages the patient to reveal conscious and preconscious thoughts, which in turn aid the practitioner in establishing a basis for the patient's difficulties. Although it varies considerably from one therapeutic style to another and from one school of hypnosis to another, cognitive learning is a common characteristic of much psychotherapy, and much hypnosis is used in a psychotherapeutic setting.

4. Catharsis, or the release of emotional tension. Here, again, Mott's elaboration is brief, but he emphasized the cathartic element in most styles of psychotherapy and the known ability of hypnosis to encourage abreaction in such a way as to permit control over the degree and intensity of affect.

5. Suggestion and persuasion, overt and covert. Mott made the point that suggestion and persuasion, while common to most forms of therapy, are especially obvious and well planned in hypnosis. Following Barrios (1970), he stressed the way in which hypnosis keeps incongruent perceptions, beliefs, and attitudes from interfering with hypnotic suggestions and, thus, with conditioning.

6. Learning new adaptive behavior and unlearning maladaptive behavior enhanced by operant conditioning and the rehearsal of new adaptive techniques. To illustrate this characteristic, Mott referred to the way in which Erickson speaks directly to the unconscious in teaching new adaptive behavior. He also emphasized the way that hypnosis generally provides an excellent ground to rehearse new adaptive techniques.

Referring to his own work in documenting the ability of hypnosis to facilitate many different styles of psychotherapy, Mott (1981) claimed that it would be more useful to avoid the term hypnotherapy altogether and simply consider hypnosis a facilitator of a specific form of therapy. In this suggestion, he was similar to Cheek and LeCron (1968) who stated that "hypnosis is not a method of treatment but a clinical tool" (p. 197).

It can hardly be denied that hypnosis can serve as a facilitator for various forms of psychotherapy. Its range of application is indeed broad, and one can find it useful in a wide variety of psychotherapeutic styles. It is likewise clear that hypnosis may be used to facilitate not only various forms of psychotherapy, but also a wide variety of other endeavors, from religious or mystical states to advertising and entertainment.

One could also use Mott's list to support the argument that hypnosis *is* a form of psychotherapy. Erickson's work is a case in point. That his techniques have been adapted by practitioners of other therapeutic styles, such as Bandler and Grinder's (1975, 1977) neurolinguistic programming and Rossi's (1979) Jungian analysis, would seem to illustrate Mott's thesis that hypnosis is a tool that facilitates therapy. On the other hand, Erickson himself always used different forms of psychotherapy, from psychoanalysis to operant conditioning, to support his use of hypnosis as a treatment method. All other methods were clearly secondary to his own particular use of hypnosis.

At the present time, it is clear that hypnosis can be a major ingredient in the psychotherapeutic process, but it is not clear whether hypnosis can be considered a form of psychotherapy. With the possible exception of Erickson, no one has applied hypnosis in a clearly defined or systematic way comparable to recognized forms of psychotherapy. However we understand hypnosis, it definitely has important uses in psychotherapy. Perhaps, for now, that is as far as we can or need to go.

HYPNOTIC TECHNIQUES AND
THE PSYCHOTHERAPEUTIC PROCESS

This section will focus on the practical rather than the theoretical aspect of hypnosis in the psychotherapeutic process. On the broadest level, hypnosis can be effective in treating a wide variety of psychological disorders, especially those that involve anxiety, depression, and habit control. It is useful in treating anxiety, partly because it is a state of relaxation. It is useful in treating depression, partly because it goes beneath the conscious, rational level, the overdevelopment of which is one of the major causes of depression. And it is effective in treating problems of habit control, partly because the habitual way of experiencing the world is surrendered in the trance state, which is conducive in itself to change.

In *Trauma, Trance, and Transformation: A Clinical Guide to Hypnotherapy*, Edelstein (1981) arranged hypnotic techniques into three basic categories: (a) uncovering techniques, (b) techniques for attenuating affect, and (c) relearning techniques.* These categories provide a useful framework for exploring the uses of hypnosis in the psychotherapeutic process.

Uncovering Techniques

One of the basic assumptions in most styles of therapy is that it is necessary to uncover either personal material that will help to delineate the patient's problems or internal resources that will help to deal with those problems.

Relaxation.   A patient who is anxious or hysterical must first be able to enter a more relaxed state of mind before it is possible to work with the problem in a coherent way. Even styles of therapy that deal neither with a patient's past nor unconscious activities find relaxation a basic resource in uncovering and working with more complex problems. Relaxation can be the specific goal of hypnosis, but it is more likely to be a means to another end, even if that is a further deepening procedure.

Dreams and fantasies.   Dreams may be used in many ways in hypnosis. They can be remembered, explored, and developed in a trance state just as in psychoanalysis, but they can also be induced, either during the trance state or as posthypnotic suggestions, for the sake of realizing specific goals. Sacerdote (1978) developed some useful procedures in which he induced dreams during trance that were repeated and developed with each repetition toward the completion of the patient's incomplete themes.

Fantasies may be used in a similar way. A number of authors have explored these possibilities (Sheehan, 1972; Kroger and Fezler, 1976,

---

*I am indebted to this book for the tripartite organization of this part of the chapter. I have elaborated Edelstein's categories somewhat differently, condensing or expanding upon his sections, and defining some of the subheadings differently. Thus, I do not mean to imply that he was saying exactly the same thing that I am in my elaboration of his basic themes.

Samuels and Samuels, 1975). Fantasy must be distinguished from imagery, which will be discussed later in this chapter under Relearning Techniques. While fantasy is used to tap a patient's revelatory and creative potential, imagery is most often used for reconditioning and relearning activities. The variety of patient responses to a single fantasized setting, either inside or outside trance, testifies to his or her ability to explore internal resources and uncover important information about the problem being treated.

Automatic writing and other expressive techniques.   To use automatic writing, the patient is provided with a pen and paper while in trance and told to write on the paper without any preconception of what is to be written. In other words, the pen is to do the writing without conscious interference from the writer. Patients who achieve a deep trance state may not even recognize what they have written after they have returned to a normal state of consciousness. The writing style of automatic writing is quite often different from that of the waking state (Kroger, 1977); its content can be a valuable resource in dealing with the patient's problems and can be used as a basis for further therapy.

Also included in this category are (a) hypnography (Meares, 1957), or working with painting in a trance state; (b) hypnodrama (Greenberg, 1974), or dramatizing a conflict while under hypnosis; and (c) hypno-plasty (Raginsky, 1962), or working with clay or other sculptural material. These techniques are especially useful with patients who are unusually visual or kinesthetic but not verbal.

Age regression.   Age regression under hypnosis not only has the advantage of recovering earlier experiences that are unlikely to be remembered in a normal state, but it is also a safer way of making that recovery. A number of protective devices can be used, such as suggestions that the patient observe the experience from behind a protective shield or watch it on a movie or television screen. Age regression can be used by itself or in combination with desensitization or other techniques for attenuating affect. As Cheek and LeCron (1968) reported: "the patient who is age regressed seems to be able to vent bottled up emotions far better than when he merely remembers some experience" (p. 199).

The following case study illustrates the use of hypnotic age regression as an uncovering technique and as a technique for attenuating effect.

A female patient had been involved in a skiing accident in which she had suffered a severe rupture of the medial collateral and anterior cruciate tendons, requiring a tendon transplant. After 7 weeks of physical therapy, including three sessions per week, she had regained flexibility of her knee from 105 to 124°, far short of the normal 155-160°. During the sessions, she would suffer intolerable pain and even attack the therapist if he tried to push her beyond her meager limits. She originally sought psychotherapy for a program of pain management, as an adjunct to her physical therapy program.

Using standard inductions and relaxation procedures, she was able in three sessions of hypnosis during the next 10 days to increase the mobility of her knee from 124° to 133°, a much greater rate of improvement than she had managed up to that point. During the fourth session, she was beginning to show signs of stress that appeared to be coming from a much deeper level than in any of the earlier sessions. Further communication indicated that the source was an earlier childhood experience. Her whimpering, for example, seemed to be an indication of a spontaneous age regression. A formal age regression procedure was employed, in which the patient turned back through time by visualizing the years as pages of a book and slowly leafing back through the pages until she came to an experience that seemed to be the source of the feelings that she was experiencing. The patient was able to relive the experience without the protection of shielding techniques. She seemed, however, to be shivering a bit, and so the therapist provided her with a blanket to help give her a sense of security. She then relived an experience in which she had been condemned for crying when injured. She was encouraged to cry for as long as she felt like it and to let the therapist know when she felt finished. She cried softly for a few minutes, undoubtedly in part her reaction to her present injury as well as her past one, and then drifted back into a deeply relaxed state. After a few more minutes, the therapist returned her to a waking state.

When she went to her physical therapy session later that day, she increased the flexibility of her knee from 133 to 138°, the greatest gain that she had experienced in any single session up to that point. During the next three sessions of hypnosis, she moved from 138 to 152°, for a total of 28° in the 3 weeks of hypnotic treatment. This rate of recovery was over three times the rate obtained before treatment in hypnosis began. The patient later credited hypnosis as the greatest single factor in recovering her ability to walk.

Techniques for Attenuating Affect

Handling potentially traumatic or even unmanageable emotions is one of the most common problems in psychotherapy. Hypnosis has some obvious advantages in this regard.

Suggestion. Affect can be reduced by either direct or indirect suggestion, which can be combined with other techniques listed below.

Because the person in hypnotic trance is already relaxed and affect is flattened, it is a good time to work with highly charged issues such as anger, grief, anxiety, panic, and phobic reactions. Direct suggestion may be useful and is simpler and more easily programmed than indirect suggestion, but it can also trigger resistance. Indirect suggestion has the advantage of bypassing many forms of resistance, because the suggestions take place below the conscious level. The following case study illustrates the use of both kinds of suggestion as well as the use of imagery:

In working with a woman with a chronically high level of anxiety, the author began with a number of stress reduction procedures, teaching the patient self-hypnosis based on sensory relaxation techniques that link suggestions for relaxation with breathing patterns and other body sensations. In the most effective of these, the author linked the relaxation with a personal mannerism that she showed quite often during situations in which she was especially self-confident. This mannerism was a slow, almost cat-like blinking of her eyes. It was suggested that when she was experiencing stress, she could enter a relaxed state by simply closing her eyes very slowly, taking a deep breath, and then slowly opening her eyes again, but this time to a different, more relaxed vision of the world.

This suggestion was simple and direct and worked well most of the time, but she complained during one session that she had had several occasions during that week where the anxiety reaction started and had grown to such proportions by the time that she became aware of it that it was "too late" for the technique to work well. The practitioner gave indirect suggestions in a conversation with her unconscious by telling a story of how, when people wake up to an alarm clock that they have set by accident on their day off, they roll over, shut off the alarm, and go back to sleep without ever coming up to the conscious level. An indirect suggestion was made that she could experience anxiety in a similar fashion, that she could roll over and shut off the alarm before the anxiety reached any conscious level. This was done by stressing how irritable the sound of an alarm clock can be, incorporating many of the characteristics of her own reports of anxiety states, but without calling attention to that comparison. Anxiety can in fact be very alarming.

As a precautionary matter, so that she could still become alarmed when the source of anxiety justified the alarm, she was also given an extended account, following Pelletier (1977), of the origins of the stress reaction in primitive societies, where anxiety might be an appropriate response if a person were suddenly confronted by a bear; she was told that anxiety is usually triggered at inappropriate times in civilized societies, where energy can usually be put to better use by solving the problem at hand than by panicking.

In her next visits she reported that the anxiety that had been troubling her earlier was in much better control and that most of the time she did not think about it at all.

This account also raises the issue of using self-hypnosis in a psychotherapeutic setting. Self-hypnosis, taught during sessions and facilitated by tapes, can be a very effective way of dealing not only with a patient's problems, but also with the therapist's own work-related stress. It is, in fact, difficult to use hypnosis with patients all day without the therapist becoming hypnotized as well, in unintentional, if not intentional, self-hypnosis.

Desensitization. According to Kroger (1977), desensitization, or the gradual and controlled exposure to a situation or object that the patient fears, falls into two basic categories: overt and covert. Overt techniques deal directly with the environment, while covert techniques use the imagination and its images. Overt techniques include flooding and implosion therapy, in which the patient is presented with intense forms of the fear, and in which desensitization takes place by repeated and intense expression until the material becomes familiar and more relaxed. Role playing, modeling, and positive reinforcement are all overt techniques that can be used in hypnotic states as well as outside them. In covert techniques, however, the patient imagines going through a carefully constructed fear hierarchy while in a relaxed state, moving from one level to another until the situation or object no longer produces the usual anxiety.

Silent abreaction. Here the emphasis is on reliving and reenacting traumatic experiences and releasing energy, such as grief or anger, that is attached to the experience. Silent abreaction overlaps to some extent with age regression in this connection, but its purpose is to release energy rather than to uncover levels of experience below the level of consciousness. Also, the emphasis with silent abreaction may be on present or future situations, rather than on the past, as is the case in age regression. There is also some overlapping with desensitization, but the focus is more on erasure by energy release rather than on control and relearning.

Relearning Techniques

Many theories have been advanced in recent years about the way in which hypnosis facilitates learning. The most recent of these involved attempts to relate hypnosis to cybernetic principles of learning (Kroger, 1977). Understanding consciousness as an open, rather than closed, system maximizes one's ability to change in order to respond, survive, and grow. Habit control goes far beyond matters of smoking, drinking, or controlling one's weight. It can even be important for the way in which therapists develop their therapeutic styles. We may be in a better position to appreciate and apply hypnosis to psychotherapeutic problems when we surrender our attachments to habitual thought forms.

Consistent with the cybernetic notions of entropy (decay) and negentropy (renewal) is Erickson's concept of the way in which hypnosis facilitates unconscious learning. The desire to maximize negentropy is one of the reasons that unconscious learning has become so important. Unconscious activity is closer to the edge of most change than is conscious activity, which tends to be more fixed and more subject to entropy. Change takes place at the unconscious level, before the consciousness becomes aware of it. Hypnosis is especially suited to the change and renewal process because of the way that it uses the more unconscious and less rational framework.

Suggestion. The classical model for learning in hypnosis is direct suggestion. The patient can be led clearly and consciously from one stage to another in the learning process, as in the learning of relaxation techniques or habit control. It has been and will doubtless continue to be a major part of the contribution of hypnosis to psychotherapy.

It is indirect suggestion, however, that is now receiving more attention in relation to the learning process. Erickson's favorite illustration is that all of us learned to walk (Zeig, 1980), a very complex behavior, at an age considerably earlier than the emergence of consciousness. His own vast reservoir of metaphors, stories, jokes, puzzles, and anecdotes, in which he rarely brings his points to a conscious level, is indeed impressive. Erickson, for example, is more apt to deal with a potential suicide by telling stories filled with images of vegetation, death, and rebirth, without even mentioning suicide, than he is to use a direct approach in which the patient is aware of learning on a conscious level. This approach suggests a host of imaginative possibilities to the psychotherapist. In the case study of the woman with the chronic anxiety, described earlier, her feeling of anxiety was indirectly linked with the irritating sound of an alarm clock, which could easily be shut off. The wording of this suggestion was modeled after similar images used by Erickson (see Zeig, 1980, for examples).

Imagery. Kroger and Fezler (1976) have done the most to promote imagery in the context of reconditioning and its relationship to hypnosis. They developed and catalogued a vast array of images—mental representations of actual objects, activities, or situations—capable of producing the same response as the actual object, activity, or situation. The basic assumption is that by putting the patient in an imaginary situation, the same learning can take place as in the real-life situation. One can learn, for example, to ski, play tennis, or shoot foul shots in basketball to a surprising level of competency simply by imagining regular participation in these activities (see Korn, 1983, chapt. 8; Singer and Switzer, 1980, chapt. 14). The application of imagery to the use of hypnosis in psychotherapy is rich in possibilities.

Rehearsal techniques.   The rehearsal of a situation can be overt or covert. In either case, a person can practice and learn difficult behaviors simply by rehearsing the activity until mastery takes place. By the time the person confronts an actual situation, unwanted energy has been discharged, difficulties have been anticipated and overcome, and mastery has been achieved through practice.

The following two short case studies demonstrate learning processes facilitated by hypnosis:

Case study 1.   A graduate student in mathematics was suffering a severe panic reaction while preparing for her qualifying examinations. This panic dated back to a particular exam in high school and had been experienced regularly since then. She strongly resisted returning to that experience through age regression, and so the decision was made to use rehearsal as the main approach. She first learned a number of stress reduction techniques and then began rehearsing the exam itself, taking one problem at a time as they emerged. She discovered, for example, that part of her panic during the last few days leading up to the exam came from the fact that her boyfriend would be returning to school at Berkeley and that he would not be available for emotional support. So she was told while in trance how a person can be present without actually being there. Some people, for example, carry photographs of loved ones that can be displayed on the dashboard of the car. It was further stated that her unconscious could learn from this account, but that it would learn in its own way. When she awakened from her trance, she announced with great enthusiasm that she often slept in her boyfriend's old shirts and that she would plan to wear one of them to the exam, which proved to be an effective device.

Case study 2.   A middle-aged man had been fired from his job and had been depressed and out of work for over a year. One part of his rehabilitation involved a homework assignment in which it was suggested that he buy a

Christmas cactus and take daily care of it, noticing even slight differences in the growth of the buds when they began to appear at the ends of the leaves. The suggestion at the unconscious level was that he pair himself with the cactus blossoms as they developed. This procedure proved to be effective, along with others, since he did experience more "growth" during that time than at any other period of his therapy. It became especially interesting when he began wearing frequently to his sessions a green sweater and a pair of socks that were the same color as the cactus. This was never mentioned to him and may, of course, have been coincidental, but he did stop wearing the sweater and socks when the cactus bloomed. When asked about it later, he stated that he did get a special kind of pleasure out of wearing the clothing despite the fact that he did not find it especially attractive. As it also turned out, the cactus did not bloom until February, which was in keeping with his own schedule of being a late bloomer in looking for his job. Eventually, he did find one.

The kind of learning by pairing behaviors that is represented by these studies is, of course, something that can be done outside of trance, but the author has found it much more effective when developed or suggested in trance. In the first case, the patient was fully conscious of the lesson; in the second, the patient was completely unconscious of it. One of the most challenging and interesting parts of working with hypnosis is the possibility of designing such learning situations. While a chapter on hypnosis and psychotherapy is only an introduction to some of the possibilities of using hypnosis in such a context, it is hoped that it will also stir some of the more creative possibilities for the reader in the development of his or her own learning processes.

SAMPLE INDUCTION

Relaxation of an anxious patient must precede any actual work in psychotherapy. Induction processes are relaxation processes in themselves, and they may also lead to further relaxation procedures as the trance state deepens.

The following induction procedure has characteristics of methods in standard use as well as some distinctive elements of the author's invention. Pacing of the induction may vary, depending on the response of the patient. The pauses can be timed to coincide with the patient's breathing patterns.

This is an exercise . . . where you don't need . . . to do anything . . . except to look at the thumb . . . of your right hand. . . . Just extend your right arm . . . straight in front of you . . . and then raise it . . . about one foot . . . above the horizontal position. . . . Extend your thumb to the left. . . . You can either close your fingers . . . against the palm of your hand . . . or leave them open. . . . That part doesn't . . . make any difference . . . so long as your thumb . . . is extended . . . and you can see it easily. . . . Now just look at your thumb . . . and focus your attention there . .ʼ. without letting your gaze . . . wander off . . . to objects in the background. . . . Just look at your thumb . . . in the same way . . . that you would look . . . at a sunset. . . . You just watch it . . . without trying to change anything. . . . You don't try . . . to make the sun go down . . . any faster . . . or any slower . . . than it does. . . . You don't try to add . . . or to subtract anything . . . from a sunset. . . . You just watch it. . . . So just watch your thumb . . . without trying to change anything. . . . And don't try to change . . . what you are thinking . . . either. . . . Just watch your thumb . . . and continue to think . . . whatever you are thinking. . . . I am not talking . . . to your conscious . . . rational mind anyway. . . . So let your conscious, rational mind . . . think whatever it likes . . . while I am doing that. . . . Just keep watching . . . your thumb. . . . You may begin to notice . . . however, . . . several interesting things. . . . One is that your arm . . . begins to feel heavy . . . very heavy. . . . Just notice that. . . . You may also notice . . . certain changes . . . in the way that things look. . . . They take on . . . a different appearance. . . . You don't have to make this happen. . . . It just happens. . . . You may also be surprised . . . to notice that . . . without making it do so . . . your thumb . . . will slowly . . . begin to move down . . . very slowly . . . almost imperceptibly at first . . . just like the sun in the sky. . . . As you continue to notice . . . how your arm is getting heavier . . . and heavier . . . it begins to move down . . . all by itself . . . toward your leg or your lap . . . and as it does . . . you feel more . . . and more relaxed. . . . You may also notice . . . that the sounds . . . that you hear . . . take on a somewhat different quality. . . . They are more like music now. . . . The sound of my voice . . . or other sounds in the room . . . or outside the room . . . go together . . . to make a kind of . . . musical accompaniment . . . to your relaxation. . . . As your thumb continues . . . to move down . . . you feel more . . . and more . . . relaxed . . . moving deeper . . . and deeper . . . into a state of relaxation. . . . As this happens . . . you also notice . . . that your eyelids feel heavier . . . and heavier. . . . Even if you want them . . . to stay open . . . they want to shut . . . all by themselves. . . . You do not have to make them do that. . . . They just do it . . . all by themselves. . . . So as your thumb gets closer . . . and closer . . . to your leg or your lap . . . and you move down . . . deeper . . . and deeper . . . and deeper . . . into the state of relaxation . . . it will be very easy . . . for your eyes . . . to shut completely . . . when your arm . . . comes to rest . . .

wherever it comes to rest . . . and you will notice . . . that you feel . . . very . . . very . . . relaxed. . . . You never know . . . just how long that takes . . . but when it does . . . you notice . . . that you feel . . . very . . . very . . . relaxed. . . . Your breathing becomes slower . . . and easier . . . as you continue to move deeper . . . and deeper . . . as far as you care to go . . . for the present . . . very . . . very relaxed.

SUMMARY

This chapter acknowledges many of the problems involved in defining both hypnosis and psychotherapy, as well as the problems of relating them to each other. The question of whether there is such a thing as hypnotherapy is left open. The focus of the chapter is on matters of practice rather than on analysis or diagnosis as such.

A three-fold division of hypnotic techniques relevant to the psychotherapeutic process has been described by Mott (1982): (a) Uncovering techniques including relaxation, use of dreams and fantasies, automatic writing and other expressive techniques, and age regression; (b) techniques for attenuating affect, including direct and indirect suggestion, desensitization, and silent abreaction; and (c) relearning techniques, including direct and indirect suggestion, imagery, and rehearsal techniques. In practice, of course, these techniques will be used in various combinations with a great deal of overlap as practitioners develop their distinctive styles and adapt their approaches to the needs of individual patients.

The chapter contains some concrete illustrations of these techniques in the form of brief case studies, but the reader is encouraged to pursue an individual program of professional training and further study. The additional readings at the end of this chapter have been chosen for their rich collection of concrete case studies as well as their further discussion of theoretical issues.

FURTHER READING

Bandler, R., & Grinder, J. (1975, 1977). *Patterns of the hypnotic techniques of Milton H. Erickson, M.D.* (2 vols.). Cupertino, CA: Meta Publications.

Edelstein, M. G. (1981). *Trauma, trance, and transformation: A clinical guide to hypnotherapy.* New York: Brunner/Mazel.

Gruenewald, D. (1981). Failures in hypnotherapy: A brief communication. *International Journal of Clinical and Experimental Hypnosis, 29,* 347–350.

Kroger, W. S., & Fezler, W. D. (1976). *Hypnosis and behavior modification: Imagery conditioning.* Philadelphia: J. P. Lippincott.

Zeig, J. K. (Ed.). (1980). *Teaching seminar with Milton Erickson, M.D.* New York: Brunner/Mazel.

REFERENCES

Bandler, R., & Grinder, J. (1975, 1977). *Patterns of the hypnotic techniques of Milton H. Erickson, M.D.* (2 vols.). Cupertino, CA: Meta Publications.

Barrios, A. A. (1970). Hypnotherapy: A reappraisal. *Psychotherapy: Theory, Research and Practice, 7,* 2-7.

Cheek, D. B., & LeCron, L. M. (1968). *Clinical hypnotherapy.* New York: Grune & Stratton.

Edelstein, M. G. (1981). *Trauma, trance, and transformation: A clinical guide to hypnotherapy.* New York: Brunner/Mazel.

Erickson, M. H., Rossi, E. L., & Rossi, S. I. (1976). *Hypnotic realities* (pp. 226-230). New York: Irvington.

Frank, J. D. (1973). *Persuasion and healing.* Baltimore: Johns Hopkins University Press.

Greenberg, I. (1974). *Psychodrama.* New York: Behavioral Publications.

Halleck, S. (1980). Seven healing factors in psychotherapy. *Practical Reviews in Psychiatry, 4,* 10.

Korn, E. R. (1983). *Visualization: The uses of imagery in the health professions.* Homewood, IL: Dow Jones-Irwin.

Kroger, W. S. (1977). *Clinical and experimental hypnosis* (2nd ed.). Philadelphia: J. P. Lippincott.

Kroger, W. S., & Fezler, W. D. (1976). *Hypnosis and behavior modification: Imagery conditioning.* Philadelphia: J. P. Lippincott.

Marmour, J. (1980). Recent trends in psychotherapy. *American Journal of Psychiatry, 137,* 4.

Meares, A. (1957). *Hypnography.* Springfield, IL: Charles C Thomas.

Mott, I. (1981). Hypnosis in the treatment of phobic disorders. *Psychiatric Annals, 11,* 36-45.

Mott, T. (1982). The role of hypnosis in psychotherapy. *American Journal of Clinical Hypnosis, 24,* 241-248.

Pelletier, K. R. (1977). *Mind as healer, mind as slayer: A holistic approach to preventing stress disorders.* New York: Dell.

Raginsky, B. B. (1962). Sensory hypnoplasty with case illustrations. *International Journal of Clinical and Experimental Hypnosis, 10,* 205-219.

Rossi, E. L. (Ed.). (1979). *The collected papers of Milton H. Erickson on hypnosis.* (4 vols.). New York: Irvington.

Sacerdote, P. (1978). *Induced dreams: About the theory and therapeutic applications of dreams hypnotically induced.* New York: Gaus.

Samuels, M., & Samuels, N. (1975). *Seeing with the mind's eye.* New York: Random House.

Sheehan, P. W. (Ed.). (1972). *The function and nature of imagery.* New York: Academic Press.

Shor, R. E. (1959). Hypnosis and the concept of the generalized reality orientation. *American Journal of Psychotherapy, 13,* 582–602.

Singer, J. L., & Switzer, E. (1980). *Mind-play: The creative uses of fantasy.* Englewood Cliffs, NJ: Prentice-Hall.

Spiegel, H., & Spiegel, D. (1978). *Trance and treatment.* New York: Basic Books.

Zeig, J. D. (Ed.). (1980). *Teaching seminar with Milton Erickson, M.D.* New York: Brunner/Mazel.

13

Use with Severely Disturbed Patients

Elgan L. Baker, PhD

The aspects of things that are most important for us are hidden because of their simplicity and familiarity. (One is unable to notice something— because it is always before one's eyes.) The real foundations of his inquiry do not strike a man at all unless that fact has, at sometime, struck him before. And this means: we fail to be struck by what, once seen, is most striking and most powerful.

—Ludwig Wittgenstein
Philosophical Investigations

In recent years, there has been growing interest in the nature of psychotic regression and the psychological treatment of severely disturbed patients. Although severely disturbed patients have long been of concern to psychiatry and psychology, the effective treatment of these problems has been delayed by the absence of a consistent and appropriate metapsychology for understanding them. Only in the past 30 years has this theoretical and conceptual base evolved to the point that efficient psychotherapeutic technique could be formulated and applied. The development of this conceptual base has been prompted primarily by the advances in ego psychology and clinical object-relations theory.

For many years, psychoanalysts paid little attention to severely disturbed patients except to conclude that they were unamenable for treatment by psychoanalysis and, therefore, by psychotherapy. This position derived primarily from Freud's (1911/1959) conclusion that the narcissistic nature of psychotic regression prevented these patients from establishing a workable transference. Although Freud never actually treated severely disturbed patients, he did analyze the well-known case of Schreiber, who provided an autobiographical account of his own psychotic episodes. On the basis of that analysis, Freud concluded that severely disturbed patients became so completely disengaged from the external world and reinvested in internal and autistic experience that they would be unable to form the working alliance necessary for psychoanalytic intervention.

However, as object-relations theory and ego psychology increasingly turned our attention to preneurotic developmental experiences and preneurotic forms of psychopathology, work with severely disturbed patients came to form the basis for the experimental development of clinical theory and technique. The evolution of the use of hypnosis in the treatment of severely disturbed patients parallels the development of psychological intervention within the larger psychotherapeutic context. The past decade in particular has been characterized by growing interest in the applications of hypnosis to the management of severely disturbed and actutely regressed patients.

The evolution of clinical techique with severely disturbed patients has come to emphasize the importance of establishing and maintaining a relatively safe, consistent, dependable, and gratifying therapeutic relationship. The development of this sort of treatment alliance is predicated on the use of a number of techniques that significantly differ from the traditional therapeutic stance of psychoanalytic psychotherapy. Research and clinical experience have suggested that neutrality and therapeutic deprivation only provoke further regression and decompensation among this population. Effective intervention recognizes the importance of establishing a modulated degree of therapeutic symbiosis and tolerating the development of a dependent and intense transference without premature interpretation and working through.

This evolving therapeutic approach has also tended to emphasize the provision of a working environment in which the therapist can lend his or her ego functions to the patient to provide support, reality testing, impulse control, and problem solving at a point when patients are not yet able to provide these functions for themselves. Therefore, even within the psychoanalytic tradition, contemporary psychotherapy with severely disturbed patients places little emphasis on formal interpretation, but rather views the therapeutic interaction as an opportunity to provide a developmental crucible and a sufficiently dependable relationship that patients can deal with the severe developmental defects that characterize the nature of their ego instability.

As clinicians have attempted to integrate the use of hypnosis into this larger therapeutic perspective, a number of significant issues have emerged. The controversy regarding the application of hypnosis with this population is not yet fully resolved. This chapter will review the contemporary literature and prevailing perspectives on issues important to the use of hypnosis with severely disturbed patients. These include hypnotic responsiveness, general treatment considerations, trance induction and principles of use, specific strategies for intervention, the nature and management of the therapeutic relationship, and specific techniques for dealing with many common problems encountered in work with these patients, including psychotic resistance and acting out.

HYPNOTIC RESPONSIVENESS

The early literature on hypnosis with severely disturbed patients focused primarily on whether or not psychotic patients could be hypnotized, and if so, whether hypnosis was contraindicated in their treatment. Research consistently demonstrated that psychotics are generally comparable to normal subjects and to neurotic patients in their responsiveness to hypnosis as measured by standardized scales (Greene, 1969; Kramer and Brennan, 1964; Vingoe and Kramer, 1966). In fact, one well-controlled study demonstrated that hospitalized shizophrenics scored higher on measures of hypnotizability than did undergraduate normal subjects (Kramer and Brennan, 1964). Although most studies tended to focus on schizophrenics, there is some evidence that the affective psychoses demonstrate comparable degrees of hypnotizability (Baker and Copeland, in press). In general, acute psychotics appear to be somewhat more hypnotizable than chronics (Whitman, 1961), and patients who demonstrate organic psychoses appear to be less amenable to trance induction, especially as their mental status becomes more deteriorated and demented. Formal measures of reality testing do not appear to correlate directly with hypnotizability (Wilson, Cormen, and Cole, 1949), and available evidence indicates that chemotherapy does not directly interfere with hypnotic responsiveness among psychotic patients unless they are so sedated that the focusing of attention is limited (Vingoe and Kramer, 1966).

A comprehensive review of the literature (Abrams, 1964) concluded that paranoid schizophrenics appear somewhat more hypnotizable than nonparanoid types, while catatonics are the least responsiveness to standard hypnotic induction techniques. Nevertheless, anecdotal reports of hypnotherapy with even catatonic patients are found in the literature. LaVoie, Sabourin, Ally, and Langolis (1976) attempted to relate the degree of hypnotizability among psychotics to clinical and intrapsychic variables. Among this population, several factors appeared directly related to hypnotic responsiveness: (a) indices of adaptive regression, (b) motivation, (c) capacity for ego involvement, (d) degree of control over dissociative processes, and (e) degree of preservation of autonomous and synthetic ego functions. On the basis of these data, LaVoie et al. concluded that the degree of regression in psychosis is inversely associated with the degree of hypnotic responsiveness. In general, then, these data suggest that acutely disturbed patients are more likely to be responsive to hypnotherapeutic intervention than chronics.

In a recent overview of the clinical and research literature, Scagnelli-Jöbsis (1983) concluded that the evidence of the past 30 years clearly supports the conclusion that psychotics can be hypnotized. Their responsiveness to hypnosis is generally comparable to that of any other patient population, although factors such as ego integrity, motivation, trust, and transference may be more powerful in determining hypnotic responsiveness in any specific situation than they would be in other, less disturbed, populations. The literature also supports the conclusion that hypnosis is a safe treatment modality for psychotics. In the entire empirical literature reported through 1980, there is not one report of harm directly associated with hypnotic induction. Although untoward experiences have been noted infrequently in the clinical literature, hypnosis has been judged to be a safe and effective intervention within the context of psychotherapy. It seems likely that the safe and judicious use of hypnosis in the treatment of these patients is predicated on the skill and sensitivity of the therapist, as is the case in psychotherapy with patients of any sort.

GENERAL TREATMENT CONSIDERATIONS
The special structural defects and dynamic concern of severely disturbed patients present several general considerations for their treatment in hypnotherapy. In particular, these patients present a developmentally determined inability to maintain a consistent and constant relationship with the external environment. For this reason, their behavior is typically viewed as labile and erratic. It is difficult for them to establish and maintain any sort of ongoing relationship with significant others. Due to this inability to maintain constancy, as well as to

conflicts around issues of trust and control, psychotic patients typically feel vulnerable in a world viewed as threatening, hostile, and potentially overwhelming. Their experiences with interpersonal relationships have been so malevolent and disappointing that an opportunity to establish a therapeutic alliance is met with great initial resistance or, at best, ambivalence. Many of the behaviors of severely disturbed patients may be viewed as attempts to insulate themselves from this threatening environment and to drive others away, so that their self-protective regression can be kept free from dangerous intrusions. Patients frequently fear that close or prolonged contact with other people will result in personal destruction through merger or incorporation. The fluid and unstable quality of the psychotic's boundaries and the extremely fragmented internal sense of self present additional dilemmas in developing an appropriate treatment program.

These specific concerns suggest that the development of hypnotic strategies must address the patient's need for stability, consistency, and security before any sort of useful therapeutic interaction can evolve. In addition, the therapeutic interactions in and out of trance must be experienced as sufficiently positive and gratifying to combat the patient's developmentally determined predisposition to dilute or destroy any form of intimate interpersonal involvement. Interpretation, demands for specific behavioral changes, and too-quickly intensified transferences are antithetical to the development of an environment in which hypnosis can be appropriately used. Therapeutic interactions must be supportive, structured, and direct. Every effort must be made to assure that the patient feels a secure sense of control, both in terms of the quality of the therapeutic interaction, and in terms of the intensity of the therapeutic process. The patient's need for distance and distancing must be respected and supported. The therapist must maintain a stable and consistent therapeutic stance, respecting the patient's need for distance while making sure that the boundaries of the therapeutic contract remain constant and dependable. At a very concrete level, this therapeutic stance translates into carefully managed, consistent, and clearly defined periods of therapeutic contact that are not altered by the patient's need to test limits before beginning to trust the dependability and availability of the therapist. It involves the regular confrontation of the patient's early resistances to forming an alliance. which are examined in terms of relevant structural and dynamic issues.

The application of hypnosis also presents an opportunity to deal specifically with some of these important issues. Experience has suggested that the presentation of hypnosis as self-hypnosis is the most efficacious way to deal with questions of control and the integrity of body boundaries. Hypnosis is presented as a way of controlling feelings of anxiety and providing an opportunity for self-mastery. Patients are often encouraged to use self-hypnosis independently of the therapist and outside of the therapy session. In addition, patients are encouraged to open their eyes during initial trance work. Because these patients have difficulty maintaining a sense of constancy in their contact with the external world, prolonged eye closure often results in unmodulated regression or dissociation and the intrusion of destructive autistic associations. Furthermore, eye closure is often perceived by these patients as increasing their vulnerability. Open-eye trance permits the patient to check to see that the therapist is still there, that the environment has been retained in a consistent way, and that there is no immediate threat to his or her safety. This experience of eye opening reassures the patient of the permanence and dependability of the therapist, so that concerns with abandonment and incorporation begin to be experientially modulated. Thus, hypnotic intervention initially needs to be permissive, yet structured, to provide the sense of stability needed for a positive experience that does not intrude too much on the patient's sense of safety and control.

These sorts of considerations generally help most patients begin to use hypnosis in an effective and therapeutic way. Patients quickly come to feel that the trance state is an opportunity to enter a safe sanctuary where they an find a respite from the pervasive sense of vulnerability that characterizes much of their waking experience. This sanctuary then provides a phenomenological opportunity for patients to begin to invest in a gratifying interaction with someone who they discover at their own pace and on their own terms to be a safe, reliable, and gratifying object. With severely disturbed patients, it is important to use hypnosis within the context of general psychotherapy. Hypnotic sessions are interspersed with verbal, insight-oriented psychotherapy to assure that the experiences developed and explicated during trance are not dissociated or defended against by the patient's relegating them to some nonconscious aspect of the fragmented ego. The experiences that the patient can recall must be discussed, explored, and evaluated at a conscious level so that they may be integrated into the evolving sense of self that will form the core for a more healthy sense of identity.

Occasionally, severely disturbed patients who find the trance experience a safe place for examining painful material will develop spontaneous amnesia for that material in the waking state. When this occurs, directed imagery, fantasy, and dreams can be used to help the patient gain access to or mastery over this material. In addition, hypnotically modulated abreaction is often useful in reducing the tension associated with repressed material, so that its gradual emergence into awareness becomes more easily tolerated by the patient.

TRANCE INDUCTION AND USE

Most severely disturbed patients are able to enter hypnotic trance without a significant modification of typical induction techniques. However, before the first trance induction, it is important to explain to patients that hypnosis will in no way compromise their ability to control their body boundaries and their need for distance from the therapist. As previously noted, self-hypnosis is introduced early and is used as the primary induction technique for the ongoing therapeutic work. Consistent with contemporary clinical technique, trance induction strategies appropriate for severely disturbed patients emphasize the development of permissive and naturalistic induction techniques that are consistent with patients' expectations and ego-syntonic capacities for altering their state of consciousness. Most often, some variation of a combined relaxation and imagery technique is useful. In addition, these patients often respond well to ideomotor techniques, which provide a sensory-perceptual grounding in physical experience for the altered phenomenology of trance. Ideomotor techniques are also useful for the therapist who may not have direct access to the patient's cognitive and associational experience and can determine compliance by observing the patient's motor responses (or lack thereof) to specific suggestions. Many patients refuse to close their eyes initially, and permission should be given for them to enter open-eye trance or to open their eyes periodically during the course of the hypnotic experience.

Unlike permissive induction with normal and neurotic patients, induction techniques with psychotics and other severely disturbed persons should emphasize clear structure and direction. When patients are given extended periods of time for self-directed fantasy or free association, they often become overwhelmed by the negative affect of spontaneous autistic associations. For this reason, work in hypnosis with severely disturbed patients should be more closely directed by the therapist than is typical in hypnotherapy with better integrated patients. In addition, the therapist should spend a larger proportion of the treatment time emphasizing suggestions for relaxation and comfort so that the experience of hypnosis can be a positive and gratifying one. This experiential element of hypnosis is a valuable means of enabling the patient to develop a positive alliance with the therapist. The sense of relaxation, comfort, and security that the patient can experience in hypnosis provides the basis for interpersonal gratification that previously has been missing from the patient's history.

Most severely disturbed patients enter trance without great difficulty. However, when patients become distressed or resist hypnotic induction, it is important to examine the reasons for this resistance. Usually, direct discussion of various dynamic issues related to fears of merger and loss of self-control are sufficient to help the patient begin to develop at least a light trance. Occasionally, however, the inability to enter trance is related to a more pervasive negative transference. When this is the case, it is important to examine and work through aspects of this negative transference before induction is reattempted. Resistance to hypnosis is most often seen with severely paranoid patients who are unable to relinquish any degree of ego control in order to participate in the dissociative and regressive aspects of trance. Continued attempts to induce a trance may intensify the negative transference to the degree that the therapist becomes incorporated into some form of defensive delusional ideation. In general, it is best to attempt hypnotic induction when the patient is interacting in a neutral or fairly positive fashion. The trance experience can strengthen the therapeutic alliance, but it initially depends on a sufficient degree of trust to allow the patient to invest in the trance without undue defensiveness or anxiety.

Once trance has been induced, the usual range of utilization techniques can be applied in the service of specific treatment strategies. There are several utilization principles, however, that should be emphasized when working with severely disturbed patients. Interventions oriented toward material that is likely to arouse anxiety should be interspersed with periodic suggestions for comfort and relaxation. This approach will prevent the patient's spontaneous dehypnotization, as well as the development of resistance rooted in intolerable negative affect and discomfort. Due to the frequency of disturbances in information processing and the personalized use of language among severely disturbed patients, it is also important to remember that these patients may respond to the wording of hypnotic suggestions in a very concrete or autistic fashion. For this reason, it is useful to verify the patient's understanding of the suggestion before requesting compliance. Furthermore, to maintain a sense of personal control and security, severely disturbed patients need the option of terminating trance spontaneously whenever they feel themselves growing intolerably uncomfortable.

It is often useful to link suggestions to the positive relationship emerging in psychotherapy between the patient and the hypnotist. Suggestions for self-control or for a sense of well-being are often best framed in terms of encouraging the patient to recall experiences of comfort and well-being that have previously occurred in trance or during psychotherapy in the hypnotherapist's office. In this way, the therapeutic alliance begins to be internalized as a source of continuing security and comfort. It can be spontaneously evoked during periods of insecurity and discomfort, and it can be used to reinforce compliance with suggestions. In other words, patients may be told that when they successfully control an impulse or when they are able to shut off a hallucinated voice, they can then experience the same sense of safety and well-being that they experience in the therapist's office. This use of the therapeutic relationship to maintain security and to restore a sense of well-being is very similar to the way in which children learn to evoke images of their parents to soothe themselves during periods of anxiety or to reinforce their personal compliance with the behavioral expectations of their parents. In more theoretical terms, the relationship becomes internalized as a core element in the patient's sense of self, as well as a crucial component in the ego ideal.

Consistent with good hypnotherapeutic technique, problem-focused therapeutic suggestion should emphasize the provision of alternatives for managing particular conflicts or feelings rather than simply the removal of a particular symptom or maladaptive behavior. Psychotic patients are particularly sensitive to the notion that hypnosis will be employed to take something away. They have experienced a number of interpersonal situations in which they have felt deprived or castrated and are, therefore, likely not only to resist such suggestions but to become distrustful and erect a more pervasive resistance based in an iatrogenic negative transference. The notion of adaptation and mastery is crucial to problem-focused interventions, so that patients begin to feel that they are gaining rather than giving up. This sense of growth and mastery is linked to the emergence of a more healthy sense of self and to the gradual development of a stable capacity for self-monitoring, self-modulation, and self-control.

The hypnotherapist must also be aware that, during trance, severely disturbed patients may experience spontaneous somatic sensory alterations that seem to serve the same defensive function as hypochondriacal concerns and somatic delusions. These sensory alterations reflect a primitive form of body narcissism designed to maintain some sense of ego integrity and to defend against the vulnerability associated with the dissolution of body boundaries and the sense of personal destruction associated with boundary diffusion. In addition, these sensory experiences may also be linked to primitive identifications with significant figures that are evoked within the context of the hypnotic regression or that represent some dynamic component of the transference interaction. Careful monitoring of the patient will help the hypnotherapist become aware of these sensory alterations when they occur. The hypnotherapist should make regular suggestions that the patient can maintain a sense of integrated body boundaries and can awaken from trance with normal sensation and experience in all parts of the body.

In general, however, the principles of trance utilization in work with severely disturbed patients are not significantly different from those in work with more traditional patient populations. The most important guiding principle to remember is that these patients are particularly sensitive to the feeling that they may be deprived of some aspect of themselves or of some aspect of control. For that reason, strategies and suggestions should support the patient's meager capacities for autonomy, while helping to reinforce the integrity of body boundaries and the nascent sense of self.

INTERVENTION STRATEGIES

There are a variety of specific hypnotic techniques that can be employed in therapeutic work with severely disturbed patients. Many patients will require a number of techniques used sequentially or simultaneously, while some patients will be most responsive to the regular use of only one form of hypnotherapeutic intervention. It is appropriate to explore many techniques with each patient and not to become discouraged if the patient is unable to use any particular aspect of hypnotherapeutic intervention.

In general, the use of hypnotherapy with severely disturbed patients can be divided into several categories: (a) to support the therapeutic alliance and to structure a positive transference, (b) to facilitate uncovering and abreaction, (c) to support the ego integrity and identity of the patient, and (d) to resolve dynamic conflicts and to restore developmentally defective character structure. In each of these contexts, the hypnotherapeutic intervention is designed to address an important issue in the therapeutic process that is in need of experiential remediation. That is to say, hypnosis is not simply employed for uncovering in the service of developing insight or interpretation. Rather, the trance is structured to provide a specific phenomenological experience that allows patients to discover something new about themselves, about their capacity to relate to someone else, or about their capacity for mastery and self-control It is this *experiential focus* that most clearly differentiates the applications of hypnotic technique with severely disturbed patients from work with a more normal population. Here, the emphasis is on the development of a relationship and an experiential context that provides a kind of corrective emotional experience, rather than more directly on the development of self-understanding or behavioral change.

Enhancement of the Therapeutic Alliance

It is impossible to engage in meaningful psychotherapeutic work of any sort unless there is a sufficient level of rapport and continuing cooperation. The specific structural and dynamic conflicts associated with severely disturbed patients and pre-oedipal forms of psychopathology make the development of such an alliance extremely difficult. One of the most useful applications of hypnosis is to support and develop a sense of security in the therapeutic alliance and to structure a positive transference free from the contamination usually associated with transferential developments among psychotics and severely disturbed patients.

A number of specific technical strategies (Baker, 1981, 1982, 1983a, b) have been described for supporting the evolution of the therapeutic alliance. These strategies are based on an object-relations theoretical approach to understanding the way in which the structuralization of the personality emerges from the internal representation of various important interpersonal experiences. The internal representation of a safe and stable relationship with the therapist provides the anchor point around which the patient's fragmented internal sense of self can begin to coalesce. This strategy also provides a foundation for the patient's beginning to generalize the gratifying and mature personal relationship with the therapist to significant others in the contemporary environment.

There are seven stages in the hypnotherapeutic approach for enhancing the therapeutic alliance:

1. While maintaining relaxed feelings of comfort and calm during trance, the patient is helped to visualize being involved in a pleasant activity. Feelings of relaxation and well-being are suggested intermittently. If the patient has difficulty imaging, the problem is examined and dealt with either by suggestion or by directed alterations in specific images.

2. The patient is instructed to open his or her eyes, see the therapist, and then close the eyes, returning to an internal imagistic representation of the self. This process, which is repeated several times along with suggestions for continued relaxation, is used to emphasize the reliability of personal boundaries while the patient develops an experience of self in relation to the therapist. The patient is reassured that the therapist continues to exist, even when he or she cannot be seen, and this process supports opportunities for the patient's development of object constancy.

3. The patient is helped to develop visual images of the therapist while maintaining continued feelings of well-being. Many patients have a good deal of difficulty experiencing a visual representation of the therapist. When this is the case, the patient is encouraged to visualize the therapist's initials written on the blackboard, his or her name on a sign, or some representative symbolic object. Often this object is chosen from the therapist's office and seems to serve the same function as Winnicott's conceptualization of the transitional object (1965). If patients experience difficulty in developing even a transitional object representation internally, then they may be given a concrete object that serves a transitional object function and asked simply to visualize this object internally. They can open their eyes and then reproduce it eidetically if they are unable to produce the image spontaneously.

4. The patient is instructed to develop visual images of the therapist, to develop visual images of himself or herself, and then to picture the two together in some kind of mutual activity. The patient is allowed to define the proximity of this togetherness, from being in the same room or in the same country, to being in universes far apart. The only requirement is that the patient and the therapist be involved together in some kind of activity. The activity may be parallel at first but it eventually should include some kind of interactional involvement.

5. Treatment then moves to the development of hypnotic fantasies involving the patient and therapist in a variety of activities designed to emphasize the nurturing, supporting, and protecting role of the therapist. With time, these suggested fantasies may move from concrete to symbolic representations as the therapist suggests that the nurturing interaction is located not only in the relationship, but also within the patient in the form of an increasing capacity for self-nurturing, self-direction, and self-mastery. Such fantasy must be

consistent with the patient's level of dependence. This internalization of positive visual images provides a cognitive-affective pairing that facilitates introjection of the therapist as a "good object" and the experience of self in relation as a "good me." These images may then be used as cues to induce or deepen trance, to reduce anxiety, to increase positive feelings of self-regard, or to provide imagistic foci for the control of hallucinations or delusional ideation. Once the object introject is well established, it becomes an important focus for gaining self-control and for the emerging capacity to see oneself in an integrated and positive way.

6. This process is followed by the controlled externalization of distorted self and object representations. The patient is encouraged to develop such imagistic representations as threatening delusional figures, the infant self who provokes mother's anger and withdrawal, or the crazy self who engages in self-mutilation. These images may be elaborated and managed in fantasy or hypnotic dreams in one of two ways. Elements that should be made increasingly ego-dystonic or that should be repressed or externalized may be elaborated in terms of their destructive effects on the patient and relegated to "an old trunk," "flushed down the toilet," "stored in the attic," or "buried for a later excavation" through directed fantasy. Elements that reflect aspects of defensive object splitting may be moved toward integration by emphasizing their similarity, by altering their symbolization in terms of their shared significant dynamic roots, and by emphasizing temporal and spatial pairing or revivification of common historical derivatives. The process of integration often results in a significant level of abreaction and catharsis.

7. As the patient develops an increasing stability of ego functioning, hypnotic fantasy may begin to include other significant objects, and guided fantasy work may move to examine past or present interpersonal experiences with an emphasis on integrating both the positive and the negative aspects of such relationships. Often, dynamic conflicts related to these relationships emerge and may be worked through with hypnotic suggestion and imagery during trance and with verbal discussion and interpretation outside of it.

This strategy, then, provides an experiential focus based on directed hypnotic imagery for helping the patient begin to internalize a representation of the therapist and the self in relation to the therapist. This new representation is important for developing the capacity of the ego for mature object relationships and for developing an integrated representation of personal identity. Directed imagery provides an opportunity for the patient actually to experience a modulated degree of gratification within the context of the therapeutic relationship. This positive experience phenomenologically evokes the emergence of positive transference and also provides a very real sense of security, safety, and gratification during trance.

Relaxation

Perhaps the most common application of hypnosis, generally, is for tension reduction and relaxation. Because most psychotic patients suffer from intense and labile anxiety, this nonspecific relaxation component of trance can be particularly therapeutic. Patients can begin to experience their own capacity for tension reduction in trance, which not only restores a level of comfort and calm but also provides them with a meaningful way to experience their own capacity for self-control. In addition, the experience and release of tension can serve a useful function in demonstrating the integrity of body boundaries and the way in which one part of the physical self is connected to other parts of the physical self. It has also been demonstrated that, as patients begin to experience a greater degree of comfort and calm, their reliance on self-destructive and primitive defenses is lessened. This reduction results in a decrease in delusional ideation, hallucinatory experience, and acting out. Furthermore, this ability to control tension is a powerful expression of the gratification that can be derived from the therapeutic relationship and, therefore, it further reinforces a positive transferential involvement with the psychotherapeutic process. Most psychotic patients can comfortably accept direct suggestions for relaxation during trance. Occasionally, however, the patient may need to be given opportunities for abreactive fantasy or for motor activity to reduce tension to the point where it is manageable by suggestion alone.

Uncovering Techniques

Occasionally, it is useful to help patients gain access to repressed memories of early negative experiences in order to work on them during trance and to learn that they can be modulated and controlled without overwhelming the ego. The traditional uncovering techniques, including projective imagery, age regression, and revivification, may all be used with severely disturbed patients in a carefully controlled and modulated way. However, it is important to consider the possibility that they may provoke an intense level of negative affect. The therapist should provide avenues for controlling such affective intensity through abreactive techniques, the use of enforced amnesias, or hypnotically suggested defenses. Uncovered material may be incorporated into guided fantasy to suggest indirectly the positive resolution of dynamic conflicts, or it may become the focus of hypnotically induced dreams to allow for abreaction and tension discharge. When remembered at a conscious level, such material may be explored, explicated, and eventually interpreted during later stages of intervention.

Mastery and Ego Building

A variety of fantasy, imagery, and indirect and direct suggestions may be used to provide the patient with an increasing sense of personal strength and self-control. These techniques may be used to suggest indirectly the resolution of dynamic conflicts or to suggest more directly the emerging capacity for various mature ego functions. It may be useful at times to allow patients to rehearse the successful accomplishment of a particular task in hypnotic fantasy or to fantasize the ability to deal with a particularly difficult relationship in an effective and positive manner.

The therapeutic relationship as well as directed imagery may be used to convey to the patient a sense of importance and value as a human being. Patients' experience of the therapist's respect and caring is often the most important factor in altering their negative self-concept and sense of personal worthlessness. The intensity of hypnosis and the degree of affect involved in trance heighten the influence of these messages of nurturance, support, and valuation. Suggestions for growth, strength, and mastery also can be interspersed throughout the course of trance communication. These suggestions are gradually assimilated by the patient when they are delivered within the context of a positive and secure environment sustained by the therapeutic alliance. Such techniques can be used to restore a sense of personal strength to the patient and to support the development of a range of ego capacities, including specific defense mechanisms and coping strategies, impulse control, reality testing, the control of intrusive psychotic defenses such as hallucinations and delusions, and the modification of specific destructive behaviors. Most treatment strategies that the therapist might use in work with other patients can be employed for these purposes. However, variations in technique may be demanded by the developmental level of the patient and should be consistent with the general principles of trance utilization previously mentioned.

In summary, the trance experience is used first to support and structure the development of a positive therapeutic relationship. Once this relationship has been established, a range of hypnotic intervention strategies can be employed to resolve conflict, to reduce anxiety and abreact negative affect, to support the emerging positive and integrated sense of identity within the patient, to modify specific problem behaviors, and to support the development of an increasing array of mature ego capacities. The controlled experience of therapeutic connectedness, the modulation of abreactive and cathartic experiences, the phenomenological experience of personal control and mastery, and the directed suggestions for increasing ego capabilities are all important curative factors in this kind of hypnotherapeutic intervention. Hypnosis provides an opportunity for directing and structuring experience and for intensifying affect in a controlled way in association with the experiences that are structured and evoked. Therefore, the patient is not simply uncovering and understanding previous conflicts but reexperiencing and working through them in a controlled fashion. For severely disturbed patients who lack the cognitive, verbal, and observing ego capacities for the intellectually modulated and structured work characteristic of typical psychotherapy, this controlled *experiential* intervention is really the only efficacious way the therapist can begin to address their pervasive character defects and dynamic conflicts.

THERAPEUTIC RELATIONSHIP

The therapeutic relationship, long considered an important curative factor in psychotherapy, is particularly important in work with severely disturbed patients, where it becomes the path for providing experiences central to the reparenting process. In discussing the therapeutic relationship, however, we are concerned not only with its transferential component but also with its contemporary nontransferential components. In other words, the therapist may be seen in terms of unfinished business with significant relationships from the patient's past and also as a separate and real object with contemporary value. It has long been noted that hypnosis tends to increase the affective involvement of the patient in the therapeutic relationship. In addition, a variety of psychoanalytic writers have commented on the way in which hypnosis tends to increase the intensity of the transference and the rapidity of its development. With severely disturbed patients who try to avoid significant involvement with others, this enhanced intensity is particularly useful.

The contemporary component is especially crucial to the therapeutic relationship, and so a good deal of effort is made from the outset to structure it, to reinforce the positive experience of it, and to direct the patient in the internal representation of a nondistorted version of it. The therapist can modulate the intensity of the transference so that the patient does not become inappropriately regressed and at the same time structure the contemporary therapeutic relationship so that it provides real and immediate opportunities for nondistorted gratification. Encouraging the patient to describe the therapist and correcting any distortions inherent in the patient's conceptualization reinforces the real stimulus value of the therapist. In addition, the hypnotic management of transference prevents contamination by negative transference phenomena that may become so strong as to overwhelm the therapeutic alliance.

To the degree that the therapist is successful in maintaining the therapeutic alliance, the patient is more likely to accept suggestions and to work cooperatively in directed hypnotherapeutic interaction. However, when the contemporary relationship is overwhelmed by negative transference or when this relationship component has not been developed sufficiently to provide a secure sense of gratification, the patient may become resistant to trance or may be unable to work productively during hypnotic sessions. Resistance to hypnosis or overwhelming negative abreaction during trance are signals to the therapist that the relationship has not been successfully structured to provide a safe and secure container for the hypnotic experience. For this reason, the therapeutic relationship needs careful and continual scrutiny and should be the focus of specific suggestion during hypnotherapeutic work.

SPECIAL CONCERNS

There are a number of special issues that arise in the therapy of severely disturbed patients. Two issues, resistance and acting out, can be managed effectively in hypnosis.

Resistance

Resistance refers to behaviors that interfere with the process and work of psychotherapy. There are three major sources of resistance in hypnosis. The first is the characterologically syntonic defenses of the patient; that is, the patient becomes anxious due to the material being uncovered or due to the experience of regression and trance and, therefore, begins to withdraw from the trance experience. Withholding material, coming late to sessions, or other behaviors that dilute the intensity of the trance experience are manifestations of resistance arising from the syntonic defenses of the patient. These sources of resistance are best managed by specific suggestion during trance and by interpretive examination in verbal waking psychotherapy.

A second major source of resistance is negative transference. The patient may become overwhelmed by anxiety rooted in the intensity or negative affect associated with the therapeutic relationship. Most often, this form of resistance becomes manifest in various types of acting out, such as premature termination of therapy or the sudden onset of self-mutilation, drug abuse, or promiscuity. The most appropriate management of this form of resistance is to provide increased structure, support, and gratification to indirectly dilute the negative transference. Increased suggestions of comfort and well-being, extra therapy sessions, hospitalization or medication, or an increased emphasis on accurate empathy can underscore the fact that the therapist is understanding, accepting, and reliable. At the same time, the therapist reexamines the acting out behaviors in terms of the patient's disappointment, anger, or fears of merger and incorporation. The therapist provides reassurance about the unrealistic nature of these concerns while allowing the patient to ventilate anger and anxiety without fear of retaliation. This process also demonstrates that intense affect can be contained within the relationship without disrupting its reliability and that strong emotions in general can be modulated and controlled without a need to resort to self-destructive defensive maneuvers.

The third major source of resistance is therapist error, which may be rooted in negative countertransference. Careful, regular, and sensitive reflection and self-scrutiny are useful in controlling this factor.

Two particular manifestations of resistance are commonly seen in psychotic and borderline patients. The first is resistance rooted in fear of merger. It is often effective to identify this fear with patients in trance and then to provide a variety of sensory and motor experiences designed to demonstrate the integrity of the patient's boundaries. A very effective example of such an experience is the "moving hands together" technique. Patients are instructed to clasp their hands together in front of them and to focus on the experience of warmth and strength and the feeling of connectedness that develops in the hands. When they are ready, the patients are instructed to allow their hands to move apart and to come to rest again by their sides or on the arms of the chair. The therapist suggests that the right hand is still the right and the left hand is still the left; that neither has been altered by having come together in close proximity for a while. This experience is then used as an analog for the therapeutic relationship: The patient and the therapist can come together when the patient chooses, and in this togetherness the patient can experience a sense of warmth, security, and strength. When the patient wants or needs to move away, he or she will still be the same, separate person, as will the therapist. Neither will have merged, and their boundaries will have proved adequate to that situation of togetherness. Other sensory-motor techniques can also provide an experience of togetherness that does not result in the dissolution of boundaries.

Conflicts related to autonomous functioning represent a second major manifestation of resistance in severely disturbed patients. Patients who perform very well in hetero-hypnosis in the therapist's office find that they are unable or unwilling to practice self-hypnosis or use hypnotic suggestions independently. This inability is often rooted in the fear that separation is tantamount to rejection and abandonment. In addition to specific suggestions about independence and fantasy rehearsal of autonomous functioning, hypnotic dreaming (Baker, 1982) is an effective technique for dealing with this sort of resistance. The patient is instructed to have a series of dreams in hypnosis and to begin to become aware of the experience of natural dreaming during sleep at home. This process of dreaming becomes a thread that binds together various aspects of ego functioning in the office and at home. The patient can dream in the office and remember the dreams at home, or dream at home and remember the dreams in the office. There is a reassuring sense of continuity between the two situations.

Specifically directed and hypnotically induced dreams can be used to resolve conflicts related to separation and autonomy. If this technique is not possible with the patient, the therapist can provide a concrete symbolic representation of the relationship in the form of a transitional object. The patient is given some small object or allowed to choose something from the therapist's office to borrow for a while. The patient is then instructed to use this object for eye fixation to induce self-hypnosis, to visualize it as an aid to relaxation, or to comply with specific suggestions that were successfully complied with in the therapist's office.

Acting Out

Problems with acting out often relate to conflicts regarding the integrity of boundaries. The patient may need to test these boundaries to fully trust them. If so, hypnotic imagery can be used to enhance the patient's sense of the integrity of boundaries by the therapist's elaborating on the strength and reliability of fences, walls, bridges, and houses to contain intense feelings and fears. Self-mutilation in severely disturbed patients is often a specific form of testing personal boundaries. Patients begin to feel that they are dissolving, and by cutting themselves they can see that there are boundaries that contain some things and keep other things out. This act is not really masochistic but, rather, a way of demonstrating that boundaries continue to exist and can be penetrated under the control of the patient's own motivation. Typically, patients feel a sense of relief in cutting or mutilating themselves because it reassures them of the integrity of their physical boundaries.

Other forms of acting out can be dealt with by specific suggestions to enhance ego-syntonic defenses for dealing with impulses or by a variety of abreactive techniques designed to relieve tension so that it need not be acted out external to the therapy session. In addition, the patient can be reassured of the reliability and availability of the therapist and of the strength of the therapist for dealing with intense and primitive affects so that these feelings need not be taken elsewhere. When the patient feels that the relationship is strong enough to contain these feelings, there is less likelihood that they will be acted out somewhere else.

Patients who have regressed to these primitive states often engage in acting out in order to provoke retaliation and thereby affirm their negative self-concepts. They find it somehow easier to confirm their sense of worthlessness than to risk the insecurity of altering their internal representational worlds by behaving in ways that might lead to reinforcement and acceptance. With these patients, this dynamic can often be managed by working more directly on the self-concept. Experiences of self-control and mastery during trance, statements about the degree to which the patient is valued by the therapist, and images designed to underscore the way in which this evaluation can be experienced and reinforced are all useful in decreasing the need to act out to provoke retaliation and punishment. In addition, this particular dynamic can be interpreted outside of trance as a repetition compulsion of early experiences in which the patient was repeatedly rejected by his or her parents and made to feel deserving of that rejection. Patients often continue to act out rather than give up hope that someday they will be accepted by their parents.

CASE STUDY

The following case vignette provides an example of a hypnotherapeutic approach with a young, acutely psychotic patient:

Carol was a 19-year-old-college sophomore who experienced an acute regression of psychotic proportions during her second year in college. Her premorbid adjustment had been marginal. She had seldom formed lasting or meaningful relationships and was described as having been shy and withdrawn since the onset of adolescence. Her adjustment to college had also been difficult for her, marked by a good deal of anxiety and almost schizoid withdrawal. She seemed to be obsessed with her grades and became distressed and debilitated when she was unable to make the highest score in the class on an examination. She was from an upper-middle-class family with no apparent history of severe psychiatric disturbance, although both her mother and father were described as being somewhat compulsive and perfectionistic over-achievers.

Carol's regression was marked by increasing withdrawal and by auditory hallucinations telling her to harm herself because she was worthless and contaminated. She began to neglect her hygiene and to spend increasing amounts of time in her room writing long essays about her sense of personal unacceptability. Shortly before her admission, she had begun to mutilate herself with a series of small cuts on her forearms and thighs made with a razor blade. These activities culminated in her making a frank suicide attempt by cutting her wrists, which resulted in her admission to the psychiatric inpatient service of a university teaching hospital. The author began working with Carol on the second day following her admission. After a couple of sessions to establish rapport, hypnotherapy was initiated to enhance the development of a positive therapeutic alliance and to begin to gain some control over the hallucinatory experience that had become the focus of Carol's conscious attention. She was at that time relatively uninvolved with the activities of the ward and other aspects of the real external environment.

The following material is taken from the second session of hypnosis, after trance had been induced by a permissive relaxation and imagery technique. Carol fantasized being at the family cabin at a nearby lake where she always felt peaceful and secure.

Therapist: *Carol, as you are just resting there comfortable and safe and relaxed, just allow your attention to focus on the waves of the lake as they gently rise and fall and rise and fall in a repetitive and rhythmic way. Allow yourself to imagine how comforting it would feel to imagine yourself in that place, just watching the continuing, repetitive motion of the water. Can you see that?*

Carol: *Yes, I see it.*

Therapist: *And can you feel yourself relaxing there?*

Carol: *A little, but the sky is gray, and the voices say, "Don't stay to play, run away, run away."*

Therapist: *There is a kind of rhythm inside of you, too; a rhythm that keeps a different beat and makes you feel somewhat uncomfortable coming into contact with someone else. But this is a safe place and, as you simply relax, you can let go of any tension and let go of any fear or discomfort because this is a safe place to be, and you can choose the rhythm. You can choose whether it is a rhythm that is yours alone. You can choose whether it is a rhythm that you share. You can allow the rhythm to go fast or you can allow the rhythm to go slowly. You are in charge of the timing. You are in charge of the beat.* Whatever decision you make, it can help you feel safe and comfortable here, because just like the rhythm of the waves and the rhythm of your rhyme, there is a natural, consistent, dependable order to things, and that sense of consistency and dependability and order can help you feel safe inside yourself and can help you feel safe inside this room with me just now. (The patient appears to visibly relax.)

Carol, as you are resting there, I would like for you to take your hand and place it on your chest so that you can feel the beating of your heart. Just go ahead and do that. (The patient slowly places her hand to her chest.) *Can you feel the rhythm of your heart beating there?*

Carol: *I feel it. It is strong.*

Therapist: *Good, because you can feel the strength inside yourself. You can feel the continuity of your rhythm beating on and on. It is you. No one else's heart is beating just that way. You don't have to make the waves move up and down on the lake. It is a natural occurrence and, in just that way, it is natural for you to find the rhythm that is most comfortable and safe and suitable for you, a rhythm that will still be yours even when you and I come together to develop new ways of being with other people. That is a good thought and a comfortable thought, and in just a moment, I would like for you to take your two hands and clasp them together in front of you very tightly, locking the fingers together. Just go ahead and do that.* (The patient puts her hands together in front of her.) *As you focus your attention on your hands, while continuing to relax, you can feel, in your fingertips, the beating of your pulse, a sign that that rhythm continues, and you can focus on it whenever you would like. But you can also feel a kind of strength from the two hands clasping onto one another. You can feel a warmth where your palms are touching. You can feel a kind of security in the strength and warmth of your hands. When you are ready, you can allow your hands to move apart, to relax, and to come to rest again on the arms of the chair. That is fine, good, and you can see that your right hand is still your right hand; your left hand is still your left hand. The right hand is still at the end of the right arm; the left hand is still at the end of the left arm. Neither has been changed, and that is how it is with you and me. When you want to, when you need to, you can come together with me and feel, in our togetherness, a safe sense of warmth and strength and security. Even when we are together, you can still feel your own rhythm and still know that you are you. But when it comes time or when you feel it is necessary, you can move away and move apart. You will still be you; I will still be me. Your right hand is still your right; the left hand is still your left. But in our togetherness, there can be a time of secure, safe comfort when we can begin to find ways for you to get well and to feel more sure of who you are and where you want to go.*

Carol: *It does feel strong, but my voices say it isn't safe.*

Therapist: *Perhaps the voices come from a place that wasn't safe in your life, but they don't come from here. In fact, when the voices come and begin to bother you, you don't have to listen to them. You can instead, focus your attention on the beating of your heart and see that you are still you no matter what the voices say, and that someday, together, we'll make sure that they don't intrude on your relationship with me, with yourself, or with anyone else.*

In this vignette, the hypnotic experience was structured to enable the patient to begin to ground her perceptions and her somatosensory phenomenology in a way similar to an infant's perceptual development. This sensory experience reinforced the patient's sense of boundaries and the continuity of her own identity so that she did not need to fear merger or incorporation by the therapist. In this way, resistance was anticipated and the anxiety, which might have interfered with the therapeutic alliance and formed the basis of a more pervasive negative transference reaction, was diffused. The experience of the relationship, the continuity of personal identity, and the security of boundaries was also used later to move the patient's auditory hallucinations to an external position where they were less likely to intrude on the evolution of the therapeutic alliance.

Work such as this demonstrates the way hypnosis is used to structure a variety of experiences that may be applied to the specific defects evident in the psychotic patient. This approach does not directly alter the internal structure of the representational world or character organization of the patient. It may, however, form a foundation for the development of the therapeutic relationship which, in time, can be used to make important changes in the intrapsychic structure of the patient.

SUMMARY

A variety of hypnotic interventions are useful in work with severely disturbed patients. Both empirical research and clinical experience have demonstrated, through several decades, that these patients are relatively easy to hypnotize and that there are no unexpected, untoward results associated with employing hypnosis as one aspect of the therapeutic regimen. Specific applications of hypnosis should be made in a relatively structured yet permissive way, with an emphasis on self-hypnosis and the opportunity for the patient to engage in open-eye trance or periodic eye opening to check on the constancy and security of the environment. Hypnotic imagery and suggestion can be used to structure and support the evolution of a positive experience of relatedness with the therapist that becomes the experiential crucible for the evolution of the therapeutic alliance. The therapist then can employ a variety of hypnotic techniques to resolve conflicts, to enhance the patient's sense of mastery and self-control, and to provide a basis for altering the patient's grossly distorted negative self-image. Various forms of resistance and acting out can also be controlled through the specific hypnotherapeutic techniques described in this chapter.

In closing, a few words of caution are appropriate. First, hypnosis is not a substitute for careful, well conceptualized, intensive psychotherapy. Rather, it provides an opportunity for additional therapeutic strategies and is particularly useful for structuring the therapeutic relationship to prevent its contamination by negative transference phenomena. It should be employed by professionals who are experienced both in the treatment of severely disturbed patients and in the intensive use of hypnotherapy. Second, hypnosis is not a panacea. Work with severely disturbed patients is difficult, complicated, and long. It requires the careful management of a variety of therapeutic variables over a long period of time, often in conjunction with chemotherapy and inpatient treatment. Intensive hypnosis of the sort described in this chapter is often best begun in an inpatient situation where there is greater control over the environment and the contingencies that affect the patient's sense of external security. However, it often can be used in an outpatient setting or continued in outpatient psychotherapy after hospitalization. The techniques described in this chapter do not automatically alter the character structure of patients but, rather, create a stable and reliable therapeutic environment in which these changes can begin to occur with time. Finally, by modulating the negative transference that is a problem in treating severely disturbed patients, hypnosis helps to keep patients in treatment and allows for the emergence of a consistent and continuing therapeutic process in which the therapist and the patient work together to examine and resolve significant conflicts.

FURTHER READING

Abrams, S. (1964). The use of hypnotic techniques with psychotics: A critical review. *American Journal of Psychotherapy, 18,* 79–94.

Arieti, S. (1974). *Interpretation of schizophrenia.* New York: Basic Books.

Baker, E. (1981). An hypnotherapeutic approach to enhance object relatedness in psychotic patients. *International Journal of Clinical and Experimental Hypnosis, 29,* 136.

Baker, E. (1982). The management of transference phenomena in the treatment of primitive states. *Psychotherapy: Theory, Research and Practice, 19,* 194.

Biddle, W. E. (1967). *Hypnosis in the psychoses.* Springfield, IL: Charles C Thomas.

Scagnelli, J. (1974). A case of hypnotherapy with an acute schizophrenic. *American Journal of Clinical Hypnosis, 17,* 60.

Scagnelli, J. (1976). Hypnotherapy with schizophrenic and borderline patients: Summary of therapy with eight patients. *American Journal of Clinical Hypnosis, 18,* 33.

Zeig, M. S. (1974). Hypnotherapy with psychotic inpatients. *American Journal of Clinical Hypnosis, 17,* 56.

REFERENCES

Abrams, W. (1964). The use of hypnotic techniques with psychotics: A critical review. *American Journal of Psychiatry, 18,* 79–94.

Baker, E. (1981). An hypnotherapeutic approach to enhance object relatedness in psychotic patients. *International Journal of Clinical and Experimental Hypnosis, 29,* 136–147.

Baker, E. (1982). The management of transference phenomena in the treatment of primitive states. *Psychotherapy: Theory, Research and Practice, 19,* 194–198.

Baker, E. (1983a). The use of hypnotic dreaming in the treatment of the borderline patient: Some thoughts on resistance and transitional phenomena. *International Journal of Clinical and Experimental Hypnosis, 31*(1), 19–27.

Baker, E. (1983b). Resistance in hypnotherapy of primitive states: Its meaning and management. *International Journal of Clinical and Experimental Hypnosis, 31*(2), 82–89.

Baker, E., & Copeland, D. (in press). Hypnotic susceptibility of psychotic patients: A comparison of schizophrenics and psychotic depressives. *International Journal of Clinical and Experimental Hypnosis.*

Freud, S. (1959). Psycho-analytical notes upon an autobiographical account of a case of paranoia. In *Collected Papers* (pp. 390–472). New York: Basic Books. (Original work published 1911)

Greene, J. T. (1969). Hypnotizability of hospitalized psychotics. *International Journal of Clinical and Experimental Hypnosis, 17,* 103.

Kramer, E., & Brennan, E. P. (1964). Hypnotic susceptibility of schizophrenic patients. *Journal of Abnormal and Social Psychology, 64,* 657–659.

LaVoie, G., Sabourin, M., Ally, G., & Langolis, J. (1976). Hypnotizability as a function of adaptive regression among chronic psychotic patients. *International Journal of Clinical and Experimental Hypnosis, 24,* 238–257.

Scagnelli-Jöbsis, J. (in press). Hypnosis with severely disturbed patients. In W. C. Hester & A. Smith (Eds.), *Comprehensive clinical hypnosis: Medicine—psychology—dentistry.*

Vingoe, F. J., & Kramer, E. F. (1966). Hypnotic susceptibility of hospitalized psychotic patients: A pilot study. *International Journal of Clinical and Experimental Hypnosis, 14,* 47–54.

Whitman, J. R. (1961). The performance of acute and chronic schizophrenic patients on a test measuring susceptibility to hypnosis. *International Journal of Clinical and Experimental Hypnosis, 9,* 163–166.

Wilson, C. P., Cormen, H. H., & Cole, A. A. (1949). A preliminary study of the hypnotizability of psychotic patients. *Psychiatric Quarterly, 23,* 247–261.

Winnicott, D. W. (1965). *The maturational process and the facilitating environment: Studies in the theory of emotional development.* New York: International Universities Press.

14
Sex Therapy

Imagination is more important than knowledge.
—Albert Einstein
The World As I See It

At one time or another, all mental health professionals and physicians work with patients who have concerns or disorders related to sexual functioning. Nearly all (90%–95%) sexual problems are psychological rather than physical in origin, and most can be alleviated without intensive therapy. Hypnosis can be an extremely effective tool, not only for the sex therapist but also for other practitioners who treat sexual problems.

The purpose of this chapter is not to encourage the reader to become a sex therapist, which requires special study and certification. Instead, the purpose is to increase the practitioner's sensitivity and effectiveness in dealing with patients who have sexual problems and to give the practitioner a better idea of what can be done within the limits of his or her knowledge and experience. The use of hypnosis in sex therapy reinforces the point Thomas made in Chapter 12—that hypnosis can facilitate the various forms of psychotherapy and that, in fact, it is a major ingredient in any psychotherapeutic approach.

RATIONALE

Before discussing hypnosis as it applies to sex therapy, it is important to understand the nature of sexual dysfunction and the rationale behind sex therapy as a profession. Sexual dysfunction was defined by Hogan (1978) as "cognitive, affective, and/or behavioral problems that prevent an individual or couple from engaging in and/or enjoying satisfactory intercourse and orgasm" (p. 58). This definition suggests the complex etiology of most sexual dysfunctions, in which misinformation, anxiety, negative conditioning from past experiences, and negative self-talk all play a part.

Sex therapists distinguish between dysfunctions and sexual variations, which, although unconventional, may be acceptable and satisfying to people. It is also important to distinguish between sexual dysfunctions and sexual concerns, which may require only information or support rather than therapy.

A specialty within the larger field of psychotherapy, sex therapy requires special skills and knowledge of specific techniques designed around sexual functioning, in addition to skill in psychotherapy and relationship therapy. Masters and Johnson's *Human Sexual Response* (1966) first drew attention to sex therapy as a specialty. Sex therapy as a separate profession emerged in 1974, when the American Association of Sex Educators, Counselors and Therapists began a program to certify interested mental health professionals as sex therapists.

Before Masters and Johnson's work, most therapists viewed sexual problems as a form of neurosis and based treatment on a psychoanalytic model. Masters and Johnson took a behavioral approach, working directly with the symptoms rather than trying to help the patient attain insight into the problem. Their treatment techniques consisted of a series of structured exercises designed to replace unpleasant and maladaptive sexual experiences with positive and pleasurable sexual interactions. In their view, the relationship must be treated, and not just the symptomatic partner, and they stress communication and cooperation between the partners in the task of mutually completing the human sexual response cycle.

Masters and Johnson's work has provided a foundation for the continued development and expansion of specific treatment techniques. Helen Singer Kaplan (1974) developed a psychodynamic approach to sex therapy that involves sexual tasks (the application of behavior modification methods) conducted within a psychotherapeutic context. Kaplan was one of the first authors to stress the importance of a patient's cognitions in sexual functioning. LoPiccolo (1978), a pioneer in the behavioral treatment of sexual dysfunction, has summarized the seven major elements in direct therapy for sexually dysfunctional couples:

1. Mutual responsibility between both partners.

2. Information, education, and permission.

3. Attitude changes from negative to positive.

4. Anxiety reduction.

5. Communication and feedback between the partners.

6. Intervention in destructive sex roles, lifestyles and family interactions.

7. Prescription of changes in sexual behavior.

In recent years, behavior therapy has "gone cognitive" (Araoz, 1982), and sex therapists have begun to recognize the role cognitions play in sexual response. In cognitive therapy, as developed by Beck (1976), the practitioner trains the patient to identify negative thoughts and correct them. One example is Meichenbaum's (1973) three-step process for countering negative covert messages that are translated into maladaptive behaviors:

1. Identifying maladaptive thoughts and negative self-statements.

2. Learning appropriate behaviors and positive self-statements.

3. Practicing by verbalizing appropriate self-instructions and rehearsing them in fantasy.

The importance of cognition in sexual functioning has been explained by Walen (1980) in her model for the sexual arousal cycle. The model includes eight cognitive elements, each of which "functions as both a cue for the next link and a reinforcer of the preceding event" (p. 89). Most dysfunctions, she states, have as common denominators "a high level of emotional distress induced by cognitive errors of evaluation, often coupled with cognitive errors of perception" (p. 96). Sex therapy today acknowledges the brain to be the most important sexual organ.

SEXUAL DISORDERS
Following the classifications of Masters and Johnson, sexual dysfunctions traditionally have been grouped into male and female dysfunctions. This system lacked a physiological rationale, however, Now, based primarily on Kaplan's (1974) explanation of the biphasic nature of both the male and female sexual response, sexual dysfunctions are classified by phases: the desire phase, the arousal phase, and the

orgasmic phase. It is common to find problems from one phase in combination with those of another phase.

Desire phase. Disorders of the desire phase range from a mild disinterest in sexual functioning to a strong aversion, in which sex is seen as disgusting, dirty, and awful. In cases of sexual aversion, which is more common in women than in men, the onset of the problem usually can be traced to a precipitating event, such as rape or incest. Sex therapists are seeing a steadily increasing number of cases of sexual aversion.

Arousal phase. Arousal is the first of the physiological phases of the sexual response in both males and females. Both the vasocongestive/erection phase in the male and the vaginal lubrication/swelling phase in the female are mediated by the parasympathetic branch of the autonomic nervous system.

The male problem of arousal is erectile dysfunction, which used to be referred to as impotence. The term "primary erectile dysfunction" is used to describe males who have never experienced successful erection and penetration. "Secondary erectile dysfunction" refers to males who have functioned successfully in the past but are now not experiencing adequate erections.

There are two female disorders within this phase: vaginismus, which involves the involuntary contraction of the outer one third of the vagina, making penetration by the male impossible, and dyspareunia, or painful intercourse, which may be caused by lack of lubrication.

Most authors agree with Wolpe (1973) that anxiety is probably the greatest culprit in disorders of the arousal phase. Anxiety, which is a sympathetic response, is physiologically incompatible with sexual arousal, which is a parasympathetic response.

Orgasmic phase. The orgasmic response is mediated by the sympathetic branch of the autonomic nervous system. Male disorders of this phase include premature ejaculation and retarded ejaculation. The definition of premature ejaculation is a relative one: If the female is functional and she is not satisfied in at least half of the coital attempts, then a condition of premature ejaculation exists. This dysfunction is one of the simplest to treat. Retarded ejaculation relates to a male's inability to ejaculate within the female's vagina, although he may be able to ejaculate by means of masturbation. Masters and Johnson (1970) found this condition to be infrequent.

Female disorders include anorgasmia, which is the absence of an orgasmic response in a woman, and preorgasmia, in which a woman is interested in sex and is erotically aroused but cannot achieve an orgasm. The term preorgasmia implies that the woman has not yet, but will soon, become orgasmic. Approximately one third of all women are routinely orgasmic with intercourse; one third are sometimes orgasmic with intercourse, and one third are never orgasmic with intercourse. This third condition is not considered a dysfunction unless the woman is upset about it and desires to change.

HYPNOTIC ELEMENTS

The evolution of modern hypnosis and of sex therapy have proceeded along roughly parallel courses. Few hypnotherapists have focused on sexual concerns, and few sex therapists have systematically employed hypnosis. There are exceptions, however. As early as 1935, Erickson reported the treatment of premature ejaculation through hypnosis. Biegel was a hypnotherapist who dealt extensively with sexual disorders. Just before his death, he was working with Johnson on the first book dealing specifically with hypnosis in sex therapy (Biegel and Johnson, 1980). Kroger and Fezler (1976) developed a hypnobehavioral model they applied to sexual dysfunction. According to them, the use of hypnosis "strengthens the standard covert desensitization models used by the behavior modifiers" (p. 86–87).

Araoz (1982) traced the development of hypnosis as it has been applied to sex therapy and the extent to which sex therapy has employed hypnotic techniques. He also integrated the technique of hypnosis with the field of sex therapy, in the definitive work on the subject. Araoz presented a convincing case that hypnotic phenomena play an important part in the clinical approach of most sex therapists. As the authors have implied throughout this book, hypnosis is an important, if often unrecognized, element in successful treatment in most medical and psychotherapeutic situations, including sex therapy.

To support his argument, Araoz (1982) demonstrated the way in which the techniques of cognitive (behavioral) therapy are basically hypnotic in nature. He defined hypnosis as "a state in which the critical mental faculties are temporarily suspended and the person uses mainly imagination or primary process thinking" (p. 9). He defined cognitions as all mental activities, both conscious and subconscious, including not only beliefs and ideas, but also mental images. Araoz rephrased negative covert messages or negative self-talk, terms used by behaviorists, as "negative self-hypnosis."

Covert conditioning techniques (Cautela, 1975), such as sensitiza-
tion, positive and negative reinforcement, and extinction, use imagery
to change behavior and are important tools of cognitive therapy. As
Kroger and Fezler (1976) pointed out in their discussion of the
hypnobehavioral model, these techniques "have been used by hypnotherapists for decades" (p. 86). Based on his view of hypnosis as a
special type of communication between human beings (see Field, 1972),
Araoz went further to state that the covert conditioning techniques are
actually a form of hypnosis: "The more one emphasizes the covert
aspect of the procedure, the more hypnosis is used" (p. 59).

Referring to studies that explore the relationship between imagery
ability and sexual arousal (Harris, Yulis, and LaCoste, 1980; Mosher
and White, 1980), Araoz goes beyond the generally accepted statement
that hypnosis can be used to intensify imagery to assert that successful
guided imagery *is* hypnosis. The authors of this book agree with
Araoz's conclusion that "hypnosis is a very effective technique to
accomplish swiftly and elegantly what sex therapy is trying to attain"
(p. 72), and that it is time to apply hypnosis in a more conscious and
systematic way to the problems of sexual functioning.

BASIC ISSUES IN SEX THERAPY

Before moving on to discuss hypnotic techniques as they apply to sex
therapy, several basic issues relating to sex therapy should be discussed.
These fundamentals apply to all practitioners, including those using
hypnosis.

P-LI-SS-IT Model

For practitioners who do not specialize in sex therapy, the issue of when
to treat and when to refer a patient is important. The P-LI-SS-IT model,
developed by Anon and Robinson (1978), provides a conceptual
scheme for the practitioner to order and treat sexual problems within a
learning theory framework. The model contains four levels, each of
which requires increasing degrees of knowledge, training, and experience on the part of the practitioner. Anon categorized the first three
levels as "brief therapy" and the fourth as "intensive therapy." There is
some overlap between levels, and they often are used in combination.
Using this model, the practitioner can adjust the approach to his or her
own level of competence, theoretical orientation, and value system.

A brief summary of the four levels described by Anon and Robinson (1978) follows. For further information, the reader may refer to
Anon's description of a brief approach to behavioral therapy (1976).

1. Permission. Often people are more bothered by the idea that a specific behavior may be "wrong" or "bad" than they are by the behavior itself. Simply being informed by a person in authority that they are not alone and that other people share their concerns can prevent a problem from evolving. At this level, the practitioner gives the patient permission to do what he or she is already doing.

2. Limited information. At the second level, the practitioner provides the patient with factual information directly related to the patient's sexual concern. For example, a young man who is concerned that his penis is too small may be greatly relieved to learn that there is a foreshortening effect when he views his own penis and that there is no correlation between flaccid and erect penis size. Limited information may or may not result in changes in the patient's behavior.

3. Specific suggestions. Before giving specific suggestions, the practitioner must take a sexual problem history, which Anon distinguished from the more comprehensive sexual history that would precede intensive therapy. The problem history focuses on the onset and course of the problem, the ways in which the patient is dealing with the problem, past treatment and outcome, and current expectations and goals of treatment. Unlike the first two levels, the specific suggestions at this level are an attempt to help the patient modify behavior in order to reach the stated goals. To work at this level, the practitioner needs to have a thorough knowledge of human sexuality, such as the information included in the major texts on the subject. Suggestions for a male with premature ejaculation problems might include the sensate focus exercises developed by Masters and Johnson (1970), the squeeze technique described by Semans (1956), or the stop and start technique described by Kaplan (1974).

4. Intensive therapy. According to Anon and Robinson's model, intensive therapy is necessary when other treatments have not been successful in helping the patient to reach his or her goals. Treatment at this level is highly individualized and should be undertaken only by an experienced sex therapist.

Anon does not discuss hypnosis in conjunction with the P-LI-SS-IT model. However, hypnotic techniques, both formal and informal, can be used effectively at all four levels. The next section of this chapter will discuss the integration of hypnotic techniques at different levels of intervention.

Systematic Approach

Most sex therapists today prefer to treat problems of sexual dysfunction within the context of the primary couple relationship. It is not necessary for a couple to be living together or married if each partner regards the other as a main partner with whom there is a significant emotional investment. In the absence of a primary relationship, treatment proceeds on an individual basis. When cost and scheduling factors permit, some couples are more comfortable if both a male and a female therapist are present.

According to the Masters and Johnson (1970) model, the relationship is the patient, not just the symptomatic partner. Such attitudes as "he's the one with the erection problem—I don't have to deal with it," or "I'll just drop her off and you fix her up, Doc," may indicate relationship problems that need to be addressed. Viewed in systemic terms, a sexual problem experienced by one member of the couple not only reflects the current functioning of the whole system, but also affects the future of that system. Therefore, all aspects of treatment, including the initial history, counseling, hypnosis, and homework exercises, are addressed to both partners.

Diagnosis

An assessment period should, as a matter of course, precede any form of therapy. In some cases, when simply articulating a problem and receiving professional feedback is all the assistance someone requires, the diagnosis becomes the treatment. A careful diagnosis also helps the practitioner determine whether the presenting problem is within his or her area of competency and expertise.

A thorough history (as distinguished from the sexual problem history described by Anon as a prelude to brief therapy) usually takes 2–3 hours and should include personal, relationship, and sexual histories and reports of previous treatment for both partners. A medical evaluation to rule out an organic basis for the problem is also strongly recommended. What appears to be a sexual dysfunction may actually be a symptom of another problem, such as a low testosterone level or a prostatic tumor. In many ways, the diagnostic process merges into therapy by providing a couple with an introduction to a process that can seem threatening and by helping the couple deal with initial embarrassment and discomfort.

The diagnostic process also serves another important function in helping the practitioner determine whether or not sex therapy is the appropriate treatment for a sexual problem. In a study on the successes and failures among 30 couples who had requested sex therapy, Chapman (1982) found that major problems in the treatment situation that fell outside the category of bona fide sexual dysfunction comprised significant impediments to the progress of sex therapy. For example, to focus on the problem of premature ejaculation when there is extremely poor communication between the partners usually results in failure of the therapy.

Based on the results of her study, Chapman (1982) devised a set of criteria to help the therapist decide when sex therapy is appropriate and when other interventions are required. When these criteria are met, Chapman concluded, the likelihood of successful sex therapy is greatly increased. The criteria, which are summarized in the following list, also provide a guideline for the kind of information that should be included in a thorough sexual history.

1. Absence of a physical problem. Recent medical examinations are strongly recommended to rule out organic problems that either cause or coexist with the sexual dysfunction.

2. Absence of other "primary" problems. The sexual dysfunction may be symptomatic of some other primary problem, such as depression, substance abuse, or difficulties in a relationship, that must be treated first.

3. Presence of a bona fide sexual dysfunction. Someone seeking sex therapy may be mistaken in the belief that he or she has a sexual dysfunction. An alteration in sexual functioning, such as a period of diminished desire, can be processed negatively to the point where the person sees it as a serious problem.·

4. Presence of "therapy-positive" factors. In order for sex therapy to be effective, the couple must have a belief in sex therapy as a potentially helpful tool, a positive attitude towards sex therapy, a motivation to profit from treatment, and an ability to afford treatment. Negative attitudes, such as the use of therapy to justify divorce, are predispositions to failure.

5. Absence of interfering situational events. Events such as a recent death in the family or an unusually heavy work load may significantly interfere with a couple's ability to have sufficient time and concentration to carry out sex therapy.

6. Presence of basic relationship requirements. In order to profit from sex therapy, the couple needs to have a relationship that is basically functional at least at a minimal level. The components of such a relationship include:
   a. Absence or arrest of significant individual pathology.
   b. A clearly established commitment agreement.
   c. A basic repertoire of communication skills.
   d. Willingness to discuss most of the material that is relevant to the relationship.
   e. Mutually compatible life and relationship goals.

   If serious problems are encountered here, relationship therapy should be initiated.

Hypnosis can be an effective technique for diagnosing a problem and determining whether someone is ready to work on it. Ideomotor questioning is one diagnostic method available to the practitioner using hypnosis. Another, described by Araoz (1982), is to have the patient visualize himself or herself naked in front of a three-way mirror and evaluate every part of the body. Noting where the patient begins and ends the evaluation and what areas are omitted or excessively described can aide the practitioner in diagnosing the problem.

Effectiveness

Sex therapy is a field with a high success rate. Although the precise figures are open to argument (Masters and Johnson, 1970, reported a 20% failure rate), most people who enter treatment are able to achieve their treatment goals.

The question of effectiveness has nonetheless been raised in relation to sex therapy, just as it has been raised in the areas of medicine and psychotherapy in general. In a review of the literature on the effectiveness of sex therapy, Hogan (1978) concluded that "there is little ˙efinitive knowledge concerning the etiology, assessment, or treatment of sexual dysfunction" (p. 79). Brown and Chaves (1980) reviewed 26 reports on hypnosis in sex therapy and concluded that they did not meet the scientific criteria necessary to isolate the effect of a specific intervention procedure. Most of the case studies lacked controls, combined several treatment techniques, or lacked clearly delineated success criteria. Brown and Chaves, like Hogan, urged controlled studies on the effectiveness of sex therapy. Levitt's (1983) update on Brown and Chaves' review largely confirmed the earlier conclusions.

Although it has been said before in this book, it should be noted again that experimental conditions cannot be duplicated in a clinical setting. Lack of solid data on the effectiveness of different therapies should not deter the practitioner who is concerned with the progress of one patient rather than the mean performance of a large sample. Furthermore, many of the important variables in a clinical interaction, such as the patient's motivation and trust in the practitioner, are impossible to isolate.

In the absence of scientific data, we must rest our belief in the effectiveness of treatment on our own experiences and those of our colleagues. With regard to hypnosis in particular, a statement by Araoz (1982) supports this approach:

> The final proof of any therapy is its long term outcome. Many clinicians, like myself, who had not used hypnosis initially, have found that clients change more quickly and more radically with this new tool, and the changes are more lasting. . . . For most clinicians—and many of us are "converts" from other approaches or theoretical schools—the comparison between one's ante-hypnosis and post-hypnosis therapeutic work is a strong enough argument in its favor. More clients have been helped more rapidly and with more lasting effects with hypnosis than before I used hypnosis. (p. 25)

A case in point is Crasilneck's (1982) use of hypnotherapy in the treatment of erectile dysfunction. He reported an 80% improvement rate with 1,875 males over a period of 29 years, and he believes that hypnosis should be a primary treatment modality for psychogenic impotency.

Hypnosis can be an effective technique for furthering the following major goals of sex therapy: (a) to reduce performance anxiety, (b) to enhance confidence and comfort, (c) to replace negative conditions with positive ones, (d) to provide successful experiences in vitro that generalize to behavior, and (e) to increase touching and communication between a couple and at the same time decrease the emphasis on orgasm to the exclusion of other aspects of sexual functioning.

A MODEL FOR HYPNOTIC INTERVENTION

Hypnosis can be used in the treatment of sexual disorders at varying levels of severity and in a variety of settings—by the physician with patients who express sexual concerns, as well as by the psychotherapist who specializes in sex therapy. The model presented in this section outlines six hypnotic interventions, which require increasing levels of knowledge and experience.

For the past several years, Pratt has taught this model, which roughly parallels the P-LI-SS-IT model, to professionals interested in introducing hypnosis into their practices. The first three levels are appropriate for the beginning practitioner of hypnosis, the fourth and fifth levels are appropriate for more experienced practitioners, and the sixth should be used only by psychotherapists experienced in both hypnosis and sex therapy. The levels are not discrete, but part of a continuum, one merging into and frequently combining with another.

There also are different ranges of applicability within each level. For example, the first step, relaxation, can be used to reduce anxiety in a patient and also as part of a more complex technique in which relaxation is transferred to a previously disturbing sexual area. The best rule for the practitioner who wishes to follow this model is to stop at the point where he or she becomes uncomfortable and refer the patient, or at the very least, obtain a consultation.

There are two important and related points that must be kept in mind when using hypnosis in the treatment of sexual problems. First, the practitioner must remember that it is the patient's inner resources and not the practitioner's "power" that will lead to the realization of treatment goals. Second, all aspects of induction and treatment must be tailored to the individual. An image that is relaxing for one person may be anxiety-producing for another. What may be a realistic goal for one case of sexual aversion may be unrealistic for another. Therefore, the techniques presented below can be used in different ways, in different combinations, and for a variety of different problems.

Level 1: Relaxation intervention.   Performance anxiety is probably the greatest causative factor in any male or female dysfunction. Relaxation is the antithesis of anxiety; it is impossible to be anxious and relaxed at the same time. Relaxation allows a patient to be more receptive to sex, reeducation, and interventions that may have less impact if the patient is anxious.

Any relaxation technique can be used to decondition performance anxiety. Jacobson's (1938) progressive relaxation technique, which involves tensing and relaxing all of the muscle groups, beginning with the feet and legs and moving up to the neck and face, is useful both in itself and as a part of hypnotic induction.

Relaxation also can be achieved by helping a patient to create and experience a pleasant, relaxing scene. What constitutes relaxing images or associations will vary among patients. Hobbies, such as fishing in a mountain stream or working in the garden, can provide the practitioner with clues. Standard images, such as a beach scene or a mountain lake, can be tailored to the individual patient (see the General Relaxation image in Chapter 5), or new images can be created out of the patient's experiences.

To be effective, an image should be more than a visual representation. Images should be developed using all of the senses. A person who feels relaxed while curled up before a fireplace could be asked to see the colors in the dancing flames, to feel the heat of the fire, to hear the wind howling outside, and to smell the burning pine logs. Kroger and Fezler (1976) developed a series of 25 structured images for the purpose of producing relaxation and deepening hypnosis.

At a more advanced level, hypnotic relaxation can be used in the treatment of specific dysfunctions. Kroger and Fezler (1976) discussed a counterconditioning procedure that pairs hypnotic relaxation with a hierarchy of fears. The patient learns to respond differently to anxiety-producing stimuli by pairing them in imagination with relaxation.

Araoz (1982) described a transfer technique based on relaxation: The patient is encouraged to relax and to experience becoming more deeply relaxed in a comfortable, beautiful, and safe place where he or she can feast all the senses. The general relaxation is then focused on the sexual area. When tension develops, the practitioner guides the patient back to the relaxing scene. When the tension is released, the focus is returned to the sexual area. The process continues until the general relaxation has been transferred completely to the sexual area.

Fuchs et al. (1978) described systematic desensitization in the treatment of vaginismus by combining relaxation with both in vitro technique (imaginary penetration of the vagina) and in vivo technique (insertion of progressively larger dilators). Relaxation training also increases body awareness because the patient must be aware of tension in order to release it.

Level 2: Focused concentration.   This technique is related to, and has the same purpose as, relaxation. It is a behavioral training technique for increasing focal awareness and decreasing peripheral awareness. It also is an induction technique. Any focal point, internal or external, can be used to focus concentration. Fixing one's eyes on an external object, concentrating on one's own breathing, or focusing on a pleasant internal image are all ways of inducing trance. The trance state, before the introduction of suggestions, has been termed "neutral hypnosis" by Crasilneck and Hall (1975) and is similar to the altered states achieved through other disciplines such as meditation and autogenic training.

Level 3: Imagery.   In addition to inducing relaxation, imagery can be used as an important change agent. The more vivid the image, the more powerful it will be. A patient who has gone through the steps of relaxation and concentration will have heightened sensory recall and a greater ability to develop positive imagery states through all five sensory channels.

Imagery can be an effective technique in the waking as well as in the trance state. Training in hypnotic techniques is not necessary for a practitioner to use imagery effectively. However, as Araoz (1982) implied in his statement that successful guided imagery *is* hypnosis, it is likely that a practitioner who is using imagery effectively is already employing hypnotic techniques.

The purpose of imagery in the treatment of sexual dysfunction is to teach the patient to replace negative images, which usually are the source of the problem, with positive ones. This process is variously termed dynamic imagery (Araoz, 1982), visualization, imagery conditioning (Kroger and Fezler, 1976), and fantasy evocation. The practitioner may direct the development of an image tailored to the patient's needs and treatment goals or may encourage the patient to take the fantasized scene to whatever conclusion he or she finds appropriate or appealing.

For example, a woman with an arousal disorder may be asked to create a scene in which she is feeling relaxed and secure. Then an attractive man approaching from a distant point is introduced into the scene, and the practitioner asks the woman to notice her interest in the man and perhaps some sexual desire. Depending on the patient's degree of comfort, the scene could stop here, with the man turning around and walking away, or it could progress to the closeness and tenderness of embracing and kissing or even to sexual union. The practitioner would observe the patient carefully for any signs of tension or distress and would tailor the specifics of the scene to meet her needs. The development of the scene might continue over a series of sessions.

Female patients who have difficulty creating sexual images may be asked to read *My Secret Garden* (Friday, 1973), or *For Yourself* (Barbach, 1975). Barbach's book is one of the most useful self-help resources for women in the treatment of preorgasmia.

Level 4: Self-hypnosis.   Through self-hypnosis, a patient can continue to work on treatment goals outside the office setting. Self-hypnosis is included at this level in the model because the practitioner need not be an experienced hypnotherapist in order to help a patient learn this extremely valuable tool. With self-hypnosis, a patient will be able to relax, to reinforce positive affirmation, and to counter anxiety and negative covert messages outside the office setting. The practice of self-hypnosis also shifts the focus of control from the practitioner to the patient.

Level 5: Suggestions.   Suggestions can take many forms. They may be direct, indirect, or even symbolic. The type of imagery described in level 3 is one suggestive technique. To treat sexual problems at this level, the practitioner needs training in hypnosis and a good knowledge of human sexuality.

There are two types of suggestions that the practitioner can use at this level: (a) suggestions focused on symptoms, and (b) suggestions that help patients focus on their own resources and strengths. Referred to as an ego-strengthening technique by Hartland (1971), the second approach is used in medical hypnosis to improve a patient's self-confidence and motivation to get well. In some cases, ego-strengthening alone can enable a patient to overcome a sexual problem.

Araoz (1982) cited the example of a 47-year-old blue-collar worker with erectile difficulties:

> Through the process of hypnotic ego-strengthening, he awakened a new positive self-esteem he had never experienced before in his life. With it, his sexual problems disappeared—which in turn reinforced his new self-esteem. (pp. 120–121)

One example of direct suggestion for symptom removal in a case of premature ejaculation was provided by Erickson (1973). During hypnosis, Erickson reassured his 38-year-old patient, who expected treatment to fail, that he would indeed fail—fail to ejaculate during a specific period of time during intercourse. As treatment progressed, the period of time during which the patient would "fail" was extended. Treatment was successful and treatment gains were maintained over a 7-year follow-up period.

Suggestions can help a patient to enhance or diminish sensations in certain parts of the body, to channel the body's energies to the sexual organs, or to visualize a problem in concrete form and then visualize a way of getting rid of it. Suggestions given under hypnosis can be reinforced through self-hypnosis and by the practitioner when the patient is in the waking state.

Level 6: Hypnotherapy.   At this level, the practitioner who is a qualified psychotherapist and sex therapist has experience with a wealth of hypnotic techniques in addition to those described above. A few of those most frequently used in the treatment of sexual dysfunction are described below:

a. Age regression under hypnosis is used to help the patient reexperience past events to uncover pertinent material that may be repressed. It also is used to help a patient reconnect with and reexperience past positive sexual or sensual experiences and positive feelings. These memories may be brought to the present to be used as overlays to the current experience. For example, the therapist might offer the following suggestion:

> As you touch your thumb and forefinger, imagine a time, using all your senses, when you felt sexually confident, comfortable, and excited. In the future, as you touch your thumb and forefinger together, you may reexperience those positive feelings and enhance your confidence.

b. Time progression can be used to project the patient forward to a time when treatment goals have been met and satisfying sexual functioning has been realized. By using positive end-result imagery in all of the senses, the patient is able to experience the result of positive change.

c. Ideomotor questioning techniques (Cheek and LeCron, 1968) can be valuable diagnostic tools because they obtain information directly from the unconscious mind through the use of a preestablished code, such as the movement of a pendulum held by the patient or the lifting of designated fingers. Questions are phrased to require a yes or no response: "Is your premature ejaculation a message from your conscious mind?" or "Is your conscious mind ready to give up this symptom?"

   Ideomotor signaling can also be used to determine whether a patient is actually experiencing suggested images, when a certain task has been accomplished, and whether the person wishes to continue the trance state.

d. Transfer techniques are used to transfer a hypnotically produced sensation or experience from one part of the body to another. In a case of erectile dysfunction, for example, the practitioner helps the patient achieve finger catalepsy and then associate the stiffness and rigidity with penile erection.

e. Time distortion can be used in the treatment of premature ejaculation. The practitioner suggests that 30 seconds of actual time will seem like several minutes, and the progressive lengthening of the sexual experience is reinforced through posthypnotic suggestion.

f. Symptom manipulation, or learning to alter symptoms, often is a first step towards the awareness that one can control symptoms. A practitioner may suggest progressive minor alterations in a symptom or encourage a patient to practice intensifying a symptom before learning to alleviate it.

g. The effectiveness of many routine sex therapy techniques can be increased when combined with hypnotic suggestion. One example is the paradoxical method of disallowing intercourse, which puts patients in the position of feeling either that they can successfully complete intercourse or that they are successfully following the therapist's recommendations.

Sex therapy has come a long way from the days when sexual problems were viewed as a form of neurosis. Behavior therapy, cognitive therapy, and other forms of psychotherapy all have proved successful in treating sexual problems. Hypnotic interactions have been important, if unrecognized, elements in most of these treatment methodologies. As hypnosis becomes more consciously integrated into sex therapy, the success rate in an already highly successful field can be expected to increase.

SAMPLE INDUCTION

Anxiety or tension that result from anger or fear associated with sexual functioning are usually antecedent to sexual dysfunction. Relaxation can be used at many levels of therapy: as a procedure to reduce performance anxiety, as an induction technique, and as part of a counter-conditioning procedure in the treatment of specific dysfunctions. The following induction uses the imagery of a beach scene to facilitate relaxation and trance.

Just sit back comfortably in your chair, . . . close your eyes, . . . and let yourself begin to relax. Feel your muscles relaxing, . . . and at the same time your mind relaxing, . . . sitting quietly and peacefully . . . more at ease . . .

and just feel your body slowing down and your mind slowing down. . . . Time is slowing down. . . . There is lots of time and you feel more at ease . . . at peace . . . at peace with the universe . . . at peace with yourself. . . . So peaceful . . . quiet . . . relaxed . . . serene . . . tranquil . . . and calm. . . . As you breathe easily and gently . . . just feel yourself relaxing more and more . . . comfortable and relaxed . . . more comfortable . . . more at peace. . . . Feel a sense of peace and relaxation spreading throughout every part of your body and mind. . . . More and more relaxed . . . at peace . . . calm . . . complete peace . . . total relaxation with peace of mind . . . at peace with the universe . . . just totally serene . . . more and more relaxed . . . at peace . . . calm . . . and at ease. . . . Just feeling as if you were floating on a soft, soft cloud . . . just floating gently and easily . . . so relaxed and calm and comfortable . . . soft . . . gentle . . . quiet . . . peaceful . . . restful relaxation. . . . Your mind and body are relaxing more and more . . . thoughts are fading away . . . feeling so relaxed and comfortable . . . so at ease . . . calm . . . at peace . . . tranquil . . . relaxed . . . at ease . . . with peace of mind. A feeling of well-being . . . as if all your cares have rolled away . . . as though nothing matters right now except relaxing. . . . As you continue to relax . . . you can easily imagine yourself sitting somewhere at a beach . . . watching the afternoon sun . . . as it moves slowly towards the horizon. . . . You can feel its warmth . . . you can feel the breeze . . . you can feel the comfort of your resting place . . . you can hear the sound of the water . . . or whatever else you may hear right now. . . . You experience a certain pleasurable sensation . . . as you continue to watch the sun . . . move lower and lower toward the horizon . . . moving closer and closer to the sunset. . . . You feel more and more relaxed . . . enjoying every moment . . . as you drift off into a state of deep relaxation. . . . It may be surprising to you . . . how easily and comfortably you experience these moments . . . moments when you don't have to do anything . . . moments when you can simply notice . . . and enjoy whatever you are experiencing right now. . . . Spending whatever time you need to complete this experience for now . . . as the sun sets . . . and the sky slowly turns to night . . . until you realize that it is time to go . . . at least for now . . . realizing that you can return later . . . when you wish . . . and you realize that the air is cooler now . . . that you have things to attend to. . . . You imagine yourself rising from your resting place . . . and walking slowly away from the scene . . . walking, however many steps it takes . . . in order to return to the world . . . that you left behind when you entered this place. . . . As you walk . . . remembering what you have seen here . . . realizing that you feel more refreshed . . . that you are breathing more easily now . . . feeling more energy to do what you choose to do . . . because you have spent a few moments doing nothing . . . but attending to yourself . . . and your need to relax . . . and enjoying yourself. . . . And when you like . . . in just a moment . . . I'd like to have you count to yourself from 1 to 5 . . . and just gently rouse yourself up . . . becoming more aware of your present surroundings . . . and as you do so . . . just feel yourself becoming more alert . . . awake . . . refreshed . . . and still calm. . . . You will now have more energy to concentrate . . . and to focus . . . Okay . . . just counting to yourself from 1 to 5 . . . as you become more and more alert . . . and gently open your eyes. . . . Welcome back.

SUMMARY

Hypnosis can be an effective tool for both the certified sex therapist and the practitioner who occasionally treats patients with sexual concerns or disorders. The most important sexual organ is the brain, and nearly all (90%–95%) sexual problems have a psychological rather than a physical origin. Sex therapists today recognize the importance of negative self-talk, or to use Araoz's (1982) term, negative self-hypnosis, in sexual dysfunction. In countering negative messages and reinforcing positive ones, most forms of sex therapy already incorporate hypnotic techniques.

Most sexual problems can be treated without intensive therapy. Anon and Robinson's (1978) P-LI-SS-IT model outlined four levels of treatment that require increasing levels of professional expertise. In some cases, a patient will need only reassurance or information regarding normal sexual functioning. Pratt developed a related model for hypnotic intervention at increasing levels of complexity. Because performance anxiety is the greatest causative factor in sexual dysfunction, relaxation techniques are an extremely valuable tool at all treatment levels. Ego-strengthening alone sometimes will enable a patient to overcome a sexual problem.

At all levels of sex therapy using hypnosis, it is important to acknowledge that it is the patient's inner resources and not the practitioner's power that will lead to the realization of treatment goals. A careful diagnosis is essential to ensure that sexual dysfunction is not a symptom of an organic problem or a larger psychological problem, such as depression. When possible, sex therapy should be approached in the context of a primary relationship and involve both partners.

Many practitioners have found that the conscious application of hypnotic techniques has greatly increased their effectiveness in treating sexual problems. It seems probable that hypnosis will continue to become an increasingly important aspect of sex therapy.

FURTHER READING

Araoz, D. (1982). *Hypnosis and sex therapy.* New York: Brunner/Mazel.

REFERENCES

Anon, J. J. (1976). *The behavioral treatment of sexual problems: Brief therapy.* New York: Harper and Row.

Anon, J. J., & Robinson, C. H. (1978). Vicarious learning in treatment of sexual concerns. In J. LoPiccolo & L. LoPiccolo (Eds.), *Handbook of sex therapy* (pp. 35–56). New York: Plenum Press.

Araoz, D. (1982). *Hypnosis and sex therapy.* New York: Brunner/Mazel.

Barbach, L. (1975). *For yourself: The fulfillment of female sexuality.* New York: Anchor Press.

Beck, A. T. (1976). *Cognitive therapy and the emotional disorders.* New York: International Universities Press.

Biegel, H. G., & Johnson, W. R. (1980). *Application of hypnosis in sex therapy.* Springfield: Charles C. Thomas.

Brown, J. M., & Chaves, J. F. (1980). Hypnosis in the treatment of sexual dysfunction. *Journal of Sex and Marital Therapy, 6,* 63–74.

Cautela, J. R. (1975). Covert conditioning in hypnotherapy. *International Journal of Clinical and Experimental Hypnosis, 23,* 15–27.

Chapman, R. (1982). Criteria for diagnosing when to do sex therapy in the primary relationship. *Psychotherapy: Theory, Research and Practice, 19,* 359–367.

Cheek, D. B., & LeCron, L. M. (1968). *Clinical hypnotherapy.* New York: Grune & Stratton.

Crasilneck, H. B. (1982). A follow-up study in the use of hypnotherapy in the treatment of psychogenic impotency. *American Journal of Clinical Hypnosis, 25,* 52–61.

Crasilneck, H. B., & Hall, J. A. (1975). *Clinical hypnosis: Principles and applications.* New York: Grune & Stratton.

Erickson, M. H. (1935). A study of an experimental neurosis hypnotically induced in a case of ejaculation precox. *British Journal of Medical Psychology, 15,* 34–50.

Erickson, M. H. (1973). Psychotherapy achieved by a reversal of the neurotic processes in a case of ejaculation precox. *American Journal of Clinical Hypnosis, 15,* 217–222.

Field, P. B. (1972). Humanistic aspects of hypnotic communication. In E. Fromm & R. E. Shor (Eds.), *Research development and perspectives* (pp. 481–494). New York: Aldine.

Friday, N. (1973). *My secret garden. Women's sexual fantasies.* New York: Pocket Books.

Fuchs, K., Hoch, Z., Paldi, E., Abramovici, H., Brandes, J. M., Timor-Tritsch, I., & Kleinhaus, M. (1978). Hypnodesensitization therapy of vaginismus: In vitro and in vivo methods. In J. LoPiccolo & L. LoPiccolo (Eds.), *Handbook of sex therapy* (pp. 261–270). New York: Plenum Press.

Harris, H., Yulis, S., & LaCoste, D. (1980). Relationships among sexual arousability, imagery ability, and introversion-extroversion. *Journal of Sex Research, 16,* 72–86.

Hartland, J. (1971). *Medical and dental hypnosis.* London: Bailliere Tindall.

Hogan, D. R. (1978). The effectiveness of sex therapy: A review of the literature. In J. LoPiccolo & L. LoPiccolo (Eds.), *Handbook of sex therapy* (pp. 57–84). New York: Plenum Press.

Jacobson, E. (1938). *Progressive relaxation.* Chicago: University of Chicago Press.

Kaplan, H. S. (1974). *The new sex therapy.* New York: Brunner/Mazel.

Kroger, W. J., & Fezler, W. D. (1976). *Hypnosis and behavior modification: Imagery conditioning,* Philadelphia: J. B. Lippincott.

Levitt, E. E. (1983). Hypnosis in the treatment of sexual dysfunction. *Journal of Sex Education and Therapy, 9,* 23–26.

LoPiccolo, J. (1978). Direct treatment of sexual dysfunction. In J. LoPiccolo & L. LoPiccolo (Eds.), *Handbook of sex therapy* (pp. 1–17). New York: Plenum Press.

Masters, W., & Johnson, V. (1966). *Human sexual response.* Boston: Little, Brown.

Masters, W., & Johnson, V. (1970). *Human sexual inadequacy.* Boston: Little, Brown.

Meichenbaum, D. (1973). Cognitive factors in behavior modification: Modifying what clients say to themselves. In C. M. Franks & G. T. Wilson (Eds.), *Annual review of behavior therapy: Theory and practice* (Vol. 1). New York: Brunner/Mazel.

Mosher, D. L., & White, B. B. (1980). Effects of committed or casual erotic guided imagery on females' subjective sexual arousal and emotional response. *Journal of Sex Research, 16,* 273–299.

Semans, J. H. (1956). Premature ejaculation: A new approach. *Southern Medical Journal, 49,* 353–357.

Walen, S. R. (1980). Cognitive factors in sexual behavior. *Journal of Sex and Marital Therapy, 6,* 87–101.

Wolpe, J. (1973). *The practice of behavior therapy* (2nd ed.). New York: Pergamon Press.

15
Weight Control

Health exists when body and mind function in harmony.

—Kenneth Pelletier
Mind as Healer, Mind as Slayer

A love-hate relationship with food permeates our culture. Social occasions are built around food or at least embellished by it. Television commercials are siren calls to visit the refrigerator for beer or the cupboard for potato chips. Yet it is fashionable to be as slim as the models who advertise fattening food products. It is obvious that we live in a country of conflicting messages. We are both enticed into overeating and preoccupied with losing weight.

In a speech before the U.S. Senate Select Committee on Nutrition, McGovern (1977) reported that one American in every five is overweight, and that one in every ten is so obese that his or her life will be shorter because of it. The medical dangers of obesity are well known. Obesity is a significant factor in the incidence of cardiovascular disease, diabetes, kidney failure, complications during pregnancy, and a wide variety of other conditions.

Overweight also has social and psychological repercussions. In a society that is prejudiced against fat, the obese person may suffer from low self-esteem and avoid social occasions. In an effort to reduce, many people fall into a diet-and-binge syndrome that, with its broken resolutions and excesses, is emotionally damaging and contributes nothing to establishing sensible eating patterns.

Although this chapter focuses on weight reduction, many of the concepts discussed here can also be applied to other eating disorders, such as anorexia nervosa and bulimia (Crasilneck and Hall, 1975;

Thakur, 1980). As stated by Mann (1980), "the pathophysiology of obesity remains an enigma" (p. 141). No one theory, whether physiological or psychological, adequately explains the causes of obesity. Because hypnosis is a technique that can modify both the physical and psychological reactions to weight loss, it holds great promise in the treatment of overweight patients.

APPROACHES TO WEIGHT LOSS

Susan Dyrenforth, of the Clinic for Eating Disorders at the University of Cincinnati College of Medicine, has said:

> Being hungry sets off an evolutionary alarm, a panic reaction far stronger, because it is more fundamental, than any motivation to become thin. "I'm going to starve!" the alarm says. The body fights back. It wants to live. ("Learning to Live with Weight," 1979)

To some people, losing weight is little more than a case of mind over matter. But what the conscious mind resolves to do, the unconscious can easily sabotage. For a person who as a child was conditioned to associate food with love, loneliness can be mistaken for hunger. For someone who has built up a protective layer of fat as a shield against emotional or sexual involvement, weight loss may be frightening. And a person who has a strong unconscious identification with an obese parent may want to lose weight but find it difficult to break a long-established pattern of overeating.

It is not surprising, then, that no single approach to weight loss has shown significant long-term success. Methods reported effective in the control of obesity in the short term include self-control procedures (Pliner and Iuppa, 1978) and self-control combined with contingency contracting (Skuja, 1976; Stalonas, Johnson, and Christ, 1978; Stunkard and Penick, 1978; Weiss, 1977). Other investigators have found that weight loss is facilitated by a treatment paradigm employing behavioral techniques and hypnosis (Aja, 1977; Hartman, 1977; Kroger and Fezler, 1976; Ringrose, 1979; Stanton, 1975).

In some instances, these methods may be more effective when used with psychotherapy (Wood and Skuja, 1979). While behavior modification was hailed with great enthusiasm in the early 1970s because of its efficacy in achieving immediate weight losses in patients, its long-term results are ambiguous (Stunkard and Penick, 1979). Group treatment can offer a shared experience and moral support for some persons in a weight reduction program. For others, individual treatment is the most effective for long-term change.

The failure rate for the clinical treatment of obesity is over 90%. Some people have records of chronic failure, of heroic efforts to lose weight that are followed by backsliding, and each time, their already negative self-images become worse. The quest for permanent weight loss has led some desperate people into drastic treatments, including intestinal bypass surgery, rigid fasts, and procedures to wire their jaws shut. Radical therapies, too, often fail, because once the weight has been lost, the well-established patterns reemerge.

RESEARCH ON HYPNOSIS FOR WEIGHT LOSS

Although many authors (e.g., Cheek and LeCron, 1968; Crasilneck and Hall, 1975; Kroger and Fezler, 1976; Stanton, 1975) have reported success with hypnosis for weight reduction far beyond that found in the majority of treatment programs, there is little hard data to support these successes. "We do not know whether hypnosis is better or worse than other techniques because there apparently have never been any controlled comparative studies" (Cohen, 1979, p. 1).

Mott and Roberts (1979) found that the literature on obesity and hypnosis between 1955 and 1978 "consists primarily of anecdotal reports and studies of selected cases" (p. 6). They identified the following methodological problems in existing studies: (a) a lack of standardization in induction procedures and treatment suggestions, (b) no replication of findings, (c) no clear determination which treatment variables are responsible for outcome, (d) lack of long-term follow-up of patients, and (e) no attempt to correlate results with hynotizability.

Two studies published since Mott and Roberts' review illustrate some of the problems inherent in attempting to isolate hypnosis as one variable in a weight-reduction program. In the first, Deyoub and Wilkie (1980) compared the effectiveness of suggestions for weight loss with and without a hypnotic induction procedure. One group received a standard eye-fixation induction, followed by suggestions for changing eating habits, increasing physical activity, recognizing internal cues for hunger, and learning methods of self-mastery. A second task-motivational (TM) group received the same suggestions without an induction. They were told that "you, like most people, are capable of imagining and visualizing things that are suggested to you. . . . You have the potential and the ability to let the suggestions become part of your thinking behavior" (p. 335).

The weight loss in the TM group was greater by 2.7 lb, although this difference was not statistically significant. In acknowledging that their study could not demonstrate the effectiveness of hypnosis for obesity as compared to alternatives, Deyoub and Wilkie noted two critical limitations of the study: (a) the failure to validate the actual presence of hypnosis in the hypnotic group, and (b) the similarity between the TM instruction and informal induction techniques.

The fact that subjects "in the hypnosis group were more nervous, distracted, less relaxed and more defensive than Ss in the TM group" (p. 338) suggests that hypnosis was not achieved. On the other hand, it is possible that the more informal, relaxed approach, combined with the positive motivation inherent in the TM instruction, resulted in a more pervasive hypnotic effect among the TM group. What the study may in fact have been comparing is the effectiveness of a formal and an informal hypnotic induction procedure. As discussed previously in Chapters 1 and 4, the very elusiveness of the hypnotic phenomenon makes it an extremely difficult variable to control for in research.

In the second study, Wadden and Flaxman (1981) compared weight loss among subjects assigned to hypnosis, covert modeling, and relaxation-attention control groups. At the end of 7 weeks, all three groups showed comparable weight losses. Unlike the Deyoub and Wilkie (1980) study, this study provided individual rather than group treatment. As in the previous study, one can argue that the treatment methods for both experimental groups were hypnotic in nature.

The major distinction between the hypnosis and covert modeling groups was the use of a formal induction procedure as opposed to progressive muscle relaxation. Both groups used personalized and standardized reducing imagery, and subjects in the hypnosis group were given direct suggestions for weight loss. Araoz (1982) argued that covert modeling procedures are hypnotic in nature, and that "the more one emphasizes the covert aspect of the procedure, the more hypnosis is being used" (p. 59). Viewed in this light, the distinction between hypnotic and covert modeling procedures for weight reduction becomes arbitrary.

Wadden and Flaxman (1981) concluded from their findings that the

> . . . efficacy of hypnosis as a weight-reduction strategy is attributable to factors shared in common with a minimum treatment condition, including positive expectancy, weekly participation in a reduction program, relaxation training, and limited dietary counseling. (p. 162)

Positive expectancy, relaxation, and regular practice with self-hypnosis are important components of clinical hypnosis, regardless of the goal to be achieved. It can be argued that when these components are present, the stage has been set for a hypnotic interaction between practitioner and patient.

In the absence of reliable scientific data on hypnosis and weight reduction, one might hypothesize that the hypnotic elements of positive expectations, relaxation, and regular practice in achieving the hypnotic state are an important part of any successful weight reduction program. Given the difficulties inherent in controlling for hypnosis as an isolated variable, the best we can do at this point is to describe on a case-by-case basis how advanced hypnotic techniques can be used to facilitate weight loss.

HYPNOTIC TECHNIQUES

Hypnosis is a tool that can facilitate most treatment methodologies. "The hypnotic relationship is in reality a teaching situation in which the patient learns to explore his full potential healthfully, constructively and creatively" (Mann, 1980, p. 143). Using hypnosis, the practitioner can help the patient make positive changes in eating and lifestyle patterns.

General Approach

During the initial session of a weight-loss therapy, the practitioner and the patient should discuss the patient's eating habits, reasons for wanting to lose weight, and weight-loss goals. Why does the patient want to lose weight? To improve health and fitness, to gain acceptability to employers, to become popular with the opposite sex, to conquer a negative set of habit patterns, to develop a better self-image?

A practitioner's first step is to foster a positive expectation that treatment will be successful. Before inducing trance for the first time, it is important to allay any fears concerning hypnosis and to correct misconceptions. The value of hypnosis in weight control can then be explained. The patient should be informed that he or she will receive instruction in self-hypnosis, relaxation techniques, and imagery conditioning, and that these procedures will lower anxiety levels and facilitate a change in eating patterns. An explanation of short- and long-term goals is helpful to set up small successes on the way to greater successes.

For health as well as psychological reasons, most physicians recommend that patients lose no more than 2 lb per week. It is strongly recommended that all patients see a physician who will conduct a physical examination to rule out any physical causes for overweight, such as hypothyroidism, and recommend a healthful eating plan. Patients who are unaware of the nutritional content and caloric value of various foods may need to familiarize themselves with food charts.

A positive approach is extremely important for the overweight person who is accustomed to failure. For many obese people, even the word diet triggers feelings of resentment and rebellion. Dieting is associated with deprivation and a weight loss that usually proves to be temporary. For this reason, Cheek and LeCron (1968) recommend that the practitioner avoid using the word diet. Instead, the practitioner should refer to the healthful changes the patient will be making in eating habits.

The focus throughout treatment should be on the patient's positive motivation for losing weight. In trance, ego-enhancing suggestions for relaxation, confidence, and enjoying life can be effectively combined with a rehearsal of the positive results of weight loss. In the context of a positive approach, it is also advisable to avoid strict prohibitions against fattening foods. Cheek and LeCron substituted the following suggestion: "You can avoid these foods most of the time, but do not feel that you must never eat a piece of candy or a slice of pie or cake. You will only do this rarely, however" (pp. 185–186).

Contracts between the practitioner and the patient are sometimes helpful. Such contracts usually include a pledge to stick to the weight-loss program, an avowal of serious intent, and an expectation of success. The patient is asked to hang the contract in a prominent place, such as the bathroom wall or refrigerator door, along with a chart for recording weight and a reinforcer of a positive self-image, such as a photograph of the patient at a time when he or she was thin.

Trance induction, the specific content of suggestions, and the end-result imagery should be individualized to the background, weight-loss goals, and personality of each patient. As the patient becomes increasingly comfortable with the hypnotic state at each session, the practitioner can introduce additional hypnotic techniques and expand upon weight-reduction scenarios. Discussing a patient's progress each week provides the practitioner with information that can be used in subsequent sessions to deal with specific problems.

All sessions should emphasize positive experiences and offer assurances that difficulties can be overcome. Weight loss usually occurs in an uneven pattern, even if a weight-loss regimen is strictly followed, and it is a rare person who does not relapse once in a while. It is important that the practitioner be supportive and encouraging.

Specific Techniques

The following hypnotic techniques can be used or combined, according to the individual needs of each patient, as part of a weight reduction program using hypnosis.

1. Hypnotic relaxation in itself can facilitate the treatment of overweight because stressful situations often exacerbate the tendency to overeat. Self-hypnosis, as an antidote to the stress response, can be an effective way of short-circuiting a conditioned reaction to reach for food.

   Mann (1973) offered the following direct suggestion to a patient in a trance; it may be expressed in indirect language by practitioners using an indirect approach:

   > Your attempts in the past to starve yourself into reducing body weight developed tension, anxiety, and frustration. That is all over. Now you have the wonderful opportunity to associate relaxation of body and mind with a relaxed attitude toward eating. You find yourself comfortably choosing only those foods that are good for you, and passing up the foods that are fattening. (p. 81)

2. Imagery conditioning can be a powerful force in the treatment of overweight. Kroger and Fezler (1976) developed several standard images that enhance recall of taste and smell and can be used to help patients gain control over the hunger drive.

   End-result imagery is one of the most effective forms of imagery conditioning. Patients in trance should be asked to visualize themselves as having already attained their weight-loss goals. For example, they may see themselves stepping on a scale that registers the correct weight or being admired for their slim figure at a social occasion. The practitioner can work with the patient to develop effective end-result images based on each person's background and interest.

   Negative conditioning, such as pairing a certain food with aversive experiences, tastes, or smells, is generally not recommended. Patients may want, however, to rehearse scenarios for overcoming unhealthful eating habits. For example, patients in trance can rehearse opening a container of their favorite food, shutting it again, and walking away feeling light and elated. A similar approach would be to visualize a chain connecting the patient with the food and then to imagine breaking the chain.

3. Time distortion can be used to expand the sense of time while eating and to contract time between meals to make it seem shorter.

4. Glove anesthesia can be used to allay hunger pangs. The patient is taught to produce numbness in one hand and transfer that sensation to the pit of the stomach.

5. Metaphors for weight control can be used effectively with a patient in trance. A story seemingly unrelated to weight reduction is understood and applied at the unconscious level, as in the following example:

> Communication between different countries or even different worlds creates a need for new styles and new constructs. During this kind of change in communication, or any other kind of change, you can find a feeling of openness and motivation to modify old styles that may be slowing the progress of important changes.

6. Age regression can be used to identify the causes of an eating disorder that has its roots in childhood.

7. Ideomotor questioning also can provide insight into the causes of overweight (Cheek and LeCron, 1968). For example, obesity may be serving some purpose, such as protection from a sexual relationship. It may result from an identification with one or both parents who are obese. Or it may stem from frequently repeated statements heard throughout childhood that had the effect of posthypnotic suggestions: "You must eat to be big and strong," or "you must eat everything on your plate."

8. Practitioners using hypnosis incorporate a wide variety of hypnotic suggestions into a weight-reduction program. The following represent a few of many possibilities.
   a. Suggestions may enhance sensory enjoyment of eating. The practitioner may suggest rolling the food from the front of the tongue to the back to extract every bit of taste or chewing food well to enjoy all the subtle factors.
   b. Suggestions may help the patient eat less, as in the suggestion to eat a small meal and feel full and satisfied before the meal is finished.

c. Kroger and Fezler offered "Could you overeat enough to lose 2 pounds per week?" and "Every time you even think of eating something you are not supposed to, you will see the number 130 *(or the patient's target weight)* in blue encircled by a blue ring, just as the price of an item is stamped on the food can in a grocery store" (1976, p. 218, italics added).

d. Brodie suggested that the patient would learn "to become a gourmet who eats with good taste in every sense of the word" (1964, p. 215).

e. Cheek and LeCron (1968) believed that "it is possible that hypnotic suggestion can affect the rate or amount of absorption of food" (p. 183) and recommended a suggestion that the patient would absorb only enough from the food that is eaten to maintain a weight considerably below the present weight (e.g., 170 lb for a 200-lb person).

CASE STUDIES

The following case studies illustrate ways in which hypnosis can be combined with other treatment methods in a weight reduction program:

Wood and Skuja (1979) reported the case of Sally, a 22-year-old licensed vocational nurse who weighed 133 lb, which she considered too much for her height of 5 ft 3 in. Personal conflicts related to self-image and sexuality played a role in her weight problem, which had begun when she was 17. During the intervening 5 years, her weight had fluctuated several times from normal to overweight, a yo-yo syndrome that revealed her inability to reach and maintain a desirable weight.

A modification of the procedures described by Kroger (1970), Ringrose (1979), and Skuja (1976), was developed for Sally's treatment. Her treatment program included contingency contracting to establish a weight-loss regimen, information about nutrition, brief psychotherapy, self-hypnosis training, and treatment employing posthypnotic suggestions for weight control, ego strengthening, and relaxation therapy. A program designed to eliminate poor eating habit patterns was also incorporated. Sally was encouraged to practice self-hypnosis once a day, giving herself suggestions designed by the therapist and herself to encourage her to stick to her diet-and-exercise program and comply with the terms of her contract.

Her psychotherapy focused on her beliefs about her present weight and ideal weight. Food consumption and daily weights were recorded during a 7-day baseline period. During the initial consultation, the rationale and plan for weight loss were discussed. Sally and the therapist reached the conclusion that a loss of 1 lb per week was desirable. The therapist emphasized that the treatment program was not aimed at changing food intake but at permanently altering eating habits.

The following contract was signed by Sally and the therapist:

I do hereby pledge to stick to the rules and suggestions of the weight-loss program. I am serious enough about losing weight to use these techniques actually to lose weight and keep it off. I understand that I will be changing many well-learned habits, and it will not be quick or easy.

The contract and weight-loss recommendations were placed conspicuously on Sally's bathroom wall, along with a weight chart for keeping a daily record of gains and losses. The specified behavior was that Sally should lose a pound every week. The behavioral requirements were that she stay below the criterion line. The therapist and Sally agreed that should she fail to keep at or below the weight maximum for 2 consecutive days (one grace day allowed), a negative contingency would be effected—to forego eating for 2 days a specific food that was part of the plan and considered a treat. Positive reinforcements arose from compliments from Sally's friends and colleagues about her improved appearance. She was encouraged to keep track of them.

Sally's goal was to reach a weight of 110 lb, with the contingency to remain in effect for 2 weeks after achieving the goal to establish maintenance of the loss. Over a period of 18 weeks, which included 3 weeks of vacation time, Sally lost 18 lb. She reported feeling better physically and mentally. During the first 4 weeks of the program, several friends and colleagues commented on her weight loss (8 lb), which increased her enthusiasm.

She lost as much as 5 lb in 1 week, sometimes lost no weight (especially during her vacation when she temporarily discontinued her program), and during 2 weeks gained ½–3½ lb. Because she had not complied with the weight-loss program during a vacation (weeks 6 and 7), the program was recycled after her return.

Weekly treatment sessions lasted approximately 30 minutes. The treatment was originally planned to last 23 weeks, but it had to be discontinued after 18 weeks, when Sally moved out of the area.

Six months after termination of the treatment, the therapist contacted Sally for follow-up. She reported that she had decided that her target weight of 110 lb was too low, and so she had raised it 2 lb. She also said that she had maintained her weight loss at 112 lb. Although she had temporarily gained as many as 6 lb when she increased her caloric intake and reduced her physical activity, she was able to "regain" her target weight by going back on her weight-loss program. Total treatment time was 8 hours.

In a case reported by Alman, Marianne W. weighed 165 lb, which was 40 lb over normal weight. Five years earlier, she had given birth to a daughter out of wedlock, and in the next 5 years, until treatment, she had ballooned from 125 to 165 lb. Eating was a nervous habit; she needed to eat as an outlet for her energy. She also stayed fat to keep people away because she had been disappointed in her interpersonal relationships. If she had a husband who would act as father to her daughter, she said, she would have someone to look good for, but since she hadn't, she ate. Her therapist, who had been treating her sporadically over an 18-month period for what he diagnosed as an obsessive compulsive neurosis, referred her for hypnosis, stating that her prognosis was good and termination of treatment near.

During the psychological treatment, her eating habits had been "up and down, depending on when I was in therapy." Though she dressed neatly, she appeared quite overweight. It was apparent that her self-concept was in disrepair, exacerbated by her lack of employment. A college graduate, she was looking for a job as a researcher in a community organization and had been unable to find one. Although she had gained much insight from her therapy, she could still be diagnosed as obsessive compulsive, and this personality characteristic bore a direct relationship to her nervous eating habits.

Marianne reported that after smoking for 4 years she had been able to quit cold turkey, but to lose weight, "I need some help, but I know I can do it." She had tried Weight Watchers, diet pills, water diets, and other weight reduction methods with little success. Her therapist felt she had come far enough to be able to lose weight with no substitute symptoms. He presented the hypnotherapist to her in a positive manner and continued treatment during the weight-loss program.

Marianne and the hypnotherapist contracted for three 50-minute sessions. During the first session, the hypnotherapist interviewed her to obtain a sense of who she was, to gather information about her problem, and to discuss her understanding of hypnosis.

During the second session, after assuring Marianne that hypnosis was a natural, internal technique, the hypnotherapist facilitated the induction of a trance, during which he presented an analogy relating weight control to research, her chosen occupation. Specifically, he discussed the value of internal processes to control external stimuli, the need for more time to be directed to development, and her involvement as a researcher in finding out how her internal processes were affected by external stimuli. He also gave her suggestions for ideomotor responses. It was hoped that she would identify food as the external stimulus, the development as weight gain, and her internal processes as her real nutritional needs, and that she would gain psychological control over this "project."

At the beginning of the third session, she reported that she was much more aware of what and how much she was eating, which had helped her to eat less and better food. She had lost 2½ lb in the intervening week. The hypnotherapist facilitated a reinduction of hypnosis, during which he made suggestions similar to those he had given her during the previous session. She agreed to do the research and necessary "footwork" for the project, as well as *to coordinate processes. The hypnotherapist explained the meaning of the metaphorical project, identifying the footwork as a 15-minute-per-day exercise period that would allow her to think more clearly about her research and to put information to work. Two posthypnotic suggestions were given: The first was that she would keep the project confidential; she could tell someone about the weight loss only if she didn't give away the whole plan. (This strategy was intended to keep her understanding at an unconscious level, thus facilitating motivation.) The second was that she was the chief researcher and experimenter on the project and could control its pace and success, promising to finish it and report the results at the end of each month for 6 months. The session ended with an agreement of termination.*

Marianne fulfilled her pledge to report at the end of each month. When last heard from, she reported that she had lost 20 lb, was only 10 lb away from her goal, and had joined a health spa.

SUMMARY

Overweight, a problem usually involving food addiction, plagues a large proportion of the population. Reasons for it are physiological as well as psychological. Short-term methods of treatment that have proved successful are self-control procedures combined with contingency contracting, hypnosis, and behavioral techniques. Long-term results are more difficult to attain. Treatment includes a diet-and-exercise program, with the goal of reaching a desirable weight and changing eating habits.

Problems with overweight are complex, and it is wise for the practitioner to develop a treatment plan that matches each patient's background, habits, goals, and personality. Imagery conditioning, glove anesthesia, relaxation, age-regression, and other hypnotic techniques can be used effectively to facilitate weight reduction. The emphasis is best placed on self-control and internal rewards. Brief psychotherapy is often essential.

Much more research must be done to find long-term methods of weight maintenance. Backsliding is all too common: Successful dieters, euphoric with their success and believing they have their problem permanently licked, go back to their old eating patterns. Self-hypnosis can be an effective tool for maintaining improved eating patterns after formal treatment has ended.

FURTHER READING

Stern, F. M., & Hoch, R. S. (1976). *Mind trips to help you lose weight.* Chicago: Playboy Press.

REFERENCES

Aja, J. H. (1977). Brief group treatment of obesity through ancillary self-hypnosis. *American Journal of Clinical Hypnosis, 19*, 231-234.

Araoz, D. (1982). *Hypnosis and sex therapy*. New York: Brunner/Mazel.

Brodie, E. I. (1964). A hypnotherapeutic approach to obesity. *American Journal of Clinical Hypnosis, 6*, 211-215.

Cheek, D. B., & LeCron, L. M. (1968). *Clinical hypnotherapy*. New York: Grune & Stratton.

Cohen, S. B. (1979). Editorial: Hypnosis for obesity? *American Journal of Clinical Hypnosis, 22*, 1-2.

Crasilneck, H. B., & Hall, J. A. (1975). *Clinical hypnosis: Principles and applications*. New York: Grune & Stratton.

Deyoub, P. L., & Wilkie, R. (1980). Suggestion with and without hypnotic induction in a weight reduction program. *International Journal of Clinical and Experimental Hypnosis, 28*, 325-333.

Dyrenforth, S. (1979, May 9). Learning to live with weight. *Los Angeles Times.*

Hartman, B. J. (1977). A hypnobehavioral approach to the treatment of obesity. *Journal of the National Medical Association, 69*, 821-824.

Kroger, W. S. (1970). Comprehensive management of obesity. *American Journal of Clinical Hypnosis, 12*, 165-176.

Kroger, W. S., & Fezler, W. D. (1976). *Hypnosis and behavior modification: Imagery conditioning*. Philadelphia: J. B. Lippincott.

McGovern, G. (1977, February 2). Speech before U.S. Senate Select Committee on Nutrition and Human Needs. Washington, DC.

Mann, H. (1973). Suggestions based on unlimited calorie, low carbohydrate diet. In *A syllabus on hypnosis and a handbook of therapeutic suggestions* (pp. 81-83). Des Plaines, IL: American Society of Clinical Hypnosis, Education and Research Foundation.

Mann, H. (1980). Hypnosis in weight control. In H. J. Wain (Ed.), *Clinical hypnosis in medicine* (pp. 141-146). Miami: Symposia Specialists.

Mott, T., & Roberts, J. (1979). Obesity and hypnosis: A review of the literature. *American Journal of Clinical Hypnosis, 22*, 3-7.

Pliner, P., & Iuppa, G. (1978). Effects of increasing awareness on food consumption in obese and normal weight subjects. *Addictive Behaviors, 3*, 19-24.

Ringrose, C. A. D. (1979). The use of hypnosis as an adjunct to curb obesity. *Public Health, 93*, 252-257.

Skuja, A. T. (1976). A self-control and contingency-contracting weight reduction program: An informal case study. *Psychological Reports, 38*, 1267-1270.

Stalonas, P. M., Johnson, W. G., & Christ, M. (1978). Behavior modification for obesity: The evaluation of exercise, contingency management and program adherence. *Journal of Consulting and Clinical Psychology, 46*, 463-469.

Stanton, H. E. (1974). Weight loss through hypnosis. *American Journal of Clinical Hypnosis, 18*, 34-38.

Stunkard, J. J., & Penick, S. B. (1979). Behavior modification in the treatment of obesity. *Archives of General Psychiatry, 36,* 801–806.

Thakur, K. S. (1980). Treatment of anorexia nervosa with hypnotherapy. In H. J. Wain (Ed.), *Clinical hypnosis in medicine* (pp. 147–154). Miami: Symposia Specialists.

Wadden, T. A., & Flaxman, J. (1981). Hypnosis and weight loss: A preliminary study. *International Journal of Clinical and Experimental Hypnosis, 29,* 162–173.

Weiss, A. R. (1977). A behavioral approach to treatment of adolescent obesity. *Behavior Therapy, 8,* 720–726.

Wood, D. P., & Skuja, A. T. (1979, November). *The use of self-hypnosis and contingency-contracting. Self-control in weight reduction: An informal case study.* Paper presented at the annual convention of the American Society of Clinical Hypnosis, San Francisco.

16

Stress Management

The mind is its own place, and in itself can make a Heav'n of Hell, a Hell of Heav'n.

—John Milton
Paradise Lost

Stress has become a byword of the 1980s. In this age of anxiety, stress and its synonyms, tension, frustration, and pressure, have become an accepted condition of modern living. Rare is the person who does not feel the effects of stress that result from political and economic, environmental, or personal causes. The list of potential stressors is endless: unemployment, rising crime, the energy crisis, changing sex roles, traffic congestion, noise pollution, a high-pressure job, a death or an illness in the family, moving, or children leaving home.

According to Cousins (1979), "the war against microbes has been largely won, but the struggle for equanimity is being lost" (p. 65). While the fear of diseases such as polio or smallpox has been largely eliminated, stress itself has become epidemic. The way we live, and not a microscopic invader, now appears to be the greatest threat to our national health. *Time* has reported the three best-selling drugs in the United States to be an ulcer medication (Tagamet), a hypertension drug (Inderal), and a tranquilizer (Valium) (Wallis, 1983).

Chronic stress is manifested both physiologically and psychologically, and both physicians and psychologists treat a multitude of stress-related problems. Studies with laboratory animals and humans have established a clear link between stress and such major illnesses as heart disease and cancer. Numerous chronic conditions, such as diabetes and asthma, are aggravated by stress. Psychological manifestations of stress include tension headache, insomnia, and anxiety. As more and more illnesses appear to be stress-related, our concept of the term "psychosomatic" is expanding rapidly.

As researchers try to understand the mechanisms by which stress is translated into organic pathology, counselors, psychologists, and physicians are identifying weapons to use in the struggle for equanimity. Hypnosis directed toward obtaining mental and physical relaxation is an effective technique for treating as well as preventing stress-related problems.

A DEFINITION

The word "stress" generally has negative connotations, as in "the stress of modern life." In our minds, stress has become synonomous with distress. However, stress is not necessarily negative. Because the nervous system needs a certain amount of stimulation to function, some degree of stress is necessary to maintain life. Like the violin string that needs enough tension to sound under the bow, but not so much that it snaps, each person needs to find the appropriate stress level for optimal functioning.

A pioneer in the area of stress research, Selye (1975) defined stress as "the nonspecific response of the body to any demand made upon it" (p. 14), thus distinguishing the stress-producing factor, or stressor, from the stress response itself. According to this definition, stress results from any action or situation that unbalances a person's equilibrium. Getting a divorce may be a stressful situation, but so is getting married. A birth or a death in the family, the loss or gain of a big account, retirement or new job—all can place demands on one's system to adapt to the change.

Experiments have shown that the absence of stress, such as during isolation or sensory deprivation, can be as harmful as an overload. The bored assembly-line worker and the aging widower who have too few challenges, friends, or outside interests live with a stress underload. Those who lack stimulation may suffer from a "disease of stagnation," such as depression or digestive disturbance. At the other extreme is the business executive who gets up at 5 A.M., works until 7 P.M., rushes home, grabs a hasty meal, reads business reports, has two or three martinis to "relax," and dozes off in a chair. He or she is suffering from stress overload and is vulnerable to "diseases of adaptation," such as rheumatoid arthritis, peptic ulcer, heart disease, anxiety, and high blood pressure.

Stress is an important component in all areas of human achievement. The athlete in training or the artist in the throes of composition both expose themselves to stressful conditions. Stress, therefore, must be distinguished from distress, which is unpleasant or harmful stress. The challenge for the practitioner is not to assist the patient in avoiding stress entirely, but to help develop appropriate responses to it.

PHYSIOLOGY OF STRESS

To understand the value of hypnosis as a tool in the treatment of stress and related diseases, it is necessary first to have a basic understanding of the physiology of the stress response. Selye's (1956) theory of nonspecificity states that, in addition to their specific effects, all stressors provoke an identical biochemical reaction in the body. Thus, the effect of a stressor is not due to its origin but rather to the intensity of the demand made on the body to adapt to the situation and maintain homeostasis, or equilibrium of the internal environment.

Selye (1956) named the sequence of changes that the body goes through in response to a stressor the general adaptation syndrome (GAS). It consists of three stages:

1. The alarm reaction, or the body's call to arms. The autonomic nervous system reacts by increasing the heart rate, releasing hormones that raise blood pressure and increase the flow of blood and oxygen to the muscles, sharpening the sense organs, and slowing the digestion. The body's preparation for vigorous action has been called the "flight or fight" response by physiologist Cannon (1953). This initial reaction to a stressor reduces the body's resistance, and if the stressor is sufficiently strong, death may result.

2. The stage of resistance. The organism cannot support a continuous state of alarm. If survival is possible, the body adapts to the situation, its functions return to normal, and its resistance increases. The body is quite capable of recovering from acute, short-term stress.

3. The stage of exhaustion. Prolonged exposure to stress destroys the body's ability to adapt. Symptoms similar to those of the initial alarm reaction reappear, but this time they are irreversible. Once adaptation energy is exhausted, the organism dies.

Through the GAS, the nervous system and endocrine glands enable people to adjust to changes and maintain homeostasis. However, repeated stress, whether it be an actual threat or only a misinterpreted situation, is destructive and causes structural changes in the body that will deteriorate with time.

In the course of his research on the psychological aspects of biological stress, Mason (1971) investigated the methods by which essentially different stimuli, such as heat and cold, provoke identical biochemical reactions in the body. He found that while different stressors may have stimulus-specific reactions, each is perceived as a threat by the organism. Thus, the "primary mediator" underlying the stress response may be "the psychological apparatus involved in emotional or arousal reactions to threatening or unpleasant factors in the life situation as a whole" (p. 329). From Mason's point of view, stress becomes primarily a psychological and a behavioral concept.

Recent research has found that the physiological response to stressful situations varies with the type and duration of the stressor and the individual's coping ability (see Borysenko and Borysenko, 1982, and Locke, 1982, for a review of related studies on behavior and immunity in laboratory animals and humans). Coping ability includes such factors as ego strength, the ability to relieve anger or anxiety, and the presence of an emotional or psychological support system.

The intensity of someone's stress response depends on how he or she perceives a stressful situation. For example, in response to the invitation, "Would you like to dance?" a person who feels awkward on the dance floor will experience more stress than the person who loves to dance. One person who has just lost a job may feel angry and helpless and go into a deep depression, while someone else, who has the support of a loving family, may respond more positively to the same situation.

The stress syndrome thus has three components: (a) the environment (or the external stressor), (b) negative thoughts ("I'll make a fool of myself," or "I'm a failure"), and (c) a physiological response (Selye's GAS). Targeting the way they respond to stressors can enable people to use hypnosis and other stress reduction techniques to modify their physiological responses.

STRESS AND DISEASE

Human physiological responses to stressful situations are the result of millions of years of evolution. The flight-or-fight response was at one time crucial to survival. Today it is useful only under certain physically threatening circumstances. In most situations, it is at best inappropriate and at worst an actual threat to survival. A traffic jam can daily evoke the same release of adrenalin in a commuter that an attacking predator evoked in a neolithic hunter.

The stresses of society continually elicit the flight-or-fight response while preventing us from discharging the response. It is not advisable, for example, to fight or run from a police officer writing out a ticket or a boss criticizing one's performance. Mason (1971) found that "even subtle psychological stimuli of everyday life can be sensitively reflected in adrenocortical activity" (p. 325). When the mind repeatedly interprets situations as threatening and thus continually triggers the GAS, the body can become taxed beyond its ability to adapt; its weakest link, whether the heart, kidneys, or gastrointestinal tract, will break down. For someone with heart problems, a strong reaction to a stressful situation can provoke a life-threatening heart attack. Thus, the mechanism that has ensured the survival of our species can lead to the destruction of the individual.

A host of stress-related diseases have been identified by the medical community. Those for which stress is clearly an important factor include hypertension, headache, backache, and stomach and duodenal ulcers. People engaged in a constant "cold war" with their environment are subject to chronic stress and, therefore, are perfect candidates for hypertension and ulcers. Headaches and backaches often result from prolonged contraction of muscles as a result of tension.

During World War II, people living in the heavily bombed cities of Great Britain experienced epidemics of "air raid ulcers"—or peptic ulcers. Those who had been badly burned manifested the same symptoms—bleeding ulcers—as did those who remained physically unharmed but who suffered great emotional shock. Both types of severe stress activated the GAS, and the resulting release of corticoids had an adverse effect on the gastrointestinal tract.

Clear cases of stress-related illnesses also have been manifested by an estimated one million Vietnam veterans. Symptoms of the "delayed stress response syndrome" (Horowitz and Solomon, 1975) include headaches, gastrointestinal and cardiorespiratory disturbances, exhaustion, mood disturbances, nightmares, psychotic episodes, and many similar problems.

Holmes and Rahe (1967) rank-ordered various life events for their stress value. The common denominator for these events is that they involve a change in the individual's ongoing life pattern. In a sampling of 5,000 persons from various cultures, Holmes and Rahe found a significant correlation between high scores on their Social Readjustment Rating Scale (see table) and stress-related illnesses. People who scored over 300 for the previous year had a 90% chance of developing a significant illness or undergoing a major health change. People who scored as low as 150 still had a 50% chance of experiencing a significant health change. Although its references to a mortgage of $10,000 are outdated, the scale remains a valid and widely used tool for measuring the level of stress in one's life.

Social Readjustment Rating Scale*

EVENT	IMPACT	SCORE
Death of spouse	100	_____
Divorce	73	_____
Marital separation	65	_____
Jail term	63	_____
Death of close family member	63	_____
Personal injury or illness	53	_____
Marriage	50	_____
Fired at work	47	_____
Marital reconciliation	45	_____
Retirement	45	_____
Change in health of family member	44	_____
Pregnancy	40	_____
Sex difficulties	39	_____
Gain of a new family member	39	_____
Business readjustment	39	_____
Change in financial state	38	_____
Death of a close friend	37	_____
Change to a different line of work	36	_____
Change in number of arguments with spouse	35	_____
Mortgage over $10,000	31	_____
Foreclosure of mortgage or loan	30	_____
Change in responsibilities at work	29	_____
Son or daughter leaving home	29	_____
Trouble with in-laws	29	_____
Outstanding personal achievement	28	_____
Spouse begins or stops work	26	_____
Begin or end school	26	_____
Change in living conditions	25	_____
Revision of personal habits	24	_____
Trouble with boss	23	_____
Change in work hours or conditions	20	_____
Change in residence	20	_____
Change in schools	20	_____
Change in recreation	19	_____
Change in church activities	19	_____
Change in social activities	18	_____
Mortgage or loan less than $10,000	17	_____
Change in sleeping habits	16	_____
Change in number of family get-togethers	15	_____
Change in eating habits	15	_____
Vacation	13	_____
Christmas approaching	12	_____
Minor violations of the law	11	_____

TOTAL   _____

If an event mentioned above has occurred in the past year or is expected in the near future, copy the number in the score column (as many times as the event has occurred or will be expected).

*Holmes and Rahe, 1967. Used with permission.

In their review of life change and illness onset studies, including complications of pregnancy and parturition, childhood leukemia, diabetes mellitus, rheumatoid arthritis, traffic accidents, and psychiatric illness, Rahe and Arthur (1978) concluded that the correlation had been so well established that further studies would be redundant. Even though they represent only a single dimension of stress, recent life changes

> . . . do reflect current environmental demands to which most persons endeavor to adjust. Psychological and physiological efforts necessary for such adjustment, if severe and/or protracted in time, appear to predispose individuals towards the development of illness. (p. 4)

Rahe and Arthur (1978) conceptualized the individual differences in stress tolerance into a model with the following steps:

1. A filter of perception that can alter the significance and intensity of life-change events.
2. Ego defenses (unconscious), which are like a negative lens and can diffract the impact of events.
3. Internalization of events into a set of psychophysiological responses.
4. Response management (conscious), such as relaxation, exercise, and "cognitive strategies," that may prevent the development of organ dysfunction and bodily symptoms.
5. Illness behavior leading to diagnosis and health records used in life change and illness studies.

Like perceptions of pain, individual perceptions of stress are influenced by prior experience and culture, as well as by emotional and cognitive factors. Therefore, while stress can be understood both psychologically and physically, it must always be put into a personal context. Not only will prolonged stress cause different problems in different people, but people will have different responses to the same potentially distressing situation. It is these intervening variables that must be studied "if one is to begin to approximate the subtle and complex reality of why some individuals fall ill at specific times" (Rahe and Arthur, 1978).

HYPNOSIS AND STRESS REDUCTION

Because chronic stress contributes to many, if not most, medical and psychological disorders, it can be argued that this entire book addresses the subject of hypnosis in stress reduction. The rest of this chapter will focus on techniques for coping with stress before it has become manifested as a serious illness. Previous chapters in this book have provided discussions in more depth on the use of hypnosis during treatment of physical and psychological disorders.

Each person develops individual ways of coping with stress. The mental and physical relaxation achieved in the hypnotic state make hypnosis an excellent means of counteracting the stress response and reestablishing physical and emotional equilibrium. By lowering the amount of steroids circulating in the system, relaxation also improves the body's ability to resist disease.

As suggested by Bowers and Kelly (1979), hypnosis can be used in several ways in an overall approach to stress management: (a) alone as a means of inducing relaxation and coping with stress, (b) as a strategy for controlling specific physical responses to stressful situations, and (c) in conjunction with psychotherapy. Even more importantly, hypnosis can be a tool for preventing disease and for promoting health. By helping people break out of the negative stress cycle, hypnosis can help to initiate a positive cycle in which they assume responsibility for their own health.

Coping with Everyday Stress

Self-hypnosis is one of the fastest and easiest ways of inducing relaxation. With practice, it can create almost immediate relaxation. As discussed in Chapter 1, neutral hypnosis, or the trance state before suggestions are introduced, is a natural antidote to the stress response. To use self-hypnosis, then, is simply to augment our natural ability to maintain homeostasis.

Hypnotic techniques are an integral part of most of the stress-reduction programs that are appearing throughout the country. Sponsored by corporations, hospitals, and groups of psychologists and physicians, the goal of most of these programs is to help people to break out of the stress syndrome by learning to recognize stress and to respond appropriately in stress-producing situations. In general, these programs use relaxation techniques and behavior modification along with exercises in time management, values clarification, or assertiveness training (see, for example, Steinmetz, Blankenship, Brown, Hall, and

Miller, 1980). Relaxation techniques include self-hypnosis, the relaxation response, meditation, and autogenic training, all of which produce the same physiological responses (see Chapter 3 and Benson, Arns, and Hoffman, 1981).

Hypnosis is frequently presented under another term, such as relaxation therapy, that is less threatening to the general population unfamiliar with hypnosis. One popular relaxation technique, progressive relaxation, is often used by practitioners as part of the induction process. The patient is asked to progressively tighten and then relax the major muscle groups, beginning with the toes and moving to the head. Using visualization (phrasing positive suggestions as mental images) is another popular technique. By vividly imagining a relaxing scene, a person is able to experience the benefits of deep relaxation. Visualization is also a common method for inducing trance; it is used extensively in hypnotherapy and in conjunction with cognitive techniques. Thus, when we talk about stress-reduction techniques, we are almost invariably talking about some form of hypnotically induced relaxation.

The following list briefly outlines a self-hypnosis procedure taught by Pratt. With a few days' practice, this procedure can be an excellent method of coping with everyday stress:

1. Write a brief suggestion incorporating positive imagery related to your desired response in a stressful situation; for example, feeling relaxed and calm when a traffic jam makes you late for an appointment, your boss criticizes you unfairly, or when your children are fighting at the dinner table.

2. Make yourself very comfortable. To create eye strain, stare at a spot on the ceiling that is slightly above your eyebrows.

3. Breathe deeply and exhale slowly while the rest of your body feels relaxed and comfortably heavy.

4. Allow your eyes to feel heavy.

5. Allow your eyes to close.

6. Roll your eyes back in your head for about 30 seconds, almost as though you were looking through the top of your head, with your eyelids slightly closed.

7. Allow your eyes to roll back to their normal position and feel a rhythmic wave of relaxation from your toes to your head.

8. Experience an image of relaxation, peacefulness, and tranquility, such as sitting on the beach at sunset or fishing in a mountain lake, in as many senses as possible.

9. Give yourself your positive suggestion (number 1) and experience your end-result image.

10. Give yourself a posthypnotic suggestion that every time you sip a beverage, open the door to your office, climb into your car, or engage in any other frequently performed activity, you will experience the same sense of tranquility.

11. Count backwards to yourself from 5 to 1 as you become more and more alert. Also, give yourself suggestions that:
    a. Each time I will go deeper.
    b. Each day I will notice some improvement.
    c. I will feel happier and more content while I count from 5 to 1, becoming fully alert, awake, refreshed and feeling great.

12. Throughout the day, repeat and affirm positive messages to yourself.

Controlling Specific Responses to Stress

In addition to inducing relaxation in a stressful situation, hypnosis can relieve many manifestations of stress, such as headache, insomnia, and minor anxiety. It also can be extremely effective as an adjunct to the treatment of medical disorders that are aggravated by stress, such as peptic ulcers, hypertension, arthritis, and allergies. Readers interested in the use of hypnosis in medical treatment are referred to Chapter 7.

Self-hypnosis (see also Chapter 6) can be used to counter all manifestations of the stress response. The two following examples demonstrate the ways that hypnotic techniques can be used in the group treatment of stress-related disorders commonly seen by the physician.

Herbert and Gutman (1980) found that stress-related disorders and their concomitants accounted for a large number of office visits in their family practice. Wishing to avoid the danger of drug dependence inherent in medicating patients suffering from stress, as well as the disproportionate amount of time required for individual counseling, these authors looked to autogenic training as an alternative. They conducted a study of 62 persons to establish whether patients with psychological disorders and self-perceived high anxiety levels could be taught autogenic training in a group setting and whether the relaxation procedure would modify their response to stress. Stress was measured by the State-Trait Anxiety Inventory (STAI) and by the participants' self-report of physical symptoms. Herbert and Gutman reported the following results.

- 79% of the subjects showed reduced trait anxiety.
- 73% showed reduced state anxiety.
- 81% reported improvement in physical symptoms.
- 86% reported improvement in psychological symptoms.

Autogenic training, which has its origins in hypnosis research, can accurately be termed a form of self-hypnosis. It focuses on a series of structured exercises and verbal formulas that promote feelings of warmth, relaxation, and heaviness and that regulate the heart rate, respiratory system, and flow of blood to the head. Like self-hypnosis, it induces a state of relaxed concentration in which the heart rate and respiratory rate are reduced, muscle tension is decreased, and alpha rhythms predominate on an EEG.

Further evidence that many relaxation techniques are essentially the same phenomena and produce the same results has been provided by Benson et al. (1978). They compared self-hypnosis and the relaxation response in the treatment of anxiety and found no difference between the two treatments. They did, however, find a significant difference between participants who were moderately or highly responsive to hypnosis versus those who showed low responsiveness.

The conclusion drawn by Benson et al. (1978), that it is not the method (in this case self-hypnosis or relaxation response) but the participants' responsiveness to hypnosis that influences outcome, may be generalized to other methods of inducing ASCs as well. As stated by Korn in Chapter 3, any of these techniques can be effective in eliciting a state of relaxation that is an antidote to the stress response.

One of many examples of the use of hypnosis to control specific responses to stress is Damsbo's (1979) study of 132 patients diagnosed as having tension headache. The patients were referred to the headache clinic established in the Department of Psychiatry at the Naval Regional Medical Center, San Diego. Damsbo used a modification of the clenched-fist technique (Stein, 1969) to help patients return to a comfortable, relaxing place when they were experiencing a headache. Ideomotor questioning techniques were used to uncover possible underlying causes of the headaches, and suggestions were given for reducing blood pressure, raising hand temperature, and balancing body chemicals. Patients were seen for three sessions in a group therapy setting at 2-week intervals. Sixty-eight percent reported total or partial improvement.

Supporting Psychotherapy

Hypnosis lends itself to all forms of psychotherapy and can facilitate the treatment of stress-related problems. Only a few examples are given here. (A more complete discussion of hypnosis and psychotherapy was presented previously in Chapter 12.)

Kroger (1977) described using hypnosis to enhance reciprocal inhibition techniques to "immunize" a patient against harmful influences of stress-related situations. The practitioner begins with the least disturbing items identified by the patient as stressful and gradually desensitizes the patient to increasing amounts of anxiety-evoking stimuli. Developed by Wolpe, this technique is effective with a wide range of psychosomatic conditions.

Hartland (1971) combined relaxation techniques with an ego-strengthening routine that enhances the patient's sense of self-esteem and control over environmental stressors. He found this approach effective in alleviating stress-related symptoms and as a prelude to the treatment of stress-related diseases, such as asthma and hypertension.

Brende and Benedict (1980) reported on the use of hypnotherapy to treat the dissociative symptoms manifested by a Vietnam veteran suffering from the delayed stress syndrome. The patient had no awareness of the relationship between past traumatic experiences and the development of symptoms. The authors used psychotherapy in combination with meditation (to loosen defenses against painful memories) and hypnotherapy (to uncover traumatic experiences). Age regression to the Vietnam experience uncovered intense feelings of fear and rage. By reexperiencing them, the patient was able to achieve ego integration of the dissociated feelings.

Although advanced problems may require psychotherapy, everyday stress can be managed through self-hypnosis. A minimum of instruction and practice can provide people with an invaluable technique for combating chronic stress—the epidemic of the 1980s.

SAMPLE INDUCTION

The following suggestions represent a modification of the clenched fist technique developed by Stein (1969). This sample verbalization was used by Damsbo (1979) during the first session of group hypnotic treatment of patients with tension headache:

With your eyes closed, roll them up as though you were looking at a spot in the middle of the inside of your forehead. Notice how much stress this puts on your eyes. Now relax them and notice how comfortable this is by comparison. Let the relaxation and comfort spread to your jaw so that it hangs slightly open. . . . Let it spread over your head, neck, and shoulders . . . out into your arms, forearms . . . hands, and fingers. Take a deep breath and feel the tension build up as you hold it while I count . . . 1, 2, 3, 4, 5. Now exhale and notice how relaxing it is to exhale. Let this relaxation spread throughout your chest . . . into your abdomen . . . to your hips . . . thighs . . . and all the way to your feet and toes.

Step into your own private time tunnel and transport yourself to a time when you were completely comfortable . . . no matter how long ago that might have been. If you prefer you can travel into the future . . . to a more comfortable time than you remember in the past. . . . When you step from the time tunnel, you can find yourself in a special place.

It can be a real place or an imaginary one . . . a place you have been before . . . or one you would like to visit . . . indoors . . . or outdoors . . . or any combination of these. The place can change with your mood of the moment. . . . When you remember the comfortable feeling . . . gently close the hand you write with into a fist . . . and reexperience those comfortable feelings all over again . . . as you enjoy your special place with all of your senses.

See the beauty of it. . . . Notice the details . . . the colors . . . the lighting . . . the shadows. . . . Notice who, if anyone, is there with you. . . . Notice what is overhead . . . and underneath you . . . and round about you. . . . Hear the sounds . . . or if it is a quiet place, enjoy the silence. . . . Smell the fragrances . . . perhaps a special flower or perfume . . . even a favorite food cooking. . . . Perhaps you can even taste it. . . . Most important . . . feel the comfort . . . and because this place is your own mental creation at this moment . . . the temperature should be perfect. . . . It can be any kind of weather . . . any season of the year . . . and you can come to this place any time it is appropriate for you to do so . . . simply by closing the hand you write with . . . and remembering how you feel right now.

Some depressed or resistant patients are unable to imagine a place. After determining the kind of places they might enjoy, the practitioner can describe a place for these patients.

SUMMARY

The flight-or-fight response is part of our psychophysiological makeup, but we need not be at its mercy. Just as we have been conditioned to tense up in a traffic jam, we can recondition ourselves to relax. The importance of learning to manage stress extends beyond comfort and quality of life: There is overwhelming evidence that stress is a major factor in most illnesses.

Psychosomatic illness is no longer limited to specific diseases, and the term is losing its neurotic connotations. Psychological stress can manifest itself in physiological responses that lead to a multitude of medical disorders, from the common cold to cancer. Stress also has psychological symptoms, including anxiety, headaches, and insomnia.

The effects of a stressor are mediated by the way one perceives a situation and by one's coping ability. Thus, hypnosis, which can have a tremendous positive impact on both one's attitude and one's coping ability, is a valuable weapon in the battle for equanimity. Hypnosis can be used to induce relaxation, to treat specific responses to stress, and to support psychotherapy.

FURTHER READING

Benson, H. (1975). *The relaxation response.* New York: Morrow.

Pelletier, K. R. (1977). *Mind as healer, mind as slayer: A holistic approach to preventing stress disorders.* New York: Dell.

Selye H. (1975). *Stress without distress.* New York: New American Library.

REFERENCES

Benson, H., Frankel, F. H., Apfel, R., Daniels, M. D., Schniewind, H. E., Nemiah, J. C., Sifneos, P. E., Crassweller, K. D., Greenwood, M. M., Koth, J. B., Arns, P. A., & Rosno, B. (1978). Treatment of anxiety: A comparison of the usefulness of self-hypnosis and a meditational relaxation technique—an overview. *Psychotherapy and Psychosomatics, 30,* 229-242.

Benson, H., Arns, P. A., & Hoffman, J. W. (1981). The relaxation response and hypnosis. *International Journal of Clinical and Experimental Hypnosis, 29,* 259-270.

Borysenko, M., & Borysenko, J. (1982). Stress behavior and immunity: Animal models and mediating mechanisms. *General Hospital Psychiatry, 4,* 59-67.

Bowers, K. S., & Kelly, P. (1979). Stress, disease, psychotherapy, and hypnosis. *Journal of Abnormal psychology, 88,* 490-505.

Brende, J. O., & Benedict, B. D. (1980). The Vietnam combat delayed stress response syndrome: Hypnotherapy of "dissociative symptoms." *American Journal of Clinical Hypnosis, 23,* 34-40.

Cannon, W. B. (1953). *Bodily changes in pain, hunger, fear and rage.* Boston: Charles T. Branford.

Cousins, N. (1979). *Anatomy of an illness.* New York: W. W. Norton.

Damsbo, A. M. (1979). Tension headache treated with hypnosis. In G. D. Burrows, D. R. Collison, & L. Dennerstein (Eds.), *Hypnosis 1979*. Elsevier: North Holland Biomedical Press.

Hartland, J. (1971). *Medical and dental hypnosis*. London: Bailliere Tindall.

Herbert, C. P., & Gutman, G. M. (1980). Practical group autogenic training for management of stress-related disorders in family practice. In H. J. Wain (Ed.), *Clinical hypnosis in medicine* (pp. 109–117). Miami: Symposia Specialists.

Holmes, T. H., & Rahe, R. H. (1967). The Social Readjustment Rating Scale, *Journal of Psychosomatic Research II*, 213–218.

Horowitz, M. J., & Solomon, G. F. (1975). A prediction of delayed stress response syndromes in Vietnam veterans. *Journal of Social Issues, 37*, 80.

Kroger, W. S. (1977). *Clinical and experimental hypnosis*. Philadelphia: J. B. Lippincott.

Locke, S. E. (1982). Stress adaptation and immunity: Studies in humans. *General Hospital Psychiatry, 4*, 49–58.

Mason, J. W. (1971). A re-evaluation of the concept of non-specificity in stress theory. *Journal of Psychiatric Research, 8*, 323–333.

Rahe, R. H., & Arthur, J. (1978). *Life changes and illness studies: Past history and future directions* (Rep. No. 76–14). San Diego: Naval Health Research Center.

Selye, H. (1956). *The stress of life*. New York: McGraw-Hill.

Selye, H. (1975). *Stress without distress*. New York: New American Library.

Stein, C. (1969). *Practical psychotherapy in non-psychiatric specialties*. Springfield, IL: Charles C Thomas.

Steinmetz, J., Blankenship, J., Brown, L., Hall, D., & Miller, G. (1980). *Managing stress: Before it manages you*. Palo Alto, CA: Bull Publishing Company.

Wallis, C. (1983, June 6). Stress: Can we cope? *Time*, p. 48–54.

17

Forensic Uses

It is a curious fact in the philosophy of the mind how prone we are voluntarily to deceive ourselves, and then firmly to believe in the self-created deception as if it were a truth not to be doubted.

—Charles Radclyffe Hall
Mesmerism: Its Rise, Progress and Mysteries

The use of hypnosis for criminal investigations is highly controversial. When it first became popular in the early 1970s, forensic hypnosis appeared to be a great boon for law enforcement and the judicial process. A few years later, however, experimental studies and court cases began to provide evidence that hypnotically elicited testimony could be unreliable. Now, opinion is shifting against the forensic use of hypnosis.

Practitioners experienced in the use of hypnosis have lined up on both sides of the issue. There have been impressive successes involving the application of hypnosis to investigative matters. The Federal Bureau of Investigation and police departments across the country have employed trained psychologists and psychiatrists and trained thousands of their own law enforcement personnel to use hypnosis for heightening the recall of victims or witnesses to crimes such as homicide, rape, and kidnapping. On the other hand, many respected researchers in this field advise caution, especially in the interpretation and subsequent use of evidence obtained from a witness under hypnosis. Still other practitioners take the position that hypnosis should not be used at all in a forensic context.

As the debate between the critics and advocates of forensic hypnosis rages, the courts are settling the issue on a state-by-state basis. In an early precedent-setting case, (*Harding v. State*, 1969), the Maryland Supreme Court accepted testimony from a rape victim who recalled the traumatic event under hypnosis. The judge instructed the jury to weigh the credibility of this testimony along with all the other testimony. At the other extreme is a recent California Supreme Court ruling (*People v. Shirley*, 1982) that disallows any testimony by a witness who has undergone hypnosis. Many states, including Arizona, New Jersey, and New York, have made major rulings on hypnosis that fall somewhere between those two extremes.

In 1897, the California Supreme Court excluded the use of evidence obtained under hypnosis, stating that "the law of the U.S. does not recognize hypnotism" (*People v. Ebanks*, p. 1053). With the Shirley decision, which found the technology of hypnosis to be generally viewed as unreliable, the scientific respectability of hypnosis has again been called into question. The purpose of this chapter is to discuss the major issues related to the use of hypnosis in investigative matters and to present guidelines proposed by experts for the use of hypnosis in this nontherapeutic context.

TRUTH AND HYPNOSIS

The use of hypnosis in a forensic setting suffers from some of the same misconceptions that can hamper its clinical uses. A major problem with hypnosis as a technique for gathering evidence is the erroneous but popularly held idea that the production of an ASC in a witness will necessarily produce the truth. An editorial by Cohen (1980) stated the problem succinctly:

> It is amazing that investigators and attorneys continue to expect to find a magical means of obtaining absolute veracity and are surprised that there is no such thing as "truth serum" and that people can lie with facility under hypnosis. (p. 71)

Two of many cases cited in recent literature illustrate how hypnosis can be both used and abused in an attempt to heighten the recall of a witness in a criminal investigation. The first case, reported by Kroger and Douce (1979) involved the much-publicized Chowchilla kidnapping. Masked men driving vans abducted 26 school children and their bus driver and buried them in the school bus. The driver and two older boys eventually were able to dig themselves out and get help.

Hypnosis was used to help the bus driver recall the license plate numbers on the vans of the kidnappers. Kroger and Douce (1979) used a team approach, with Kroger, a physician and well-known authority on clinical hypnosis, inducing and deepening the trance and then transferring rapport to Douce, an agent-interviewer trained in criminal investigation and forensic hypnosis. Through the use of age regression and imagery conditioning, the driver reexperienced the event in such detail that he suddenly called out two license plate numbers, one of which matched that of the van driven by the kidnappers. The authors also report that he "abreacted with considerable affect, sobbing and crying as he reexperienced the ordeal" (p. 368). The information he provided under hypnosis contributed to the capture of three suspects who subsequently were convicted and sentenced to life imprisonment.

Another example reported by Cohen (Gravitz, 1980) showed how hypnosis can lead to misunderstandings and, in this case, conviction because of false information. The key to the conviction of seven men for the murder of a physician couple was the testimony of a 19- or 20-year-old girl whose memory "was refreshed by a professional who happened to have a doctorate after his name" (p. 111). Her testimony later proved to be clearly false, and all seven convictions were overturned. Whether the girl lied deliberately, attempted to please the hypnotist by providing the desired information, or simply confabulated a memory based on bits of information or her own preconceptions, is unknown. It is clear, however, that the use of hypnosis does not guarantee the truth.

These cases raise several issues regarding the nature of memory in general and of hypnotic recall in particular. Some criminal investigators believe that the memory functions much like a tape recorder, and that hypnosis is simply a tool for facilitating the retrieval of information. This assumption makes hypnosis appear to be an effective tool for getting at the truth.

According to memory theorists, however, memory is constructive. In other words, a memory of an original event can be modified by subsequent information. As discussed by Hilgard and Loftus (1979), experts in the theory of memory divide the memory process into three stages: (a) the *acquisition stage*, in which information is entered into someone's memory system; (b) the *retention stage*, or that period of time between the acquisition and recollection of certain information; and (c) the *retrieval stage*, during which the person recalls the stored information. It is this third or retrieval stage that is of interest here, because the recollection of information is the object of most uses of investigative hypnosis.

Based on their review of several studies concerning the reconstructive processes in memory, Hilgard and Loftus (1979) concluded that the progressive changes in memory, which include elaboration, rationalization, and transformation, are important considerations in obtaining any eyewitness account and are "particularly relevant to witness testimony which may have to be repeated at various times subsequent to the original observations" (p. 345). As these authors made clear, all memories, and not just those elicited under hypnosis, can be contaminated during the retrieval stage.

In the Shirley decision (*People v. Shirley*, 1982) the California Supreme Court stated that hypnotically aided recall was inadmissible because the technique of hypnosis itself is scientifically unreliable. The issue, however, is not the scientific respectability of hypnosis, but the extent to which it can reliably be applied to the process of criminal investigation. What may be beneficial in a therapeutic context where the goal is growth or change can be disastrous in a forensic context where the goal is to obtain valid and reliable information.

The two major hypnotic techniques for heightening the recall of a witness are age regression and the direct suggestion of hypermnesia, both of which are used with great success in a therapeutic context. However, Orne (1979) pointed out that practitioners using age regression in a clinical setting do not try to corroborate the accuracy of a patient's description of past events. A useful therapeutic experience may involve fantasy as well as history. Therefore, reliving a past event through hypnosis "may jog the subject's memory and produce some increased recall, but it will also cause him to fill in details that are plausible but consist of memories or fantasies from other times" (p. 317).

There are several documented cases in which the suggestion of hypermnesia resulted in information that had no basis in fact. In *People v. Kempiniski* (1980), for example, a witness who was hypnotized during a murder investigation described a suspect who was viewed in semidarkness from 250 feet away. The person matching the description spent 5 months in jail awaiting trial until an opthamologist testified that it would be impossible to see someone clearly under those conditions at more than 30 feet. We need not assume that a subject who provides erroneous information is lying deliberately, although that is a possibility investigators must take into consideration. It is more likely that conscious or unconscious preconceptions, the desire to please on the part of the witness, or cues from the hypnotist produced a confabulation that satisfied the desire of both to help solve the crime.

Several experts (see Putnam, 1979; Orne, 1979; and Worthington, 1979) stressed that once a witness has confabulated plausible material under hypnosis, he or she has great confidence in that memory as the truth. At that point, it is beyond the ability of even a highly trained expert to distinguish between the confabulation and an actual memory. Zelig and Beidleman (1981) added that responsiveness to hypnosis correlates with confidence in, but not accuracy of, hypnotically enhanced recall. Because of the contaminating effect of hypnosis on recall, Diamond (1980) argued that "testimony by previously hypnotized witnesses should never be admitted into evidence" (p. 315).

Watkins (1983) took this discussion a step further by pointing to recent research (Sturm, 1982) that suggests that the key factor in the contamination of memories is not the induction of hypnosis but the person's susceptibility to hypnosis. In a study using 101 subjects, Sturm found that those who were highly susceptible to hypnosis had the greatest amount of memory contamination when hypnotized but the least amount when not hypnotized. In other words, in the normal waking state, people who were highly susceptible to hypnosis had less memory contamination than unhypnotized controls had. Furthermore, those in the intermediate range of hypnotic susceptibility had the greatest amount of memory contamination when they were not hypnotized but less than unhypnotized controls when they were.

If these findings hold up, Watkins (1983) stated:

> The State Supreme Court should require *all* witnesses to take hypnotic susceptibility tests. High susceptibles (as per earlier studies) would not be considered credible if they had been hypnotized; but by the same reasoning, the intermediates (about two-thirds of all witnesses) would not be considered credible unless they *had been* hypnotized. (p. 4)

As Watkins' statement suggests, research has only begun to explore the relationship between hypnosis and memory. Until there is more conclusive evidence, however, the best approach is a cautious one. Because of the reconstructive nature of memory, eyewitness testimony, even without hypnosis, can be affected by the way questions are worded and the desire to provide needed information. With hypnosis, in which motivation and expectation play an important role and in which critical judgment is suspended, eyewitness testimony should be subject to extremely close scrutiny. While hypnotically aided recall may be useful, as in the Chowchilla case, it is not infallible, and without independent verification it can be dangerously misleading.

GUIDELINES FOR THE USE OF FORENSIC HYPNOSIS

In a 1978 affidavit to the U.S. Supreme Court, Orne (1979) proposed minimal guidelines to be used in obtaining evidence by hypnotic means. These guidelines and the rationale behind them remain an excellent statement for those interested in the use of hypnosis for criminal investigation. Each of Orne's safeguards is summarized in the following sections, which include a discussion of relevant issues. A final recommendation, added since Orne's affidavit, is also included.

Use of an independent practitioner trained in hypnosis. A qualified psychiatrist or psychologist should conduct the hypnotic procedure. To ensure objectivity, the practitioner should be a friend of the court, with no involvement in the case, and should be informed of the facts of the case only by a written memorandum.

Orne's recommendation that hypnosis should be carried out by a psychiatrist or psychologist with special training in its use is by no means a criterion accepted by all involved in the field of forensic hypnosis. Martin Reiser, director of the Behavioral Science Services of the Los Angeles Police Department and founder of the Society for Investigative and Forensic Hypnosis, has written a manual for training law enforcement personnel to use hypnosis in police investigations. In this *Handbook of Investigative Hypnosis* (1980), Reiser asserted that because police officers already have been trained in interrogation techniques, they are better qualified than health professionals to employ hypnosis during investigations.

Perry and Laurence (1982) refuted this view, pointing out that, as in any psychological procedure, there can be complications using hypnosis. Only the broadly trained professional is likely to be able to deal effectively with the release of anxiety or abreactions that may accompany reliving a traumatic memory. Another book by Hibbard and Worring (1981), which proposed training police investigators to use hypnosis for the interrogation of witnesses, was similarly refuted by Watkins (1982). He concurred with Perry and Laurence that only a practitioner is equipped to handle potential problems and also pointed out that "hypno-investigators" (as Perry and Laurence referred to them) cannot truly be objective because police and prosecutors are rewarded for capturing and convicting criminals and not for exonerating innocent persons.

Bernaur W. Newton (1978), former chair of the Ethics and Standards Committee of the Psychological Hypnosis Division, American Psychological Association, agreed, adding that the bias of the police investigator may "lead to the development of 'pseudo-memories' damaging to the credibility of a witness" (p. 5). The case for employing only health professionals for interviewing witnesses under hypnosis is further supported by the FBI policy, since 1968, of employing only professionals trained in medicine, psychiatry, dentistry, or psychology for questioning victims and witnesses of a crime (Ault, 1979).

Detailed records of all interactions.   A videotape should be made of the entire interaction between the professional using hypnosis and the witness or victim, from the preinduction evaluation to the concluding comments. The initial evaluation provides a record of the witness's beliefs and recall before hypnosis. The practitioner should avoid adding any new elements to this description for fear of altering or constraining memories.

When hypnosis is used in law enforcement to "refresh" someone's memory or to help a witness recall events that may have been forgotten or repressed because of traumatic circumstances surrounding the events, it becomes necessary to employ safeguards so as not to lead the witness to certain answers.

Studies have indicated that the techniques of questioning a victim or witness are extremely important to the outcome of an interview. The interviewer must be aware of the unreliability of information gained by asking leading questions—questions that by either form or context suggest or lead a witness to an answer desired by the interviewer. To ask, "What did the suspect look like?" may elicit quite a different response than the more leading question, "Did the suspect have blue eyes and blond hair?"

Putnam (1979) reported a study in which hypnotized subjects made more errors when they answered leading questions than did subjects in a normal waking state. There were no significant differences between the groups on nonleading questions. The questions pertained to a videotaped recording of a car-bicycle accident. Six of the fifteen questions were leading questions ("Did you see the stop sign at the intersection?") designed to suggest a specific answer. Putnam's findings support the hypothesis that people are more suggestible in the hypnotic state and more easily influenced by the leading question. In a similar study, Zelig and Beidleman (1981) also found that although hypnosis did not enhance recall for nonleading questions, "the subjects in the hypnosis group responded more frequently in the direction implied by the leading questions, and thus were led into erroneous responses" (p. 407).

In their overview of studies on eyewitness interrogation, Hilgard and Loftus (1979) concluded that free reports from hypnotized eyewitnesses provided greater accuracy but less detail than reports obtained through directed inquiry. On the other hand, increased recall of details obtained through specific questioning was accompanied by a greatly increased degree of inaccuracy. Hilgard and Loftus suggested that the optimal combination of the two approaches would be to begin with free reports from the witness and then proceed to more specific questioning. Orne (1979) concurred:

> . . . the patient has a higher likelihood of producing uncontaminated memories if allowed to initially relive the events without much questioning by the hypnotist. Further details can then be elicited by questioning the second or third time the material is brought forth. (p. 325)

It is evident that a witness can be cued in many ways by an interrogator. Therefore, a videotaped recording of all statements and conversations between the witness and the professional employing hypnosis is a necessary and useful tool for permitting a detailed review of what has occurred and for determining the reliability of testimony.

Privacy of the hypnotic session.   To avoid the subtle communication of expectations by observers, no one but the practitioner and the person to be hypnotized should be present in the room either before or during the session. Prosecution or defense attorneys may observe the session through a one-way screen or television monitor.

While this particular guideline seems to make an obvious point, the privacy of an interview during hypnosis has not been automatic. As Gravitz (1980) explained:

> It is very nice . . . to be able to have a one-way screen, adequate facilities, etc. But more often than not, most of the situations in which I have worked have involved having a heat-generating video-camera, cables thick as an arm all around, police artists sitting, attorney quite adequately and rightfully protecting the safeguards of the person I was working with and others including bodyguards carrying very awesome weapons. (p. 106)

Gravitz questioned the impact of this entourage on the responses of the person being interviewed and on the hypnotic process itself. Furthermore, according to Worthington (1979), the tendency for an interrogator to phrase questions that in some way suggest an expected response is compounded when there is another person present at the session who is involved in the interaction and who "has his own theory about the case about which the subject's memory is purportedly being enhanced" (p. 414).

Records of prior interrogations.   Tape recordings should be made of all interrogations before the hypnotic session to be certain that information that surfaces under hypnosis has not been previously suggested.

The memory process is such that subsequent bits of information can be incorporated into an original recollection. A number of other factors, including issues of countertransference and the witness's wish to please, may also affect the outcome of any interview. Therefore, all interviews with the witness, including those that may take place with another investigator before the induction of hypnosis, should be taped so that the content and procedures may be examined and evaluated if necessary.

Corroboration of information.   Warner (1979) presented one other major point that has been added by the court to Orne's guidelines: There is a clear need to corroborate any information gained during hypnosis or as a result of posthypnotic suggestion in the same way that leads obtained through other means must be double-checked. The case upon which this guideline is based, *State v. White* (1979), involved a first-degree murder charge. The defense moved for an order to suppress certain statements of the main witness for the prosecution because that witness's statements were a "product of hypnosis" that had affected or created some or all of the witness's testimony. During a lengthy hearing concerning this case, Orne testified as the court's witness, and the court used his guidelines as a basis for forming an opinion. As explained by Warner (1979), the court ruled that statements made under hypnosis would be suppressed "if there was unnecessary suggestiveness in the hypnotic session and if the totality of the circumstances of the information-seeking process did not prove the reliability of the statements made" (p. 428). The court also added a supplement to Orne's safeguards by stating that "consideration should be given to any other evidence tending to corroborate or challenge the information garnered during the trance or as a result of post-hypnotic suggestion" (Warner, 1979, p. 429).

One danger of enhanced recall produced through hypnosis is that it may be inaccurate or misleading—just as evidence gained without the use of hypnosis may also be inaccurate or misleading. As stated by Kroger and Douce (1979), "even deeply hypnotized subjects may be capable of purposely lying; they may also inadvertently distort versions of actual fact, can confabulate, have screen memories, or fantasize" (p. 366), and thus lead to questionable or false testimony. Only independent corroboration of testimony that has been produced through hypnosis can safeguard against this possibility.

APPROPRIATE USES OF HYPNOSIS

Even with the guidelines formulated by Orne and the courts, there remains the question of who should be hypnotized and for what purpose. All of the discussion above has concerned obtaining information from victims or witnesses to crimes. Although there are cases reported in which hypnosis was used with a suspect, or in which a witness became a suspect while under hypnosis, hypnosis is not generally used with suspects. Statements made by a hypnotized suspect are inadmissible as evidence under the Fifth and Fourteenth amendments to the U.S. Constitution. Similarly, a confession given under hypnosis would most likely be inadmissible because such testimony would be considered either involuntarily given or otherwise in violation of a defendent's constitutional rights.

Warner (1979) cited the Canadian case of *Rex v. Booher* (1928), in which a criminologist who practiced hypnosis visited the accused in jail. After his last visit, the criminologist told the police that a confession would be forthcoming from the accused. The defendant's subsequent confession was held inadmissible as involuntary in the absence of proof that he did not confess under the influence of a posthypnotic suggestion by the criminologist.

Orne (1979) identified three contexts in which hypnosis may be used to enhance the memory of a victim or witness: (a) to provide leads in a situation where the facts are not known, (b) to prepare a witness for court testimony after a suspect has been identified, and (c) to help a witness who has given confusing or conflicting statements remember "what really happened."

In Orne's view, hypnosis is not appropriate "in an investigative context, with the sole purpose being to obtain leads" (p. 327). When the facts are not known, hypnotically enhanced recall may produce valuable information that can help investigators construct a case. Use of hypnosis in the second and third instances, however, is replete with dangers. A witness trying to remember important details may easily be led to create a memory. Hypnosis used in an attempt to validate the reliability of a witness's testimony may also produce a witness who can convincingly relate a confabulation that he or she believes to be fact.

The Shirley decision provides a good example of the problems involved in using hypnosis to clarify vague or self-contradictory testimony. In *People v. Shirley*, the defendant was charged with the rape of a 32-year-old woman bartender. At the preliminary hearing, the testimony of the victim, who had been under the influence of alcohol at the time of the alleged rape, was vague and self-contradictory. The day before the trial, a deputy district attorney hypnotized her to enhance her memory of the circumstances surrounding the assault. Under hypnosis, the victim's account contradicted much of her previous testimony. Although the defendant was convicted, the conviction was later reversed by the California Supreme Court, which held that all testimony of previously hypnotized witnesses, with the exception of defendants, was inadmissible in court.

As argued by Fulgoni (1983), a Los Angeles deputy district attorney, the Shirley decision ignores the difference between the Shirley case and other cases in which there is no suspect and in which hypnosis is used to obtain leads:

> In cases where the pre-hypnotic statement is identical to the proffered testimony, it makes little sense to preclude the testimony. Where there is corroboration of the hypnotically adduced statements by subsequently acquired evidence, preclusion is absurd. (p. 5)

In 1978, SCEH adopted a resolution on the use of forensic hypnosis. The International Society of Hypnosis adopted an almost identically worded resolution in 1979. Each society

> . . . views with alarm the tendency for police officers with minimal training in hypnosis and without a broad professional background in the healing arts employing hypnosis to presumably facilitate recall of witnesses or victims privy to the occurrence of some crime.

The societies have based their concern on two points. First, "there is no known way of distinguishing with certainty between actual recall and pseudo memories except by independent verification." Second, police officers are trained to solve crimes, and this orientation, in the absence of a broader understanding of psychology, may influence their interaction with a hypnotic subject. Therefore, the statements conclude, only "trained psychiatrists or psychologists with experience in the forensic use of hypnosis should be employed," and all necessary safeguards should be followed (SCEH, 1979, pp. 452–453).

Hypnosis has not proved the secret weapon for eliciting the truth in a criminal investigation that some early advocates hoped it would be. Since research on hypnosis and recall is not conclusive, there are no definitive answers to the questions of when, how, or even whether hypnosis can be used effectively in the legal process. It does not follow, however, that hypnosis should be banned entirely. Instead, while promising new areas of research are being explored, practitioners should proceed cautiously, using hypnosis only when other investigative techniques have failed, and scrupulously following Orne's (1979) guidelines to reduce the possibility of memory contamination.

CASE REPORT

The following case is an instance in which hypnosis was used with a defendant following a conviction for first-degree murder. The transcript of the hypnotic interview contributed to a larger psychiatric profile of the defendant that the defense attorney used to influence sentencing in the case.

The attorney for the defense asked Pratt to employ hypnosis to enhance the defendant's recall of events surrounding his wife's death. Court testimony had been unable to account for the strange angle at which one of two bullets had entered the head of the deceased woman. The defendant, who had developed an amnesia block from the trauma of the incident, insisted that he did not remember firing a second shot.

The hypnotic interview was held in the county jail, with only Pratt, a psychological assistant, and the defendant present. Officials would not allow the interview to be videotaped, and so only a cassette recorder was used. The sequence of events during the 2½-hour interview was as follows: (a) an explanation of the cassette taping procedure, (b) a description of the psychologist's role during the interview, (c) a definition of hypnosis, (d) discussion of any questions the defendant had about hypnosis, (e) the defendant's description of his wife's death at a nonhypnotic level, (f) induction, (g) the defendant's description of his wife's death at a hypnotic level.

The defendant was in a highly emotional state both before and during hypnosis and abreacted consistently to references to his son and deceased wife. Before hypnosis, his memory of the entire event was spotty, and he could remember nothing after the first shot.

Pratt used a combination of approaches, including progressive muscle relaxation, fractionation, and relaxing imagery to induce trance. To control his abreactions and return himself to a safe and relaxing place, the defendant was taught to associate his dominant (left) hand with a place of serenity. At various points during the hypnotic session, when he would begin crying hysterically, he would open and close his hand to regain the calm he associated with being in the mountains. The nondominant hand was used to release tension and negative emotion.

Pratt regressed the defendant to the time of the shooting, where the man reported that his wife had threatened him several times, that she had run to the garage to get the gun, that he believed she was going to shoot him, and that after hearing a loud roar, he saw his wife lying on the ground. Asked to "back up the tape for just a moment and replay it," the defendant was able to describe struggling with his wife for the gun, hearing a second shot, and falling backwards.

The transcript of the hypnotic interview was used as part of a psychiatric profile of the defendant that was sent to the district attorney. The events described by the defendant were confirmed by the coroner as an adequate explanation for the second bullet's angle of penetration. With no data to indicate premeditation, the charge against the defendant subsequently was reduced from first-degree murder to second-degree manslaughter.

This case highlighted the importance of using a clinical practitioner to conduct a hypnotic interview in a forensic setting. The extreme abreactions of the defendant, a large and muscular man, required sensitive handling on the part of the psychologist. A police interrogator with training in hypnosis would not have been qualified to handle the intensity of emotion and overwhelming expression of guilt elicited by a regression to the time of the shooting.

The case also demonstrated the importance of corroborating evidence. The information retrieved during the hypnotic interview and Pratt's assessment of the defendant were consistent with a previously developed psychiatric profile. The events described by the defendant under hypnosis were also consistent with the coroner's findings. Thus, it was not hypnosis alone, but hypnosis in the context of a total picture developed through several methods of inquiry, that resulted in a reduction of the sentence.

SUMMARY
Hypnosis has been used for criminal investigation with mixed success: An excellent therapeutic tool is not necessarily a good investigative one.

Since the mind is not an "exact copy" tape recorder, hypnosis cannot be used as a truth serum. Memories reported by a witness under hypnosis may blend actual recall with pseudomemories and in some cases deliberate lies. The fact that hypnosis is not an infallible technique for enhancing recall does not mean it cannot be used effectively in a forensic context.

There is a strong correlation between the way questions are phrased and the kind of responses they elicit. Research data (Putnam, 1979; Zelig and Beidleman, 1981), suggest that hypnotized subjects demonstrate a higher degree of inaccuracy to leading questions than do subjects in a waking state. By cuing the witness, an interrogator can actually facilitate the development of a confabulated memory that the witness in the waking state will accept and defend as real. Even the unstated expectations and biases of an interrogator or observers in the room may affect a hypnotized witness's responses to questions. Other research (Sturm, 1982) has suggested that responsiveness to hypnosis rather than hypnosis itself may be the key factor in the reliability of a witness's testimony.

Hypnosis should be viewed as one among many potentially useful techniques for developing leads in a criminal investigation. It should be used only with witnesses and victims, not suspects, and it should be used cautiously, employing the following safeguards set forth by Orne (1979):

1. Hypnosis should be carried out by a clinical practitioner with special training in its use.

2. All contact between practitioner and witness should be videotaped.

3. No one else should be present in the room before or during the session.

4. All prior interrogation should be tape-recorded.

5. All information obtained under hypnosis should be corroborated in the same way that evidence obtained through other means is corroborated.

Finally, the practitioner should proceed cautiously in this area and carefully follow future research on the accuracy of hypnotically induced memory.

FURTHER READING

Orne, M. T. (1979). The use and misuse of hypnosis in court. *International Journal of Clinical and Experimental Hypnosis, 27,* 311–341.

REFERENCES

Ault, R. L. (1979). Guidelines for use of hypnosis. *International Journal of Clinical and Experimental Hypnosis, 27,* 449–451.

Cohen, S. D. (1980). Editorial: Finding facts with hypnosis. *American Journal of Clinical Hypnosis, 23,* 71–72.

Diamond, B. L. (1980). Inherent problems in the use of pretrial hypnosis on a prospective witness. *California Law Review, 68,* 313–349.

Fulgoni, D. (1983, April). Shirley: A bad decision. *American Psychological Association, Division 30: Psychological hypnosis, Newsletter,* pp. 5-6.

Gravitz, M. A. (1980). Discussion. *American Journal of Clinical Hypnosis, 23,* 103–111.

Harding v. State, 5 Md. App. 230, 246A. 2d 302 (198), *cert. den.,* 395 U.S. 949, 89S. Ct. 2030, 23 L. Ed. 2d 468 (1969).

Hibbard, W. S. & Worring, R. W. (1981). *Forensic hypnosis: The practical application of hypnosis in criminal investigations.* Springfield, IL: Charles C Thomas.

Hilgard, E. R., & Loftus, E. F. (1979). Hypnosis in criminal investigation. *International Journal of Clinical and Experimental Hypnosis, 27,* 342–357.

Kroger, W. S., & Douce, R. G. (1979). Hypnosis in criminal investigation. *International Journal of Clinical and Experimental Hypnosis, 27,* 358–374.

Newton, B. W. (1978, December). *American Psychological Association, Division 30: Psychological Hypnosis, Newsletter,* p. 5.

Orne, M. T. (1979). The use and misuse of hypnosis in court. *International Journal of Clinical and Experimental Hypnosis, 27,* 311–341.

People v. Ebanks, 117 Cal. 652, 49 P. 1049 (1897).

People v. Kempiniski, No. W80CF 352 (Cir. Ct., 12th Dist, Will Co., Ill., October 21, 1980, unrep.).

People v. Shirley, 31 Ca. 3d 18 (1982).

Perry C., & Laurence, J. R. (1982). Review of Martin Reiser's *Handbook of investigative hypnosis. International Journal of Clinical and Experimental Hypnosis, 30,* 443–448.

Putnam, W. H. (1979). Hypnosis and distortions in eyewitness memory. *International Journal of Clinical and Experimental Hypnosis, 27,* 437–448.

Reiser, M. (1980). *Handbook of investigative hypnosis.* Los Angeles: LEHI.

Rex v. Booher, 4 D.L.R. 795 (1928).

Society for Clinical and Experimental Hypnosis (SCEH). (1979). Resolution adopted October 1978. Reprinted in *International Journal of Clinical and Experimental Hypnosis, 29, 452–453.*

State v. White, No. J-3665 (Cir. Ct., Branch 10, Milwaukee Co., Wisc., March 27, 1979, unrep.).

Sturm, C. E. (1982). *Eyewitness memory: Effects of guided memory and hypnotic hypermnesia techniques and hypnotic susceptibility.* Unpublished doctoral dissertation, University of Montana, Missoula.

Warner, K. (1979). The use of hypnosis in the defense of criminal cases. *International Journal of Clinical and Experimental Hypnosis, 27, 417–436.*

Watkins, G. (1982). Review of Hibbard and Worring's forensic hypnosis: The practical application of hypnosis in criminal investigations. *International Journal of Clinical and Experimental Hypnosis, 30, 449–450.*

Watkins, J. G. (1983, April). The baby and the bath water. *American Psychological Association, Division 30: Psychological Hypnosis, Newsletter,* pp. 4, 7.

Worthington, S. (1979). The use in court of hypnotically enhanced testimony. *International Journal of Clinical and Experimental Hypnosis, 27, 402–416.*

Zelig, M., & Beidlemen, W. B. (1981). The investigative use of hypnosis: A word of caution. *International Journal of Clinical and Experimental Hypnosis, 29, 401–412.*

PART IV

THE FUTURE OF HYPNOSIS

T he practice of the ancient art of hypnosis is more widespread and more widely accepted today than ever before. Hypnosis helps in the cure of the sick and enhances the lives of the well. It is now considered scientifically respectable, if not entirely understood, and it is achieving a professional and public acceptance unparalleled in its long history.

The current popularity of hypnosis can be attributed primarily to solid advances in the state of the art, rather than to vagaries in the public taste. Experiments are being conducted to determine its nature and how it works; laboratory studies quantify and evaluate its effects; and breakthroughs are constantly occurring in the application of hypnosis to medical and psychological problems and to our everyday lives. In the future, it is probable that advances will continue on both the experimental and clinical levels.

Membership in organizations such as ASCH and SCEH has been growing rapidly. Professionals from a wide variety of fields have joined these organizations to gain a place on the leading edge of the art. Some have done so at the request of patients aware of the benefits of hypnosis.

Quo vadis hypnosis? It is safe to say that hypnosis is here to stay, because we now recognize that hypnosis is, and always has been, an inherent human ability. The following chapters reflect the biases and hopes of the authors of this book and of other practitioners actively involved in clinical hypnosis. Its actual future will depend on those to whom this book is dedicated: the present and future students and practitioners of clinical hypnosis.

18

Hypnosis: A Bona Fide Brave New World?

If the medicine of imagination is best, why should we not practice the medicine of imagination?

—Charles d'Elson
Observations sur le magnétisme animal

T he mind-body dualism characteristic of much Western thought since the time of Plato is being reexamined. A holistic view of humankind that owes a debt to Eastern religious thought holds that emotional, psychological, and physical health come from within and that processes once considered unconscious can be consciously self-controlled to promote health. The concept that many physical disabilities have a psychological basis has roots in antiquity. The unity of mind and body is reflected in the Bible: "For as a man thinketh in his heart, so he is." William Osler (1849–1919), considered to be the father of modern medicine, said "the care of tuberculosis depends more on what the patient has in his head than what he has in his chest." As we learn more about the potential of hypnosis, we will capitalize on the wisdom of the past while we take advantage of modern research.

PERSONAL CONTROL

In *Brave New World,* Aldous Huxley presented a picture of a future in which people are happy to get what they want and never want what

329

they cannot get. They are well off, safe, never ill, unafraid of death, and blissfully ignorant of passion and old age. Strong feelings are unknown to them. They have no family members or lovers to care about. They are so conditioned that they cannot help behaving as they ought to behave. And if something should go wrong, there is always soma, a mind-altering cure-all.

We can project a much more optimistic future influenced by the widespread use of hypnosis. Unlike Huxley's world, in which control is imposed from without, our world will be characterized by control arising from within each person. According to this scenario, people using hypnosis are happier, if not always happy. They actively work toward what they want. They are likely to be well off, unafraid of risk for positive change, and more secure in themselves. They are rarely ill, and when they are, they can control the pain and facilitate the healing process. They are less afraid of death, can more readily tap their intelligence from birth through old age, and are better able to relate to and communicate with their loved ones. If anything should go wrong, there is always the knowledge of the ways that they can, within limits, take control of and improve an undesirable situation.

Only recently have those on the forefront of hypnosis recognized that self-hypnosis has long been practiced routinely by human beings, although they were probably not aware of doing so. The farmer in the field who concentrates on cultivating the ground for hours without a break, often with a hypnotically steady rhythm, is probably in a self-induced trance. All of us enter such states a number of times each day while we are driving, absorbed in a task, or daydreaming. Some people instinctively put themselves in a light trance when faced with an unpleasant medical or dental procedure. As we realize that this condition *is* hypnosis and that we use it regularly, we can harness it to create many more opportunities for change and control.

"All hypnosis is self-hypnosis" is a popular refrain among practitioners of modern clinical hypnosis. With the individual as the focus, the range of hypnotic techniques has increased tremendously in recent years, and this trend will continue. The notion that there is no one who cannot be hypnotized is fast becoming a practical truth. The question is not whether a patient can achieve a trance state, but how to assist patients to explore their own unconscious abilities. Whether or not someone does well on a hypnotic susceptibility test has become less significant as methods of hypnotic induction have become more individualized. Techniques can be found for everyone, and everyone can benefit from hypnosis, which is fast becoming one of the most powerful agents for personal change, both physical and emotional.

Many people today are turning back to themselves for help with physical and emotional problems. Instead of depending on the external world for solutions to health problems, for example, people now look to their own capacity to control mind-body functions, a feat that seemed impossible in the past, at least in the Western world. While hypnosis may be used more often and more efficiently by practitioners in both new and established disciplines, its greatest influence may be on ordinary people who regularly practice self-hypnosis to meet a variety of personal needs.

EXPANDED APPLICATIONS

Professionals new to hypnosis often are surprised by the variety of applications represented in hypnosis journals. Yet hypnosis has been, and remains, one of the most underused treatment methodologies in psychology, medicine, and dentistry. Its potential in such areas as athletic performance and creativity has been neither well researched nor applied on a broad scale. This deplorable state of affairs is fast being remedied.

Hypnosis is no longer a medical stepchild. Mind-body interactions are being vigorously explored by practitioners and researchers alike. New fields, such as psychoneuroimmunology, will continue to validate clinical experience. As hypnosis becomes a more widespread and accepted treatment alternative, more practitioners will be willing to report the significant results patients have achieved through hypnosis.

Most hospitals today have on staff an anesthesiologist, surgeon, nurse, or therapist who is able to use hypnotic techniques to put patients at ease and in some cases even facilitate pain control and healing. This was not the case a decade or so ago. With its focus on the whole person, hypnosis holds great promise of becoming a humanizing force for the field of medicine as a whole. Practitioners familiar with hypnotic techniques will acknowledge that a bedside manner can be a potent healing tool. Realizing that even unconscious patients hear and remember information that pertains to them, physicians, surgeons, nurses, and anesthesiologists will communicate more effectively with comatose, critically ill, and anesthetized patients, thus replacing fear and isolation with encouragement and positive expectations.

Hypnosis will continue to assume an increasingly greater role in modern psychology, which is undergoing a transformation that began with the insights of such leaders as Freud, Adler, Perls, and Rogers. Hypnosis is increasingly being used for self-discovery and self-analysis in short-term therapies lasting 6–8 weeks. As patients proceed through understanding of the emotional as well as the intellectual experience of a hypnotic session, perhaps experiencing catharsis, they begin to work on goals and directions for a more positive and rewarding future.

In long-term therapy, emotional blocks impervious to other approaches often yield to hypnotic techniques such as age regression. The future should see refinements in these uses of hypnotic techniques during long-term therapy.

Psychotherapists will use hypnosis to an even greater extent to enhance the ways in which people relate to each other, to take patients on journeys through open discussion while in trance, to treat sexual dysfunction, to modify habit patterns, and to alleviate nervous conditions such as tics, ulcers, allergies, and hypertension.

The human potential movement, which had its genesis in California, has been often satirized for some of its popular manifestations. However, it has made people aware that, through techniques such as hypnosis, they are capable of much more awareness and creativity than they might have thought possible.

Hypnosis is being brought into the home, the work place, the school, and even the playing field to help people reduce stress, gain clarity, and realize maximum potential. As the public becomes more familiar with the effectiveness of hypnotic techniques, these techniques will become more widespread. For a great many people around the world, hypnosis may very well become as much a part of everyday life as brushing their teeth.

The secret of mental, emotional, and physical health remains unknown, yet we are closer to the answers—which probably lie in a complex interrelation of factors such as body chemistry and neurology—than we have ever been. Hypnosis, with its own secrets, may play a part in discovering those answers. As we find out more about new applications of hypnosis and new ways of individualizing hypnotic induction, we will become more adept at tapping the resource that we all possess but that we have used very little. More and more, people will become proficient at self-hypnosis and more sophisticated in its use, and perhaps they will be successful enough to make many clinical applications obsolete.

Although we can make reasonable judgments about the future of hypnosis, we cannot absolutely predict it. We do know one thing: Its role as a disreputable and mysterious phenomenon on the fringe of the study of consciousness is over.

19
Other Voices

Nature affords a universal means of healing and preserving men.

—Franz Anton Mesmer
Dissertation on the Discovery of Animal Magnetism

T o present future trends and applications of clinical hypnosis more clearly and in balance, the authors of this book invited opinions from outstanding practitioners of hypnosis in various clinical fields. Those who responded offered a variety of predictions on the future direction of hypnosis in their professions. Most agreed that hypnosis has found a niche in medicine, dentistry, and psychology. Although some expect cyclical variation in the popularity of hypnosis, all believe that continued scientific efforts and the increasing professionalism of practitioners will assure overall growth in its scientific respectability, proliferation of its uses, and even greater success in its applications.

David Spiegel, MD, Herbert Spiegel, MD

We stand at a crossroads in the field of hypnosis, a period of both opportunity and danger. Medicine and psychotherapy are threatened on all sides by demands for efficiency and accountability on the one hand and for increasing sensitivity to emotional problems and holistic care on the other. The field of hypnosis has survived two centuries of mysticism, cultism, derision, and finally, scientific exploration. Our hope is that those who work with hypnosis will be able to combine the discipline of the scientific laboratory with the wisdom, intuition, and sensitivity that are the heritage of our collective clinical experience to reconcile these two opposing challenges. From recent developments in the laboratory and the clinic, we can learn to use the measurement of hypnotic capacity as a means of making more systematic treatment decisions and of solving complex problems of differential diagnosis. What is emerging as a promising byproduct is a method of personality style that enhances the therapist's ability to resonate with the patient's language. From the clinical tradition, we can draw on a variety of ingenious strategies to simplify hypnotic intervention, using the trance state as an occasion not to control or manipulate the patient but rather to teach the patient to become a cotherapist. With this enhanced control, the patient can learn to explore and use his or her own hypnotic capacities to reach a variety of goals. The hypnotic mode provides an opportunity for a kind of third way, emotionally sensitive and yet scientific, in the field of psychotherapy. Furthermore, the phenomena of hypnosis are at the interface of the mind-brain problem, and we look forward with excitement to the use of hypnosis in the further investigation of the relationship between consciousness and brain function.

Harold B. Crasilneck, PhD

The future of hypnotherapy in medicine and psychology is, in my opinion, quite good. In the years ahead, classes in hypnotherapy will be taught in all medical and dental schools at the undergraduate level, followed by specialized and intensive training during the periods of residency. Similar training will be a part of the curriculum in graduate schools offering training in clinical psychology. Such legitimate teaching is, in my opinion, the most plausible solution to the required training and practice of hypnotherapy. Therefore, laws will eventually legally limit the practice of hypnotherapy to those officially trained in medicine, psychology, and dentistry.

There will be a concerted research effort to establish a neurological basis explaining the depths of trance. With more elaborate instrumentation, this research could well help us understand the age-old question of why a person becomes hypnotized.

I believe most hospital staffs will have persons trained in the use of hypnotherapy. We are now seeing the use of hypnotherapy as a method of choice for several conditions such as smoking, obesity, and psychogenic impotency. In the near future, further clinical applications of hypnotherapy to a wide variety of clinical problems will continue to prove the extraordinary values of this therapy in both organic and functional types of illness.

Karen Olness, MD

My view of hypnosis is that it is a tool, albeit a poorly defined tool, that will facilitate our understanding of human potential for using psychophysiologic controls. As we develop more precision in monitoring and measuring changes occurring during hypnosis, we will understand how it may be applied and recommended to patients more precisely.

I envision the next quarter-century witnessing a coming together of discoveries in physics, neurophysiology, and molecular biology in ways that will negate many current theories of causality, pathophysiology, and psychodynamics. Techniques involving positron emission transaxial tomography (PETT) scans, neuropeptide assays in all body areas, precise nutritional assays, elimination of "noise" in remote perceptual processes, 1-week micromonitoring of physiologic processes including variations in circadian rhythms, incorporation of concepts of antimatter and tachyons—and other discoveries and abilities of which I cannot yet dream—will perhaps make it possible to understand what is generic to "hypnosis," "meditation," "prayer," "progressive relaxation," "daydreaming," and many other names attached to exercises or procedures that are descriptive and not explanatory. I believe we will understand more objectively how therapists and patients communicate in nonverbal ways and how they affect one another.

I see the potential for our grandchildren who have the opportunity to retain their innate skills in imagery, eidetic imagery, or remote perceptions, and to use these not only to improve their health but to enhance their creativity, ego strength, and happiness. I see their abilities in these areas facilitated routinely by their parents, teachers, physicians, dentists, psychologists, and coaches who will know how to encourage the special abilities of children.

I see potential for more peace and understanding in the world as we apply what we learn about communication between people who are teaching or learning hypnosis or its generic counterparts to programs in Third World Countries, to diplomatic relations. I see a generally reduced craving for exogenous medicines, alcohol, and illegal drugs.

And I see our successors laughing at some of the old ideas about cause and treatment, and perhaps at some of the statements in these paragraphs. If so, I hope the laughter will be because I was not bold enough in my guesses about the future of hypnosis, rather than because I have overstated them.

Lillian E. Fredericks, MD

The future of hypnosis, in my opinion, will be very bright. I foresee that hypnosis or its techniques will be used by all physicians, since it really is the essence of the art of medicine. Today, so many physicians are involved in the pure science and technology of medicine and completely forget that the human being consists of both a body and a soul. We all know, but often forget, that a patient's mood, outlook, and state of mind greatly influence his or her physical condition. There is good evidence that many diseases are precipitated, if not caused, by stress, fear, and anxiety. As anesthesiologists, we see the distinct difference between patients who come to the operating room calm, full of hope, and confident that the outcome will be successful and those who are pessimistic and tremble with fear. Medical hypnosis is an ideal tool to approach and influence patients' attitudes and effect a change from depression and hopelessness to a positive outlook. By teaching patients self-hypnosis, we give them a tool they can use to actively participate in their cure.

Hypnosis will have to be incorporated in the early curriculum of medical schools to teach students to pay attention to the mental attitudes and psychological state of their patients and to communicate effectively with them. The choice of words we use when talking to our patients and the changes in mood achieved with the use of hypnosis can make the difference between a cheerful, confident, and involved patient and one who is riddled with fear and immobilized by it, unable and unwilling to participate in the course of treatment. By learning hypnosis, students will learn how to treat human beings and not just diseases.

As more and more courses are taught throughout the world and misconceptions are removed through research and greater understanding, more physicians, psychologists, and other professionals will recognize the tremendous potential of this valuable modality.

S. W. Chiasson, MD

I believe that hypnosis has finally come into its own. We are on the threshold of a big breakthrough, and I feel that we will soon know what hypnosis really is and how it works. We already know that it *does* work. However, many of its uses are still untapped. We must rekindle in our colleagues a desire to excel in this modality and to acquire the ability to use hypnosis for the benefit of their patients or clients.

Clyde W. Jones, MD

I am most gratified that, as I have helped to wage the war for the acceptance of hypnosis as a recognized medical modality, I have seen greater acceptance by more and more physicians, including such realists as orthopedists. By the number of consultations I receive, I am convinced that excellent progress is forthcoming. It is my feeling that as more is learned about the brain and how the mind works, greater use of techniques such as hypnosis that make use of the vast and largely untapped powers of the mind will gain greater popularity in an effort to more comprehensively and completely assail human ills. The immense area of psychoimmunology promises to be exciting.

Most of all, I hope that practitioners who choose not to use formal hypnosis in their practice will realize that the relationship with patients is by its very nature hypnoidal, and that careful attention will be paid to the suggestions given, verbal and nonverbal, that have significant and often devastating effects upon the patient, often far beyond the knowledge of both therapist and patient alike. The times ahead will be times of great excitement in the field of hypnosis.

A. David Feinstein, PhD

Three trends that I believe will continue to shape the field of hypnosis are increased precision, broader application, and wider ownership. With continuing advances in such fields as biofeedback, behavior therapy, and neurochemistry, the emergence of increasingly sophisticated and precise hypnotic applications seems inevitable. Increased precision may also be expected in the therapist's ability to match personality factors with the most effective hypnotic procedures, a result of the growing understanding of the relationship between individual traits and hypnotic responsiveness. This increased ability to tailor the use of hypnosis to different individuals and to address specific goals with greater reliability will lead to a growing demand for hypnosis in such diverse fields as medicine, business, and government.

Increased precision and broader application will be accompanied by the development of sophisticated computer programs capable of processing medical, psychological, and other data along with objectively tested personality variables and then recommending appropriate hypnotic strategies, as well as pointing out possible hazards or pitfalls. These programs will become available for use in clinics, hospitals, business, and even private homes. With the broader applications and information bases, it is also inevitable that hypnosis-related activities will become more and more commonplace. Increasing numbers of private individuals will come to consider themselves competent in hypnosis. Naturally, it will be beyond the scope of professional hypnosis to prevent the indiscriminate use of hypnosis among nonprofessionals and members of the general public. However, the field will be challenged to find ways of assisting the public in using hypnosis wisely, safely, and with an understanding of its capabilities and limitations. While there will continue to be a role for competent hypnotherapists, the need for skilled educators, consultants, and researchers is likely to expand.

Michael Jay Diamond, PhD

I see hypnosis as playing a very important role in the future development of psychology in several areas: namely, experimental, clinical, and forensic. The last, of course, is receiving increasing publicity as hypnosis is helping us sort out some of the problems in eyewitness testimony. Experimentally, we are beginning to see important advances in the use of hypnosis as a tool to increase our understanding of how the mind works in such areas as cognition, information processing, and perception. This book itself bears evidence to developments in clinical hypnosis.

I think it is becoming clearer to us that hypnosis taps into and involves what are perhaps best called naturally occurring processes. That is to say, we don't see them in the normal waking state or in other states of mind outside of hypnosis. We have found, however, that hypnosis often accentuates, facilitates, evokes or potentiates certain aspects of these naturally occurring processes so that we can see them more fully and begin to use them for clinical, experimental, or forensic purposes. I am referring here to such processes as imagery, suggestion, dissociation, selective attention, and affect arousal, as well as to processes that have to do with relationship, such as transference, archaic involvement, rapport, and atavistic regression.

I believe that the burgeoning interest in hypnosis will help us to unravel the mysteries in the fields of consciousness and interpersonal relationship as they apply to human experience outside of the domain of hypnosis. I am referring specifically to the *nature of the hypnotic experience*, that is, the nature of the alterations in consciousness occurring in hypnosis, and the *nature of the transference* that occurs in hypnosis.

We are beginning to see a much more investigatory outlook towards the *nature of the hypnotic experience*. Researchers are beginning to discern many of the subtle cognitive processes that we see in ordinary waking as well as in hypnotic mental processing. We finally are beginning to see the development of a methodology for exploring the phenomenological nature of hypnotic experiencing. I am particularly impressed with the methodology of Peter Sheehan and Kevin McConkey (in their new book *Hypnosis and Experiencing*), which relies on videotape recordings of subjects' hypnotic experiences played back following trance termination. At any point in watching the tape, the subject can stop the tape and describe to the experimenter what was occurring internally during that time. As a result, we are beginning to see how active the hypnotic subject is and to realize the importance of the hypnotic relationship.

So we are taking hypnosis out of the realm of stereotype, myth, and misconception. Hypnosis no longer is seen as something that is done to a passive subject but rather as an experience that follows the ordinary processes of persuasion, communication, perception, and learning. The nuances of the hypnotized individual's active mental processes are something that we are going to be able to understand better in years to come. We're also witnessing additional methodological advances concerning the internal experience of hypnosis. Erika Fromm and her colleagues at the University of Chicago are conducting studies in which self-hypnotic experiences are phenomenologically described by the subjects. These studies emphasize what actually happens in hypnosis rather than inferring from behavior what is occurring internally. I think this very important direction in hypnosis research parallels other methodological developments in psychology over the past 50 years that again are focusing on the mind as the center of human experience.

The second important direction in hypnosis research, particularly from the clinical perspective, concerns the investigation of the subtleties, nuances, and complexities of *the relationship* between the hypnotized person and the hypnotherapist. Many researchers, including Eva Banyai and her colleagues in Hungary, Elgan Baker and Eugene Levitt in Indiana, Michael Nash and Steven J. Lynn in Ohio, and Peter Sheehan and Kevin McConkey in Australia, are seriously studying the relationship aspects of hypnosis. I think we are going to see greater emphasis on this aspect of hypnosis and less on the induction techniques and creative maneuvers of the hypnotherapist that have characterized the field, particularly with the "Ericksonian movement," over the past decade. I think we're going to come to the understanding that the essence of hypnosis can be understood in terms of the relationship between hypnotherapist and patient—where the patient can feel a strong alliance with the hypnotherapist, where the hypnotherapist can become a more positive transference object, where the real relationship can be strengthened, and where the idealized elements of the relationship can play a particular role in hypnotherapy.

So we are beginning to explore the relational aspects of hypnosis and their implications for clinical and experimental research. In my recent presidential address for Division 30 of the American Psychological Association, I attempted to differentiate four dimensions of the hypnotic relationship. I have discussed some implications and described various interventions that may tap into and make use of these dimensions in ways that are appropriate for particular kinds of patients, such as pre-Oedipal or borderline psychotic patients. I think we are going to see a lot of work in this area.

I believe that the major trends in hypnosis are going to blend very well with the holistic approach to health. Hypnosis will contribute to our understanding of how the mind and body interact: How, for example, the hypnotized person experiences the hypnotherapist as being inside rather than outside, just how that perception affects the hypnotized person's own experience of his or her body, and what the implications are for the control of pain or for psychosomatic conditions. I think that as hypnosis is investigated in these ways and as it is seen to parallel more of the ordinary psychological processes that we see in the waking state, more and more clinicians of various persuasions are going to become interested in and I hope influenced by the potency of hypnosis as a procedure for utilizing more of these ordinary human processes. The relationship between hypnosis and psychology as a whole is likely to change radically. It isn't going to be the odd bedfellow of science or the rejected cousin of psychoanalysis, but rather part and parcel of scientific and clinical psychology. This trend is going to rest on the training and thinking of open-minded, scientifically oriented clinicians entering the discipline of psychology.

Ann Damsbo, PhD

Hypnosis is a natural state that occurs spontaneously in both children and adults. It is especially evident in children who have not yet been conditioned to suppress the creative, imaginative states that we now recognize as hypnoidal. Thus, children will naturally spend many of their waking hours in these altered states.

Artists, inventors, actors, and other creative individuals have successfully resisted the adult world's efforts to stifle their creativity. Madison Avenue and the media are well aware of the advantages of using hypnotic techniques in merchandising. Cult leaders and others actively engaged in brainwashing techniques have capitalized on the naivete of young adults. Unskilled in the arts of hypnosis and untrained to resist the subtle and often not-so-subtle abuses of hypnosis, they become unwitting victims of such tragedies as the Jonestown massacre.

With the current renaissance of clinical hypnosis, it is hoped that children of the future will be more strongly encouraged to utilize and develop their natural hypnotic skills. Children who are taught to use these skills will be able to improve their academic achievement, increase their ability to learn languages, compete more successfully in sports, and perhaps even develop ways of attaining the level of relaxation they might otherwise seek to experience through the use of illegal drugs. Ideally, it would be possible for children who learn to master this natural gift to grow into adults who have no need for tranquilizers, alcohol, and other external means of reducing stress or achieving an altered state of consciousness.

Joan Murray-Jobsis (formerly Scagnelli), PhD

It seems valuable to look at the future of hypnosis from a historical point of view. When seen in its historical context, it seems apparent that hypnosis has gone through cycles of high popular interest and activity and wide usage, alternating with periods of scientific disrepute and loss of popular interest and clinical usage.

At present, we appear to be riding the crest of one of these cyclical upswings. There is currently a great deal of popular interest in hypnosis and clinical use and scientific exploration of hypnosis are expanding. Twenty years ago, those dedicated to the cause of hypnosis felt the need to expand the interest in and use of it. Now, many of us who are clinicians, educators, and researchers feel the need to restate the constraints and limitations of hypnosis because of excessive public interest in and expectations of hypnosis and the possible backlash that this can produce, once again, as in the past.

If history does indicate the pattern of the future, hypnosis may again run its course and enter into a period of some abuse of the process and some reaction to overexpectations. It already appears that the courts may be pulling back from according admissibility to hypnotically produced testimony because of some abuses and lack of safeguards in this area. There is also likely to be a popular reaction to the extravagant claims of lay hypnotists who offer effortless miraculous changes in body and character. Thus, hypnosis may follow its previous historical pattern into a recessive period.

However, the sound clinical gains and reputable research work of the past two decades may have established a solid advance for hypnosis that will not be eroded by popular shifts in attitudes. It is, therefore, the hope of this writer that the future will see the continued growth of sound clinical and scientific work in the understanding of and use of hypnosis. Further, it is hoped that hypnosis, as a clinical and research tool, will be taught in increasing numbers of medical schools and university programs and that questions concerning the phemonenon of hypnosis, its theoretical constructs, and the parameters affecting its successful application will be resolved successfully.

Elliot V. Feldbau, DMD

The future will undoubtedly see an increased acceptance of hypnosis into the realms of other psychodynamic therapies. While the use of relaxation as a therapeutic modality and mental image formation as a means of gaining psychological control of physiological processes have long been associated with and understood in the hypnotic context, they have also been described as an integral part of a multiplicity of other therapies. Although each of these has a different label and origin, they all show distinctly similar effects upon people who learn how to use them. Thus, progressive relaxation, Eastern meditation, and autogenic training all show commonalities that may, in the context of the physio-logical parameters of Benson's relaxation response, become integrated into the fundamental constructs of hypnosis. Similarly, the placebo phenomenon and the techniques of biofeedback have a unique relation to the therapeutic suggestive methods of hypnosis in the control of physiologic functions. It will be the exploration of the unities of our therapeutic experiences that will provide creative insight in the future of hypnosis. The integration of ideas, rather than the separation and duplication of them, will bring about the greatest enrichment in our ability to understand therapeutic strategies and will allow us to transcend the boundaries and limits of individual disciplines.

The need for an integrated view of a complex problem is apparent in the clinical management of chronic pain. Only through a multidisci-plinary approach and effort by physicians, psychologists, dentist, osteopaths, and other health professionals will we be able to offer diagnosis and treatment that deal effectively with psychophysiological complexities.

I believe that the hypnotic state will continue to be a vehicle for our therapeutic communications and will gain in popularity as our knowledge of fundamental truths evolves. The phenomenology of this altered state of consciousness may indeed provide the unifying ideas for the integration of much of our understanding of mind-body processes. Only then will we gain new insight into the needs of our patients and the best treatment for their problems.

Eric Steese, PhD

The future of hypnosis is excellent. In general, the increasing emphasis on a holistic approach to patient care meshes smoothly and productively with the use of hypnosis, particularly for practitioners who maintain a model that holds that all hypnosis is self-hypnosis. This model of hypnosis generates an emphasis on the capacities and capabilities that lie within each individual, and the ways in which these internal resources can be used to promote self-care and healing.

For example, the growing work on brain chemistry and the presence of naturally occurring pain modifiers within the brain provides a potential scientific basis for the successes that some clinicians have long held possible in alleviating pain with the use of hypnosis. Increased understanding in this area leads directly into the broader issues of placebos and spontaneous remissions and the truism that the healing professions have only begun to understand the resources available within the human mind and body. It is these resources that hypnosis is ideally suited to explore and develop.

To maintain this future there is a need to learn from the past. Mesmer's basic error was an inability to *explain* his results, and the consequences of this error still cloud discussions of hypnosis. In the process of assisting patients with hypnosis, we must hold a balanced view, insisting on what is possible, yet not inflicting it on those patients and professionals whose world view rejects such forms of help. It is also necessary to ensure that there will be a well-trained and capable body of professionals available to offer hypnosis to the public within their own disciplines. Inevitably there will be those who misuse this powerful tool either willfully, for their own gain, or through a mistaken belief that hypnosis is a panacea. Only competent professionals, willing to speak out, can offer a defense against these abuses and ensure that the future of hypnosis continues to be bright beyond the current wave of popularity and popularizing. The real future of hypnosis is based on the process of responsible exploration and learning, which will provide the additional knowledge and understanding necessary for even further expansion and development of its techniques and capabilities.

PART V

ADDENDUM: CURRENT TRENDS

B ecause the field of hypnosis is growing so rapidly, the following chapter has been added to bring the reader up to date on recent trends and clinical applications. At present, there are 18 hypnosis journals published in 10 countries,* a steady stream of new books on all aspects of clinical hypnosis, and in recent years, new editions of classic texts. Even the most experienced practitioner needs to step back once in a while to assess where we are now and where we are going.

Five years ago, several distinguished practitioners made bold predictions about the future of hypnosis (see Chapter 19). If anything, recent years have lent greater credibility to these predictions. A. David Feinstein, Ph.D., for example, pointed to three trends that would shape the field of hypnosis: "increased precision, broader application, and wider ownership." Hypnosis is being used more effectively with more people than ever before in its history. As Lillian Fredericks, M.D. stated, hypnosis "really is the essence of the art of medicine." Ongoing research on the mind-body connection is for many the most exciting frontier in medicine and psychology today, and hypnosis is at the interface of the mind-body connection.

Karen Olness, M.D. envisioned the opportunity for future generations to use innate skills in imagery in all aspects of their lives.

---

*Gravitz, M. A. (1987) Two centuries of hypnosis specialty journals. *International Journal of Clinical and Experimental Hypnosis*, 35, 265–276.

Today, hypnosis is increasingly being seen as the property of Everyman, a tool not only for healing but also for enrichment. This broader application and wider ownership of what Daniel Araoz, Ed.D., in his Introduction termed this "glorious helping method," makes it increasingly important that hypnosis be used in a climate that harbors neither unnecessary fears nor excessive expectations. It may be that in the future practitioners will be called upon to step outside their roles as physicians and therapists and help educate the public in the safe and effective uses of hypnosis.

20
Present Findings and Applications

A man is limited only by the thoughts he chooses.
—James Allen
As A Man Thinketh

T he introduction to Part I states, "with the merging of many disciplines and fields of study, we appear to be on the verge of new breakthroughs in our understanding of human potential." Today, the field of clinical hypnosis is more exciting than ever as it continues to build on past knowledge and identify and explore new frontiers.

Because of the vitality in the field, it is impossible to explore in the space of a single chapter all of the research, case reports, and debates of the past several years. Instead, this chapter will provide an overview of the art and science of hypnosis, touching on ongoing controversies, apparent trends, and exciting areas of current practice and potential future research.

In the past several years, there has been a growing use of hypnosis in psychotherapy, medicine, and dentistry, not only in the number of practitioners using hypnotic techniques, but also in the wide range of applications. A recent survey (Kraft, Rodolfa, and Reilley, 1985) has identified current trends. One hundred and sixty-one members of the American Society of Clinical Hypnosis, including 77 psychologists, 64 physicians, and 20 dentists, responded to an extensive questionnaire asking them to identify theorists who most influence current trends, areas relevant to hypnosis that offer promising new applications, and areas that require further research.

The survey results showed that Milton Erickson continues to have a profound and pervasive influence on the field of hypnosis. Respondents listed Erickson by a ratio of 10 to 1 over any other theorist as the one whose views on hypnosis most closely parallel the respondents' own. This finding suggests that the techniques for which Erickson is best known, including his client-centered therapy, indirect and naturalistic induction techniques, and use of metaphor, are being favored over more ritualistic and authoritarian approaches. The survey also identified several areas relevant to hypnosis that offer promising new applications: behavioral medicine, psychotherapy, cancer treatment, educational/school problems, neurological/neuropsychological disorders, pediatrics/child problems, and forensic issues. These findings are consistent with current trends as evidenced by recent literature.

Recently, the public, as never before, has embraced hypnotic techniques, under a variety of names, for such purposes as improved performance and self-healing. Hypnotic techniques are being popularized in management training, secondary education, and team sports. Perhaps because of its rapid expansion on many fronts, the field of hypnosis is entering a period of self-scrutiny, marked by surveys, retrospectives, self-criticism, and a need to caution both practitioners and the public against potential abuses.

THE ONGOING SEARCH FOR HYPNOSIS

Any discussion of hypnosis should begin by reminding the reader that hypnosis is no better defined now than it was several years ago. In fact, as our understanding of hypnosis has evolved over the more than 140 years since the time of James Braid, who is considered to be the father of modern hypnosis, its definitions have become less precise and more controversial. One school of thought holds that hypnosis is a clearly defined phenomenon: One is either hypnotized or one is not, and some people are more hypnotizable than others. At the other extreme are those who consider a wide variety of interactions to be hypnotic in nature, and believing that everyone can benefit from hypnosis, show little concern for the hypnotizability of their clients.

These different points of view are expressed by two well-known practitioners in the field, Daniel Araoz and Andre Weitzenhoffer. Araoz first put forth his definition of what he terms the New Hypnosis in 1982 and has recently elaborated on his analysis. Araoz (1985) includes within the realm of hypnosis "all mental activities which bypass left hemispheric functioning, whether induced or spontaneous" (p. xx). Neither a school nor a therapy, the New Hypnosis "comprises an attitude, a willingness to recognize in a practical way the influence of the inner mind—the subconscious—in every aspect of a person's life, and an effort to learn how to use that influence of the subconscious to the best advantage" (p. xxii).

In the formulation of his understanding of the New Hypnosis, Araoz notes in particular the clinical contributions of Milton Erickson and the research of T. X. Barber (1969), who, along with Hilgard (1977), have shown that hypnosis is a naturally occurring experience. Historically, Araoz traces the New Hypnosis back to the Nancy school (of which Liébeault and Bernheim were the founders) through Coué, and then to Coué's disciple Baudouin, of the New Nancy school, which flourished from the late Nineteenth Century to the early 1930s. (See Chapter 2 for an overview of the history of hypnosis.) The development of this view of hypnosis is expressed by two statements: Bernheim's "There is no hypnotism, there is only suggestion," and Coué's "There is no suggestion, there is only self-suggestion." It is in the New Nancy school that suggestion became dissociated from hypnotism and the hypnotist became a teacher or guide who helped others use self-suggestion effectively. "All hypnosis is self-hypnosis" is a tenet of much modern clinical practice, and imagery has become recognized as a form of suggestion.

Araoz (1985) also notes that the New Hypnosis shifts the emphasis from clinical hypnosis, which focuses on the hypnotist-client relationship, to "personal enrichment, a logical consequence of the insistence on self-suggestion" (p. 5). This concept of hypnosis becomes an umbrella term, encompassing other techniques and therapies that are hypnotic in nature, including cognitive-behavior modification, guided imagery, and covert modeling procedures. This forms an historical basis for the movement of hypnosis, or at least the New Hypnosis as defined by Araoz, outside the clinic and into the public domain.

While Araoz's understanding of hypnosis is characterized by its pragmatism (if a client does not respond, the practitioner changes the method), Weitzenhoffer (1985) argues for a more narrow and scientifically acceptable definition. He finds that as a result of the growing clinical applications, the concepts of hypnotism and hypnosis have become increasingly diluted, and that "Today, these concepts have become so diffused as to have ceased to be meaningful" (p. 73). If "hypnosis is everything," as Bandler and Grinder (1979), the founders of neurolinguistic programming, have stated, then, Weitzenhoffer argues, hypnosis is also nothing. He laments this evolution and reminds us that there is no foundation for it in the scientific literature, which has added little about the essential phenomenology of hypnosis since 1900.

Weitzenhoffer bases his view of hypnosis upon the work of de Puységur and Braid. Braid saw hypnotism as an all-or-none condition in which a person is most influenced by verbal suggestions, and which is always accompanied by spontaneous amnesia for the hypnotic event. Weitzenhoffer argues that "whereas for de Puységur and Braid, artificial somnambulism was the whole, entire state, by 1947 artificial somnambulism was merely viewed as the upper range or segment of a scale" (p. 69). He concludes that hypnosis is now defined to encompass behavior which Braid would not have considered hypnotic. It is not surprising that he traces the history of these changes back to Liébeault and Bernheim.

While Araoz refers to the New Hypnosis as "hypnosis without hypnosis," or hypnosis without the rituals traditionally associated with trance induction, Weitzenhoffer challenges researchers to "get back to basics," and be more stringent in what they accept as hypnotic behavior. He suggests that all scientific inquiries begin with the observable facts of hypnosis, such as individual response to suggestions and the somnambulism of de Puységur, and the well-defined procedures associated with hypnotic response, so that future scientists will know what hypnosis is.

Although the gap between the views—hypnosis as an art and hypnosis as a science—is wide indeed, many prominent practitioners have voiced the need to bridge it. Baker (1987) reminds us that clinical hypnosis owes a great debt to the work of researchers who, by establishing hypnosis as a measurable phenomenon, enabled it to achieve acceptance in the scientific community. "It is clear," Baker states, "that the recent explosion of clinical hypnosis is rooted in the growing respectability achieved through careful research" (p. 204). Erika Fromm (1987) believes that "Clinical intuition and scientific exploration must walk, and now *do* walk, hand in hand" (p. 215) and stresses the importance of testing clinical insights on statistically significant samples of patients. Finally, Frankel (1985) speaks for many when he refers to "the unavoidable complexity, uncertainty and ambiguity in our field as I see it, and the need for us to tolerate the situation while we still struggle to understand what it is that we accomplish with the use of hypnosis" (p. 16).

While acknowledging the importance of ongoing research to establish the scientific underpinnings of the phenomena we call hypnosis, the remainder of this chapter will use hypnosis in the broader sense as set forth by Araoz. Only with this broader definition can we encompass all of the therapeutic and nontherapeutic uses of hypnosis that deserve attention, if for no other reason than that they are affecting, and will continue to affect, the modern practice of medicine and psychotherapy, as well as our society as a whole.

MEDICINE

As described in Chapters 7 and 8, hypnosis has a long history of documented effectiveness as an adjunct to traditional medicine. In fact, this history has recently been expanded and strengthened with the recent report that the first documented use of hypnotic anesthesia for surgical intervention in the United States predated by two years John Elliotson's first documented case of surgical hypnoanesthesia (Gravitz, 1988). Looking at the present and future uses of hypnosis, the field of behavioral medicine, in particular, is generating excitement in both the medical and psychological communities (Fromm, 1987). Hypnosis may become one of the essential tools for behavioral medicine, which combines an understanding of autonomic physiological processes with strategies for voluntary self-control. It is impossible to identify any single impetus for this growing interest in mind-body phenomenon. Instead, it appears to be the result of a coalescing of several factors: the holistic movement in health care, which focuses on the whole person instead of just the diseased organs or body systems, the self-help impetus in our culture, and the significant and still accumulating body of research on mind-body interactions. As Achterberg (1985) states, "The role of the imagination, long dethroned, is now reappearing in medicine" (p. 96).

Frankel (1987) has identified three levels of application within medical hypnosis, which can provide a useful framework for discussion. The first level is primarily functional. At this level, hypnosis is used to manage chronic pain and the discomfort of various medical procedures, as well as reduce the stress and anxiety accompanying hospitalization and surgery. The second level is primarily structural, in which hypnosis is used in the management of such diseases as hemophilia, diabetes, and seizure disorders. Although the two levels are not distinct, the first emphasizes patient management, while the goal of hypnosis at the second level is to intervene in the disease process itself. At the third level, hypnosis is used to slow down or to reverse the extension of the pathophysiology. This use of hypnosis represents an exciting frontier and one that is not only being explored scientifically but also being embraced by the public. As we will see, a common denominator among the uses of hypnosis at all these levels is the returning of control back to the patient.

There have been and continue to be many examples in the literature of the effectiveness of hypnosis at the first level of intervention. What is new is a growing awareness that not only the physician, psychotherapist, or anesthesiologist, but also the nursing staff and other hospital personnel can positively influence a patient's experience. A few small changes can have wide-ranging positive effects in the way patients respond to treatment, as examples from recent literature show.

Zastowny, Kirschenbaum, and Meny (1986) examine the effects of coping-skills training on children's distress before, during and after surgery. They randomly assigned 33 children, aged 6 to 10 years, and their parents to one of three groups: (1) a group receiving information on typical surgical and hospital experiences, (2) a group in which parents learned relaxation procedures to help them reduce their own distress and thus be more supportive of their children, and (3) a group receiving training in how to help children use coping self-talk and related techniques for dealing effectively with hospitalization and surgery. The children in this third group learned how to relax and visualize a happy event and received reinforcement from their parents. In other words, the children used what amounted to self-hypnosis and parents offered positive suggestions. The authors found that both the anxiety reduction and coping skills groups reduced the children's self-reported fearfulness and the parents' distress. However, only children in the coping skills group exhibited fewer maladaptive behaviors during hospitalization and less problematic behavior before and after hospitalization.

In a recent discussion of the applications of relaxation/mental imagery in pediatric emergencies, Kohen (1986) describes how the emergency room physician can quickly establish rapport with a patient while, at the same time, assessing and managing the clinical problem. The way in which the physician becomes both a model and teacher, simultaneously giving over personal control of discomfort to the patient, is a good example of hypnosis without hypnosis. The techniques Kohen describes include nonverbal reassurances, direct distraction, story telling, and other imagination-stimulating approaches.

For example, Kohen determined that an eight-year-old boy with a head laceration was interested in football. The hypnotic induction became an invitation to "close his eyes and daydream so well [about football] that he could forget about being here until it was time to go home." While Kohen informed the boy of each surgical procedure, including washing the cut and injecting the local anesthetic, he reinforced the imagery and deepened the trance by suggesting the boy concentrate on getting the signals right and running the proper pass pattern. This case is one example of how imagery is suggestion. According to Fromm (1987), imagery has assumed an increasingly larger role in hypnosis, and is now being employed in all hypnotic treatment approaches.

Another case of a 12-year-old boy in the emergency room for upper gastrointestinal bleeding demonstrates the importance of positive suggestions in a supportive atmosphere. Kohen (1986) reports that he found the boy in "a spontaneous, albeit unhappy, trance." The emergency room personnel were discussing the difficulty of inserting the nasogastric tube into his stomach and complaining that the boy wouldn't cooperate. In other words, the boy was receiving negative suggestions and responding with anxiety and tension, making the task of inserting the tube even more difficult. The author first substituted positive suggestions for the negative ("Isn't it good to know that you're going to be OK?") and explained that the purpose of the tube was to clear the blood from the stomach, so "then you can begin to get better." When the boy was more relaxed, the author suggested he "find the switches in your brain that turn off hurts" and then find the one for his nose and mouth, and when it's off "the helping tube will go down easily." The tube was inserted without any further problems.

One sign that there is a growing awareness of the hypnotic elements in all medical settings is the still small but growing extent to which articles addressing these issues appear in mainstream medical journals. For example, in a recent issue of *Resident and Staff Physician,* Amen and Simms (1986) discuss techniques for helping surgical patients deal constructively with their anxieties. The authors note that little has been written on the subject by clinical physicians and state that "this dimension of the patient's response has long been overlooked in the surgical literature and training and that it is imperative for both the surgical team and the surgical nursing staff to develop ways to assist the patient constructively" in dealing with the emotional stress inherent in surgical procedures (p. 87).

The authors recommend three techniques appropriate for the busy clinician. First, provide the patient with as much factual information as possible about what to expect before, during, and after surgery. Second, use systematic relaxation techniques to reduce anxiety and accompanying muscle tension and enhance feelings that the patient still has some control over his or her reactions to the environment. In this instance, the clinician can provide the patient with an audiotape of relaxation exercises and explain to the patient the ways in which relaxation can reduce pain and promote healing. Third, the clinician can use simple therapeutic techniques to improve rapport with the patient. For example, the clinician can use the consent form for surgery as a springboard for discussing anxieties, providing information, and determining which patients are at increased risk because they lack a support system and may require more time from both doctor and staff. The authors also note that it is important for the rest of the hospital staff to provide a supportive atmosphere for the patient.

Is this interaction hypnosis? Although the term hypnosis is not used in the article, the elements of relaxation, a supportive environment, and suggestions that patients can affect both their level of pain and the healing process, are all essential parts of a hypnotic interaction. Even so, how, as Frankel (1987) asks, do we sort out the therapeutic gains attributed to hypnosis from those derived from nonspecific factors in a clinical encounter? The answer is, we can't, but that realization should not stop us from welcoming this important dimension of healing back into medicine.

Another encouraging sign is the increasing attention given to hypnosis in nursing. Referring to "the potent effect of a prepared mind on a healing body," Achterberg (1985) discusses a technique called the *sensory information approach,* developed for nurses by Jean Johnson. Nurses using this approach provide patients with information on the sensory aspects of their treatment, as well as the usual cognitive information. The sensory information technique, explains Achterberg, is "a modified version of guided imagery, and one that in many respects is more palatable to the standard world of health care than various other imagery techniques" (p. 92).

A recent book by Zahourek (1985) explores the role of hypnosis in all aspects of nursing, from initial contact with a hospitalized patient to the use of therapeutic suggestion in an outpatient clinic. Zahourek discusses how much nurses not trained to be therapists can do, for example, by helping patients reframe their negative expectations into positive ones, and incorporating positive suggestions into routine procedures, such as turning a patient. Again, the emphasis is on suggestions integrated into ongoing procedures and not on hypnosis as a separate procedure.

The second level identified by Frankel (1987) is that of structural change. Whereas the first level is primarily patient management, hypnosis at the second level is used to intervene in the disease process itself. Clinical evidence of the effectiveness of hypnosis in positively influencing the pathophysiology of systems disorders, such as hemophilia, diabetes, and neurological disorders, continues to mount.

Swirsky-Sacchetti and Margolis (1986) studied the effects of a comprehensive self-hypnosis training program on the use of Factor VIII coagulant for patients with severe hemophilia. The authors found that over an 18-week follow-up period, the treatment group (n = 15) significantly reduced the amount of factor concentrate used to control bleeding compared to controls. Moldawsky (1984) reported the successful use of hypnosis to decrease the involuntary movements of Huntington's disease—movements commonly thought to be outside the realm of conscious control. Kohen and Botts (1987) had similar success in diminishing the frequency of tics in four children, age 6 to 10 years, with Tourette Syndrome. These latter reports emphasize the importance of the patients' growing sense of self-mastery, the sense of being in control of a situation that before had made them feel helpless.

Gould and Tissler (1984) reported two case studies in which hypnosis was used to produce a decline in the subjective level of pain and the severity of recurrent genital herpes over periods of three and seven months. Surman and Crumpacker (1987) conducted a two-year study of six patients with recurrent genital herpes, with mixed results. Five weekly sessions and three follow-up sessions included suggestions for relaxation, improved well-being, and strengthening the immune system to give them freedom from recurrent lesions. Results of the study were inconclusive: one patient had an extended remission, two had mild to moderate improvement, one had no significant change, and two had an incomplete follow-up. The authors cite a number of confounding variables that should be controlled in any future studies. These include degree and chronicity of illness, demographic variables, hypnotizability, and psychosocial status.

Hypnosis has been shown again and again to be effective in managing chronic disorders. However, as Frankel (1987) states, "The clinical belief that hypnosis helps has not been disproved; however, it has not been proven either" (p. 243). Frankel again raises the question of whether hypnosis is the significant variable in a treatment situation, or whether any compassionate, reassuring approach would have the same result. For clinicians, it may be enough to know they are integrating hypnosis into a holistic approach to medicine that works with patients to foster positive expectations and a sense of self-control.

As we move from level 2 to level 3, we step into less familiar territory. To move from a belief that hypnosis can help a patient manage pain or alleviate the effects of a chronic disease, to the idea that hypnosis can facilitate the regression or elimination of a disease such as cancer, is a great conceptual leap. In an earlier chapter, we stated that "alteration of the disease process is the new frontier in medical hypnosis." It remains the new frontier, although in the past few years, we have familiarized ourselves with a little more of the terrain. In this area, the importance of behavioral medicine and hypnosis can clearly be seen.

A recent review of the literature between 1960 and 1985 on hypnosis and cancer (Steggles et al., 1987) clearly shows that most of our efforts in the past 25 years have been at the first level of intervention. Of the 69 annotated entries, 39 referred to the use of hypnosis to control the pain and anxiety associated with the disease and to reduce the side effects of treatment, such as the nausea and vomiting resulting from chemotherapy. Ten articles addressed the use of hypnosis to improve the quality of life for the terminally ill. Only 12 articles addressed the use of hypnosis to prevent disease, to strengthen the immune response, or to promote healing. In light of current trends, we expect the focus to shift toward healing and prevention in the next 25 years.

In recent years, a significant body of research has indicated that psychosocial factors affect immunity. (In addition to sources cited in Chapters 7 and 16, see Levy et al., 1985; Pettingale et al., 1985; Laudenslager et al., 1983; Derogatis, Abeloff, and Melisartas, 1979; and Kiecolt-Glaser et al., 1984). In addition, the public itself is turning increasingly to unconventional or alternative therapies to supplement conventional medical treatment. A study of 660 patients by Cassileth et al. (1984) found that more than half integrated conventional and nonconventional therapies, and that more than 60 percent of the providers for the nonconventional therapies were physicians.

The growing body of research and increased public acceptance does not mean, however, that the theory that semantic input is decoded as somatic output, or that mind can move molecules, is generally accepted in medical circles. In fact, at this level, where issues of life and death are brought to the surface, the gap between clinical experience and hard scientific evidence generates even more controversy.

Writing in *Resident and Staff Physician*, Borysenko (1987), a leading researcher and author in the field of mind-body interaction, acknowledges that this is an area in which emotions run high. As an example, she cites a study by Cassileth et al. (1985), which concluded that once a disease is established, psychosocial variables do not affect its prognosis. A flood of letters in response to the study took issue with both its methodology and its conclusions. As Borysenko points out, "The number of factors that affect prognosis and the different types of cancer studied present a matrix that will take years to develop" (p. 52). That does not mean, however, that patients should be deprived of interventions that may be medically as well as psychologically beneficial.

In a recent book, Rossi (1986) helps close the gap between theory and research by drawing together the threads of evidence from many sciences to make the neurophysiological links between mind and body more accessible to all readers. Although it is impossible to summarize fairly Rossi's closely reasoned explanations, we can highlight some of his major points. Drawing on the theories and research of Bernheim, Selye, Bowers, Ader, and many others, Rossi explains the process of information transduction, or the conversion of energy from one form to another, just as a windmill converts wind energy to mechanical energy. He stresses that instead of being separate, the mind and body are two facets of a single information system, and that biology is a process of information transduction from one to the other. The limbic-hypothalamic system, in which state-dependent memory, learning and behavior processes are encoded, is the major anatomical connecting link between the mind and body. State-dependent memory and learning refers to the theory that what is learned and remembered is dependent on one's psychophysiological state at the time.

The therapist's task is to learn how to access and use the mind-body mechanisms. Rossi equates our current level of understanding of these mechanisms to that of "the average driver who knows there is an engine somewhere that does something when we turn on a key and push the gas pedal" (p. 155), but does not yet have the knowledge to fix the engine if it breaks down. Rossi's basic premise for his therapeutic approach is that "Every access is a reframe" (p. 68). This premise refers to the fact that the mind is in constant flux, always incorporating new information, and that every time we review, or access a problem, the mind reframes the problem as it seeks an answer. Hypnosis, of course, is a powerful tool for accessing memories. The hypnotherapeutic approaches Rossi offers for mind-body communication are all aspects of "the basic accessing formula" as described by Erickson and Rossi (1976/1980).

Araoz (1985) has also written eloquently about ways in which the New Hypnosis can activate the healer that resides within each person. His five-step process is reminiscent of the Simonton's pioneering work in the use of imagery with cancer patients, and like Rossi's based on replacing negative thoughts or images (negative self-hypnosis) with healing images. The five steps are as follows:

1. Ask the patient to concentrate on the mental images related to the disease.

2. Ask the patient to imagine the medical treatment and how the image of treatment modifies the images of disease.

3. Have the patient produce an image of the internal healing forces at work in the body.

4. Have the patient intensify the healing images and combine them with images of the medical treatment to make an impact on the images of the disease.

5. Daily practice at home of each of the four steps.

Araoz takes his discussion a step further by suggesting that more than a means of fighting disease, hypnosis, as a natural and healthy activity of the mind, can and should also be used to maintain health.

It is fair to conclude that medicine is in a period of transition and that hypnosis is an important part of that transition. At present, many theories, therapies, and lines of research are converging. As researchers continue to attempt controlled studies to measure the effects of hypnosis, clinical hypnosis may be approaching its next frontier: to move beyond its current emphasis on disease control and begin to focus on promoting and maintaining health.

FAMILY THERAPY

Hypnosis is used to facilitate various forms of psychotherapy, and its range of applications is extremely broad, from treating bipolar, affective disorders using suggestions for electrochemical regulation (Feinstein & Morgan, 1986) to using hypnotic reconstruction of memories in the treatment of phobias (Mott, 1986). The reader is referred to Chapters 12 and 13 for an overview of the ways in which hypnosis can facilitate various psychotherapeutic approaches.

Family therapy, one area of psychotherapy not addressed in the first edition of *A Clinical Hypnosis Primer*, has received increasing attention in recent years. On the surface, the two seem incompatible, for hypnosis works with the subconscious and family therapy deals with patterns of interaction. In practice, however, modern, naturalistic techniques are ideal for working with both intrapsychic and interpersonal concerns.

As cited by Braun (1984), the many general benefits to the use of hypnosis with families include the following: (1) a shared pleasurable experience, (2) the introduction of calm into an escalating family system, and (3) helping family members tune into themselves and each other, thus facilitating communication. More specifically, hypnosis can be used to work on one family member's problem and at the same time help other family members to understand the problem. Age regression can be used to explore past events and to bring them into proper perspective. Other methods available to the therapist include relaxation, age progression, so a couple can experience themselves looking back on their problems after many years together, shared fantasies, and hypnotic role reversals.

Araoz (1985) goes even further to say that not only does hypnotherapy facilitate family therapy, but that family therapy must be hypnotic to be effective. He points to two recent outstanding contributions to family hypnotherapy as reflected in the work of Calof (1985), Ritterman (1983), and the Lanktons (1983): (1) that families use hypnosis, and (2) that hypnotic principles and techniques are essential to help families become functional. These insights are based on the premise that reality is subjective, and that the path to change is through right hemisphere processes (inner experience) and not rational insight.

Ritterman (1983) was the first to clarify that hypnotic-like interactions exist within the family and that mutual hypnosis, consisting of constructive or destructive suggestions, takes place among family members. In dysfunctional families, hypnotic interactions are being used in a negative way. Using an approach she calls "hypnotic family therapy," she searches for connections between individual mental sets and interpersonal contexts and then helps the family to produce new frames of reference, both intrapsychic and interpersonal. In other words, she takes what the family is doing ineffectively and turns it around to their benefit.

In order to detect "family hypnosis," the therapist must develop keen observation skills (Araoz, 1985). Family members' figures of speech, language style, important statements, and somatics all provide clues for entry into a families' inner experiences. The therapist can then proceed, using hypnotic techniques, to help family members alter their frames of reference by developing new ways of seeing and behaving.

Braun (1984) reminds us that therapists using hypnosis in family therapy must be prepared to deal with the unexpected, including strong abreactions and spontaneous age regression, especially in teenagers. In other words, only practitioners with formal training in both family therapy and hypnosis should attempt to use hypnosis in the complex dynamics of family therapy.

POST-TRAUMATIC STRESS DISORDERS

The 1980s have seen increased interest in post-traumatic stress disorders and increased awareness of what Haley (1985) terms "the deforming impact of catastrophic stress, particularly combat, on psychic structures" (p. 54). The set of symptoms now identified as post-traumatic stress are triggered by dehumanizing or catastrophic experiences: natural disasters, such as earthquakes, tornados, floods and fires; coercion, such as that experienced by terrorist hostages, kidnap victims or prisoners of war; and extraordinary human aggression, such as that experienced by combat veterans and victims of rape, assault or incest. Motor vehicle accident victims have also been shown to suffer from post-traumatic stress disorder due to the "incidence, severity and complications of their accident" (Bowden & Posthuma, 1987). Hence, "the concept of PTSD has widened far beyond the war setting, railway trains, and accidents at work" (Trimble, 1985). A post-traumatic stress disorder is manifested by both intrapsychic and interpersonal difficulties and can be either acute or chronic, immediate or delayed. These difficulties are succinctly described by Kilpatrick, Veroner and Best (1985) in their discussion of how traumatic events produce PTSD.

Hypnotherapy emphasizing cartharsis, abreaction, and integration has been used successfully with Vietnam veterans (Balson and Dempster, 1980; Brende and Benedict, 1980; Spiegel, 1981; Brende, 1985; Sax, 1985; Scurfield, 1985; Shatan, 1985; and Silver & Kelly, 1985). Additionally, Scurfield (1985) suggests that not only is hypnosis of benefit in the treatment of combat related PTSD symptoms, but hypnosis is also of benefit in treating individuals experiencing PTSD symptoms due to other dehumanizing or catastrophic experiences, extraordinary human aggression, coercion, work related injuries or the outcomes of motor vehicle accidents. Fromm (1987) predicts rapid development in the field of hypnotherapy for post-traumatic stress disorders in the next 10 years, as the number of reported incest cases increases and as more and more Vietnam veterans, treated for such secondary symptoms as drug addiction or marital dysfunction, are recognized as suffering from post-traumatic stress.

Recently, some authors have shifted the focus from hypnotherapy as a treatment method to hypnosis as a way of preventing post-traumatic stress disorders. An article by Balson, Dempster, and Brooks (1984) discusses the use of hypnosis as a defense against coercive persuasion. The authors studied victims who successfully survived coercion experiences without developing post-traumatic stress disorders. They concluded that these survivors spontaneously used self-hypnosis to defend themselves against the coercive techniques of their captors. Similar to the way a patient uses hypnosis to control pain, the authors explain, captives can use self-hypnosis to increase tolerance for unpleasant or painful stimuli. At the same time, dissociation, fantasy, and illusion can help compensate for the loss of interpersonal relations and physical comfort or gratification. The use of these techniques blocks the development of a bond between prisoner and captors, who attempt to gain control over the captive by becoming the primary source of reinforcements. Based on their findings, the authors propose a training program for civilian and military personnel at high risk of terrorist kidnaping or capture. The program would contain three components: awareness education, auto-hypnosis training, and simulation training. They stress the importance of simulation training as an experiential method for testing skill mastery in coercive situations.

Wood, Farley, and Sexton (1987) agree with the value of prior training for survival in captivity, but they take issue with the use of self-hypnosis during interrogation or torture, where a prisoner's seeming detachment from the situation may bring repercussions from an interrogator. Instead, these authors stress the use of self-hypnosis to enhance a prisoner's coping abilities during confinement. They propose a 4- to 6-hour training program in self-hypnosis and hetero-hypnosis as an adjunct to existing captivity training programs. Hetero-hypnosis would be taught as a means of teaching hypnosis to other captives, and the training program would include ego-strengthening techniques to reduce feelings of helplessness, loneliness, and isolation.

This new use of hypnosis as a preventive measure against post-traumatic stress disorders is still in the theoretical state of development. However, it is a reminder that self-hypnosis can be a powerful ally for individuals facing circumstances beyond their control.

FORENSIC USES

One of the most controversial applications of hypnosis has been its use in criminal investigations. The application of hypnosis to forensic issues has spurred continuing scientific inquiry into hypnosis and memory distortion. Practitioners have been prompted to continue to refine and expand guidelines established by Orne (1979) for its use, as well as look at the practical question of jury attitudes towards hypnosis and how these attitudes may influence jury decisions.

The issues of forensic hypnosis center around who should use hypnosis—police investigators or health professionals—with whom should it be used—victims, witnesses or defendants—and for what purpose—to heighten recall, to develop investigative leads, or to produce new evidence? Most of the controversy has centered around the basic question of whether hypnosis enhances or distorts a person's memory of past events. Recent research by Sheehan and Tilden (1986) has further supported the prevailing view that "Memories in hypnosis may be distorted in distinctive fashion" (p. 134).

As discussed in Chapter 17, any hopes that hypnosis could function as a truth serum have been dispelled by research that shows that memory is not like a tape recorder but instead a constructive process. In other words, the mind is not passive, but active, continually synthesizing new information that colors old memories. In a psychotherapeutic context, the constructive nature of memory can be an asset, enabling a client to identify a memory that encodes a problem and then "reframe" the memory in a way that resolves the problem. The difficulty arises when hypnosis is transferred from the therapeutic context, where objective truth is not the goal, to a forensic context that focuses on "evidence." The police, the courts, and practitioners called in to use hypnosis with witnesses, victims, or defendants have had to face the question: To what extent can a hypnotized person lie or confabulate?

Hibler (1984) has taken the discussion of forensic hypnosis back to the basics by asking the question "Are there circumstances that ought to influence the decision to use hypnosis in the first place?" In answer to this question, he presents guidelines developed by federal investigative agencies to ensure the appropriate use of hypnosis in the forensic context. According to these guidelines, hypnosis should be used in the following instances:

1. As a last resort, only after all traditional investigative methods of law enforcement have been used.

2. Only for serious offenses that warrant the investment of time and resources.

3. Only when there is a clear potential for further recall, and not as a "fishing expedition."

4. Only when there is a strong likelihood of independent corroboration of information recalled under hypnosis.

According to the federal guidelines, hypnosis should *not* be employed in the following instances:
1. When a case is already flawed by forensic errors; hypnosis cannot correct previous and potentially damaging mistakes.

2. When a suspect has already been identified, because the a priori knowledge may prejudice the witness or influence opinions or conclusions. (There are exceptions to this rule.)

3. When the credibility or motives of the person to be hypnotized is in question.

4. When the person to be hypnotized does not want to participate.

These guidelines emphasize the role of hypnosis in the investigative process, as a tool to be used sparingly only when traditional investigative methods have been exhausted.

Appellate Court rulings regarding hypnosis have been varied and remain everchanging. As summarized by Mutter (1984), they fall into four categories: (1) all testimony from a previously hypnotized witness is disallowed, (2) the use of hypnosis is judged not on its admissibility but on the weight and credibility of the evidence it produces, (3) testimony from hypnotized witnesses is allowed if certain safeguards have been followed, and (4) a witness who has been hypnotized may testify as long as there is a record of the witness's prehypnotic memory. In June of 1987, the Supreme Court made an important ruling that affects decisions in the first category. The court overturned the Rock vs. Arkansas decision, in which a defendant was barred from testifying about the details of a shooting incident that she recalled under hypnosis. The court ruled that the decision was an arbitrary restriction on a defendant's "constitutional right to testify in her own defense." Thus states may no longer absolutely bar criminal defendants from testifying about details they have recalled only under hypnosis.

This decision will focus increased attention on the use of hypnosis with defendants. Mutter (1984) has suggested a procedural outline to ensure the credibility of the hypnotic process when it is used with criminal defendants. The following is a brief summary of his major points, some of which overlap the general guidelines established by Orne (1979).

1. The hypnotist should be a private practitioner who is knowledgeable about the hypno-investigative procedure but who has no vested interest in the case.

2. Hypnosis should be performed only with written consent and in the presence of the defendant's attorney.

3. A full clinical evaluation, including family history, personality structure, and mental status should precede hypnosis.

4. Prehypnotic recall should be recorded, including what the defendant has read or heard in the news about the case.

5. Tests should be used to determine if the subject is actually in trance.

6. Data retrieval should be conducted with great care to lessen the likelihood of confabulation or fantasies. The examiner should take care not to lead the subject or make direct demands for information.

7. Before terminating the trance, the practitioner should ask the subject for permission to enable him or her to remember the experiences described during trance, so that these may be discussed with the attorney. If the experience has been traumatic, the defendant may be asked to remember only those experiences that he or she is able to deal with emotionally.

8. Posthypnotic testing can be used to assure the court that a hypnotic trance has occurred.

9. The entire session should be videotaped.

These guidelines and the case studies Mutter presents make it clear hypnosis with defendants must be conducted as professionally, carefully, and objectively as hypnosis with witnesses or victims, for the practitioner's responsibility is to the validity of the process itself, not to the outcome.

A study by Wilson, Greene, and Loftus (1986) raises another important issue—that the beliefs people hold about forensic hypnosis may have an impact on both witnesses and juries. The authors administered a written survey to 357 undergraduates enrolled in an introductory psychology course and conducted a telephone survey of 238 registered voters selected at random from a list of county residents. They found that more than 70 percent of the students were favorable towards the use of hypnosis by police, compared to 50 percent of the potential jurors. On the other hand, both groups reported they would place less faith rather than more faith in the testimony of a witness who had been hypnotized. The study also showed that substantial numbers of students believed common myths about hypnosis: 47 percent agreed that hypnotized persons can be made to do things against their will and 46 percent believed that people cannot lie under hypnosis. The authors conclude that because accurate knowledge about hypnosis on the part of the jury cannot be assumed, court cases involving hypnotically enhanced testimony would benefit from expert testimony on the nature and limitations on hypnosis.

Finally, a survey by Reilley et al. (1987) on the ethical uses of hypnosis found that the majority of the respondents (121 members of the American Society of Clinical Hypnosis) agreed that it is ethical for ASCH members to hypnotize victims or witnesses of crimes, with their permission, but that ASCH members should not train police officers in the use of hypnosis. It appears that practitioners are proceeding with caution in the area of forensic hypnosis, stressing importance of education, safeguards, and keeping hypnotic procedures in the hands of professionals qualified to deal with the potential problems associated with release of anxiety or abreactions that may accompany hypnotic regression.

OUTSIDE THE CLINIC

Hypnotic techniques are being widely used outside the clinical setting in such diverse fields as management training, sports, and education, and for both personal enrichment and team and organizational development. In most instances of nonclinical application, however, the word "hypnosis" is taboo. Still, the techniques, whether relaxation, mental imagery, visualization, or any number of "new" methods with newly coined names, all fall within the broad parameters of the New Hypnosis, as defined by Araoz (1985). They all represent powerful new ways of learning and of taking control over our lives.

The power of the imagination, the belief, as Emerson stated, that "Man is what he thinks all day long," has been expressed by many popular authors, including Dale Carnegie (1944) and Norman

Vincent Peale (1974). The increased public consciousness of these issues as they relate to physical health is reflected in the popularity of such books as the bestseller *Love, Medicine, and Miracles* by Bernie Siegel, M.D. (1987), which focuses on exceptional cancer patients who get well when they aren't supposed to, and *Minding the Body, Mending the Mind,* by Joan Borysenko (1987), a cancer researcher and psychotherapist.

The fact that in popular books, the word "hypnosis" is seldom used, even by authors who are practitioners of the art, is indicative of the fact that the word still has negative connotations for the general public. This view is supported by Hendler and Reed's (1986) study of 105 outpatient chemotherapy patients. The cancer patients were randomly assigned to three groups receiving identical descriptions for a behavioral procedure but different labels: Hypnosis, relaxation, and passive relaxation with guided imagery. The authors found that patients faced with an intervention labeled "hypnosis" had less faith in the procedure, and were significantly less likely to agree to try it, than were patients in the two other groups. In other words, the patients were afraid of the label "hypnosis" with its lingering connotations of mind control, and not the procedures that were described. Hendler and Reed concluded that practitioners should keep the hypnotic procedures and change the label. Practitioners who are applying the techniques of hypnosis outside the clinic appear to be taking their advice.

Sports.   In traditional medical circles, the importance of psychological factors on physical health is far from widely accepted. In the arena of sports competition, however, it is no longer a question of *if* psychological variables affect physiological performance, but what combination of strategies are most effective. Athletes and coaches are looking to sports psychologists to give them a competitive edge. Suinn (1980) was one of the first to report the professional use of imagery with athletes. His system, called visual-motor behavior rehearsal (VMBR), is essentially the use of relaxation and imagery to strengthen motor skills. Howard and Reardon (1986) describe an approach that combines cognitive-experiential therapy with hypnosis and imagery, which they used to improve performance of weightlifters. (The reader should note that some authors define cognitive therapies as hypnotic in nature.) The process includes reviewing negative emotional states in trance, refocusing on and experiencing more positive physiological and behavioral responses, and then using imagery to enhance physiological processes.

Krenz (1984) uses a technique based on Standard Autogenic Training (SAT), originated by Schultz and popularized by Luthe (1969), which is recognized by most authors as a form of self-hypnosis. Unlike SAT, which involves mastery of a progressive series of exercises over a period of 3 to 10 months, Krenz's Modified Autogenic Training (MAT) takes 7 weeks to complete. This program uses relaxation, post-hypnotic suggestions, mental rehearsal, and dissociation techniques. In one use of dissociation techniques, the athlete mentally "steps in-side" the body of a model who is performing a task perfectly, experi-encing each movement as it is completed, and then "steps out" of the model's body and allows the model to "step inside" the athlete's body to perform the task. Finally, the model "steps out" and watches the athlete perform, giving suggestions for improvement. After an initial learning period, the athlete uses MAT on his or her own for problem-solving and self-coaching.

Most of the clinical and experimental use of hypnosis to enhance physical performance has been with individual athletes. However, in team sports, cohesiveness is an important factor that can be fostered through hypnosis. As Korn (1986) states, "Just as group hypnosis has proven to be as or more effective than individual hypnosis, imagery may be shown to be at least equally effective when used in a team situation" (p. 180). Pratt and Korn (in press) provide a working proce-dure for using the dynamics of group imagery as a tool for enhancing team performance. Their group imagery procedures include the fol-lowing five steps:

1. Create a state of relaxation in a quiet setting.

2. Develop a level of control over autonomic functions, such as pulse rate and breathing, to demonstrate the effectiveness of concentra-tion and focus.

3. Introduce positive process and end-result imagery.

4. Use imagery to access past successes for the purpose of breaking slumps or overcoming performance anxiety.

5. Use imagery to develop "cues" that create relaxation or focus dur-ing competition.

The authors suggest that the therapist use permissive and choice-oriented language to promote more individualization of the imagery by the players.

The authors give two examples of this process. The first is a professional basketball team with low team morale, injuries, and a poor mid-season record. Pratt and Korn designed an imagery program that stressed team cohesiveness by associating team colors and activities with confidence, comfort, and security.

For a college football team that was playing erratically, the authors had the players imagine a thermometer that goes from 10 to 1000, and find their own individual level of personal readiness. Subsequent sessions worked on controlling the thermometer, pumping it up or down as needed to maintain each player's optimum stress level for playing effectively.

Pratt and Korn also point out the important role a coach plays in focusing a player or team on positive expectations. It is likely that successful coaches unconsciously used hypnotic techniques in the form of positive suggestions. Beyond the use of sports psychologists to work directly with athletes and teams, the next step in team development may be to teach these techniques to the coaches themselves.

Business.   According to Araoz (1984), all techniques involving mostly the imagination are hypnosis. Looked at in this light, hypnotic techniques have long been used in management training and development, although the field as a whole still emphasizes outward rehearsal, such as role playing, instead of inner rehearsal. Based on his theory of negative self-hypnosis, Araoz (1984) has developed a strategy for the use of hypnosis in management training. Negative self-hypnosis is engaging in negative self-talk, or negative imagery, of which the person may be consciously unaware, but which leads to actions that are self-defeating. Araoz uses the term "dynamic imagery" instead of hypnosis to refer to the activation of right-hemisphere activity, or use of the mind bypassing critical-analytical thinking. He applies the dynamic imagery technique to the business setting in four ways:

1. To change negative beliefs (counteract negative self-hypnosis) by identifying negative thoughts and substituting positive ones.

2. To mentally rehearse difficult situations a client must face, until the situation becomes so familiar it no longer produces anxiety.

3. To counteract resistance to change by reliving a similar situation in the past, juxtaposing it in the mind with a situation in which whatever had given rise to the resistance was enjoyed or

accomplished, and then connecting the positive feelings with the current situation.

4. To reinforce, maintain, or even generalize the gains made to other areas of functioning.

These same general techniques are incorporated into a recent popular book by Korn and Pratt (1987), both practitioners of hypnosis. Their book presents the AIM strategy, a plan for converting destructive stress into productive energy by using one's natural abilities: *A*ctive relaxation, *I*magery of the end result, *M*ental rehearsal of the process of achieving an objective. Without using the word "hypnosis," the AIM strategy employs such hypnotic techniques as cueing and reframing through the use of imagery. Even the language is in the permissive style used by hypnotherapists. For example, the authors state "In some cases you may notice an increase in comfort and confidence very quickly, and in others it may take some time before results are observed or felt."

Education.   Education is a natural arena for the New Hypnosis. Klauber (1984) notes that in addition to helping children overcome test anxiety and improve concentration and study habits, hypnosis can also affect a child's attitude and expectations toward learning. He relates the experience of the Forsythe School, a private preschool and elementary school in St. Louis, which uses goal setting, relaxation, visualization, and other "programming for success" techniques as an integral part of its overall approach to education. As described by Mary Dunbar, the founder of the school, "Normal children became 'gifted,' achieving amazing scores on standardized tests at an early age. Learning disabled children overcame their problems and the least achievement was scoring average on standardized tests. In 1980, five from a graduating class (1974) of twelve were National Merit Scholarship winners. . . . This method of overcoming learning disabilities and accelerating learning should be tried in all schools" (pp. 604–605).

These techniques are particularly appropriate for students who have been convinced by negative suggestions throughout their school lives that they are slow, or bad, or failures. Who believe they cannot learn to read, or cannot do math. Who cannot envision a future, and will probably continue to be swept along in the system until they drop out. Unfortunately, education today, with its "back to basics" emphasis on the 3 Rs is on the whole not amenable to right hemisphere learning, and many teachers are uncomfortable with techniques that empower students and reduce their own authority and control. However, it is possible to find examples of hypnotic techniques in school curricula.

The *One-of-a-Kind* curriculum package by Mark Scharenbroich (undated) is one example of the innovative materials available to help high school students improve self-image and prepare for the future. It uses videotapes and films, student activities, and a workbook to improve self-esteem and move beyond self-imposed limitations by reframing negative thoughts into positive images. These materials specifically teach relaxation and visualization techniques and encourage students to practice them at home.

Seek Out Success (SOS), a pilot project of the San Diego City Schools (1987), is based on the hypothesis that another round of remedial classes will not help children with low expectations and low self-esteem. Directed to junior high school students in danger of dropping out, with a special emphasis on minority females, the SOS curriculum empowers students by teaching them techniques for building self-esteem, setting goals, and visualizing the completion of their goals in a supportive environment. In this program, the teacher is no longer an authoritarian figure but rather a guide or facilitator, who helps to maintain a nonjudgmental classroom atmosphere in which students can learn to trust each other as well as themselves. Although it may not be possible to counter years of negative suggestions and negative self-hypnosis in the space of a single semester, SOS and similar programs suggest that the powerful techniques of "hypnosis without hypnosis" may eventually become more integrated into our educational system.

This brief review of some of the nontherapeutic uses of hypnosis makes it apparent that the basic techniques of communicating with the unconscious through the use of imagery, or right hemisphere thinking, are widely applicable to a variety of fields. The wonder is not that "hypnosis without hypnosis" is being used outside the clinic, but that it is not being used even more.

ADVERSE REACTIONS

When properly used, hypnosis is an extremely safe tool for the healing professions. However, indiscriminate and unprofessional use of trance induction and suggestion may produce adverse reactions in some people. Recent literature draws attention to the adverse effects of hypnosis produced by stage hypnotists, lay hypnotists, and professionals operating outside their specialty. These reports are an important reminder that despite the fact laypersons are using hypnotic techniques for self-improvement in many fields, hetero-hypnosis should be used only by qualified practitioners in appropriate settings.

In a study to assess the impact of performances by a stage hypnotist on a college campus, Echterling and Emmerling (1987) found that 4 of the 18 participants had a negative trance experience and some negative aftereffects, 32 percent of the audience described the demonstration in such negative terms as "exploitative" and "offensive," and that two members of the audience reported negative aftereffects of feeling apprehensive, frightened, and controlled. The authors conclude that the risks of stage hypnosis outweigh its potential entertainment value.

Kleinhauz and Beran (1984) identify a number of occurrences during hypnosis by an untrained or uncaring hypnotist that may result in posthypnotic trauma.

> Even a seemingly neutral suggestion may have intense emotional meaning to a particular person and may symbolically fulfill a hidden, unconscious desire, and thus persist as a post-hypnotic symptom. Symbolic meanings, suggested responses or suggested age regression may re-evoke an earlier trauma or "resolve" an unconscious conflict. . . . Techniques of induction or dehypnotization may be faulty or detrimental to a particular personality. (p. 283)

The authors cite six cases of complications, four of which resulted from a person's involvement in stage hypnosis. In one case, a woman had experienced 10 years of fatigue, irritability, and periods of childish behavior during which her perceptions were distorted. The source of the problem was traced back to a stage performance 10 years earlier, when she was regressed to age 11 years, a traumatic period of her life during the Nazi occupation of Germany. Through hypnosis she was able to discharge her anger against herself and the stage hypnotist and restore her sense of control and dignity. This and other cases lead Kleinhauz and Beran to speculate that there are other persons with such symptoms as sleep disturbances, compulsive behavior, and depression that can be attributed to posthypnotic trauma and who cannot be adequately treated until the source of the disturbance is identified.

Kleinhauz and Eli (1987) remind practitioners that although complications are rare, hypnosis can have deleterious effects even in a clinical setting. They cite four examples, including an unexpected abreaction, a dangerous literal interpretation of a posthypnotic suggestion, and an incomplete dehypnotization. In one case, a dentist using hypnorelaxation with a patient complied with her request to provide direction suggestions to stop smoking. The patient's underlying psychological conflicts, which the dentist was not qualified to assess, led to the development of an anxiety/depressive reaction, which improved only after the dentist, during a hypnotic session, "allowed her" to smoke again.

A series of case reports by MacHovec (1987) highlights other potential areas for complications. In one case, a high school teacher using guided imagery suggested that her students imagine circling earth in a spaceship. The session was interrupted by the bell signalling the end of class. One boy remained in trance, frozen in fear, believing the bell to be an alarm signaling an emergency for the spaceship. In another case, a woman undergoing psychotherapy facilitated by hypnosis attempted to use the procedures she had learned to relieve her husband's dental pain. During the deepening technique of arm levitation, her husband's fingertips "stuck" to his head, and a therapist had to intervene to end the trance state.

These dangers are real and should be taken seriously. What steps should the practitioner of clinical hypnosis take to prevent both abuse and careless use of hypnosis? Kleinhauz and Eli (1987) recommend the following safeguards for the professional:

1. The professional using hypnosis should stay within his or her area of expertise.

2. The clinician should be trained to assess psychopathological profiles and to recognize and cope with possible psychological reactions during the hypnotic intervention.

3. Realizing that suggestions may be interpreted literally, the professional should phrase them carefully.

4. Permissive techniques should be used in giving suggestions.

5. Dehypnotization procedures should be carefully completed.

6. Psychological services should be available in case of need.

On the other hand, the potential abuse of hypnosis should not be used as a rationale to discourage the use of hypnotic techniques outside of the clinic to improve the performance of normal people in such fields as education, sports, and management training and development. Mott (1987) has suggested that professionals should assume a larger role in ensuring the safe use of hypnosis by promoting the teaching of safe hypnotic techniques, and, even further, by informing the public of the possible dangers of the misuses of hypnosis by untrained people, such as stage entertainers and lay hypnotists.

SUMMARY

Clinical hypnosis appears to be in a period of self-assessment, as if having made great strides, we are pausing to get our bearings before proceeding. What is our proper role as clinicians in furthering the experimental study of hypnosis? What is our role in relation to the nontherapeutic uses of hypnosis? There are no easy answers, for, like a child with warring parents, the field of hypnosis is being pulled in two directions—practical application and scientific documentation.

On the whole, the trend is toward the pragmatic approach, with less focus on intellectual understanding of what is happening in hypnotic states and interactions, and more on the use of hypnosis as a vehicle for positive change. Araoz (1985) has eloquently expressed this view in his analysis of the New Hypnosis, which moves away from a formal approach that emphasizes the personality and skill of the practitioner and toward the naturalistic approach associated with Erickson that focuses on a client's innate ability to overcome illness, resolve psychic conflicts, and improve performance.

The field that is generating the most excitement in both the medical and psychological communities is behavioral medicine. A significant body of research strongly suggests, if not scientifically proves, that psychosocial variables influence physiological functioning, or as Rossi (1986) puts it, mind can move molecules. We have taken several steps into the new territory of treating such diseases as cancer through psychological means. The next frontier may be the use of the mind to maintain and promote health.

One conceptual advance in our understanding of hypnosis has been to recognize the hypnotic elements at work in medical settings, in families, in schools, on athletic teams, and in most interpersonal interactions. A physician dealing with a seriously ill patient can pronounce a death sentence or give hope; a teacher can instill in a student the expectation of failure or the expectation of success; a coach can confuse a batter by telling him not to strike out, or encourage him by suggesting he drive a fastball. Suggestion, with or without trance, in the clinic or in everyday life, is a powerful force.

Are we as clinicians to be close and cautious keepers of the flame, or guides and teachers, not only with our clients but also in a larger sense, with the public at large? The answer is that we do not entirely have a choice. Practitioners of clinical hypnosis need to be involved, not only to warn against the potential abuses of hypnosis by arm-flapping stage hypnotists and unqualified lay hypnotists, but also to provide guidance for the safe and effective use of hypnotic techniques, such as visualization and guided imagery, that are widely available to an increasingly aware public. It's an exciting time, and we look forward with great anticipation to new discoveries and new applications of clinical hypnosis as we approach the year 2000.

REFERENCES

Achterberg, J. (1985). *Imagery in healing.* Boston: New Science Library.

Amen, D. G., & Simms, G. R. (1986). Emotional stress and the surgical patient. *Resident and Staff Physician, 32,* 76–78, 83, 87.

Araoz, D. L. (1982). *Hypnosis and sex therapy.* New York: Brunner/Mazel.

Araoz, D. L. (1984). Hypnosis in management training and development. In W. C. Wester, II and A. H. Smith, H. Jr, (Eds.), *Clinical hypnosis: A multidisciplinary approach.* Philadelphia: J.B. Lippincott Co., 558–573.

Araoz, D. L. (1985). The new hypnosis. New York: Brunner/Mazel.

Baker, E. L. (1987). The state of the art of clinical hypnosis. *International Journal of Clinical and Experimental Hypnosis, 35,* 203–214.

Balson, P., & Dempster, C. (1980). Treatment of war neuroses from Vietnam. *Comprehensive Psychiatry, 21,* 167–175.

Balson, P. M., Dempster, C. R., & Brooks, F. R. (1984). Auto-hypnosis as a defense against coercive persuasion. *American Journal of Clinical Hypnosis, 26,* 252–260.

Bandler, R., & Grinder, J. (1979). *Frogs into princes.* Moab, Utah: Real People Press.

Barber, T. X. (1969). Hypnosis: A scientific approach. New York: Van Nostrand Reinhold Co.

Borysenko, J. (1987). Behavioral considerations in the development and management of cancer. *Resident and Staff Physician, 33,* 52–55.

Borysenko, J. (1987). *Minding the body, mending the mind.* Reading, Massachusetts: Addison-Wesley.

Bowden, C., & Posthuma, A. (1987). Post-traumatic stress disorder in motor vehicle accident victims: incidence, severity and complications. Paper presented at the Annual Meeting of the Society of Traumatic Stress Studies, Baltimore, Maryland.

Braun, B. G. (1984). Hypnosis and family therapy. *American Journal of Clinical Hypnosis, 26*, 182–186.

Brende, J. O. (1985). The use of hypnosis in post-traumatic conditions. In W.E. Kelly (Ed.), *Post-traumatic stress disorder and the war veteran patient.* New York: Brunner/Mazel, 193–210.

Brende, J. O., & Benedict, B. D. (1980). The Vietnam combat delayed stress symptom: Hypnotherapy of "dissociative symptoms." *American Journal of Clinical Hypnosis, 23*, 34–40.

Brown, D. P., & Fromm, E. (1987). *Hypnosis and behavioral medicine.* Hillsdale, New Jersey: Erlbaum.

Calof, D. (1985). Hypnosis in marital therapy: Towards a transgenerational approach. In J.K. Zeig (Ed.), *Ericksonian psychotherapy, vol. 2: Clinical applications.* New York: Brunner/Mazel.

Carnegie, D. (1944). *How to stop worrying and start living.* New York: Simon and Schuster.

Cassileth, B. R., Lusk, E. S. et al. (1984). Contemporary unorthodox treatments in cancer medicine: A study of patients, treatments, and practitioners. *Annals of Internal Medicine, 101*, 105–112.

Cassileth, B. R., Lusk, E. S., et al. (1985). Psychosocial correlates of survival in advanced malignant disease? *New England Journal of Medicine, 312*, 1551–1555.

Derogatis, L., Abeloff, M., & Melisartas, M. (1979). Psychological coping mechanisms and survival time in metastatic breast cancer. *JAMA, 242*: 1504–1508.

Echterling, L. G., & Emmerling, D. A. (1987). Impact of stage hypnosis. *American Journal of Clinical Hypnosis, 29*, 149–154.

Erickson, M., & Rossi, E. (1976/1980). Two-level communication and the microdynamics of trance and suggestion. In E. Rossi (Ed.), *The collected papers of Milton H. Erickson on hypnosis, I. The nature of hypnosis and suggestion.* New York: Irvington, pp. 430–451.

Feinstein, A. D., & Morgan, R. M. (1986). Hypnosis in regulating bipolar affective disorders. *American Journal of Clinical Hypnosis, 29*, 29–38.

Frankel, F. H. (1985). Hypnosis—both poetry and science. In D. Waxman, P.C. Misra, M. Gibson, and M.A. Basker, (Eds.), *Modern Trends in Hypnosis.* New York: Plenum Press.

Frankel, F. H. (1987). Significant developments in medical hypnosis during the past 25 years. *International Journal of Clinical and Experimental Hypnosis, 35*, 216–231.

Fromm, E. (1987). Significant developments in clinical hypnosis during the past 25 years. *International Journal of Clinical and Experimental Hypnosis, 35*, 203–214.

Gould, S. S. & Tissler, D. M. (1984). The use of hypnosis in the treatment of herpes simplex II. *American Journal of Clinical Hypnosis*, 26, 171–174.

Gravitz, M. A. (1988). Early uses of hypnosis as surgical anesthesia. *American Journal of Clinical Hypnosis*, 30, 201–208.

Haley, S. (1985). Some of my best friends are dead: Treatment of the PTSD patient and his family. In W.E. Kelly (Ed.), *Post-traumatic stress disorders and the war veteran patient.* New York: Brunner/Mazel, 54–70.

Hendler, C. S., & Reed, W. H. (1986). Fear of hypnosis: The role of labeling in patients' acceptance of behavioral interventions. *Behavior Therapy*, 17, 2–13.

Hibler, N. S. (1984). Forensic hypnosis: To hypnotize or not to hypnotize, That is the question! *American Journal of Clinical Hypnosis*, 27, 52–57.

Hilgard, E. (1977). *Divided consciousness: Multiple controls in human thought and action.* New York: Wiley-Interscience.

Howard, W. L. & Reardon, J. P. (1986). Changes in the self concept and athletic performance of weight lifters through a cognitive-hypnotic approach: An empirical study. *American Journal of Clinical Hypnosis*, 28, 248–257.

Kiecolt-Glaser, J. K., Ricker, D., et al. (1984). Urinary cortisol level, cellular immunocompetency, and loneliness in psychiatric inpatients. *Psychosomatic Medicine*, 46, 15–23.

Kilpatrick, D. G., Veroner, L. J., & Best, C. L. (1985). Factors predicting psychological distress among rape victims. In C.R. Figley (Ed.), *Trauma and it wake.* New York: Brunner/Mazel, 113–141.

Klauber, R. W. (1984). Hypnosis in education and school psychology. In W.C. Wester, II and A. H. Smith Jr. (Eds.), *Clinical hypnosis: A multidisciplinary approach.* Philadelphia: J.B. Lippincott Co.

Kleinhauz, M., & Beran, B. (1984). Misuse of hypnosis: A factor in psychopathology. *American Journal of Clinical Hypnosis*, 26, 283–290.

Kleinhauz, M., & Eli, I. (1987). Potential deleterious effects of hypnosis in the clinical setting. *American Journal of Clinical Hypnosis*, 29, 155–159.

Kohen, D. P. (1986). Applications of relaxation/mental imagery (self-hypnosis) in pediatric emergencies. *International Journal of Clinical and Experimental Hypnosis*, 34, 283–294.

Kohen, D. P., & Botts, P. (1987). Relaxation-imagery (self-hypnosis) in Tourette Syndrome: Experience with four children. *American Journal of Clinical Hypnosis*, 29, 227–237.

Korn, E. R. (1986). The uses of relaxation and mental imagery to enhance athletic performance. *Imagery*, 4, 173–182.

Korn, E. R., & Pratt, G. J. (1987). *Hyper-Performance: The A.I.M. strategy for releasing your business potential.* New York: John Wiley & Sons.

Kraft, W. A., Rodolfa, E. R., & Reilley, R. R. (1985). Current trends in hypnosis and hypnotherapy. *American Journal of Clinical Hypnosis*, 28, 20–26.

Krenz, E. W. (1984). Improving competitive performance with hypnotic suggestions and modified autogenic training: Case reports. *American Journal of Clinical Hypnosis*, 27, 58–63.

Lankton, S. R., & Lankton, C. H. (1983). The answer within: A clinical framework of Ericksonian hypnotherapy. New York: Brunnel/Mazel.

Laudenslager, M. L., Ryan, S. M., et al. (1983). Coping and immunosuppression: Inescapable but not escapable shock suppresses lymphocyte proliferation. *Science,* 221, 568–570.

Levy, S. M., Heberman, R. B., et al. (1985). Prognostic risk assessment in primary breast cancer by behavioral and immunological parameters. *Health Psychology,* 4, 99–113.

Luthe, W. (Ed.) (1969). *Autogenic Therapy* (Vols. 1–5). New York: Grune & Stratton.

MacHovec, F. (1987). Hypnosis complications: Six cases. *American Journal of Clinical Hypnosis,* 29, 160–165.

Moldawsky, R. J. (1984). Hypnosis as an adjunct treatment in Huntington's disease. *American Journal of Clinical Hypnosis,* 26, 229–231.

Mott, T. H. (1986). Editorial: Current status of hypnosis in the treatment of phobias. *American Journal of Clinical Hypnosis,* 28, 135–137.

Mott, T. (1987). Editorial: Adverse reactions in the use of hypnosis. *American Journal of Clinical Hypnosis,* 29, 147.

Mutter, C. B. (1984). The use of hypnosis with defendants. *American Journal of Clinical Hypnosis,* 27, 42–51.

Orne, M. T. (1979). The use and misuses of hypnosis in court. *International Journal of Clinical and Experimental Hypnosis,* 27, 311–341.

Pratt, G. J., & Korn, E. R. (in press). Imagery with groups: Applications for team sports. In A. Sheikh and E. Korn (Eds.), *Imagery in Sports and Physical Performance.* Farmingdale, New York: Baywood.

Peale, N. V. (1974). *You can if you think you can.* New York: Fawcet Crest.

Pettingale, K. W., Morris, T., et al. (1985). Mental attitudes to cancer: An additional prognostic factor. *Lancet,* 1, 750.

Reilley, R. R., Dupree, J., Rodolfa, E., & Kraft, W. (1987). Attitudes toward the ethical use of hypnosis: An interdisciplinary study. *American Journal of Clinical Hypnosis,* 30, 132–138.

Ritterman, M. (1983). *Using hypnosis in family therapy.* San Francisco: Jossey-Bass.

Rossi, E. L. (1986). *The Psychobiology of Mind-Body Healing.* New York: W.W. Norton.

Scharenbroich, M. (Undated). "One-of-a-kind" Owatonna, Minnesota: Jostens, Inc.

San Diego City Schools (1987). "Seek out success (SOS): Teacher's Manual" San Diego: San Diego City Schools.

Sax, W. P. (1985). Establishing a post-traumatic stress disorder inpatient program. In W.E. Kelly (Ed.), *Post-traumatic stress disorders and the war veteran patient.* New York: Brunner/Mazel, 234–248.

Scurfield, R. M. (1985). Post-trauma stress assessment and treatment: Overview and formulations. In C.R. Figley (Ed.), *Trauma and its wake.* New York: Brunner/Mazel, 219–256.

Shatan, C. F. (1985). Have you hugged a Vietnam veteran today? The basis wound of catastrophic stress. In W.E. Kelly (Ed.), *Post-traumatic stress disorders and the war veteran patient.* New York: Brunner/Mazel, 12–28.

Sheehan, P. W., & Tilden, J. (1986). The consistency of occurrences of memory distortion following hypnotic induction. *International Journal of Clinical and Experimental Hypnosis, 34,* 122–137.

Siegel, B. S. (1986). *Love, medicine, and miracles.* New York: Harper and Row.

Silver, S. M., & Kelly, W. E. (1985). Hypnotherapy of post-traumatic stress disorder in combat veterans from WWII and Vietnam. In W.E. Kelly (Ed.), *Post-traumatic stress disorders and the war veteran patient.* New York: Brunner/Mazel, 211–233.

Spiegel, D. (1981). Vietnam grief work using hypnosis. *American Journal of Clinical Hypnosis, 24,* 33–40.

Steggles, S., Henderikus, J. S., Fehr, R., & Aucoin, P. (1987). Hypnosis and cancer: An annotated bibliography 1960–1985. *American Journal of Clinical Hypnosis, 29,* 281–290.

Suinn, R. M. (1980). Body thinking: Psychology for Olympic champs. In R.M. Suinn (Ed.), *Psychology in sports: Methods and applications.* Minneapolis: Burgess.

Surman, O. S., & Crumpacker, C. (1987). Psychosocial aspects of herpes simplex viral infection: Report of six cases. *American Journal of Clinical Hypnosis, 30,* 125–131.

Swirsky-Sacchetti, T., & Margolis, C. G. (1986). The effects of a comprehensive training program on the use of Factor VIII in severe hemophilia. *International Journal of Clinical and Experimental Hypnosis, 34,* 71–83.

Trimble, M. R. (1985). Post-traumatic stress disorder: history of a concept. In C.R. Figley (Ed.), *Trauma and its wake.* New York: Brunner/Mazel, 5–14.

Weitzenhoffer, A. (1985). In search of hypnosis. In D. Waxman, P.C. Misra, M. Gibson, and M.A. Basker (Eds.), *Modern Trends in Hypnosis.* New York: Plenum Press.

Wilson, L., Greene, E. & Loftus, E. F. (1986). Beliefs about forensic hypnosis. *International Journal of Clinical and Experimental Hypnosis, 34,* 110–121.

Wood, D. P., Farley, R. L., & Sexton, J. (1987). Self-hypnosis in captivity survival. Paper presented at the Annual Convention of the California State Psychological Association, Coronado, California.

Zahourek, R. P. (Ed.) (1985). *Clinical hypnosis and therapeutic suggestion in nursing.* New York: Grune & Stratton.

Zastowny, T. R., Kirschenbaum, D. S., & Meny, A. L. (1986). Coping skills training for children: Effects on distress before, during and after hospitalization for surgery. *Health Psychology, 5,* 231–247.

APPENDIX

Alman-Wexler Indirect Hypnotic Susceptibility Scale (AWIHSS)

MAIN PROCEDURES*

The following instructions are to be presented verbatim.

1a. Head Heaviness

Now I don't want you to become deeply hypnotized quite yet . . . because listening to suggestions can affect your experience whether you are hypnotized or not. Responding to suggestions is within your own experience and can be an aid in taking care of yourself. Please find a position that is most comfortable, in your chair. . . . As you allow your eyes to close and relax, that's right, just let them close now . . . you can feel sensations of comfort beginning to move in a soothing motion. I wonder exactly where it starts for you. Now that you have found the position that is most comfortable for you and your eyes are feeling so relaxed that there is no need to try and do anything at all . . . all you need to do is allow this to happen . . . more and more relaxed.

You may be surprised to notice, or perhaps more pleased than surprised, to notice how easy and comfortable it is for your head to feel just a little bit heavier—just from thinking about it. That's right. Using your own natural experiences, your own imagination. I don't know exactly when your head will begin to feel heavier, beginning to fall just a little bit forward, and it doesn't really matter; what does matter is your own relaxation and comfort. Just

---

*Numbering of the main procedures corresponds to the numbering of the *Harvard Group Scale of Hypnotic Susceptibility*, Form A (Shor and Orne, 1962).

imagining, in your own particular way, your head falling forward, like a comfortable weight attached to your neck just lightly guiding your head downward, heavier and heavier, falling forward, more and more, as you begin to feel more relaxed, with your own imagination and creativity, just allowing it to happen, more and more forward, falling forward, heavier and relaxed, perhaps, and what a pleasant relief it is to allow yourself to feel satisfied and comfortable just by letting your head fall more and more forward, easily, comfortably without any effort at all, in your own way, more and more relaxed, heavier, feeling better and better, taking good care of yourself, your own natural abilities, heavier, forward, forward. *NOW* . . . that's right. And whenever you're ready, you can just sit up and let your eyes open again. You *can* sit up and open your eyes now, can't you? That's right. You may be pleased, or perhaps surprised, to notice how your own imagination can change your experience in your own particular way. You may find that you can allow yourself to experience some things that you already know how to do—you've done it so many times before.

Accepting suggestions is all up to you, . . . and how comfortable this can allow you to feel.

2a. Eye Closure

Now you are continuing to notice how one experience can lead to another. . . . No need to try to do anything. You may be more surprised than curious or more curious than surprised to find how physical events coincide with psychological events. . . . You probably haven't even noticed that your blood pressure has been altered, your pulse rate has been altered, and your breathing has been altered. All without trying to do anything—all within your own natural abilities.

I want you to realize that I am going to ask of you only the things that are actually possible for you to do. There are many things that we can do of which we are unaware. We can attend a lecture, and because the lecturer is interesting and simulating we don't even notice the passage of time and are just interested in what he is saying. But if we attended a lecture where the lecturer was dull, boring, and tiresome, one would feel the hardness of the seat of the chair, and yet it is the same chair in which you could sit and listen to an interesting lecturer and never feel all the discomforts and distress of not moving and the hardness of the seat. With the good lecturer you don't even hear anything except his *voice*. Now you are here to listen to me. You are here to experience certain things. In your lifetime of experience you have felt things and you have not felt some things that you could have felt if you had paid attention to them. You have had much experience in forgetting things that would ordinarily seem to be unforgettable.

For example, you are introduced to somebody and you reply, "I am very pleased to meet you, Mr. Jones," and 2 seconds later you are thinking to yourself, "What on earth is his name?" You have forgotten just as fast as you heard it. In other words, you can do any of the things that I will ask of you. You know how to move. You also know how not to move. You can lower your blood pressure, but you don't know how you do that. You can slow down your heartbeat, but you don't know how you do that. You can alter the rhythm of your breathing, but you don't know how you do that; but all of the things I ask you to experience, every one of them, will be within the range of your experience, so just listen carefully, knowing that I will ask of you only those things that I *know* you can do.

First of all, I want you to enjoy feeling very comfortable. Now, I'd like you to notice how much more comfortable you can feel by just taking one very big, satisfying deep breath. Go ahead . . . big, deep, satisfying breath . . . that's fine. . . . How warm your neck and shoulders can feel . . . and notice, too, how, when you *exhale*, you can just feel that relaxation beginning to sink in. . . . Good, that's fine. . . . Now, as you naturally continue breathing, comfortably and deeply and in rhythm, you can begin to picture in your mind . . . a staircase, indoors, outdoors, wooden stairs, or maybe concrete, carpeting or not, maybe it has a banister, it doesn't really matter . . . with 10 steps, and you at the top. . . . Now, you don't need to see all 10 steps at once, you can see any or all of the staircase, any way you like . . . that's fine. . . . Just notice yourself at the top of the staircase, and the step you're on, and any others you like. . . . However you see it is fine. . . . Now, in a moment, but not yet, I'm going to begin to count, out loud, from 1 to 10, and . . . as you may already have guessed . . . as I count each number I'd like you to take a step down that staircase . . . see yourself stepping down, one step for each number I count . . . and all you need to do is notice, just notice, how much more comfortable and relaxed you can feel at each step . . . one step for each number that I count . . . the larger the number, the farther down the staircase . . . the farther down the staircase, the more comfortable you can feel. . . . And I wonder exactly when it is that your eyes will become so heavy and relaxed that they feel like closing, when the feelings of deep comfort that you may or may not be feeling all over will allow your eyelids to *just drift closed*. It doesn't really matter. . . . It may be the first stair, or the fourth, or the ninth, I don't really know. . . . And what better way to express your *own* individuality than to let yourself choose, in your own way, on exactly which step your eyes will feel so comfortably heavy that you will allow them to just naturally close, remembering that this is your experience, not mine, and your creativity. . . . At what particular step, you will get so tired of staring, eyes closing, at which stair, heavy from staring on the staircase. . . . That's right. . . . You can begin to get ready. . . . Now, I'm going to begin. . . . 1 . . . one step down the staircase . . . wondering whether your eyelids have already chosen to close. . . . that's right. . . . 2 . . . two steps down the staircase . . . that's fine. . . . 3 . . . three steps down the staircase . . . perhaps your shoulders feel more relaxed than your neck . . . perhaps the pleasant, heavy sensations are more noticeable in your right eyelid than in your left. I don't know, and it really doesn't matter. . . . Perhaps they have already closed. . . . 4 . . . four steps down the staircase. . . . I wonder if the deep, relaxing, restful heaviness in your forehead is already beginning to spread and flow . . . down, across your eyes, down your neck, deep, restful, heavy . . . heavier, and heavier, tired from staring, perhaps. . . . 5 . . . five steps down the staircase . . . halfway down, and already beginning, perhaps, to really enjoy your relaxation and comfort . . . perhaps beginning to notice that the sounds that were distracting become less . . . that all the sounds you can hear become a part of your experience of comfort and relaxation. . . . 6 . . . six steps down the staircase. . . . That's fine. . . . I wonder whether you notice one arm feeling heavier than the other. . . . Perhaps your left arm feels a bit heavier than your right . . . perhaps your right arm feels heavier than your left . . . I don't know, perhaps they both feel equally comfortable . . . just letting yourself become more and more aware of that comfortable heaviness . . . or is it a feeling of lightness? . . . I really don't know, and it really doesn't matter. . . . Just knowing your own ability to satisfy yourself, how good it may feel to let your eyes close at just the right time, for you. . . . 7 . . . seven steps down the staircase . . . perhaps noticing that, even as you relax, noticing the tingling in your fingers . . . breathing comfortably, slowly, and deeply . . . perhaps wondering what might be happening, perhaps wondering whether anything at all is happening . . . and yet, knowing that it really doesn't matter, feeling so pleasantly restful . . . 8 . . . eight steps down the staircase . . . noticing, maybe, that as you feel increasingly heavy, more and more comfortable, there's nothing to bother you, nothing to disturb you, as you become more and more deeply relaxed. . . . 9 . . . nine steps down the staircase . . . almost to the bottom of the staircase . . . nothing to bother, nothing to disturb you, . . . eyes feel heavier and heavier, more and more relaxed, elying on your own natural skills at letting things happen at just the right moment. . . . That's right . . . just noticing . . . and now . . . 10 . . . the bottom of the staircase . . . deeply, deeply relaxed, deeper with every breath you take . . . eyes closed . . . Nowwww! . . . And even if you have not completely closed your eyes by now, you certainly may or may not have noticed some other changes, and that's fine. So just go ahead and let them close now.

3a. Hand Lowering

As you notice yourself becoming even more and more relaxed, you may be surprised to notice how easy it will be for you to *make yourself as comfortable as you possibly can*, adjusting yourself whenever you may or may not need to. That's right.

You may find, from now on, that you are perfectly capable of experiencing just as many experiences as you feel comfortable experiencing, and you may or may not already have experienced some of these. And that's just fine. The only really important thing is your own ability to be *comfortable* and allowing yourself to be relaxed . . . nothing to bother you, nothing to disturb you . . . just listening to the sound of my voice . . . knowing the entire time that this is *your experience, not mine*, and *your creativity*. Just let happen whatever you find is happenng, even if it is not what you expect.

Now it probably would be perfectly comfortable for you to allow yourself to *extend one of your arms straight* out in front of you. That's right. It doesn't really matter which arm, I don't know for sure, the important thing is you let one of your arms extend straight out in front of you, up in the air, with your palm down. That's right, so easily, your own experience of allowing one of your arms to extend out in front of you, palm down. Now, notice how easy it is to allow your attention to focus in this extended hand, whichever one it is, just notice the feelings and sensations. The warmth and coolness, the light and dark feeling, heaviness, and more pleasant heaviness. Perhaps a tingling sensation, maybe a twitching in some of the fingers . . . and I wonder how pleased you'll feel to begin to notice the heaviness in this hand, whichever one it is, how those pleasant heavy feelings may begin in the ring finger and extend back to the wrist, or may begin on the back of the hand, pulling the fingers along with, that's right, you may even picture a weight pulling on it, getting heavier and heavier, at just your own pace, noticing it begin to move downward from that weight like something you may have experienced before, the relief of allowing your hand to respond to the heavier, heavier, heavier feelings, that's right, getting more and more heavy, your hand drifting down, how easy that is, to just respond to the heaviness, taking good care of yourself, more and more heavy, down, down, that's right, pleased to notice the feelings of more and more weight, down, down, down, further down, your own experience, down, down, down, heavier and heavier, all the way down, at your own pace, . . . NOW. *(Allow 10 seconds.)*

That's fine. Now feel free . . . to let the lightness return to your hand, letting your hand, in its own particular way, return to its original resting position, probably noticing how heavy and tired your arm and hand may have felt, and how pleasant it feels right now, how it may have been much heavier than it ordinarily would have been if you held it out. And how interesting it is to notice your own ability to respond to the sound of my voice to make yourself feel so comfortable. Nothing to bother you, nothing to disturb.

4a. Arm Immobilization

And as you continue on your own peaceful, relaxing experience . . . your awareness can be far away and detached while your body responds to your own desires. Whether you care to do a lot or a little . . . the only thing that matters is that you create your own experience for more and more comfort . . . deeper and deeper relaxation. . . .

You can allow your own relaxed sensations to travel all around, over and through like the warm sensations running through a river or a stream. As you may notice one arm may feel heavier than the other. Your right arm may begin to feel heavy, wooden-like, or perhaps your left arm is feeling numbness and heaviness. It doesn't matter if your right arm is feeling heavier and heavier, or if your left arm feels more and more wooden, that's right. You know which arm—shoulder—hand—feels which way and you can just allow it to happen. Heavier . . . more weighted down . . . as you notice perhaps a little later you would like to see how heavy your hand is . . . so heavy to move . . . but perhaps even with the weighted experience you could lift your arm . . . or it may be just too heavy to do right now. . . . You can feel how heavy it is. . . . Just try to lift up your hand; you can attempt this now . . . try it. (Allow 10 seconds.)

That's fine . . . no need to try and do anything now. . . . Just allow yourself to feel even more comfortable and relaxed. . . . Now you can just notice any heaviness disappearing and allowing your own natural experience to be present and available. Feeling your own self relax . . . relaxing completely . . . relaxed. . . .

5a. Finger Lock

And as you continue to relax, I'd like you to notice how easy it is to just *put your fingers together*. That's right, put your fingers together. Interlock your fingers together. You *can* interlock your fingers together and you may, . . . this is your own experience, not mine . . . feel your hands pressing tightly together. And I'm sure you can imagine other times when it is very important to keep your hands pressed tightly together. That's right . . . your own imagination, not mine . . . your own fingers together, interlocking, hands pressed tightly together. . . . You may be more surprised, or perhaps more amused, possibly even more pleased . . . I don't know for sure, and it doesn't really matter . . . to notice how *tightly* your hands are pressed together, so *tight* that, perhaps, even if you wanted to, it would probably be just *too much effort* to pull them apart . . . so amused at how pleasantly and *tightly* pressed together they are . . . trying to pull them apart, probably just too *much effort*. . . . Go ahead and try to pull them apart. *(Allow 10 seconds.)*

That's right. Very good. I wonder exactly when it is that you'll begin to notice how good it feels to have the normal feelings return to your hands, pleasant and comfortably relaxed, returning to their normal resting position . . . able to separate freely and easily. That's right. Deeper relaxed. Nothing to bother you, nothing to disturb you. . . .

6a. Arm Rigidity

Either arm can be more comfortable by extending one out in front of you, up in the air with the fist in a clenched position. Allow an arm to be straight out . . . that's right . . . in front of you. Feeling the tightness of your fist and the heaviness of your experience. The stiffness of an iron bar or piece of solid wood can now transfer into your whole arm . . . stiffer and stiffer . . . and you can notice the changes happening and the natural stiffness, like a bar of iron, straight and rigid, that's right . . . it can be very difficult to bend one of these . . . as you know . . . more and more solid. You can easily become more aware of how stiff a bar of iron is . . . testing the rigidity by trying to bend it, you can try . . . go ahead and try it. *(Allow 10 seconds.)*

That's fine. You need not try to do anything else. Just allow your arm to relax and feel even more and more comfortable. You may have found how one sensation can change. You may be surprised at how easily and naturally your body responds and can respond to your own experiences and even desire for changes. As you notice more and more totally relaxed feelings, that's right, it's natural to feel your whole body relax.

7a. Moving Hands Together

Now you can try holding both hands up in the air straight out in front of you. Both hands can feel just as comfortable and deeply relaxed straight out in front of you, palms facing inward. And you'll probably find that the most comfortable position is about a foot apart. That's right. Arms straight in front of you, palms inward, about a foot apart.

Now I wonder exactly how it is that you will be able to imagine a force attracting your hands toward each other, pulling them toward each other . . . and whether you'll be more pleased than surprised to notice whether you imagine a magnet *pulling your hands together*, so easily and comfortably, closer and closer, at your own pace, slowly at first, moving together, so many ways to bring yourself comfort, that's right, moving hands closer and closer together, like something you've experienced before, closer, closer, closer, that's right. *Nowwwwwwww. . . . (Allow 10 seconds.)*

That's fine. What an interesting discovery to see, or perhaps feel, how imaging a movement can allow you to make the movement, so comfortably, easily, delightfully. You can find your hands relaxing now to their original resting position, your hands, all of you, relaxing, nothing to bother you, nothing to disturb you. . . .

8a. Communication Inhibition

The heaviness and deeply relaxed sensations are all part of your experience. There's no need to communicate in any way. In fact, movement of any kind may be as distant as when you're in a deep, deep sleep. I wonder whether, if you were to try to shake your head to say "no," whether any movement could take place . . . how trying can make it more difficult . . . that's right. Sometimes it's just *too much effort*, no matter how hard you try, so deeply relaxed. . . . Attempting to shake now—the response of no . . . you can try. *(Allow 10 seconds.)*

That's fine . . . no need to try anything else—you can just feel more and more comfortable. If you'd like to shake your head no—you'll probably find it very easy right now. Do whatever you'd like, with comfort and deeper relaxation . . . easy, satisfying deep relaxation.

9a. Hallucination (Fly)

You probably haven't even noticed some of the changes and events that have already taken place without your even realizing it . . . and that's fine. Now I wonder whether you'll be surprised or pleased to notice that you haven't yet noticed the fly that has been buzzing around you . . . until now. When I call your attention to it, beginning to hear the buzzing, just a little at first, I don't know exactly at what point you will, or already have, noticed the annoying buzzzzzzing . . . hearing the buzzing getting just a little louder, more, probably annoying you, maybe even imagining what it looks like, as the buzzing increases all around you, closer and closer, beginning to realize how much more comfortable you can again feel if you'd just take your hand, either one, it does not really matter, and just shoo the fly away. You'll probably be surprised to notice how good it feels to just shoo the fly and the buzzing noise away . . . go ahead, you can get rid of it if you want to. . . . *(Allow 10 seconds.)*

That's fine, noticing the fly and the noise fading away, replacing it with the comfortable, calm feelings, feeling satisfied with your own ability to take good care of yourself. Deeper relaxed, again, nothing to bother you, nothing to disturb you.

10a. Eye Catalepsy

You probably haven't even noticed how comfortably closed your eyes are, having been so, probably continue to be, easily and comfortably closed and relaxed. Like some of the other changes that you may not have noticed, you may not have noticed how tightly shut they are. Very tight, very comfortable. . . . And you may not even be aware of it yet, but in just a few moments, not quite yet, I'm going to ask you to try to open them. And wouldn't it be interesting noticing a sign of how deeply comfortable and relaxed you have already become, that it would be *just too much effort* to open them, they're glued so tightly shut. Even if you were able to open them, you would, of course, probably only do so momentarily and then immediately close again and relax, so as not to disturb your concentration. You're probably not even completely aware of how satisfying it feels to have your eyes so tightly shut, so comfortable and relaxing, so that it's probably *too much* effort, so heavy, to open them. Perhaps you'd like to go ahead and try now to open your eyes for a moment, even though they're just so relaxed and deeply, tightly closed that it's probably *just too much effort* to open them. That's right. See what it feels like to *try* to open them, even though they seem to want to stay shut. *(Allow 10 seconds.)*

That's fine. Perhaps you're ready to relax, even deeper again. Letting your eyes rest comfortably, letting the feeling of trying just fade away, comfortably. Deeper and deeper relaxed, so easily. Eyes resting normally again, closed and comfortable. That's right. Nothing to bother you, nothing to disturb you.

11a. Posthypnotic Suggestion (Scratching Back of Neck): Amnesia

And remaining as deeply relaxed as you'd like and continuing to relax comfortably, that's right. In just a few minutes you can hear me counting backwards from 10 to 1. You can gradually feel yourself awakening, but for most of this count you can remain as relaxed as you feel right now. As you hear the number 6 or 5 or 4, whichever you'd prefer, you can open your eyes, slowly waking yourself. When I get to 1, you can feel refreshed, awake, alert. You can then feel as if you've taken a long nap or slept for a while. However, right now and later there is no need to remember anything at all—in fact, forgetting is easier and more comfortable right now. When you hear the word "memory" you *can* remember everything easily and comfortably and only the word "memory" or the spelling of this word in your own mind can connect the whole experience. Right now you can allow this to be stored away with all else, easily, that's right.

I wonder if you'll be more surprised than curious or more curious than surprised . . . to notice a feeling you'll be pleased to notice . . . that in a short while when you hear the question, "How do you feel right now?" you can satisfy some discomfort you may be feeling . . . perhaps a desire for increased comfort can allow you to automatically find yourself . . . scratching an area on the back of your neck. . . .

When you hear that question, your hand can move upward first or your arm can . . . it doesn't really matter . . . to satisfy this itch you can scratch . . . all to increase your natural experience of refreshing satisfaction with your whole self. . . . You may be surprised at how easy this can be. . . . I don't know exactly how it will seem. . . . I only know, as perhaps you also know . . . that feeling some itching on the back of your neck and then scratching can be so pleasant, so comfortable, all by responding to the question when I ask it in a few moments . . . "How do you feel right now?"

It doesn't really matter . . . nothing matters but your own experience of comfort and relaxation . . . that's fine. With no need to remember anything until the word "memory" is heard by you. . . . Naturally you know, the mind forgets in order to remember—so you can allow all of this to be stored away. You may forget to remember all the time like most of us . . . you may remember what you had for lunch yesterday although you may forget what you had a month ago, yesterday. And that's perfectly natural . . . comfortable, relaxed, that's right.

And now as you become more and more ready to feel as if you've taken a long nap or slept for a while . . . you can easily feel more awake the closer we get to 1, that's right.

You can do this at your own . . . ready to feel more awake than perhaps you felt all day . . . naturally refreshed—ready—10 . . . 9 . . . 8 . . . feeling more alert at your own pace . . . 7 . . . 6 . . . perhaps stretching out to wake yourself . . . 5 . . . half-way up and awake . . . 4 . . . 3 . . . that's right . . . more and more refreshed . . . 2 . . . comfortable . . . and 1. Eyes open and awake. That's fine. Any remaining drowsiness can pass within a few moments, naturally.

(A clear question is now asked: "How do you feel right now?" Allow 10 seconds.)

SUBJECT INDEX

SUPPLEMENTAL SUBJECT INDEX

NAME INDEX

SUPPLEMENTAL NAME INDEX